INTERIOR DESIGN CHOICE

EDITION

A publication of
Indecs Publishing Inc.

President and Publisher:
David Jaeger
Marketing Director:
Andrea Howell

Cover and title pages design:
Taylor & Browning Design Associates
Cover Photography:
Ron Baxter Smith
Backdrop: Kurtz Mann
Chair Design: Mark Griffis
Production:
Berdj Bulbulian/Indecs Publishing Inc.
Typesetting:
XY Typesetting Services

Printed in Hong Kong

ISBN 0-9692019-5-8
ISSN 0829-5298

Published annually by
Indecs Publishing Inc.
78 Laird Drive
Toronto, Ontario
Canada M4G 3V1
Tel.: (416) 421-5227
Fax: (416) 421-8418

Distributed in Canada by:
Firefly Books Ltd.
250 Sparks Avenue
Willowdale, Ontario M2H 2S4
(416) 499-8412

All other countries:
Rockport Publishers Inc.
5 Smith Street
Rockport, Massachussets 01966
USA
(508) 546-9590

The book you are holding has a great reputation. Past editions have won

prestigious awards for graphic presentation, it enjoys a high recognition factor

in the interior design field, and is in demand internationally.

Most importantly this handsome book has a function.

Indecs Publishing produces Interior Design Choice to help decision makers who

must make "places work for people". It is a resource guide to the Canadian Interior

Design Industry.

Choice introduces to you the outstanding professional interior design firms across

Canada — experts at retail, health care, hospitality, residential and corporate

environments. The firms profiled in Choice have chosen to show their work in the

pages of this source book to acquaint you with their talents, services and areas of

specialization.

.   .   .   u s e   i t !

If you are responsible for the comfort, efficiency or profitability of a large office or public space of any kind, Choice will help you find the right design team.

Whether you are a specifier or in a position to hire consultants, Choice will make you aware of the trends and possibilities in today's interiors.

Design decisions demand knowledge of the marketplace. The scope of choice in every product from seating to lighting, tiles to files, systems to custom-made is immense. The resource section of Interior Design Choice brings to your attention the major manufacturers, the new products and a wide range of services related to interior design.

When your firm explores new premises, refurnishing or renovation, whether you need an expert or an inspiration, consider Interior Design Choice your desktop consultant.

Thirty five hundred copies of Interior Design Choice are distributed on a complimentary basis to key specifiers of design consultants, products and services. To be considered for future editions write to the publisher at 78 Laird Drive, Toronto, Ontario, Canada M4G 3V1.

INTERIOR
DESIGN
CHOICE

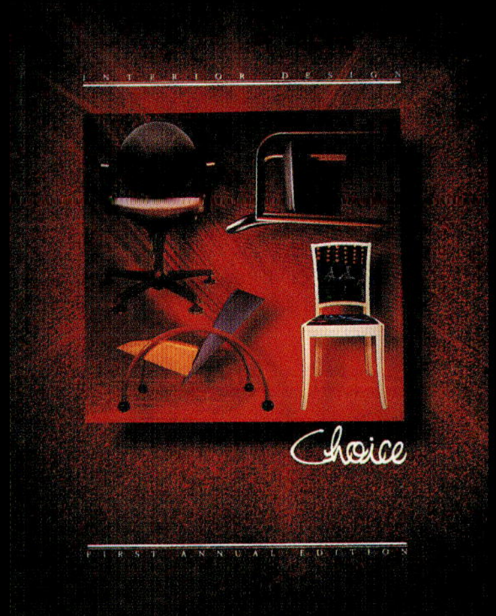

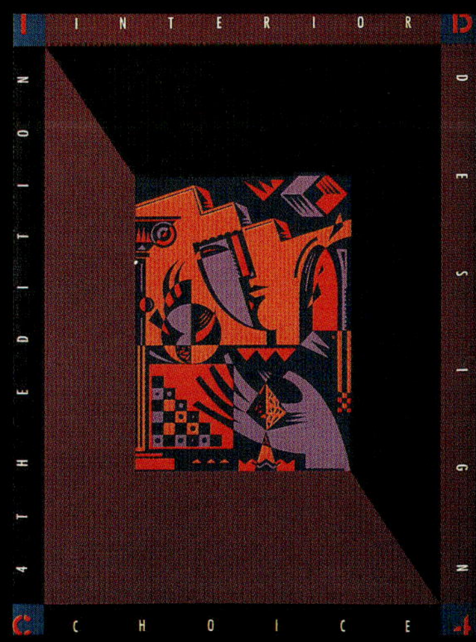

A VERY VISIBLE AND
VALUABLE PORTFOLIO
OF THE CANADIAN
INTERIOR DESIGN INDUSTRY

It's a sophisticated game. Lots of players, strong opponents, few rules.

Marketing your talent, or service, or product is an important aspect of
business development. You can knock on doors, enter competitions, mail
literature, rely on reputation, purchase advertising.

The skill is in choosing a clever mix.

Urbane and beautiful, Interior Design Choice is an opportunity for clever
marketing. Choice is an annual, hard cover, full colour glossy book. An
impressive portfolio of the Canadian Interior Design industry with a high
recognition factor as a source book and as an image maker.

The Interior Design Choice marketing package is comprehensive - including reprints of your presentation in the book, a copy of Choice for each
purchased page and a printout of the carefully researched distribution list.

The strength of Choice lies in its visibility and longevity. Choice offers long
term, widespread exposure in the context of a graphically superb promotional medium.

Thirty-five hundred thoroughly researched, key decision-makers receive

Interior Design Choice annually. Developers, major corporations, financial

institutions, hospital boards, retail directors, government departments and

foreign trade offices, architectural firms and interior designers. Addressed

by name to the premises director, facilities manager, leasing agent or prin-

cipal of the firm, Choice becomes a desk-top consultant. The introduction

encourages recipients to use the book when decisions regarding space,

renovation, relocation or refurnishing are made.

Sixty-five hundred additional copies of Interior Design Choice have an

international distribution in Japan, Hong Kong, Europe, South America and

the United States. Choice is also available in selected Canadian and U.S.

bookstores.

(Both Indecs Publishing's new book Arkitex and Interior Design Choice

are represented annually at the ABA and the Frankfurt Book Fair.)

Choice continues to be the quintessential point of contact between the

best creative talent and an increasingly design enlightened end-user.

Two exciting format changes will be introduced in the sixth edition.

The 1990 Choice will be restructured as a hardbound, two volume set - encased in a sleeve.

Book one - Interior Design Choice will profile interior design firms only, allowing the entire volume to become an inspired portfolio of both well respected names and emerging, young firms.

Book two - Choice - The Resource Edition will be a true resource compendium. A unique, upscale publication allowing major manufacturers to reaffirm their position and new companies to introduce themselves to the design community. (The resource volume will have a secondary distribution on its own to insure maximum exposure to architects and designers.)

This two volume set will have an impressive presence coupled with Indecs' continued commitment to state of the art reproduction and cover design.

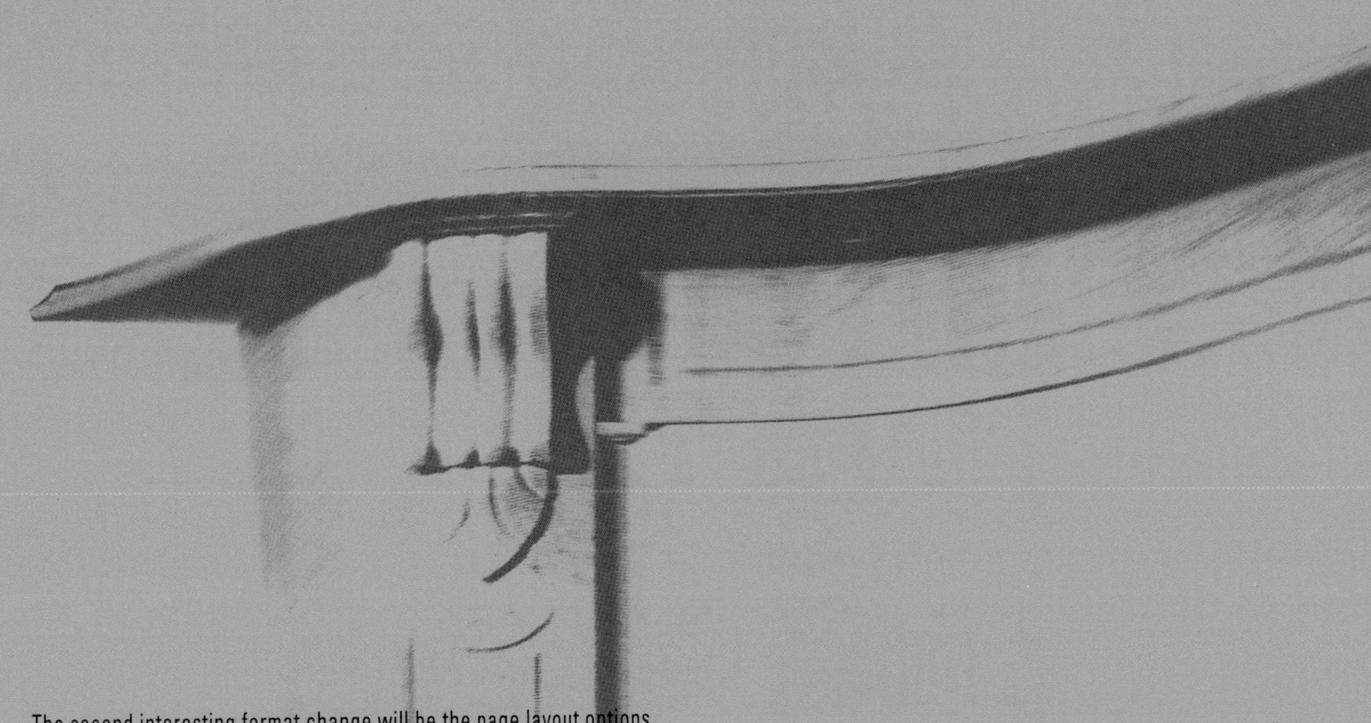

The second interesting format change will be the page layout options.
More bleeds will allow more creative freedom within the book and exciting
reprint possibilities.

Multiple page presentations can evolve into unique brochures with verti-
cal, angular or zig-zag folds; interesting cuts or poster potential. Single
pages will offer increased image area and allow for full bleed 8-1/2" x 11"
reprints.

Without doubt, these new format directions will enhance the visual dynam-
ics of Choice. Your firm deserves to be represented in the sixth edition of
Interior Design Choice.

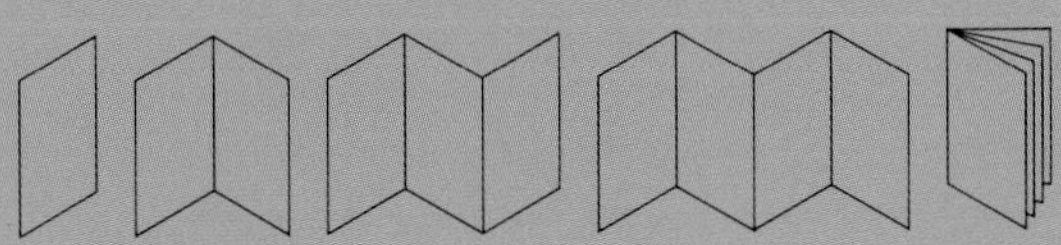

INTERIOR
DESIGN
CHOICE
FIFTH
EDITION

Award winning   Urbane   Unique   New formats

Unlimited reprint potential

Should you decide that your firm and your clients would appreciate your

corporate presence in Interior Design Choice contact:

Indecs Publishing, 78 Laird Drive, Toronto, Ontario M4G 3V1

(416) 421-5227

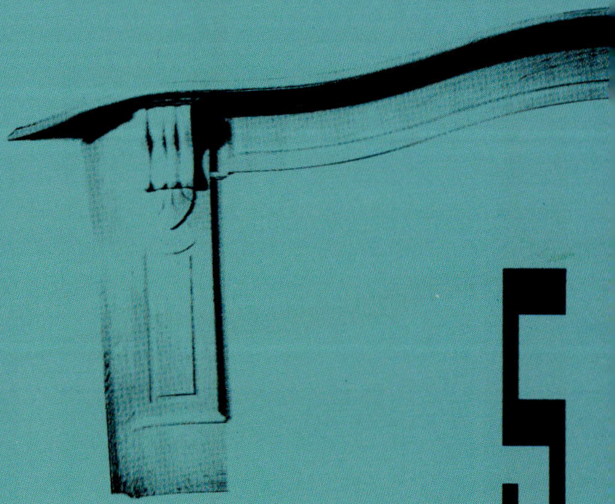

CONTENTS BY CATEGORY

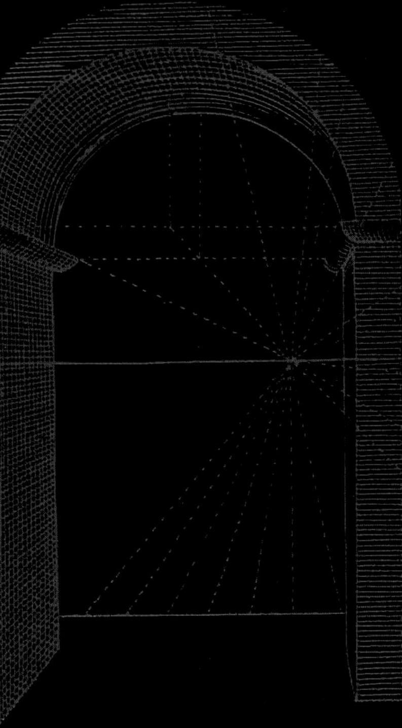

The success of Angus Wright Interior Design Consultants Ltd. has been our ability to listen to the client.

Our team of twelve design professionals can offer their experience and expertise to transform your space into an efficient and impressive workplace environment.

We are convinced that good design is good business.

New offices of Angus Wright Interior Design Consultants Ltd.

ANGUS WRIGHT
INTERIOR · DESIGN · CONSULTANTS · LTD.

306 Mount Royal Village, 1550 – 8th Street S. W., Calgary, Alberta T2R 1K1 (403) 229-2717

Parlee McLaws

Barristers and Solicitors, Calgary

37,000 sq. feet

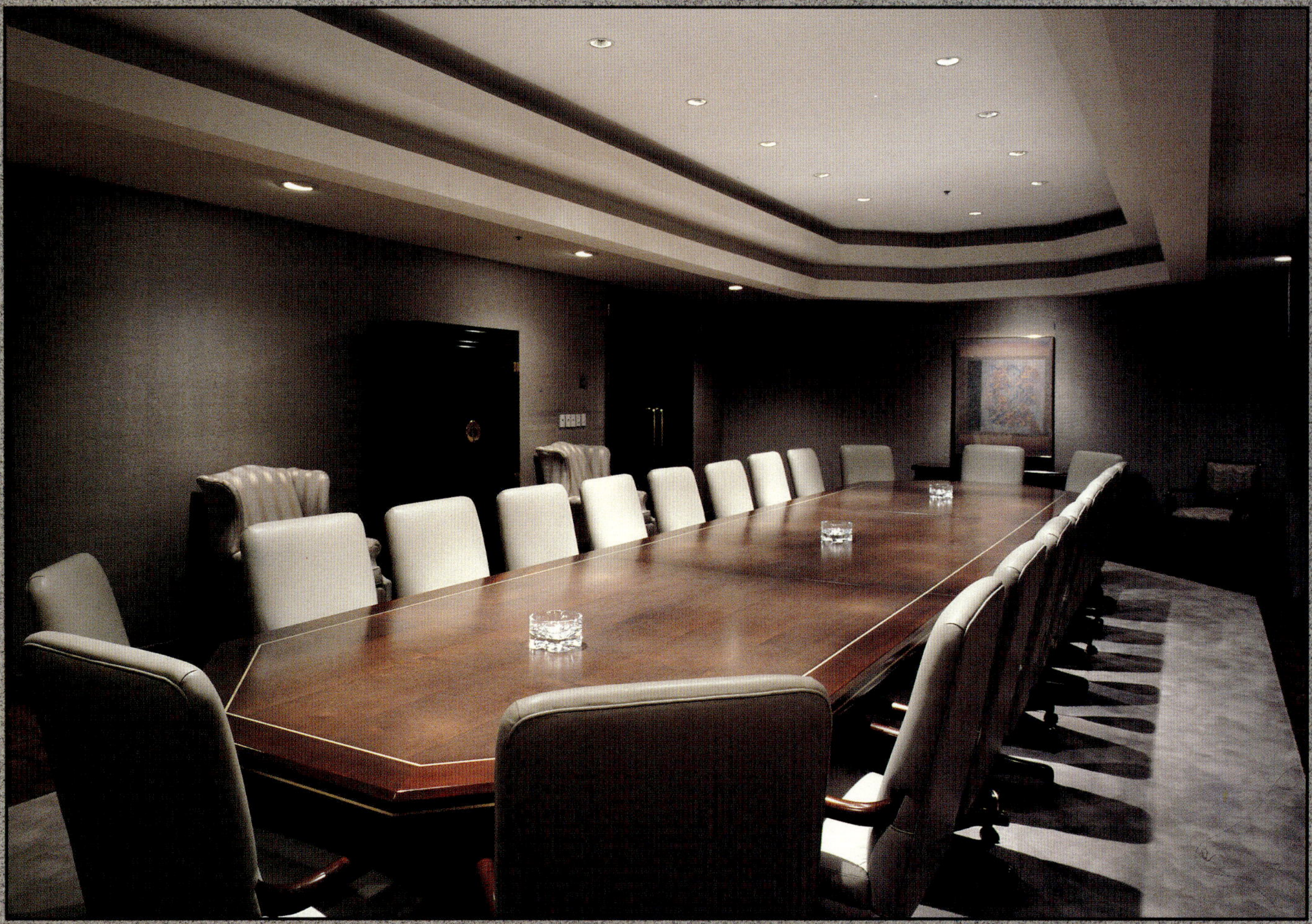

Fogler, Rubinoff
Barristers & Solicitors

Boardroom
Reception
General office

Acorn Design

Partners
Sandra Cohen
Olga Mihailovich ARIDO IDC ASID

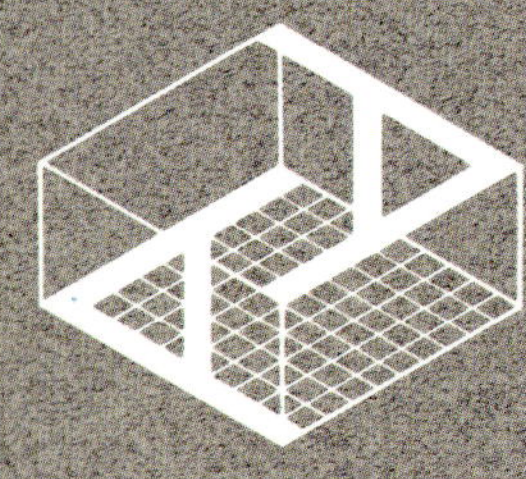

Corporate/Commercial Interiors

• Space Planning

• Interior Design Concepts

• Furnishings Selection

• System Specialists

• Project Management

Client List
– Bastedo Cooper & Shostock
  Barristers & Solicitors
– Canadian Bar Association
– Capp, Shupak, Elie
  Barristers & Solicitors
– Carewell Corporation
– Edison Group
– Grubner, Krauss
  Barristers & Solicitors
– Nadler & Company
– Nutri/System

67 Mowat Avenue, Suite 142, Toronto, Ontario, Canada M6K 3E3   Telephone: /416/537-0090 Fax: 537-5790

ATKINSON McKEE DESIGN CONSULTANTS INC.

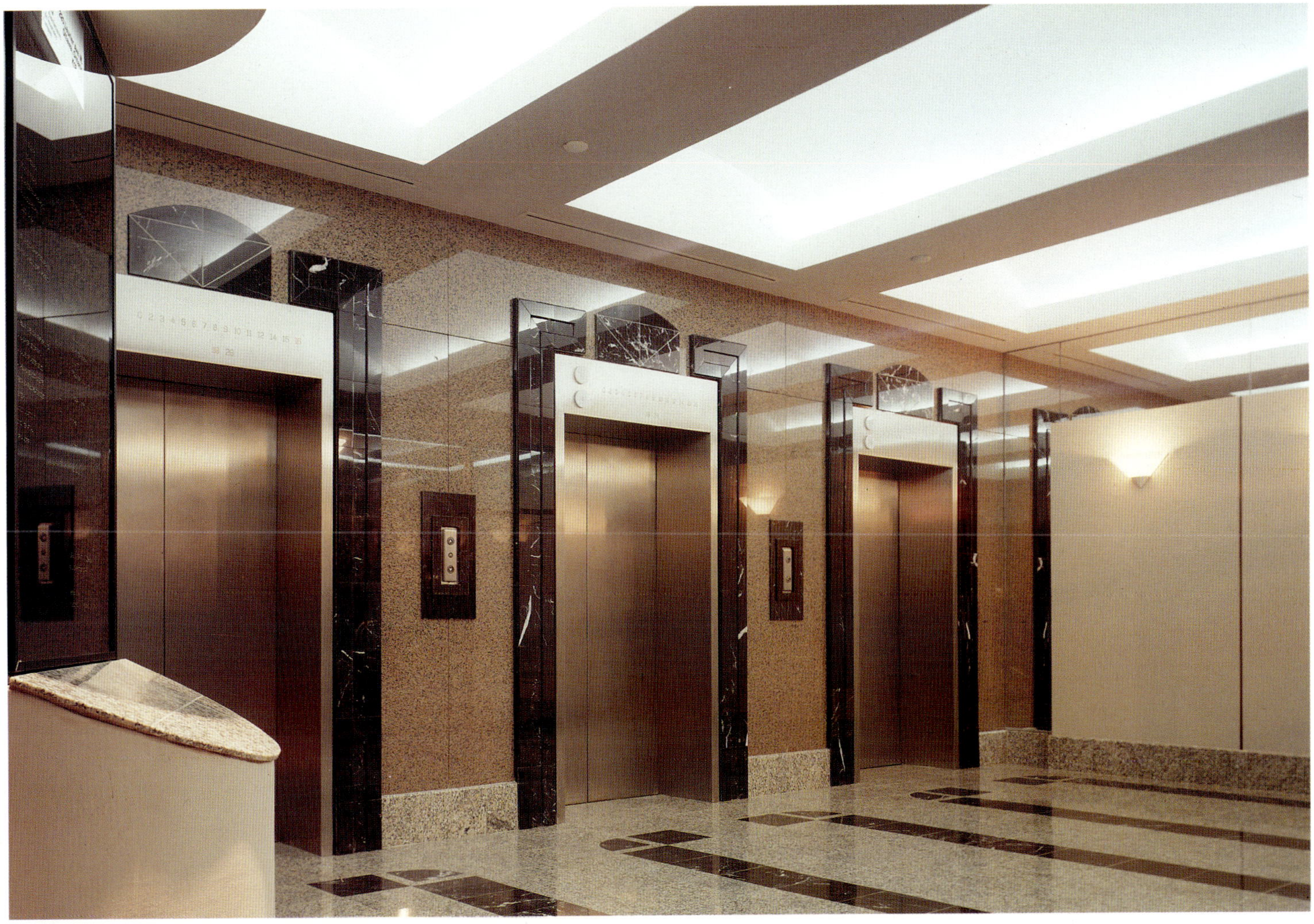

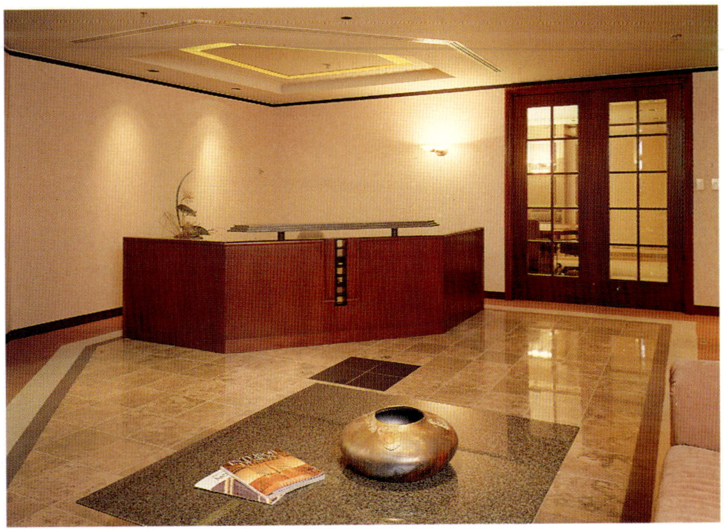

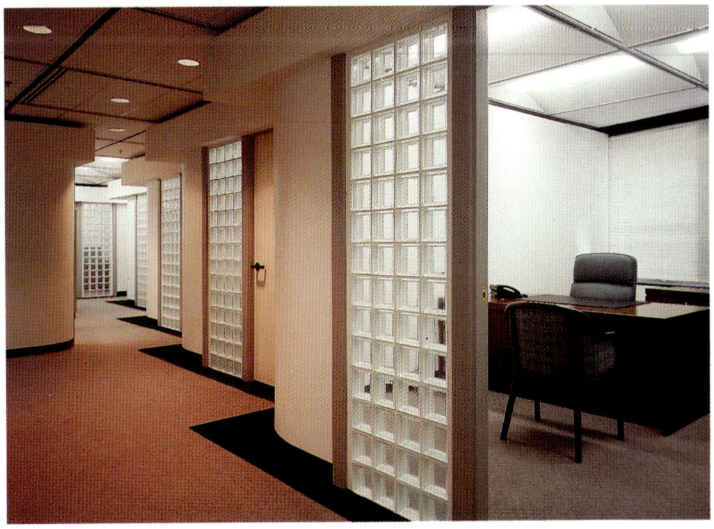

Highly motivated consultants skilled in providing services from Lease Assistance Space Planning to Project Management.

Designing creative solutions guided by a responsible approach to Client Schedules and Budgets.

We are committed to the leading position in our profession through the functional and visual reflection of design excellence.

Atkinson McKee
Design Consultants Inc.
Suite 1415, 360 Albert Street
Constitution Square, Ottawa
Ontario K1R 7X7
(613) 563-3797

atkinson mckee

D E S I G N C O N S U L T A N T S I N C

INTERIOR PLANNING AND DESIGN

Arthur Andersen & Co.

Management Station

McMaster Meighen

Boardroom

Inger Bartlett and Associates provides the full range of design services and project management; from initial planning of the design concept through working drawings to construction and installation of the client. Our objectives are to complete the project with integrity, on budget and within the planned time schedule.

Inger Bartlett and Associates Limited, 2A Gibson Avenue, Toronto, Canada M5R 1T5   *Tel. (416) 926-8247 Fax (416) 926-7587*

INTERIOR PLANNING AND DESIGN

Guardian Trust

Executive Office

Atlantique Image et Son

Reception Desk

Inger Bartlett and Associates projects the unique corporate image of each client into a clear, well thought out scheme. Individual style and character are critical to the success of every project. Architectural themes and custom designed furniture reflect the consistency of the design solution. Thorough and astute project management ensures that corporate style responds to budget demands.

Photographers from left: David Whittaker, Ian Samson, Fiona Spalding-Smith, David Whittaker

481 University Avenue
Toronto, Ontario M5G 2H4
Telephone (416) 596-2299
Telecopier (416) 586-0599

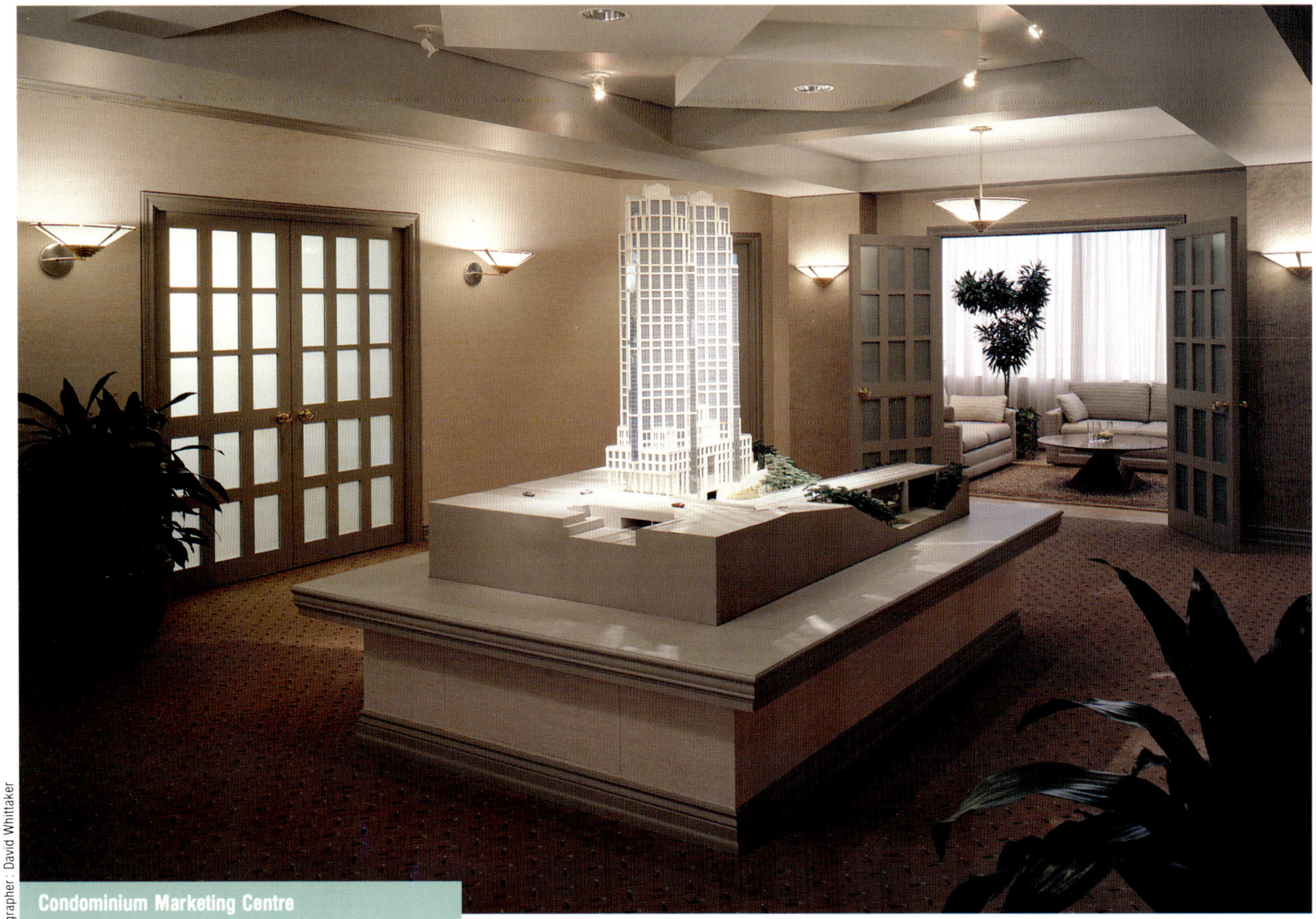

Photographer : David Whittaker

Condominium Marketing Centre
York Trillium Development Corporation

B + H INTERIOR DESIGN

B+H Interior Design

481 University Avenue
Toronto, Ontario M5G 2H4
Telephone (416) 596-2299
Telecopier (416) 586-0599

**World Trade Executive Offices
Northern Telecom Limited**

Photographer: David Whittaker

TO AMBROSE CARR LINTON KELLY INC....

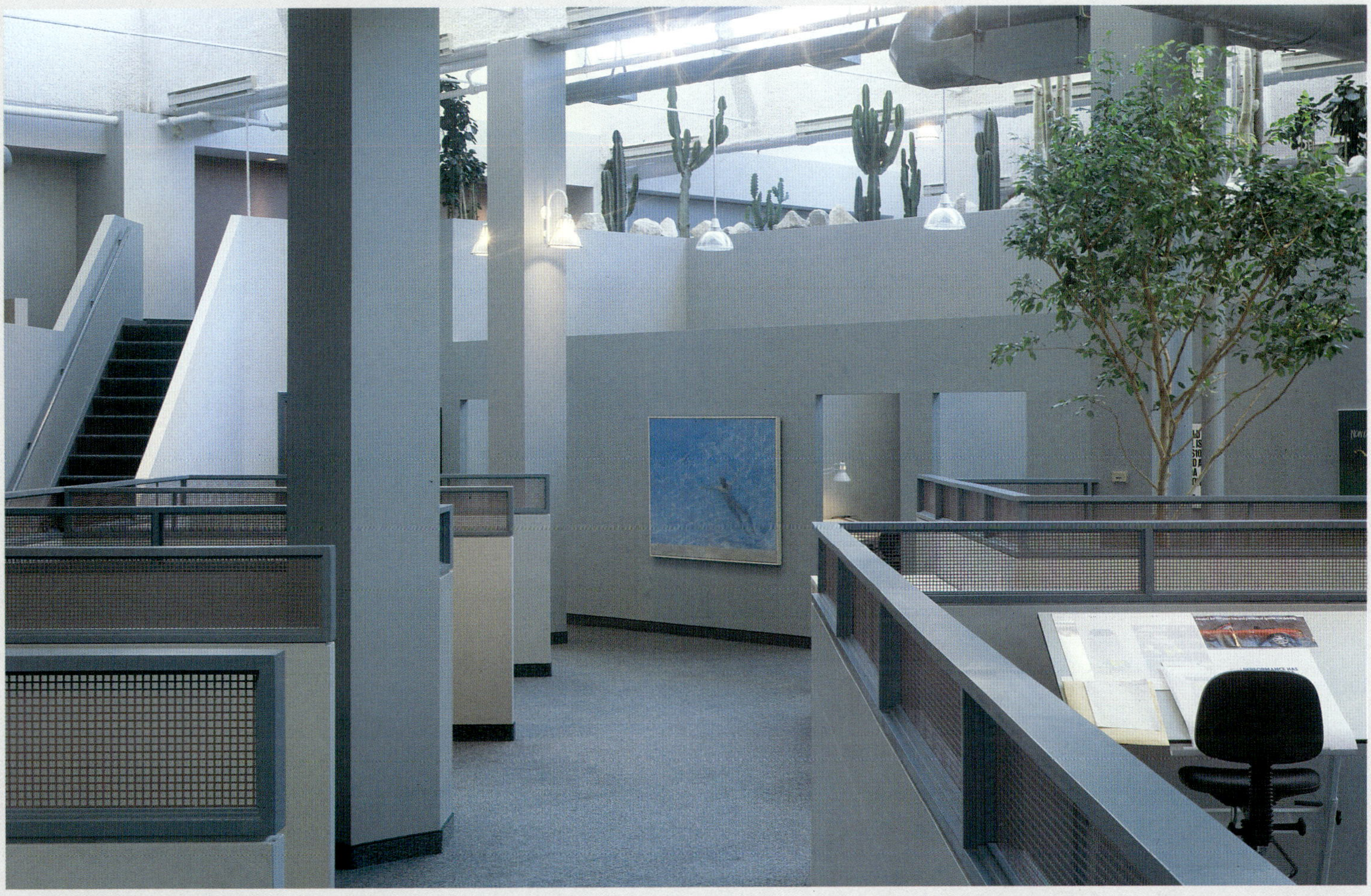

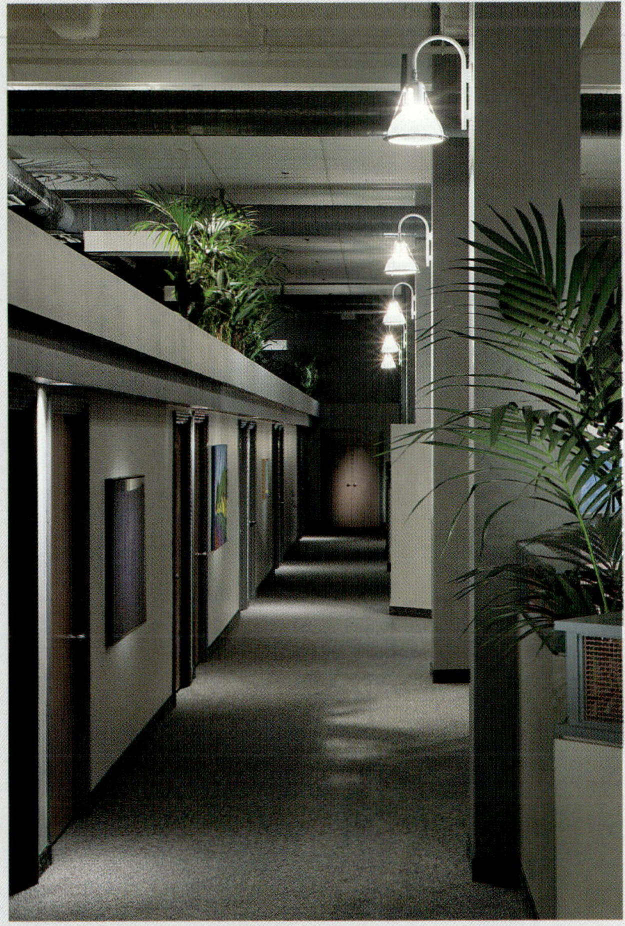

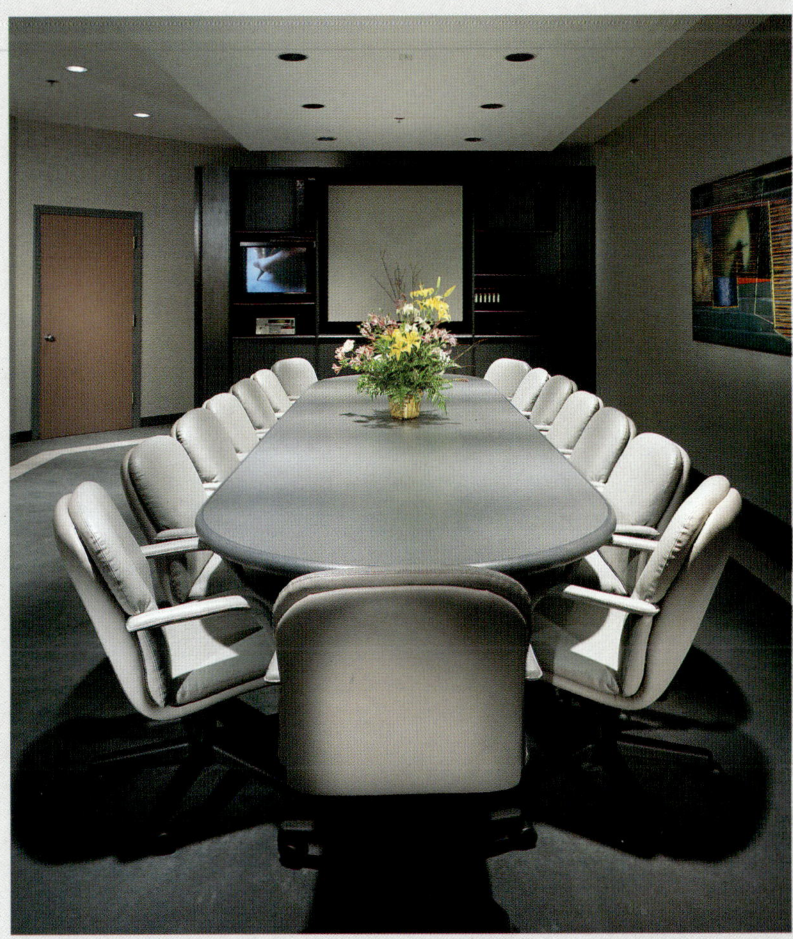

CECCONI

EPPSTADT

SIMONE

DESIGNERS

THE TORONTO WORLD TRADE CENTRE LEASING OFFICES

A CAMROST DEVELOPMENT AND YORK HANNOVER PROJECT

Melançon, Marceau, Grenier et Sciortino, avocats

Gazoduc TQM

Gazoduc TQM

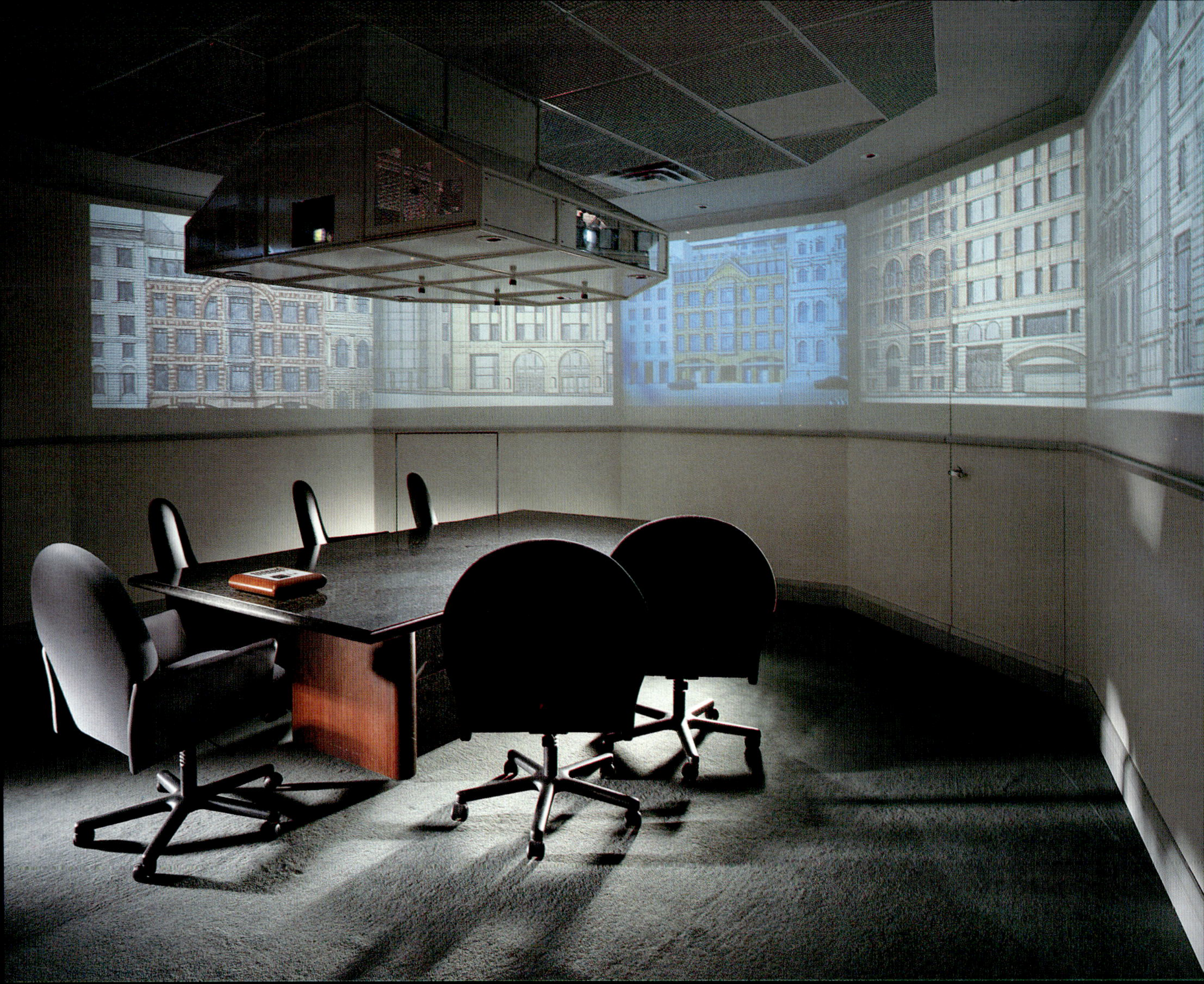

Société de promotion du Centre
de Commerce Mondial de Montréal

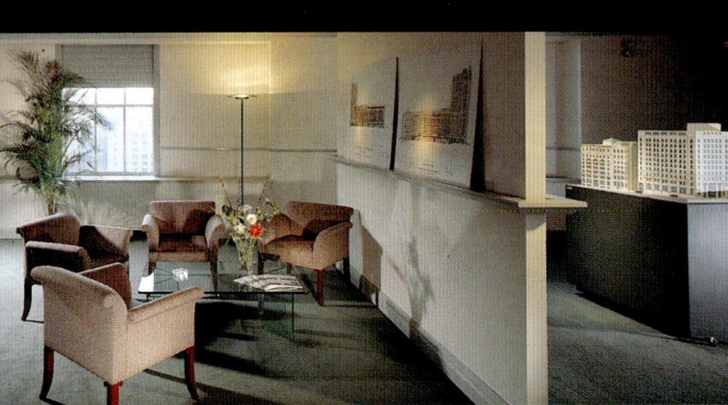

Photographies: Pierre-Louis Mongeau

FORREST DESIGN GROUP

The Forrest Design Group have a commitment to design excellence based on satisfying functional requirements on a qualitative basis: to deliver projects on time and on budget. We are in the forefront in the application of new office technology.

Acknowledged as one of Canada's most professional interior design firms, Forrest Design Group enjoys an enviable reputation in a very specialized field. We are leaders in design research and innovation. It is typical of our approach to every project – a solution individually tailored to the requirements of the client. Good design solutions make good business sense.

We offer professional consulting services
in interior design to the corporate,
commercial, retail and hospitality
communities. Our intrinsic knowledge of
building systems has established the
Forrest Design Group as specialists in
lease assistance, space planning, and
design development. User needs studies
are conducted either for new buildings
or in order to assess appropriate space
requirements in existing structures.
Our creative design approach coupled
with cost planning and management
assures the realization of most
preliminary planning. Through the proper
furniture selection and specification
a maximum cost benefit is achieved for
a newly planned business environment.

The Forrest Design Group, formerly known as Forrest Bodrug Partners Inc. has operated continuously since 1962. We are in the forefront as specialists in:
- Interior Design
- Architectural Programmes
- Space Planning
- Facilities Planning
- Ergonomics

Through our subsidiary company, Forrest Project Management Inc., we offer project and construction management services.

Forrest Project Management Inc. provides high performance project and construction management of the design and implementation programme for new tenant and corporate facilities renovations. This is a professional management service which specializes in business science techniques in cost engineering, scheduling and quality control.

FPM will assume full responsibility at the project concept phase, and maintain the required level of services throughout the planning, execution and start-up operational phases. Projects are monitored to achieve the desired schedule and cost reporting to meet budget stipulations.

Just as a single beam of light passing through a prism offers the spectrum of colour, Fielding and Associates takes a concept and breaks it into a creative, practical and cost efficient working environment. Quite simply . . . Fielding and Associates add new dimensions to your vision of the future.

Fielding
and
Associates

300 North Queen St., Suite 204
Etobicoke, Ontario M9C 5K4

416-626-6767

Photography: Elaine Kilburn

FRANKLAND·RUSZNYAK
associates limited
interior design consultants

228 GERRARD STREET EAST
TORONTO, ONTARIO, M5A 2E8
928-7422

- Power Financial Corporation

- Interprovincial Pipe Line Ltd.

- Seagram Distillers Ltd.

- Bolton Tremblay Group

THE ART OF DEFINING SPACE

Intefac Inc.
255 Matheson Blvd. West
Mississauga, Ontario L5R 3G3

Tel: 416.890.3000
Fax: 416.890.7321

It's the art of approaching a client without preconceptions. Without the will to force-fit a solution that doesn't suit their needs.

It's the art of listening. And of following it up with a design aesthetic of the highest order. On time. On budget.

GSM DESIGN

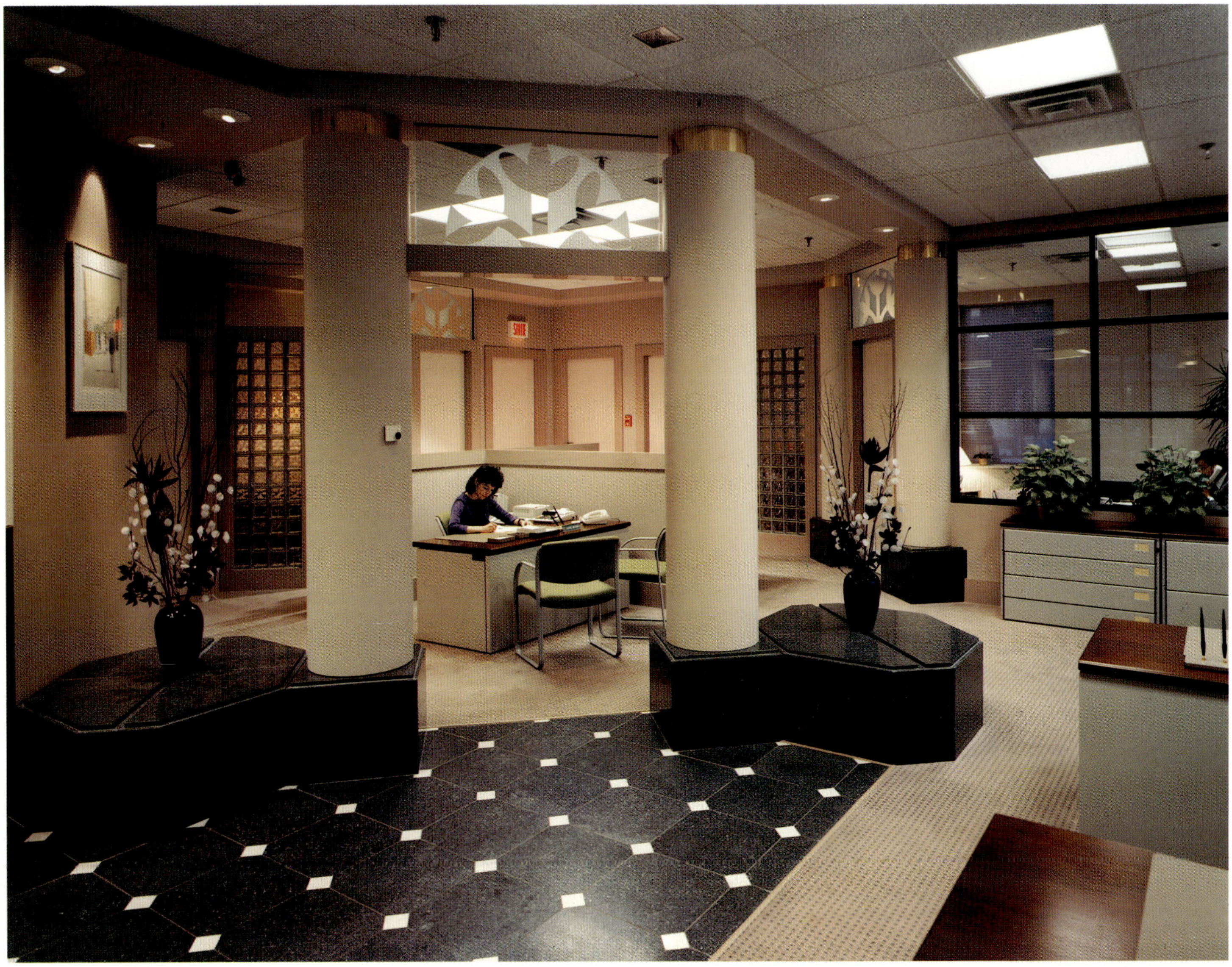

Customer Services
Montreal Trust
Westmount Branch
(Montreal)

Reception Area
Unigesco Inc.
Montreal

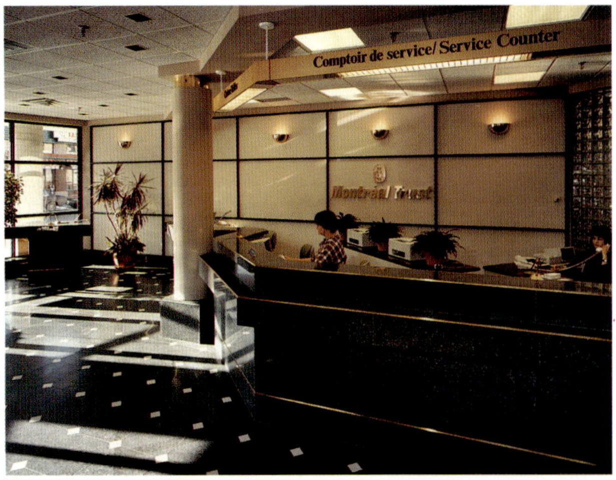

Teller Counter
Montreal Trust
Westmount Branch
(Montreal)

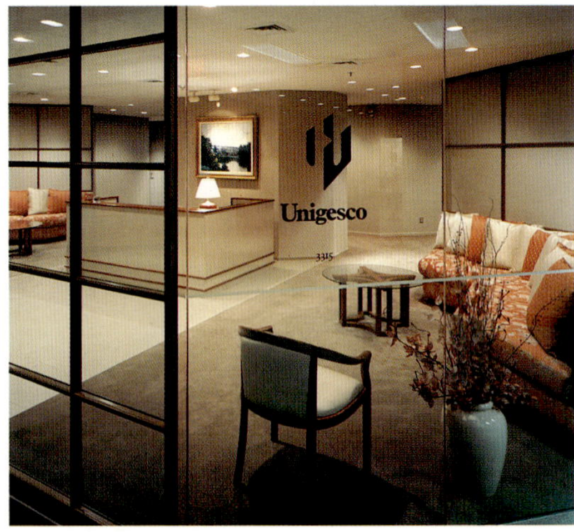

GSM DESIGN

Chief Representative's Office
The Nomura Securities Co. Ltd.
Montreal

Reception Area
The Nomura Securities Co. Ltd.
Montreal

Conference Room
The Nomura Securities Co. Ltd.
Montreal

GSM Design
Interiors, Visual Communications
and Exhibitions Inc.
317, Place d'Youville
Montréal, Québec
H2Y 2B5
Telephone: (514) 288-4233
Telefax: (514) 288-3820

A multidisciplinary firm offering
comprehensive design services
in the field of interior design
and visual communications.

HEFELE MAKOWKA DESIGN ASSOCIATES INC.

1,3 Toshiba of Canada Limited

2 Bratty & Partners

4 Private Residence

- Corporate
- Commercial
- Hospitality
- Residential
- Furniture Design
- Special Projects

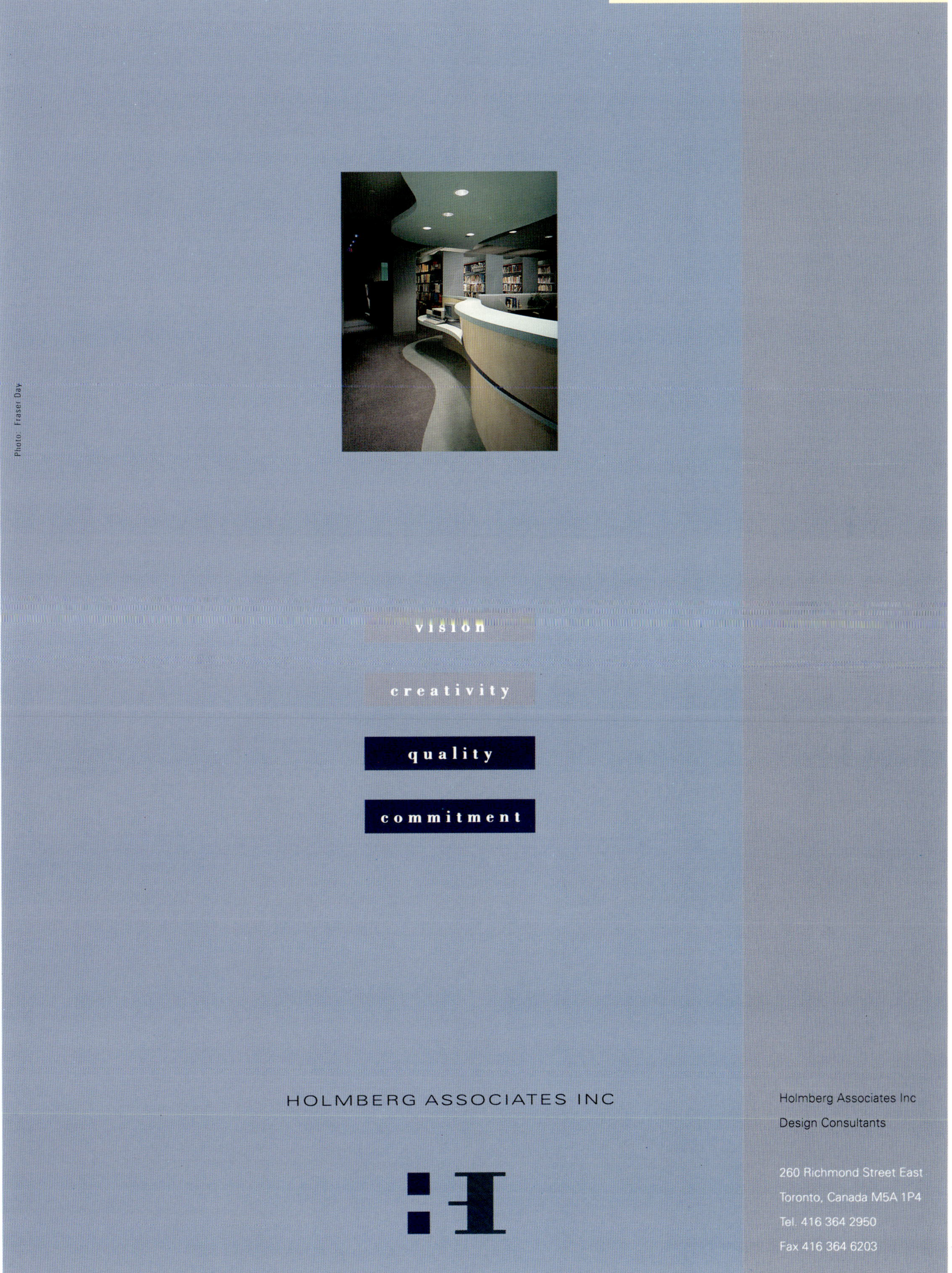
Photo: Fraser Day
vision
creativity
quality
commitment
HOLMBERG ASSOCIATES INC
Holmberg Associates Inc
Design Consultants
260 Richmond Street East
Toronto, Canada M5A 1P4
Tel. 416 364 2950
Fax 416 364 6203

HOWLETT DESIGN
CONSULTANTS

Interior Planning and Design

C. Howlett Design Consultants Limited
8 Market Street, Suite 500
Toronto, Ontario M5E 1M6
416-363-5281 · Fax 416-363-6259

Corporate Offices
Health Care

Carole Howlett ARIDO IDC
Judy Newcombe ARIDO IDC

JEFFREY/BULLOCK DESIGN CONSULTANTS INC.

ROYAL BANK OF CANADA, ONTARIO HEADQUARTERS DESIGN TEAM

PHOTOGRAPHY: DAVID WHITTAKER

Design Consultants Inc.
8 Market St.
Suite 300
Toronto Canada
M5E 1M6

Tel: 416 868·1616

INTERIOR DESIGN & PROJECT MANAGEMENT FOR FINANCIAL INSTITUTIONS & CORPORATIONS

KUBIK·ZDOBINSKY & ASSOCIATES INC.

Coca-Cola Ltd.
Concorde Corporate Centre

Touche Ross
5140 Yonge St.

- Feasibility Studies
- Interior Design
- Computer Aided Drafting
- Renovations
- Furniture Installations
- Project Management

KUBIK·ZDOBINSKY & ASSOCIATES INC.

119 Spadina Ave., suite 1103
Toronto, Ontario M5V 2L1
Tel. (416) 977-4222

Borden & Elliot
Scotia Plaza

Concorde, Don Mills, Teron International
Won 1987 T.H.B.A., Grand S.A.M. Award
and 1987 A.R.I.D.O Bronze Award

buildable details save time and money.
Our commitment to excellence goes
beyond a job well done, reaching for new
plateaus with each and every project.

Vogue International, North York,
Penta Stolp Corp., Won 1989 C.H.B.A.,
National S.A.M. Award,
Best Sales Centre over 1,000 sq. ft.

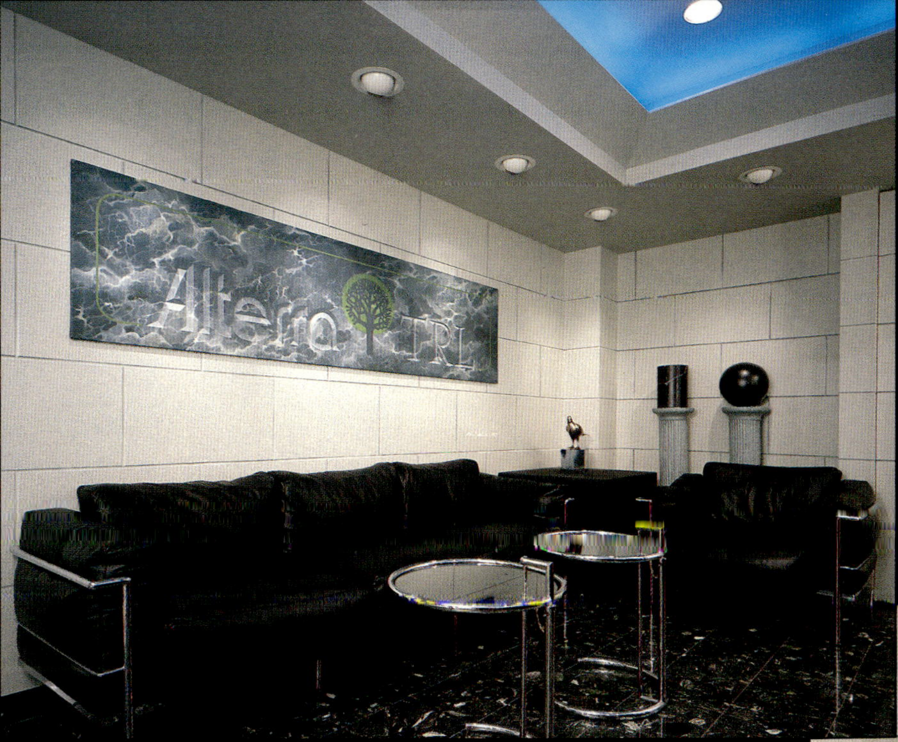

Alterra TRL Corporate Offices, Toronto

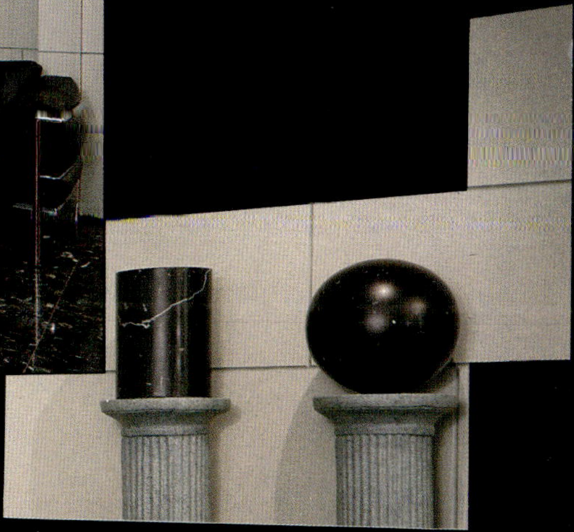

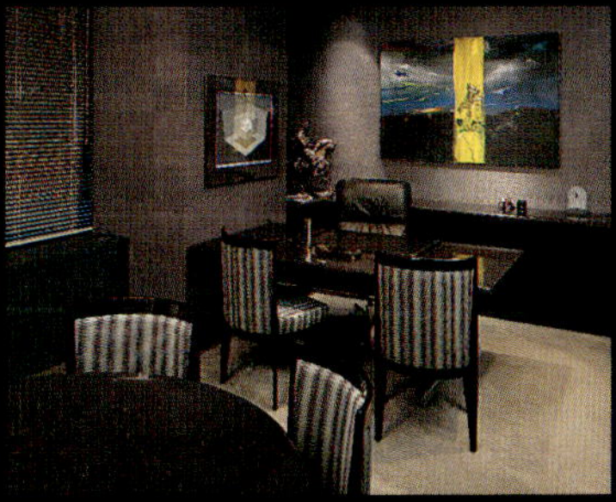

L'image Design

Suites 1 and 2, 7100 Warden Avenue

Markham, Ontario, Canada, L3R 8B5

Tel 416 475 7703, Fax 416 475 8926

See also Model Suites and Public Areas section within book

MARSHALL / MOORE / GOYETTE DESIGN INC.

Reception Area

Typical Bay

Conference Room Entry

Reception Area

■ **Winners** of the prestigious 1989 AMOCO International

Design Award for

Commercial Office Interiors

for the office of

Hemens, Cornish, Quesnel, Levac & Hindle,

Attorneys, Montreal, Quebec

Design Team:

Michael Moore

Cathy MacHutchin

Brenda Kelly

Holly Wiebe

Conference Room

Dedicated to excellence in design, costs control and on–time delivery, we have undertaken the following recent projects:
- Hemens, Cornish, Quesnel, Levac & Hindle
- The United States Consulate, Montreal
- Joseph E. Seagram & Sons Head Office
- Duschesne & Fils

Centre Manuvie
2000 Mansfield, Bureau 1505
Montréal, Québec
H3A 3A3
Tél.: (514) 843-3344
Fax: (514) 499-8495

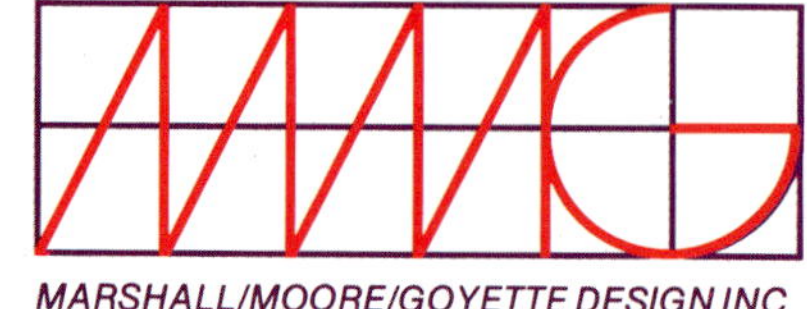

MARSHALL/MOORE/GOYETTE DESIGN INC.

PATRICIA McCLINTOCK & ASSOCIÉS INC.

Patricia McClintock & Associés inc.

Designers-conseil
Design Consultants

4040-A chemin Trafalgar
Montréal, Québec H3Y 1R2
Tél.: (514) 932-1860
Fax: (514) 939-2726

- Hotel/Restaurant Design
- Corporate Interiors
- Retail Planning & Design
- Image Development

Corporate Philosophy:

- Professionalism
- Functionalism
- Design creativity, integrity and timelessness
- Financial responsibility
- Total client involvement and awareness
- Comprehensive project management with CAD assistance

LEDUC-LEBEL
Law Firm
1130 Sherbrooke St. W.
Montreal, Quebec
Project 1988

Counter-clockwise from top:
– Conference Room
– View to Reception
– Secretarial Stations
– Design Details

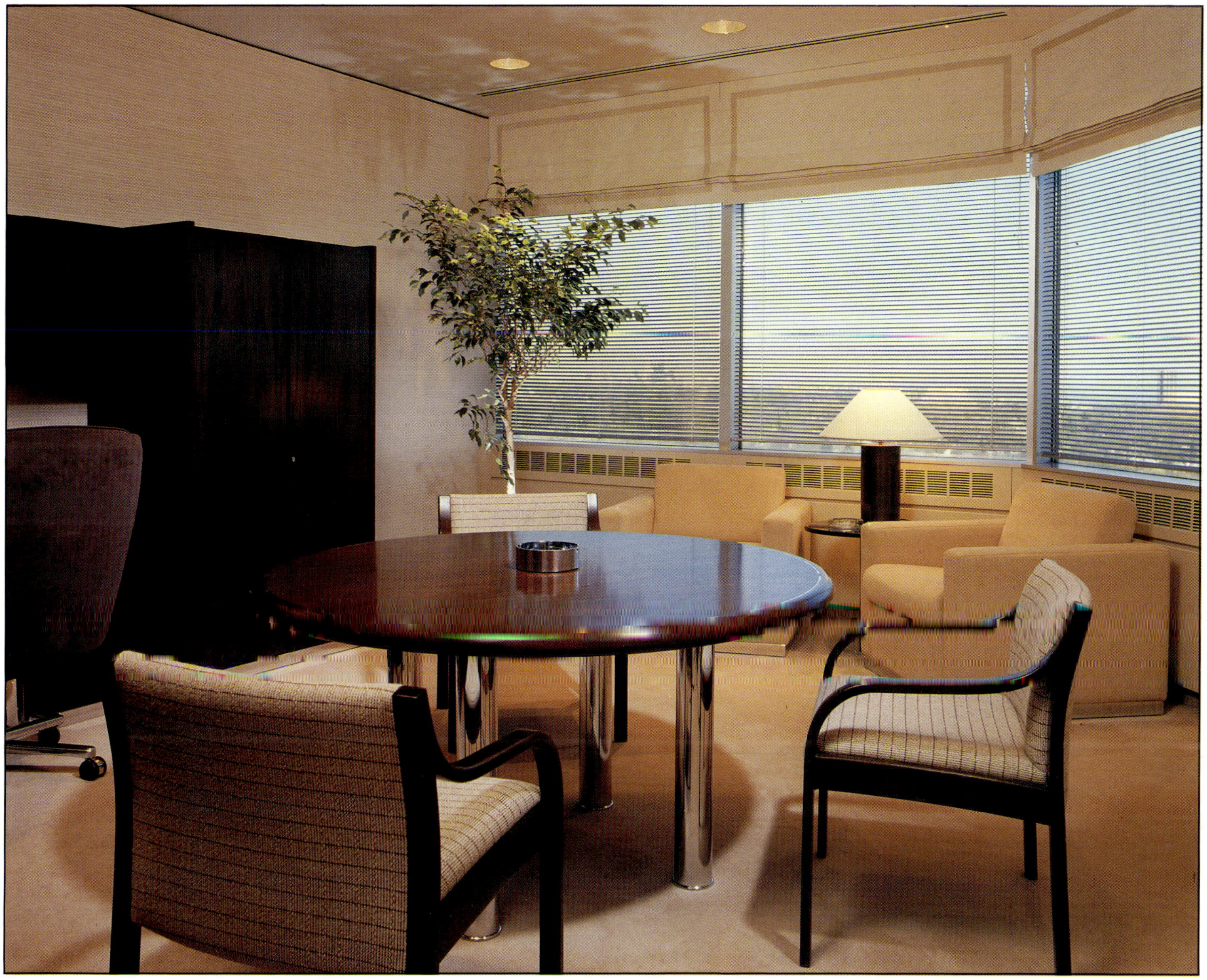

Interior Design / Corporate

Senior Project Designer: Kathryn Lange   Photo: Design Archive

Anthony Meyrick-Eastick
Design Group Inc.

430 King Street West
Suite 200
Toronto, Ontario
Canada M5V 1L5
(416) 593-8844

Founding member of Impetus International Corporate Designers Inc.

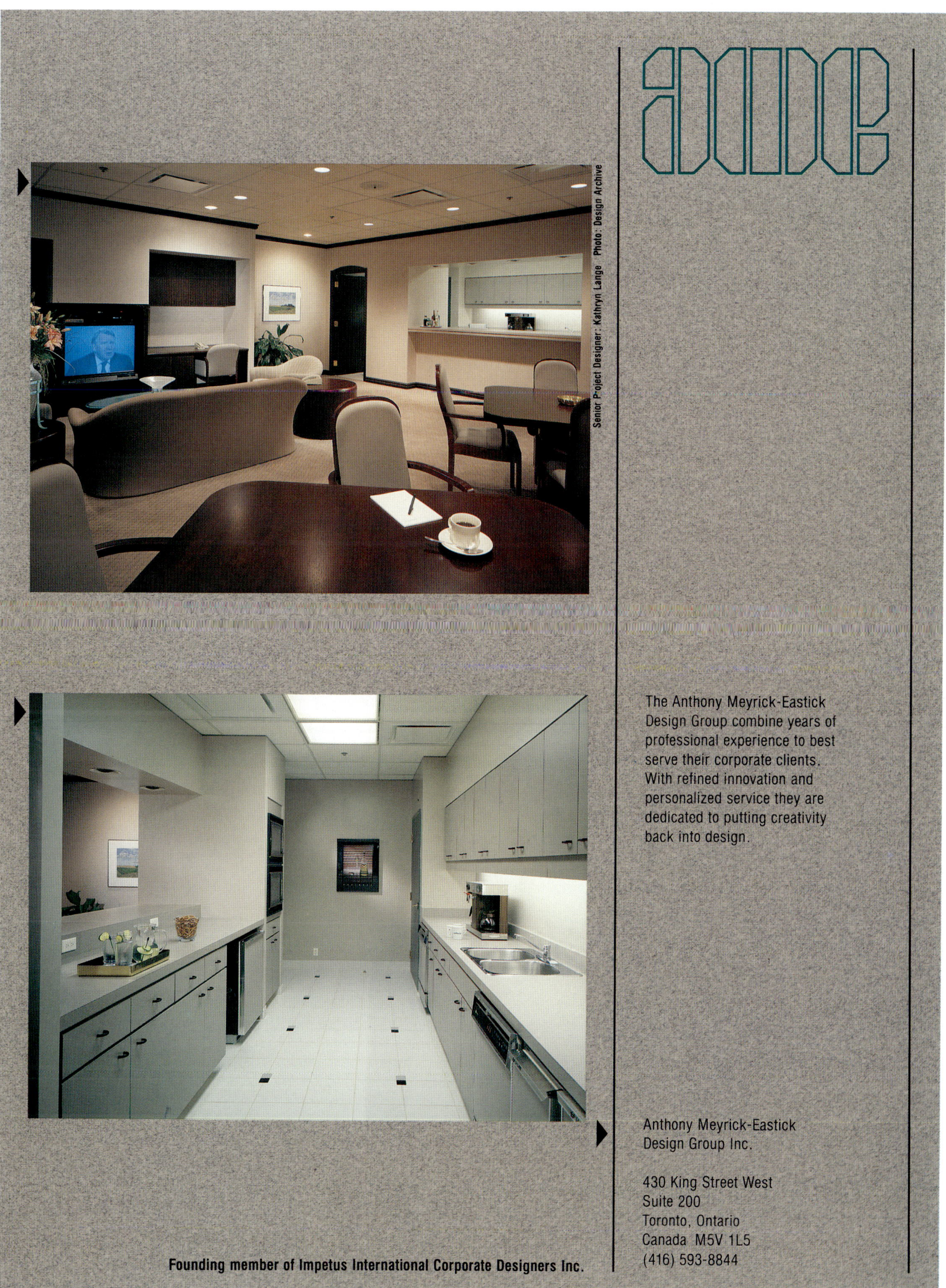

Senior Project Designer: Kathryn Lange   Photo: Design Archive

The Anthony Meyrick-Eastick Design Group combine years of professional experience to best serve their corporate clients. With refined innovation and personalized service they are dedicated to putting creativity back into design.

Anthony Meyrick-Eastick
Design Group Inc.

430 King Street West
Suite 200
Toronto, Ontario
Canada M5V 1L5
(416) 593-8844

Founding member of Impetus International Corporate Designers Inc.

MOLE·WHITE & ASSOCIATES LTD.

Rowntree Ltd.
• Reception Area
• Office
• Conference Room

• Feasibility studies
• Space analysis
• Interior design concepts
• Working drawings
• Furniture programes
• Project management

Mole·White & Associates Ltd.

260 King Street East
Suite 320
Toronto, Ontario
M5A 1K3
(416) 867-1414
Fax (416) 368-7142

Le Groupe S.B.I.
Compagnie de gestion
Property investors
and developers

Charette Fortier Hawey
Touche Ross
Comptables agréés
Chartered accountants

En collaboration avec:
In conjunction with:
Marie-Josée Paquet, Arch.

National
Cabinet de relations
publiques et publicité
Public relations
and advertising

Wyatt
Actuaires
Actuaries

Stikeman Elliott
Avocats
Lawyers

Clarkson Gordon
Comptables agréés
Chartered accountants

En collaboration avec:
In conjunction with:
T.P.L. Arch.

Wajax Limitée
Bureau chef
Head office

Westcliff Management
Promoteur immobilier
Developer

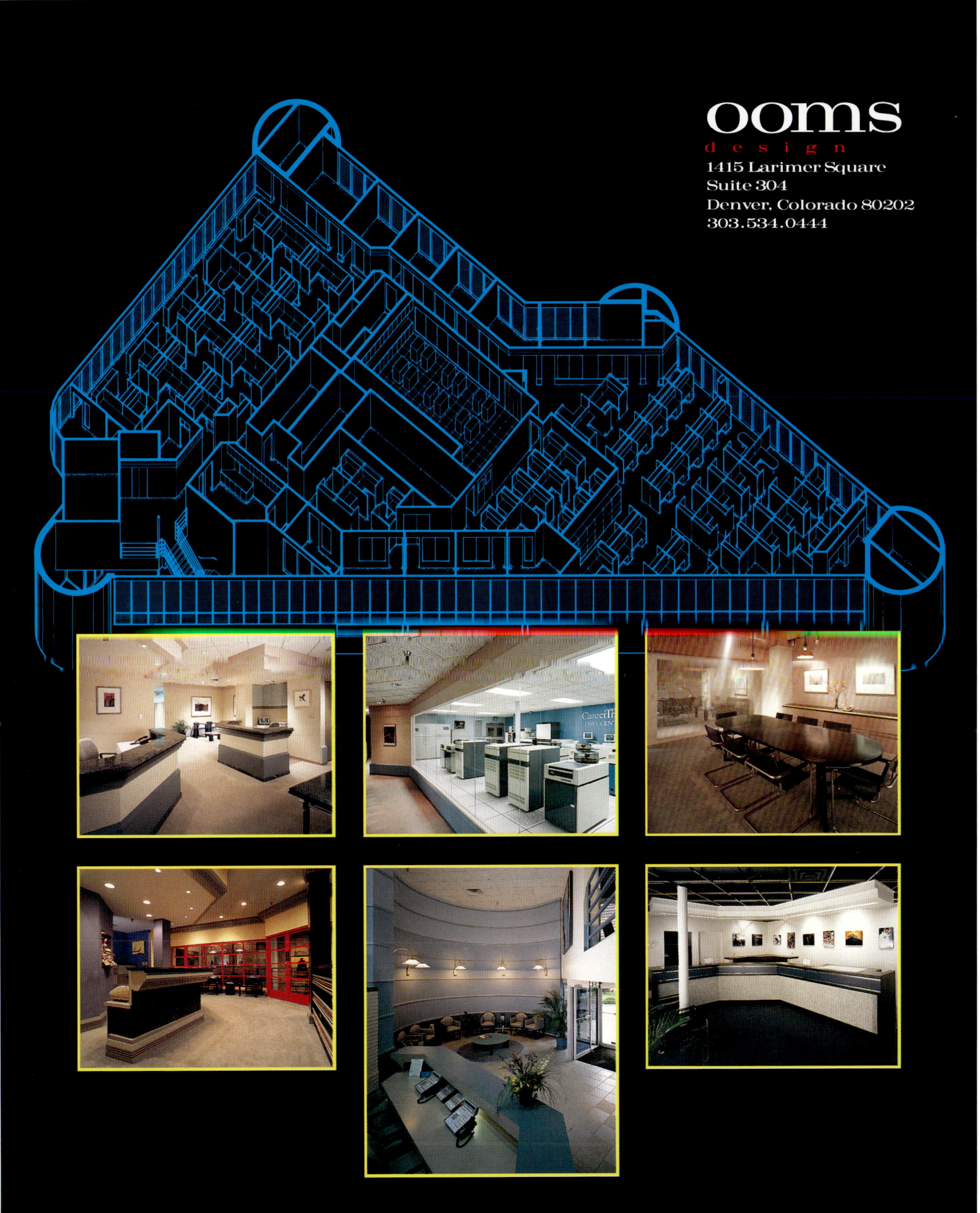

ooms
design
1415 Larimer Square
Suite 304
Denver, Colorado 80202
303.534.0444
ARCHITECTURE, INTERIOR DESIGN, PROGRAMMING, SPACE PLANNING, FURNITURE DESIGN & ACQUISITION

Ove

Ove Design intérieurs inc.
356, rue Le Moyne
Vieux-Montréal, Québec, Canada H2Y 1Y3
514 844-8421 Fax. 514 844-8978

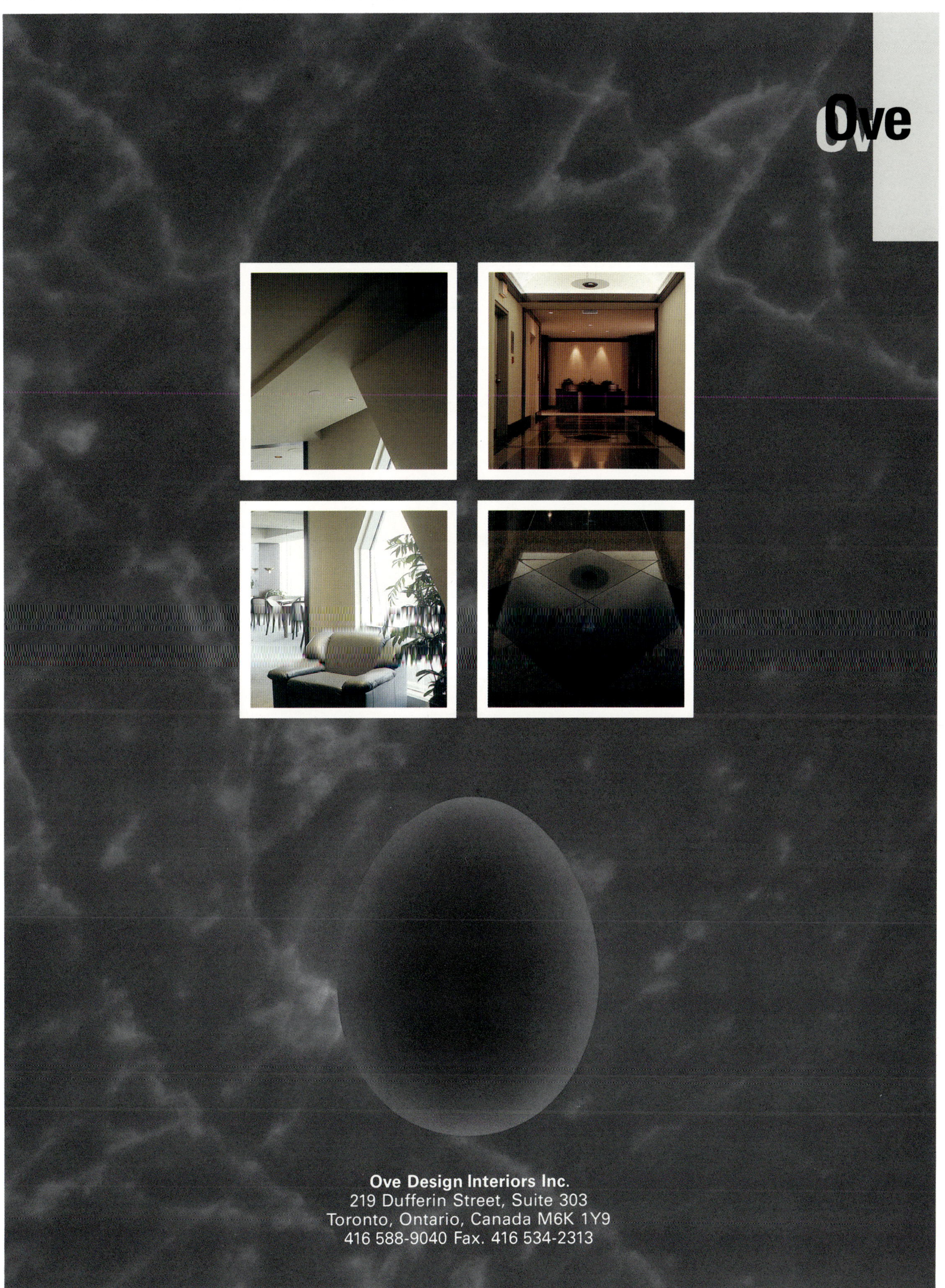

Ove Design Interiors Inc.
219 Dufferin Street, Suite 303
Toronto, Ontario, Canada M6K 1Y9
416 588-9040 Fax. 416 534-2313

PULSANN COMMERCIAL INTERIORS INC.

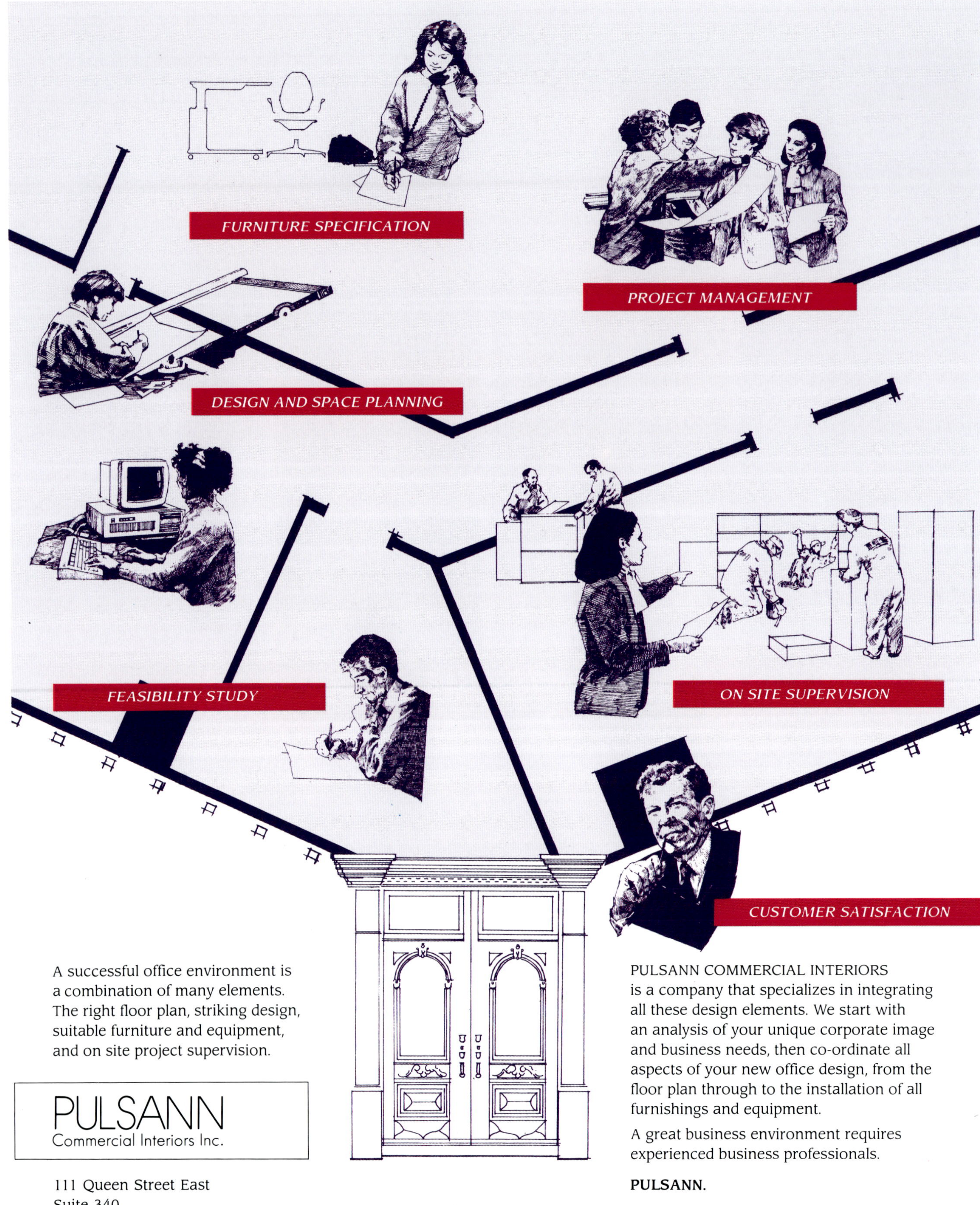

A successful office environment is a combination of many elements. The right floor plan, striking design, suitable furniture and equipment, and on site project supervision.

PULSANN
Commercial Interiors Inc.

111 Queen Street East
Suite 340
Toronto, Ontario M5C 1S2
865-1196
FAX: 865-9808

PULSANN COMMERCIAL INTERIORS is a company that specializes in integrating all these design elements. We start with an analysis of your unique corporate image and business needs, then co-ordinate all aspects of your new office design, from the floor plan through to the installation of all furnishings and equipment.

A great business environment requires experienced business professionals.

PULSANN.

RAYMOND TIPPING CHIAPPETTA INC.

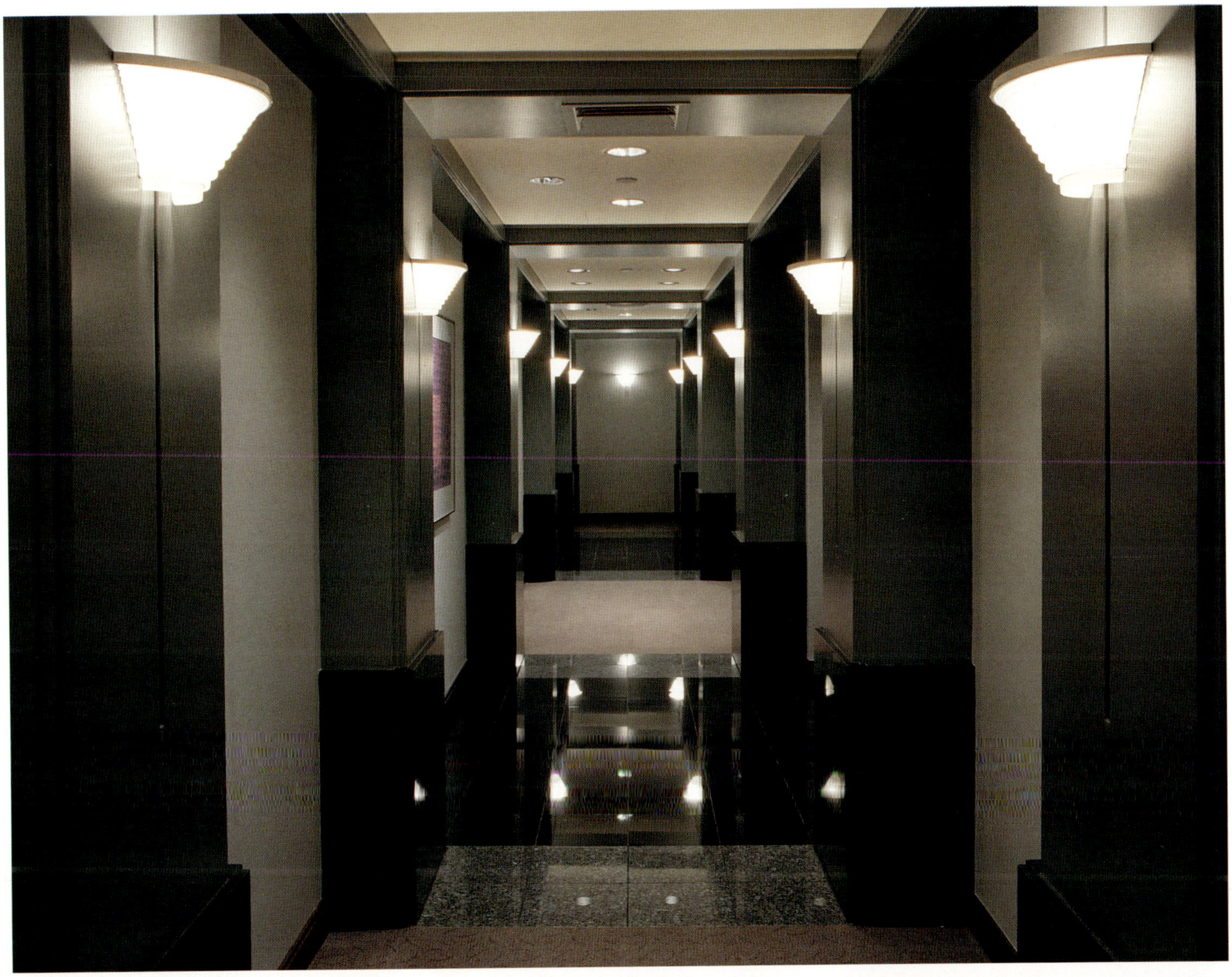

Photography by David Whittaker

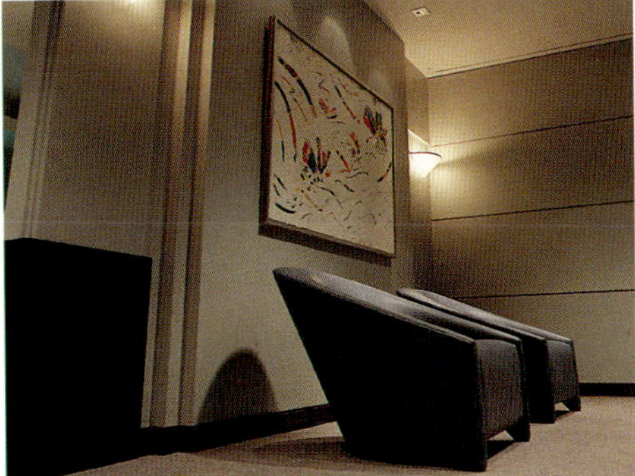

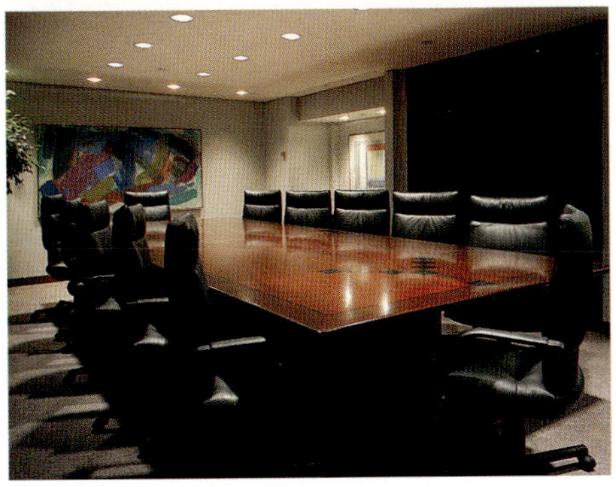

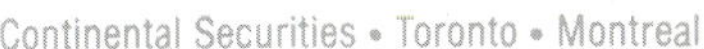

Continental Securities • Toronto • Montreal

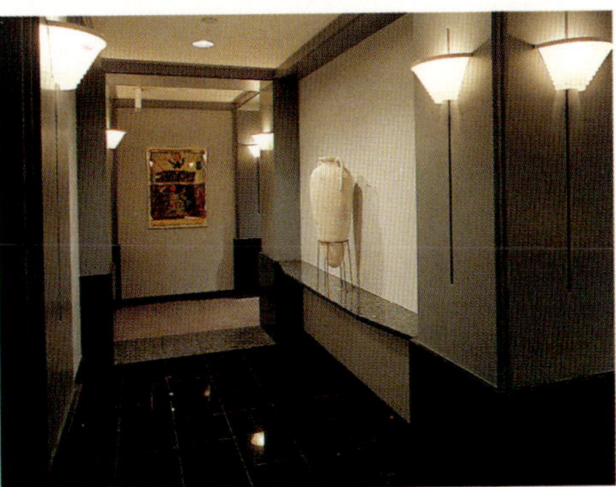

ARIDO Awards • Silver Recipient

RAYMOND
TIPPING
CHIAPPETTA

DESIGNERS / PLANNERS

550 Queen Street East, Suite 320, Toronto, Canada M5A 1V2 Telephone: (416) 368-6819 Fax: (416) 368-1387

WESCO
Westinghouse Sales Distribution Inc.
Reception Area
Conference Room

Paul A Stocks Limited

Professional Interior Design
Commercial Space Planning
Systems Specialists
Project Management

35 Coldwater Road, Don Mills, Ontario   M3B 1Y8   (416) 449-9733

COMPLETE
ARCHITECTURAL
+ DESIGN
SERVICES
FOR THE
SPACE USER

ANALYSIS

PLANNING

DESIGN

CONTRACT DOCUMENTS

CONSTRUCTION MANAGEMENT

Leopold

ARCHITECTURAL DESIGN INC.

SPACE PLANNING + ARCHITECTURE

C O M P U T E R   A I D E D   D E S I G N = S P A R C

PHILOSOPHY: We represent exclusively the interest of the corporate and industrial user of space.

GOAL: We shall translate your company's requirements into functional spaces that delight the senses and optimize your productivity.

TEAM: We are professional architects and designers using state-of-the-art CADD technology (computer aided design and drafting).

COMMITMENT: We shall provide comprehensive management of your project to ensure maximum possible savings and quality.

LEOPOLD ARCHITECTURAL DESIGN INC.
1180 Drummond, Suite 600, Montréal, Québec H3G 2S1
Tél.: (514) 393-1636   Fax: (514) 393-1447

Leopold

ARCHITECTURAL DESIGN I

TOTAL ENVIRONMENTAL PLANNING LIMITED

total environmental planning limited

265 hood road, markham, ontario l3r 4n3 (416) 474-0510 • ludwig o. schindler, arido, i.d.c. • susan papov, arido, i.d.c.

Chris Yen Designs Inc. offers design, space planning, project management and consultation to corporate, institutional and commercial clients.

Chris Yen Designs Inc.
Planning and Design
120 Carlton Street, Suite 315
Toronto, Ontario M5A 4K2
Telephone: (416) 323-3888
Fax Number: (416) 323-3814

ÉTUDES DE FAISABILITÉ • CORPORATIONS/DÉTAIL
COMPUTER ASSISTED DESIGN • SPACE ANALYSIS

LE GROUPE DMR INC., SIÈGE SOCIAL / DMR GROUP INC., HEAD OFFICE

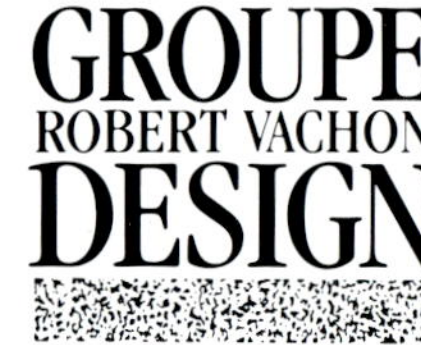

DESIGN ASSISTÉ PAR ORDINATEUR • CONSULT
PRE LEASE CONSULTATION AND PLANNING • CO

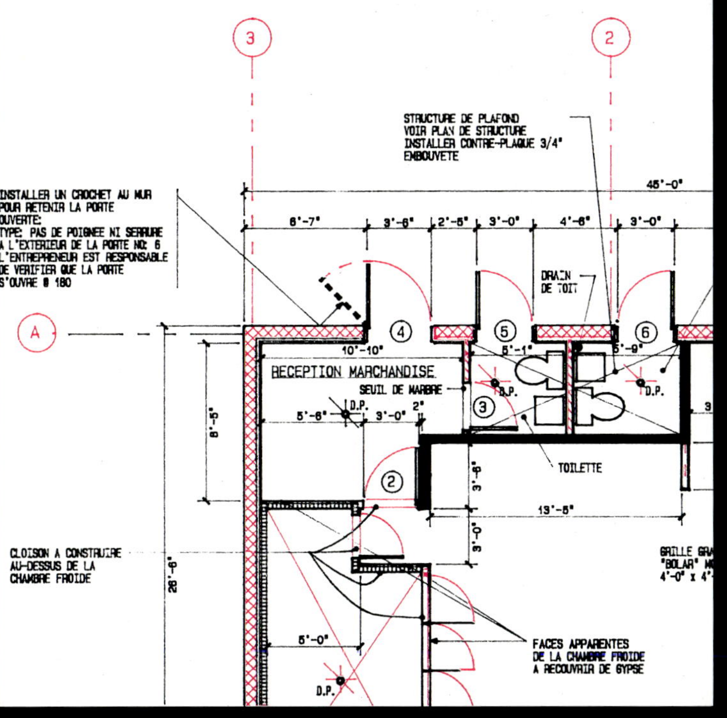

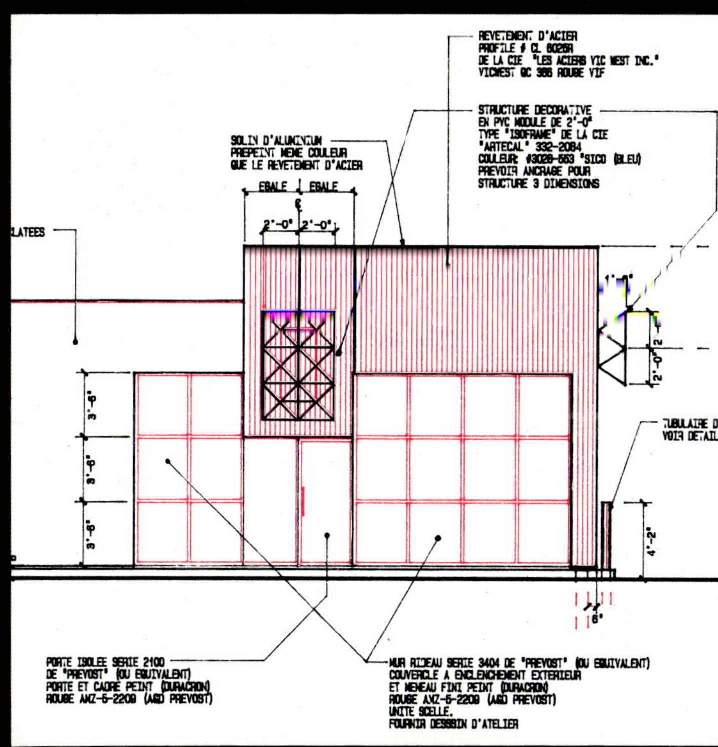

PROVI-SOIR, DÉPANNEUR/CONVENIENCE STORE

GROUPE
ROBERT VACHON
DESIGN

Le Groupe Robert Vachon Design inc.
360, rue St-François-Xavier, Bureau 401, Vieux-Montréal (Québec) H2Y 2S8
Tél.: (514) 843-3505   Télécopieur: (514) 843-4372

ZEIDLER ROBERTS INTERIORS LIMITED

THE RAYMOND F. KRAVIS CENTER FOR THE PERFORMING ARTS, PALM BEACH COUNTY*

We believe that our client's interests are best served by the harmonious blend of two areas of expertise: architecture and interior design. Our reputation for producing exciting yet functional, successful and aesthetically pleasing projects is complemented by a team which specializes in the design of interior spaces.

NUMBER ONE DUNDAS LOBBY, TORONTO

CADILLAC FAIRVIEW TOWER, TORONTO[+]

ZEIDLER ROBERTS INTERIORS LIMITED

- Offers full range of interior design services for corporate, commercial and health care facilities.
- Provides innovative, cost effective design solutions which reflect the client's image and objectives.

QUEEN'S QUAY TERMINAL, TORONTO

COLLEGE OF PHYSICIANS & SURGEONS, TORONTO

- Produces a long-term investment in terms of efficient, comfortable and classic interior spaces.
- Approaches each project with imagination and careful attention to detail and budget, thereby creating quality results for our clients.

THE CANADIAN RED CROSS SOCIETY HEAD OFFICE, OTTAWA

COLLEGE OF PHYSICIANS & SURGEONS, TORONTO

THE CANADIAN RED CROSS SOCIETY HEAD OFFICE, OTTAWA

PREMIERE DANCE THEATRE, TORONTO

THE HOSPITAL FOR SICK CHILDREN, TORONTO++

COLLEGE OF PHYSICIANS & SURGEONS, TORONTO

ZEIDLER ROBERTS INTERIORS LIMITED

315 QUEEN STREET WEST, TORONTO, ONTARIO M5V 2X2
TEL: (416) 596-8300
TELEX: 06-22224 ZEIDROBTSTOR
FAX: (416) 596-1408

*   Associate Architect: Schwab, Twitty & Hanser Architectural Group, Inc.
+   Joint Venture Architect: Bregman + Hamann Architects
++ Hospital Consultant: Karlsberger + Associates Architects Inc.

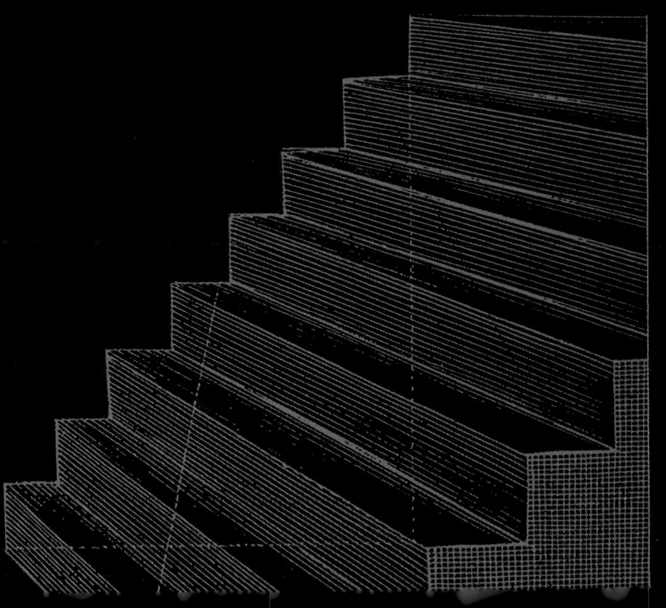

BJARNASON + ASSOCIATES

Bjarnason + Associates, under the direction of its principal, Brenda Bjarnason, offers complete space planning and interior design services in the areas of health care, retirement communities, and corporate/office and commercial design. The practice has a close association with affiliated companies, The Heinrichs Group and Victor J. Heinrichs, Architect. Collectively, we offer a comprehensive range of professional services including not only space planning and interior design, but also development and financial consulting, feasibility and space utilization studies, architecture, and project management. Creative and constructive communication between the client and project team plays an important role in the design process, resulting in innovation and functionally cost efficient solutions.

BJARNASON ◼ ASSOCIATES

Brenda Bjarnason, BID, ARIDO, IDC
Space Planning & Interior Design

11 Church Street
Suite 300
Toronto. Ontario
M5E 1W1
Tel.: (416) 368-4040
Fax.: (416) 367-2884

Affiliated Firms:

The Heinrichs Group
Development Consulting & Management
Ron Sawatsky, PhD
Tel.: (416) 368-8744

Victor J. Heinrichs, Architect
Architecture & Development Consulting
Vic Heinrichs, BArch, OAA
Tel.: (416) 860-1001

**Partial List of Health Care
& Retirement Community
Projects in Ontario:**

Canadian Mothercraft Society - Toronto
Colonel By Seniors Apartments - Smith Falls
Leamington Heritage Village - Leamington
Heritage Village Delhi - Delhi
Heritage Village Vineland - Vineland
Specialty Care Inc./Cedarvale - Keswick/Georgina
The Wellington Seniors Condominiums - Bowmanville

**Partial List of Corporate/
Office & Commercial Projects
in Ontario:**

Air Canada - Toronto
CHEX/Kawartha Broadcasting - Peterborough
Enroute - Mississauga
Knowlton Realty - Toronto
Montreal Trust - Toronto
Standard Trust - Peterborough
TVOntario - Toronto

HOWLETT DESIGN CONSULTANTS

HOWLETT DESIGN
C O N S U L T A N T S

Interior Planning and Design

C. Howlett Design Consultants Limited
8 Market Street, Suite 500
Toronto, Ontario M5E 1M6
416-363-5281 · Fax 416-363-6259

Health Care
Corporate Offices

Carole Howlett ARIDO IDC
Judy Newcombe ARIDO IDC

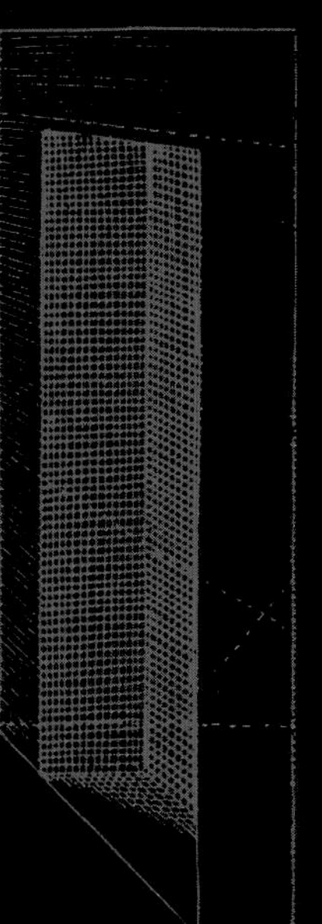

Our reception desk   Design: Rick Armstrong/DAG   Photo: Deborah Samuels

A unique consulting firm that has provided competent support to Shopping Centre Developers since 1980.

Labyrinth
Design and Development Consultants

TORONTO
262 Avenue Rd.,
Toronto, Canada
M4V 2G7
(416) 968-1750

VANCOUVER
Richmond Square
Suite 21
6551 Number 3 Rd.
Richmond, B.C.
Canada, V6Y 2B6
(604) 270-8456

MAJOR PROJECTS/CLIENTS
HAZELTON LANES, TORONTO/YORK HANNOVER • **RICHMOND CENTRE, VANCOUVER/**CONFEDERATION LIFE • **TORONTO INT'L AIRPORT, TERMINAL III/**AIRPORT DEVELOPMENT CORPORATION • **EATON SHERIDAN PLACE, MISSISSAUGA/**J.D.S. INVESTMENTS • **EATON SQUARE, BRANTFORD/**CAMPEAU CORPORATION • **WHITEOAKS SHOPPING CENTRE, LONDON/**THE WHITEOAKS GROUP • **11 SUPERCENTRES IN ONTARIO & THE MARITIMES/**I.P.C.F. PROPERTIES (LOBLAWS) • **BAYERS ROAD SHOPPING CENTRE, HALIFAX/**MAREX PROPERTIES • **UNICENTRE SHOPPING, BUENOS AIRES/**CENCOSUD, S.A. • **KOZLOV CENTRE, BARRIE/**CHEZ BELLE LIMITED •

MARIA
MANOLIU
AND
ASSOCIATES
DESIGN CONSULTANTS LIMITED

SUITE 1702, 372 BAY STREET, TORONTO, ONTARIO M5H 2W9 PHONE: (416) 860-1511 FACSIMILE: (416) 860-0898

MARIA MANOLIU AND ASSOCIATES

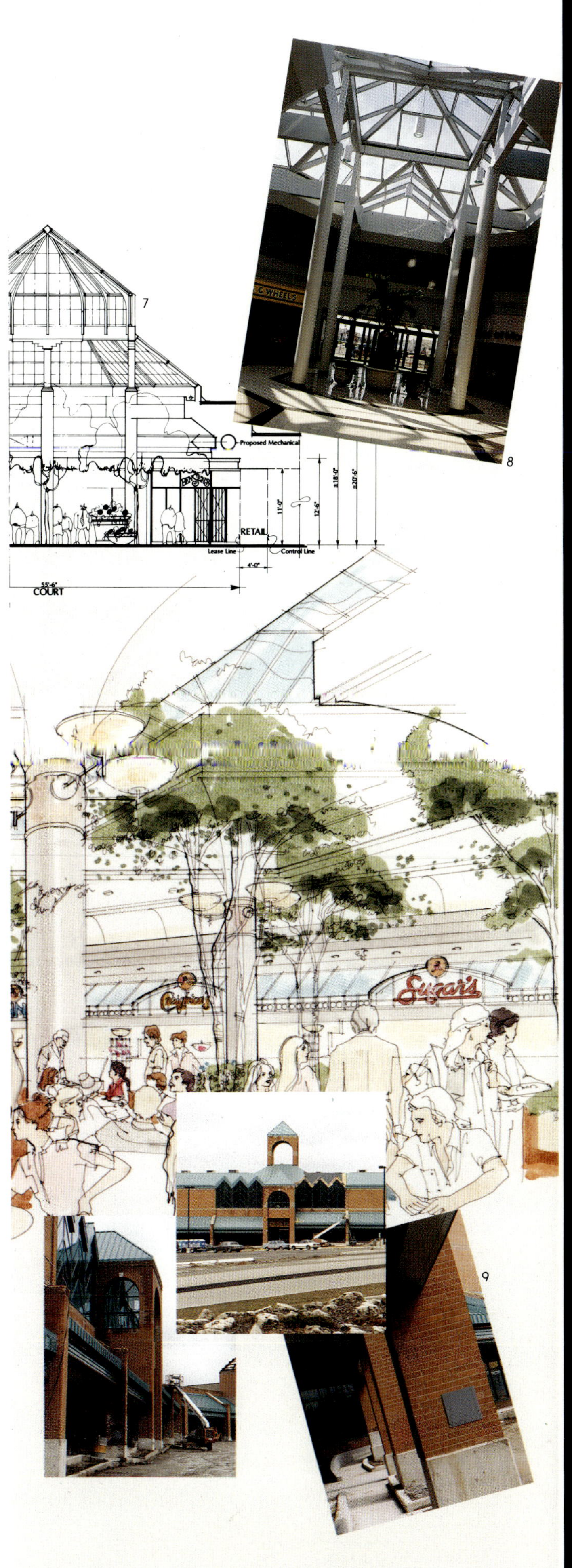

Established in 1982 the company has developed through hard work and professionalism. Numerous satisfied customers are evidence of our strong ability to serve all corners of the market. Our projects extend from coast to coast and the client base is stable; once with us they remain with us. Servicing the client's needs is of the utmost importance. Our consultants offer a comprehensive range of services and are fully committed to economically successful design.

• PLANNING

This is an exercise in mixing and matching business requirements with the art of retail planning. We have to stress the great importance of planning. It is this part of a project that begins a success story. If the planning is excellent the rest follows naturally. Our office thrives on planning some of the most dificult sites. The accent is on traffic flow, tenant visibility, ease of servicing, project identity, as well as flexibility. We are confident in our ability to present plans which maximize business volume.

• MERCHANDISING LAY-OUT

A sound merchandising concept and marketing strategy will set the project ahead from the start. This part of our work is done in coordination with the client's leasing group. Grouping theme areas, dividing the leasable area in well proportioned stores as well as the ability to match efforts with different market conditions account for our office's success.

• DESIGN CONCEPT
• DESIGN DEVELOPMENT
• PRESENTATION DRAWINGS

At any point in today's design process we have to deal with our ultimate critic, the consumer. We strive to harmonize design with market requirements while integrating economical solutions. The right design approach is always elusive. There are parallel interests between universal culture and form and continuity in culture means continuity in design. No sudden turn is allowed.

• STOREFRONT DESIGN CRITERIA
• SIGNAGE AND GRAPHICS CRITERIA
• TENANT DESIGN APPROVAL

All limitations and objectives of tenant's design, signage and graphics are formulated to encourage creative use of their setting. The intention is to allow each tenant to fully express the individuality and character of the store. We make it our business to ensure that the fine line that separates originality from fad is not crossed.

1 Malvern Town Centre, Scarborough, Ontario (ICSC Canadian Award for Innovative Construction and Design) • 2,4,5,6,7 Richmond Centre, Richmond, B.C. • 3 Market Square, Toronto, Ontario • 8 White Oaks Mall, London, Ontario (1988 Expansion) • 9 Victoria Park and Lawrence Strip Centre, Toronto, Ontario (Under construction)

NEW BAYWALL
CLG & 131-6" AFF
BRASS PERFERATED
& ILLUMINATED CAPS
PERF, BRAS
Open View
Existing Column

AND WITH OUR FULL RANGE OF
TALENT, WE CAN INTEGRATE
YOUR 3-DIMENSIONAL DESIGN
NEEDS WITH ARCHITECTURAL
GRAPHICS, IDENTITY/LOGOS,
LEASING BROCHURES, AND
SPECIAL PROMOTIONS FOR
A COMPLETE MARKETING
PROGRAM. WE KNOW HOW
TO COMMUNICATE. WHY
NOT GIVE US A CALL?
TAYLOR & BROWNING
DESIGN ASSOCIATES,
TEN PRICE STREET,
TORONTO, CANADA
TEL: (416) 927-7094
FAX: (416) 928-6713

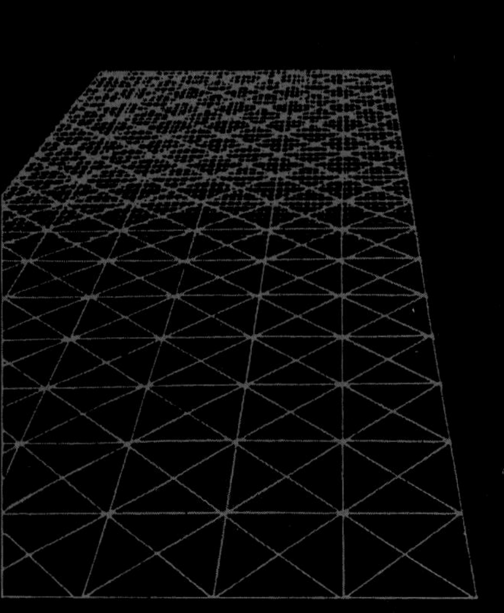

EUROPENEXTDOOR

Belcourt • Bell Canada • Cadillac Fairview
Clifton • Crown Life • First Quebec • Ivanhoe • Marathon • Olympia and York • Présud Ass. • I.T.T. • Transport Canada • Trizec • Westcliff

Shopping centres   Stores   Hotels   Restaurants

Offices:
Santa Monica
• Montréal

• 711 de la Commune ouest
Montréal, Québec, Canada
H3C 1X6

Tél.: (514) 874•1234
FAX: (514) 874•1704

Nos compétences:
c'est notre équipe

Notre qualité:
ce sont nos designers

Our approach:
Your needs
are our parameters

Our solutions translate:
your image
personality
efficiency
and
profitability

CAMDI
INTERNATIONAL
DESIGN & MARKETING

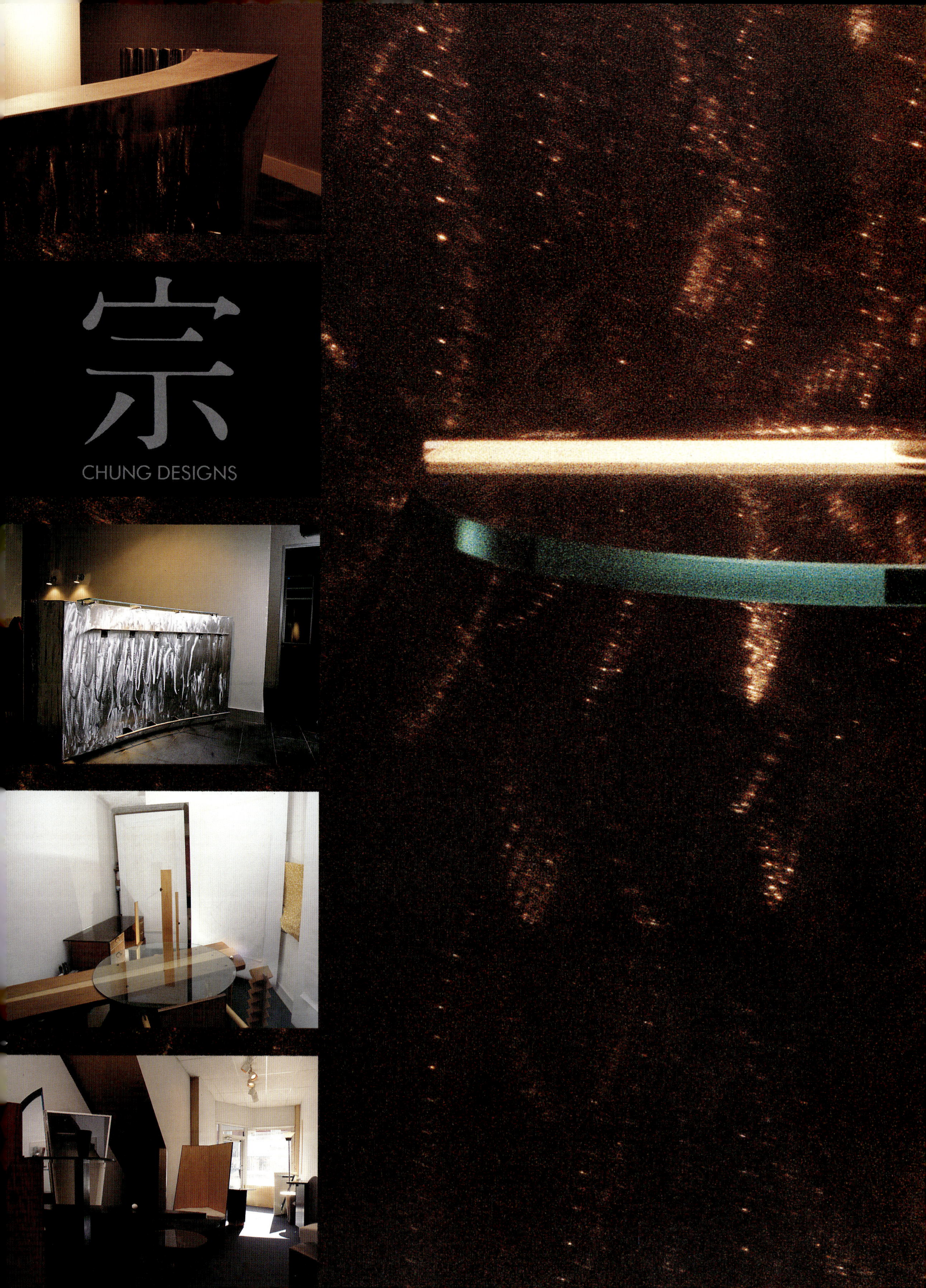

宗
CHUNG DESIGNS

722 QUEEN STREET WEST, TORONTO, ONTARIO, CANADA M6J 1E6 TEL: (416) 862-8282 FAX: (416) 862-2625

Hirschberg Design Group provides unique design specifically formulated to help you succeed.

Design Challenge:
Meld the great outdoors with indoor elements to provide a design to market the client's leisure wear line.
Design Solution:
Create a cottage, complete with a screen door framing a landscape photo mural, a boat dock cash desk and shower stall fitting rooms. Result: a casual, serene retail setting reflecting the outdoors.

MARTIN HIRSCHBERG DESIGN ASSOCIATES LTD.

An outstanding design service providing quality and innovation, Martin Hirschberg Design creates the ideal environment to suit each client's needs.

334 Queen St. E., Toronto, Ontario
M5A 1S8 416-868-1210

NEWS
DESIGN CONSULTANTS INC.

121 AVENUE ROAD
TORONTO CANADA M5R 2G3
416·925·6484

NEWS
DESIGN CONSULTANTS INC.

121 AVENUE ROAD
TORONTO CANADA M5R 2G3
416 • 925 • 6484

PAVELEK & ASSOCIATES

Pavelek & Associates Ltd. have been able to maintain a steady growth of business through a continuing network of satisfied retail, hospitality, corporate and professional clients. Our success is derived from the dedication of talented individuals who combine their diverse skills and expertise to meet project objectives.

As Retail Design Specialists, Pavelek & Associates provides a complete service from design concept through working drawings to project administration. Our scope of work includes but is not limited to:

- Feasibility studies for merchandizing.
- Developing a unique retail image.
- Fixturing sources.
- Space planning.
- Access to knowledgeable retail contractors.

Clockwise from top:

Ming Wo – Burnaby, B.C.

Can Ski – Whistler, B.C.

Stone's – Vancouver, B.C.

PAVELEK & ASSOCIATES
1101 West Georgia Street
Vancouver, B.C.
V6E 3G4

Telephone (604) 687-4566
Fax (604) 687-5833

P A V E L E K

JJ. Farmer Showroom, Montreal, Quebec

SHULIM RUBIN DESIGN INC

**Retail / Commercial / Corporate
Architecture & Interior Design**
400 McGill, 5th Floor
Montréal, Québec H2Y 2G1
(514) 393-1862

We believe that architectural
and design work are interrelated,
therefore we provide a team of
architects and designers capable
of turning ideas into reality –
with attention given not only to
aesthetics but also to budget.

Hydro Store

Japan Camera
1 hour photo

G.L.SMITH
PLANNING & DESIGN INC
260 KING ST. E., SUITE 502, TORONTO, ONT.
M5A 4L5 TEL (416) 360-1158 FAX (416) 360-5823

HIRSCHBERG DESIGN GROUP INC.

The selection of Hirschberg Design Group may be the most important business investment you ever make.

Design Challenge:
Transform a dark, narrow single level useable space into an open Mediterranean restaurant.
Design Solution:
Create an architecturally clean, tri-level terrace with hand painted and terra cotta tiles, french doors, decorative staircase, street lighting. Features include wood oven, open display kitchen and fireplace. The romance of Europe.

MARTIN HIRSCHBERG DESIGN ASSOCIATES LTD.

An outstanding design service providing quality and innovation, Martin Hirschberg Design creates the ideal environment to suit each client's needs.

334 Queen St. E., Toronto, Ontario
M5A 1S8 416-868-1210

MICHAEL LERCH INTERIORS INC.

Michael Lerch Interiors Inc.
1442 Sherbrooke Street West
Montreal, Quebec
H3G 1K4
(514) 287-0851

H. Michael Lerch
Kimberly McKinlay
Lorna McBain

Harry's New York Bar
Les Cours Mont-Royal
Montreal, Quebec

CENTRO, Grill and Wine Bar

MOMENTUM
HOSPITALITY DESIGN CORPORATION
2533 YONGE ST., TORONTO, ONTARIO
M4P 2H9 CANADA 416/485-3000

TDI ASSOCIATES DESIGN INC.

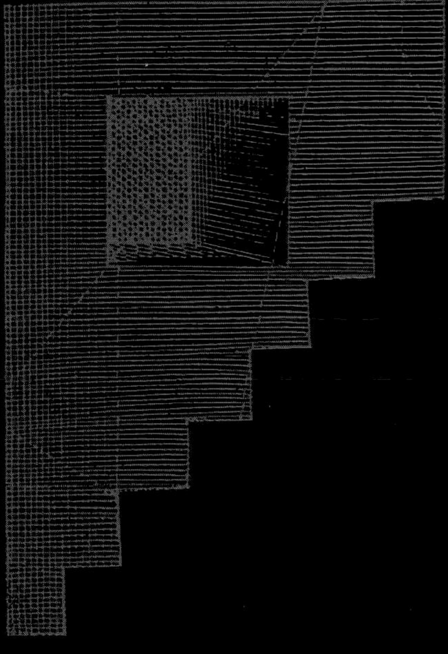

ALEX CHAPMAN DESIGN LTD.

A showcase for the talent of Alex Chapman Design Ltd.

Somerset House, a luxurious three-tower residential de

opment targetted at mature audiences in the sophisticat

Washington, D.C. market. This assignment included the desi

of a free-standing tri-level club house and recreation cen

The Company draws on a detailed understanding of the Nor

American condominium market to offer suite planning a

finishes, public space imaging and execution, and sales offi

and model suite design. Alex Chapman has spent two decad

A

Alex Chapman Design Ltd., 49 Spadina Ave., Suite 507 Toronto, Ontario, Canada M5V 2J1, 416.597.1576

N K

NORMA KING DESIGN INC.

Queens Common, Whitby, Ontario

Saddlebrook, Unionville, Ontario

Sablewood, Unionville, Ontario

The award winning work of Norma King Design consistently creates

dynamic interior environments in a wide range of styles and layouts which

realize the full potential of the spatial parameters.

Cover photo, The Horizon, New York, New York

Harbor House, Stamford, Connecticut

Carlton House, Larchmont, New Y[ork]

Harbor House, Stamford, Connecticut

Whatever the desired ambience, Norma King Design brings more than

a decade of experience to the creation of outstanding models. We deliver

consistent excellence–on time, on budget and to specifications.

L'image Design

Blooreast, Toronto,
Guided Investments Ltd.

Towne I, Mississauga, Tridel,
Won 1988 Gold Toronto Life/A.R.I.D.O.
Special Projects Award

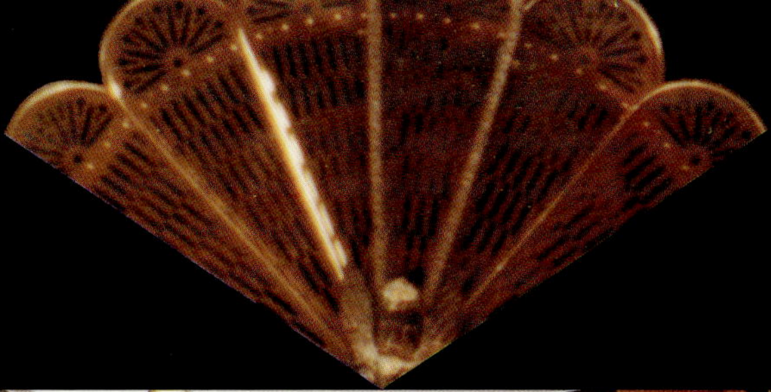

Kingsmere on the Park, Mississauga,
United Lands Development Corp.

Grandview, Huntsville,
Bruce S. Evans Ltd., Won C.H.B.A. 1987,
National S.A.M. Award,
Best Sales Centre over 1,000 sq. ft.

Grand Harbour – Rylar Development Ltd.   Architects: Matsui, Baer, Vanstone Inc.

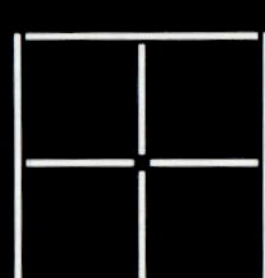

TANNER HILL ASSOCIATES INCORPORATED

73 Laird Drive, Suite 306, Toronto, Ontario   M4G 3T4   Telephone: (416) 429-1600 Fax: (416) 429-4285
Paul Maggiacomo, A.O.C.A., ARIDO, A.S.I.D., I.D.C., President

MICHAEL LERCH INTERIORS INC.

Michael Lerch Interiors Inc.
1442 Sherbrooke Street West
Montreal, Quebec
H3G 1K4
(514) 287-0851

H. Michael Lerch
Kimberly McKinlay
Lorna McBain

PLUS 5 INTERIORS

DAVID THOMAS INCORPORATED

DESIGN · DECORATION

24 ADMIRAL ROAD · TORONTO · ONTARIO · CANADA · M5R 2L5

416 · 961 · 9949   FAX · 416 · 961 · 4536

DAVID THOMAS INCORPORATED

R.C. DAWSON CO. LTD.

R.C. Dawson Co. Ltd.
544 Egerton Street,
London, Ontario   N5W 3Z8
(519) 451-1980
(416) 283-2385

Clockwise from top left:
– C.F.P.L. – T.V. – London
  London, Ontario
– V & G National Trust
  ''Bank of the Future''
  Guelph, Ontario
– Daytun Inc., London, Ontario

CREATING OFFICE ENVIRONMENTS THAT PRODUCE RESULTS

SPACE PLANNING · INTERIOR DESIGN · PROJECT MANAGEMENT · FURNISHINGS

Simpsons Commercial Interiors and Design is a division of Simpsons Limited. Our head office and Toronto branch are located in Don Mills, with regional offices throughout Ontario and in Montreal. We are in the business of office interiors, furniture and design, and have been as long as this has been a business in Canada. Our operating philosophy embraces entrepreneurship. We demonstrate the flair, knowledge and skils that provide you with a blend of creativity, functional utility and a level of customer service that is rare in our industry.

Simpsons
Commercial
Interiors
& Design

A Division of Simpsons Limited

SIMPSONS COMMERCIAL INTERIORS & DESIGN

```
1 | 2 | 3
    4 | 5
```

1. Corporate reception area
2. Corporate cafeteria entrance
3. Conference/meeting room
4. Executive office
5. Executive lounge

Branch offices located in:
**Kingston, London, Montreal, Ottawa
Sudbury, Toronto.**

Our experience in furnishing and designing office interiors is wide ranging and comprehensive. We know that each project calls for a specific kind of problem solving. We also know that all solutions have in common the goal of optimizing the way people feel, perform and interact in a specific environment. We incorporate this extensive experience into your special solution by adding the creative ingredient that turns your office space into an exciting workplace where your people can achieve excellence.

TORONTO BUSINESS INTERIORS LTD.
Offices That Work
TEL. (416) 890-1580   FAX (416) 890-6237

PRODUCT DESIGN

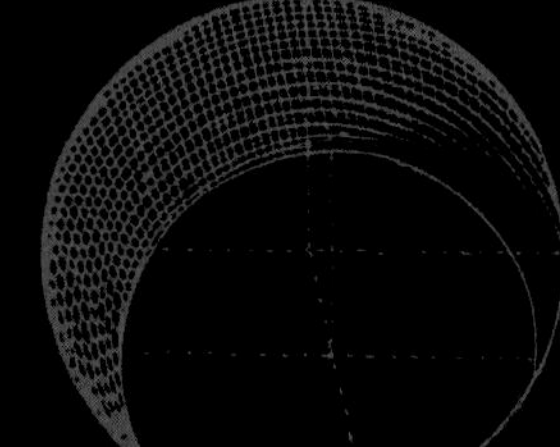

Designwerke

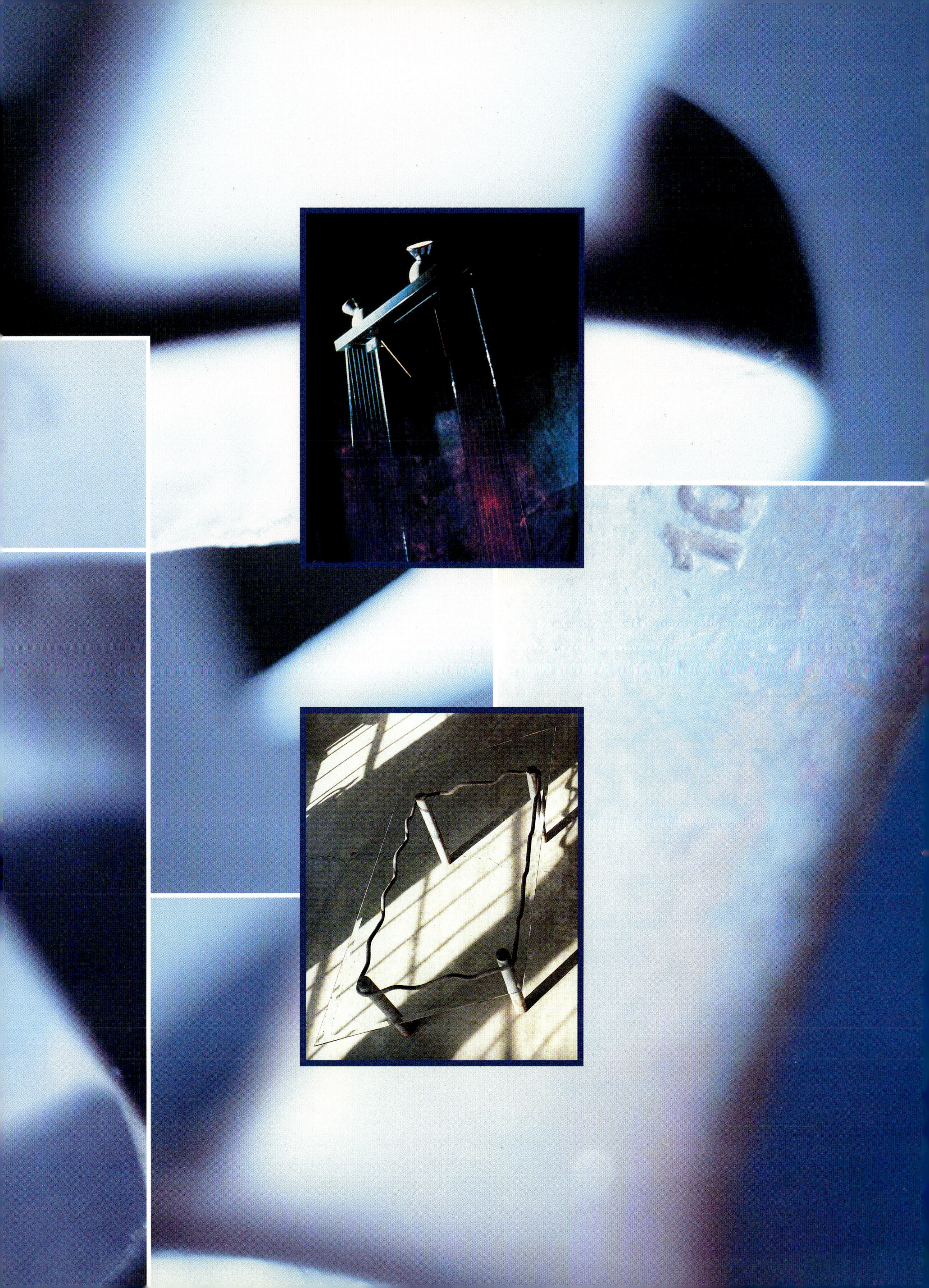

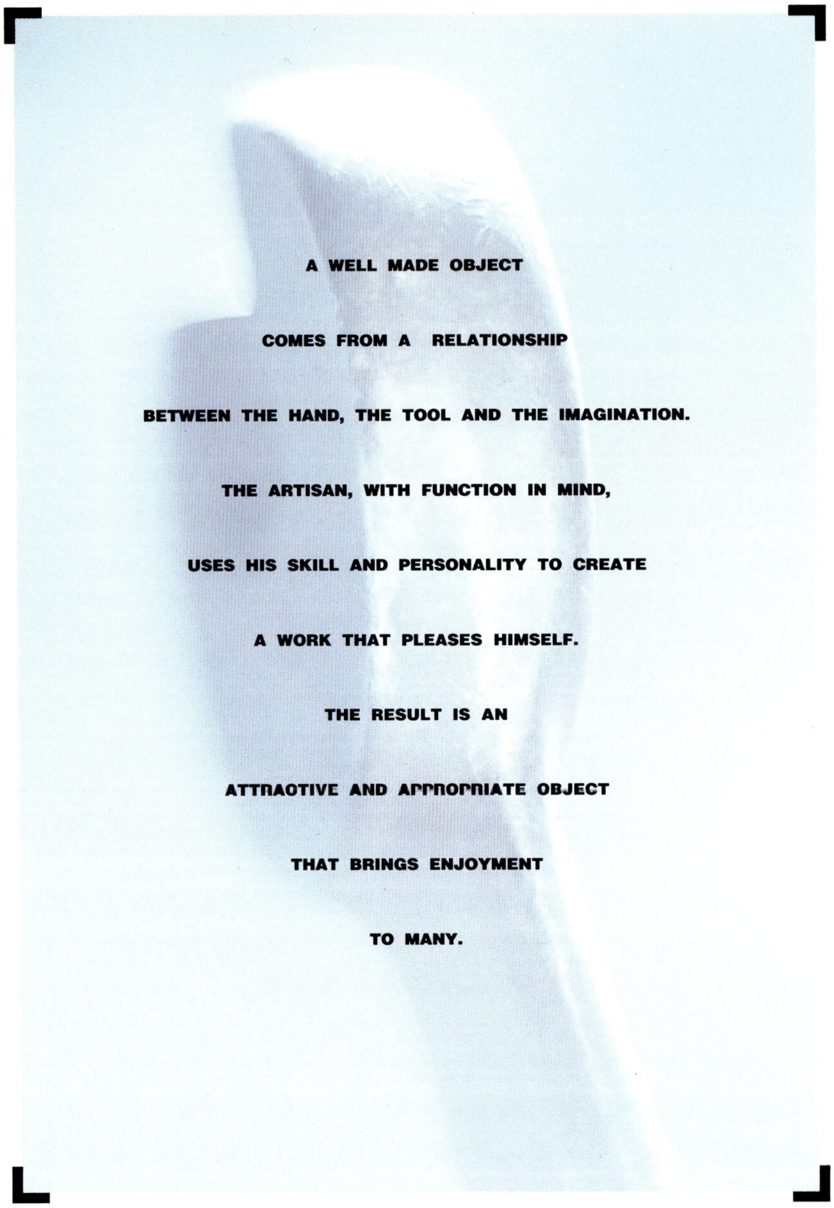

A WELL MADE OBJECT

COMES FROM A RELATIONSHIP

BETWEEN THE HAND, THE TOOL AND THE IMAGINATION.

THE ARTISAN, WITH FUNCTION IN MIND,

USES HIS SKILL AND PERSONALITY TO CREATE

A WORK THAT PLEASES HIMSELF.

THE RESULT IS AN

ATTRACTIVE AND APPROPRIATE OBJECT

THAT BRINGS ENJOYMENT

TO MANY.

Designwerke

52 Power Street

Toronto Ontario

M5A 3A6

Telephone 362 6000

OTTOMAN EMPIRE
Manufacturers

Ottoman Empire Inc., 11-25 Davies Avenue
Toronto, Canada M4M 2A9 (416) 466-0872
Contact: **Rose Anne Schoof, Catherine Thomas**
Toronto • Montreal • New York • Quebec City • Detroit

宗

CHUNG DESIGNS

EXHIBIT • SIGNAGE
CORPORATE IMAGE DEVELOPMENT

DISPLAY ARTS
OF TORONTO

Display Arts of Toronto is famous throughout North American shopping centres and retail chains as the creator of highly-original displays, innovative promotional props and vibrant hand-painted silk banners.

Whimsical shopping centre Santa settings, eye catching fashion show backdrops, customized seasonal promotional decor and original furniture pieces are all within the creative realms of Display Arts of Toronto – specialists in "Creating New Environments".

233 Carlaw Avenue, Toronto, Ontario, Canada   M4M 2S1

Telephone: (416) 461-2787 Fax: (416) 461-2535

Corporate Identity

Christmas Promotion

Poster-Massey College (GDC Best of 80's show)

Canadair chalet - '89 Paris Airshow

The Moniz Design Group is a **full-service creative design firm.** Our skill in the integration of two and three dimensional design allows us to provide you with a **complete communications program.** Whether they take the two-dimensional form – **annual reports, corporate identities, sales promotion, brochures,** or take on the three-dimensional form – **architectural signage exhibits, interiors, packaging design,** we develop solutions that best meet your objectives.

473 Queen Street East
Toronto, Ontario
M5A 1T9
Tel (416) 941-9840

AS A FULL-SERVICE DESIGN FIRM, TAYLOR & BROWNING

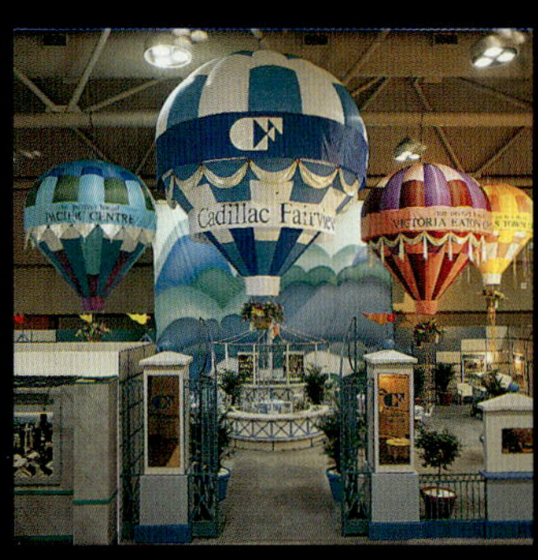

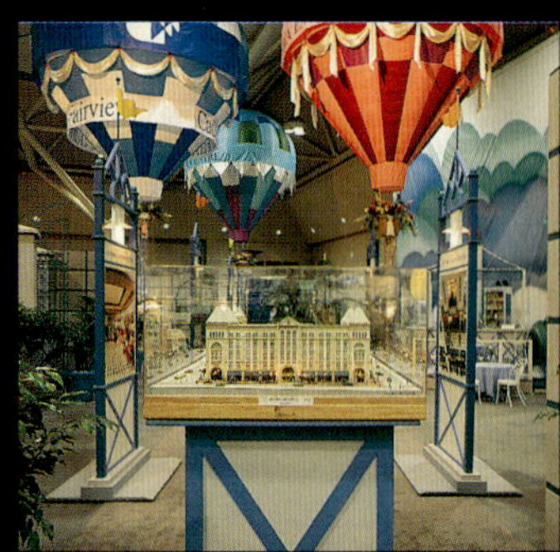

UNDERSTANDS HOW IDENTITY INTEGRATES WITH SIGNAGE AND

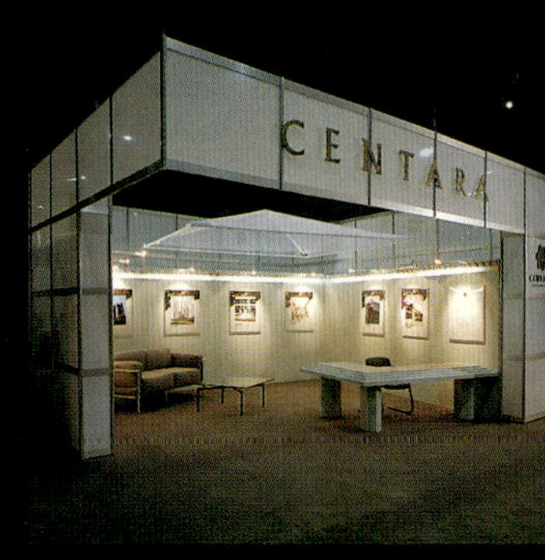

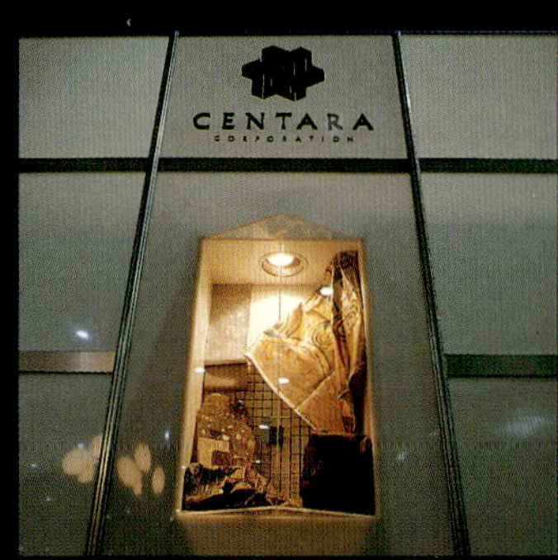

EXHIBIT DESIGN. WE'VE BEEN BLENDING COMMUNICATIONS

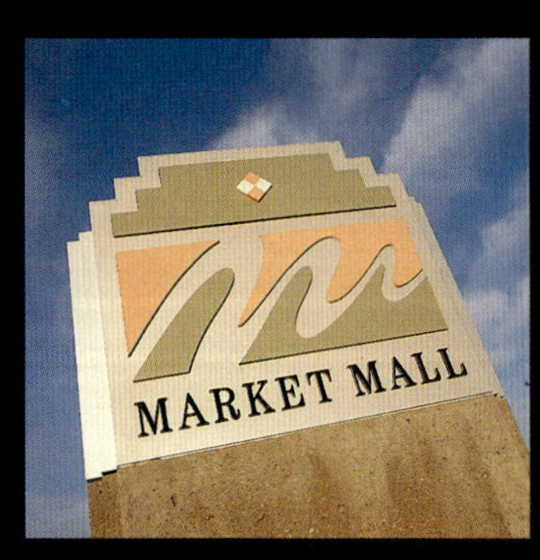

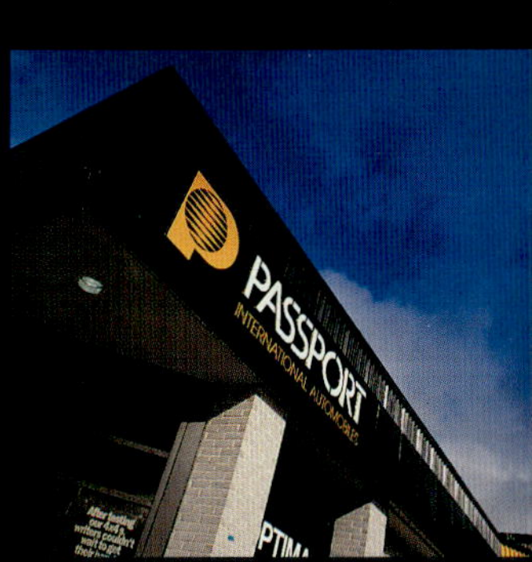

OBJECTIVES WITH THREE-DIMENSIONAL DESIGN TO PROVIDE

THE LINKS AT
ERIN MILLS

COMPREHENSIVE IMAGE PROGRAMS FOR DEVELOPERS

AND THEIR LEADING REAL ESTATE PROJECTS SINCE 1982.

TAYLOR & BROWNING DESIGN ASSOCIATES, 10 PRICE STREET,

TORONTO, CANADA M4W IZ4. TEL: (416) 927-7094 FAX: (416) 928-6713

TECHNISIGNS INC.

CUT OUT LEATHER LOGO
WITH BRUSHED ALUMINUM
STYLIZED LETTERS
BRISBIN BROOK BEYNON
ARCHITECTS

CANADA LIFE LOGO
36" DIAMETER x 1" THICK
STAINLESS STEEL CIRCLE WITH
HANDCUT CHROME LOGO
SMITH GRIMLEY BERG INC.

CUSTOM MANUFACTURING

AND INSTALLATION

OF COMPLETE INTERIOR

AND EXTERIOR SIGNS,

SIGNAGE SYSTEMS

AND DIRECTORIES.

WE WILL FABRICATE

SIGNAGE IN VIRTUALLY

ALL MATERIALS.

TECHNISIGNS SPECIALIZES

IN CORPORATE, COMMERCIAL

AND BASE BUILDING

SIGNAGE.

CUSTOM CUT 15"
BRUSHED CHROME
LOGO-STYLE LETTERS.
KUBIK ZDOBINSKY
& ASSOCIATES LTD.

THE BOARD
OF TRADE
OF METROPOLITAN TORONTO
Country Club
1845

POLISHED BRASS
LETTERS WITH 24"
CUT OUT CUSTOM LOGO.

Coca-Cola Ltd.

technisigns inc

MANUFACTURING & INSTALLATION

5510 AMBLER DR. UNIT 1
MISSISSAUGA, ONTARIO L4W 2V1
PHONE: (416) 238-9322
FAX: (416) 238-6754

SPECIAL EFFECTS

Private Residence
Swimming Pool
Trompe L'oeil Detail

Private Residence
Alex Chapman Design
Trompe L'oeil Detail

Private Residence
Molody Bongarts Design
Wallglazing • Sky • Faux Window

What We Do

Wallglazing

Sponging • Ragging

Guilding

Stenciling

Marblizing

Antiquing

Trompe L'oeil

Murals

Reproduction

General Fakery

Private Residence
Alex Chapman Design
Franagard Reproduction • Wallglazing • Stencil

EXCLUSIVE WALL GLAZING AND TROMPE L'OEIL
ALL WORK DONE THROUGH FINE DESIGNERS IN CHICAGO AND TORONTO

42 VICTORIA PARK AVENUE • TORONTO • ONTARIO • M4E 3R9 • (416) 691-8971

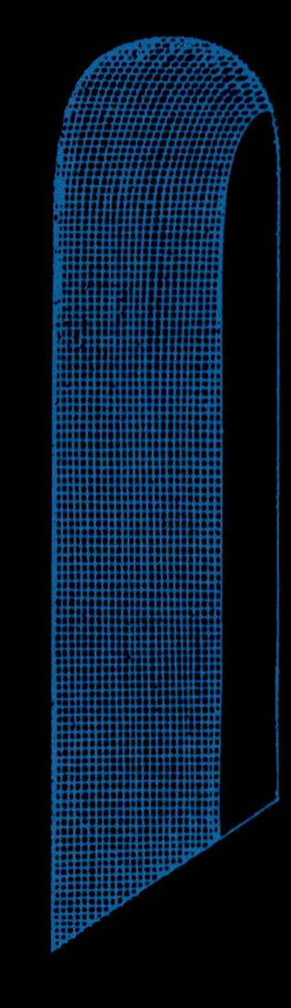

C.A.S. Interiors Inc.
549 Oakdale Road
Downsview, Ontario
M3N 1W7

CLIENT: Merit Investments
Boardroom
Lobby/Reception
ARCHITECT: Crang and Boake

C.A.S. Interiors Inc.
A Company Specializing in
Commercial Interiors:
Corporate
Institutional
Retail

A Company that relates
to its clients' needs and
requirements.

"A Company who's growth
has been built on Customer
Satisfaction".

Specialized

Interior

Builders

C.A.S. INTERIORS INC.

BEGG & DAIGLE

CONSTRUCTION MANAGEMENT • COMMERCIAL & RETAIL INTERIORS • MILLWORK MANUFACTURERS • GENERAL CONTRACTORS

Installations throughout Canada, United States, Bermuda and the Caribbean

Elizabeth Kay
The International Design Group Inc.

Marks & Spencer Building Group
Marks & Spencer

Lawleys of London
NEX/F

Robert Meiklejohn Design Associates
Fairweather

Active Minds
Coles

Robert Meiklejohn Design Associates
Fairweather

Ogilvy's
Retail Environments Design Ltd.

195 Nantucket Blvd.
Scarborough, Ontario M1P 2P3
Tel.: (416) 285-8500
Fax: (416) 285-8684

BEGG & DAIGLE

CONSTRUCTION MANAGEMENT   •   COMMERCIAL & RETAIL INTERIORS   •   MILLWORK MANUFACTURERS   •   GENERAL CONTRACTORS
Installations throughout Canada, United States, Bermuda and the Caribbean

CAMERON – McINDOO INTERIORS LIMITED

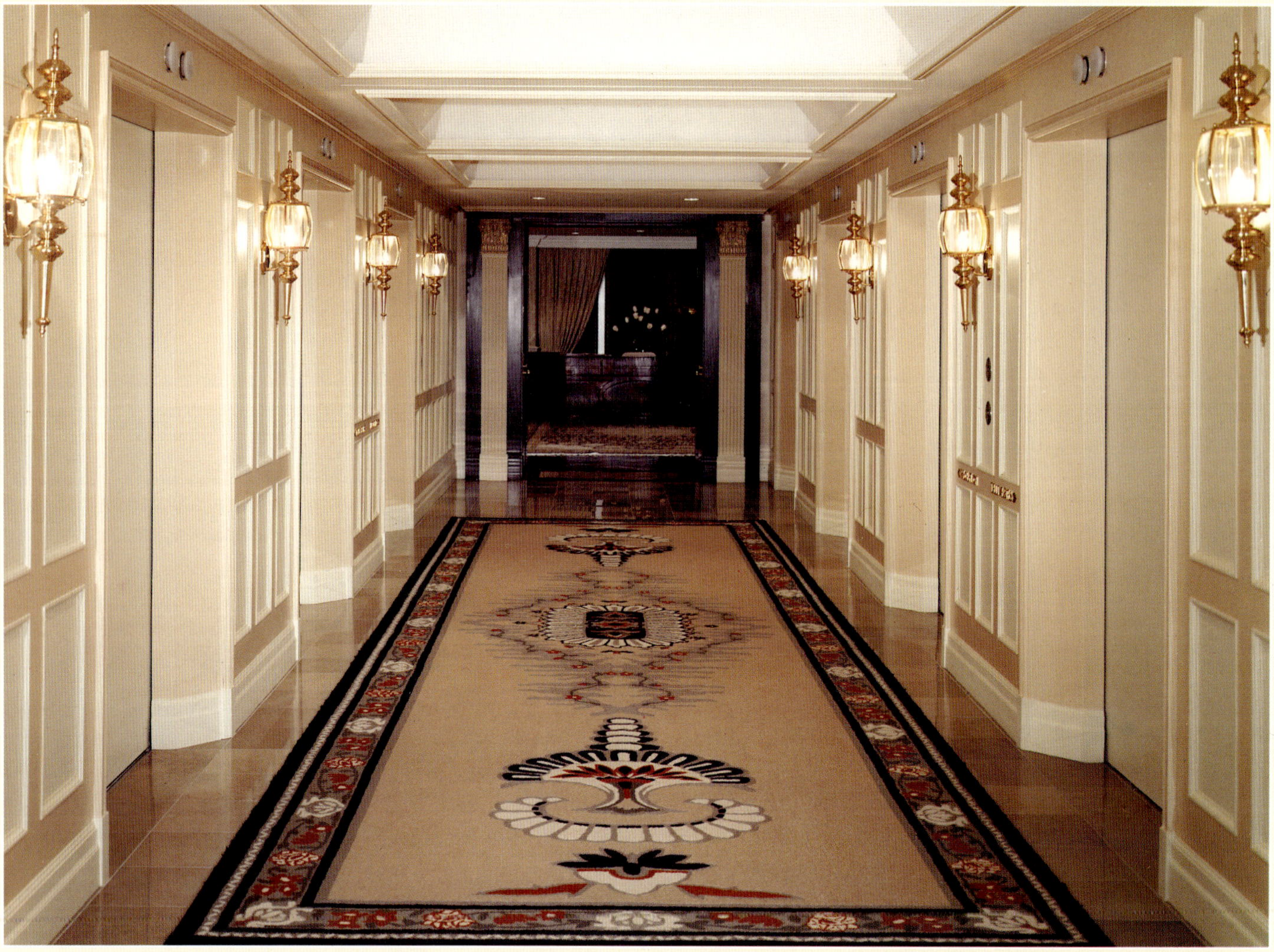

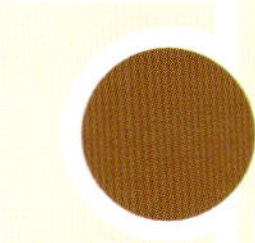

Cameron-McIndoo Interiors Limited
20 Upjohn Road Don Mills, Ontario M3B 2V9 (416) 447-3301 Fax 447-6358
General Contractors specializing in Corporate • Institutional • Retail Interiors

Partial Client List
AT & T
Bank of Canada
Bell Canada
Bramalea Limited
Hongkong Bank of Canada
Imperial Life Assurance
Lavalin Inc.
Manufacturers Life Insurance
Ministry of Government Services
Royal Bank of Canada
Royal LePage Real Estate
STM Systems Corporation
St. Michael's Hospital
Shoppers Drug Mart
Smart & Biggar
Toronto Real Estate Board
Tandem Computers Canada
Wellington Insurance

CORPORATE NATIONAL
CONSTRUCTION LTD.
21 KERN ROAD
DON MILLS. ONTARIO
M3B 1S9
(416) 449-1991   FAX 449-3889
CORPORATE · COMMERCIAL · INSTITUTIONAL

Design: Forrest Design Group Photo: David Whittaker

DECORA CONTRACTING INC.

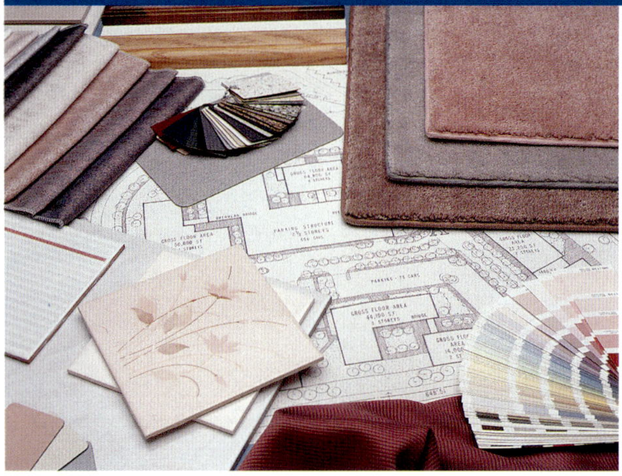

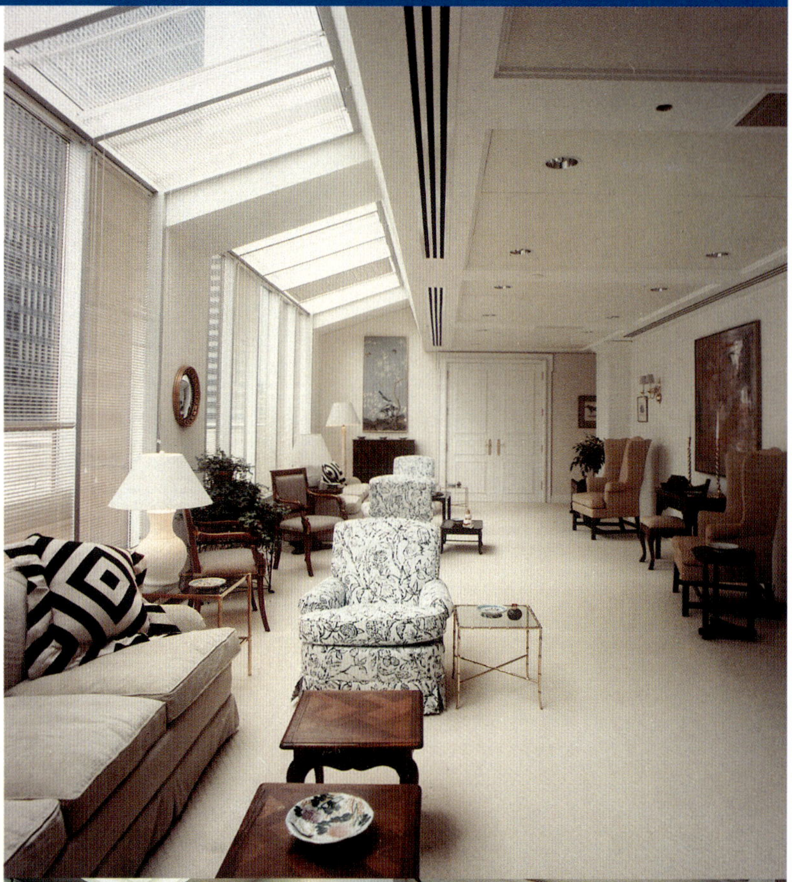

Decora Contracting has been responsible for many of the most prestigious customized office and commercial environments throughout Metropolitan Toronto and vicinity.

As interior general contractors, Decora's management-oriented people have satisfied the needs of the most discriminating designers and their clients – from initial consultation to project delivery and follow-up.

Working with your design team, Decora's personnel will enhance your concepts, expedite the budgeting/design process and provide exacting quality and cost controls at every stage of construction.

Decora Contracting Inc. Polished performance and superior results, on schedule and on budget.

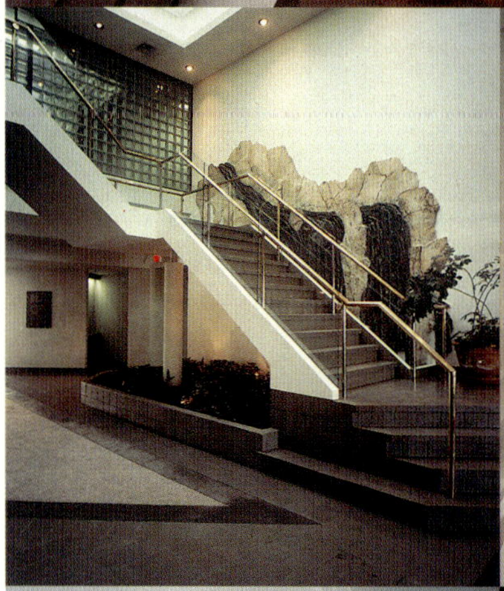

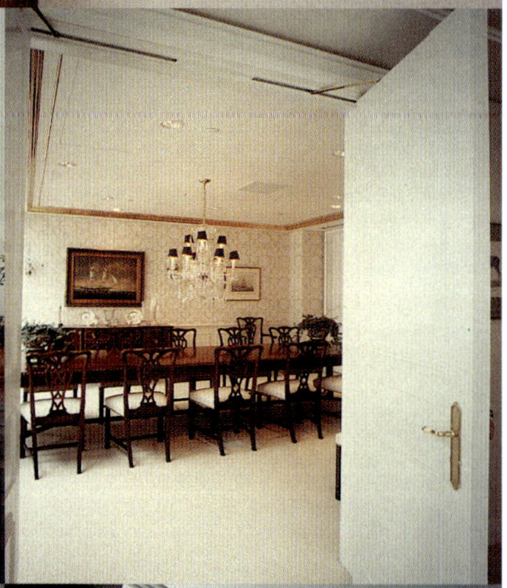

ENVIRONMENT CRAFTSMEN
DECORA
Inc

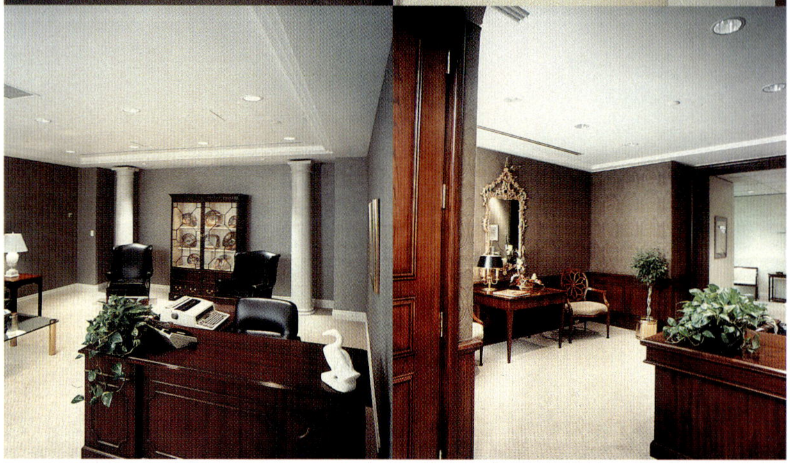

160 TRADERS BLVD., SUITE 116, MISSISSAUGA, ONTARIO L4Z 3K7 (416) 568-4211

PATELLA INDUSTRIES INC.

Los Angeles
Suite 201
1240 East Locust
Ontario, CA 91761
Tel.: 714/947-6168
Fax: 714/947-2650

Montreal
161 Stirling Avenue
LaSalle, Quebec H8R 3P3
Tel.: 514/364-1964
Fax: 514/364-4177

New York
113 E. Centre Street
Nutley, N.J. 07110
Tel.: 201/284-0400
Fax: 201/661-4151

Toronto
124 Bermondsey Road
Toronto, Ontario M4A 1X5
Tel.: 416/752-7750
Fax: 416/752-5147

Vancouver
Suite 203
1104 Hornby Street
Vancouver, B.C. V6Z 1V8
Tel.: 604/683-4240
Fax: 604/688-8612

1 **Client:** York Trillium Development Group
Corporate Offices
Design: Yabu Pushelberg
Photographer: Interior Images

2 **Client:** York Trillium Development Group
Condominium Marketing Centre
Design: B + H Interior Design
Photographer: David Whittaker

3 **Client:** Canlyte Inc. – Lighting Concept Centre
Photographer: Shin Sugino
Design: Marshall Cummings & Associates

4 **Client:** Croydon – Toronto Showroom
Design: Mark Campbell and
Susanna Schneider

General Contractor: Urbacon Limited

U

URBACON LIMITED

Project and Construction Management
Devoted to producing excellent work for discriminating clients.
5 Lower Sherbourne St., Toronto, Ontario M5A 2P3 Phone: (416) 865-9405 Fax: (416) 865-9429

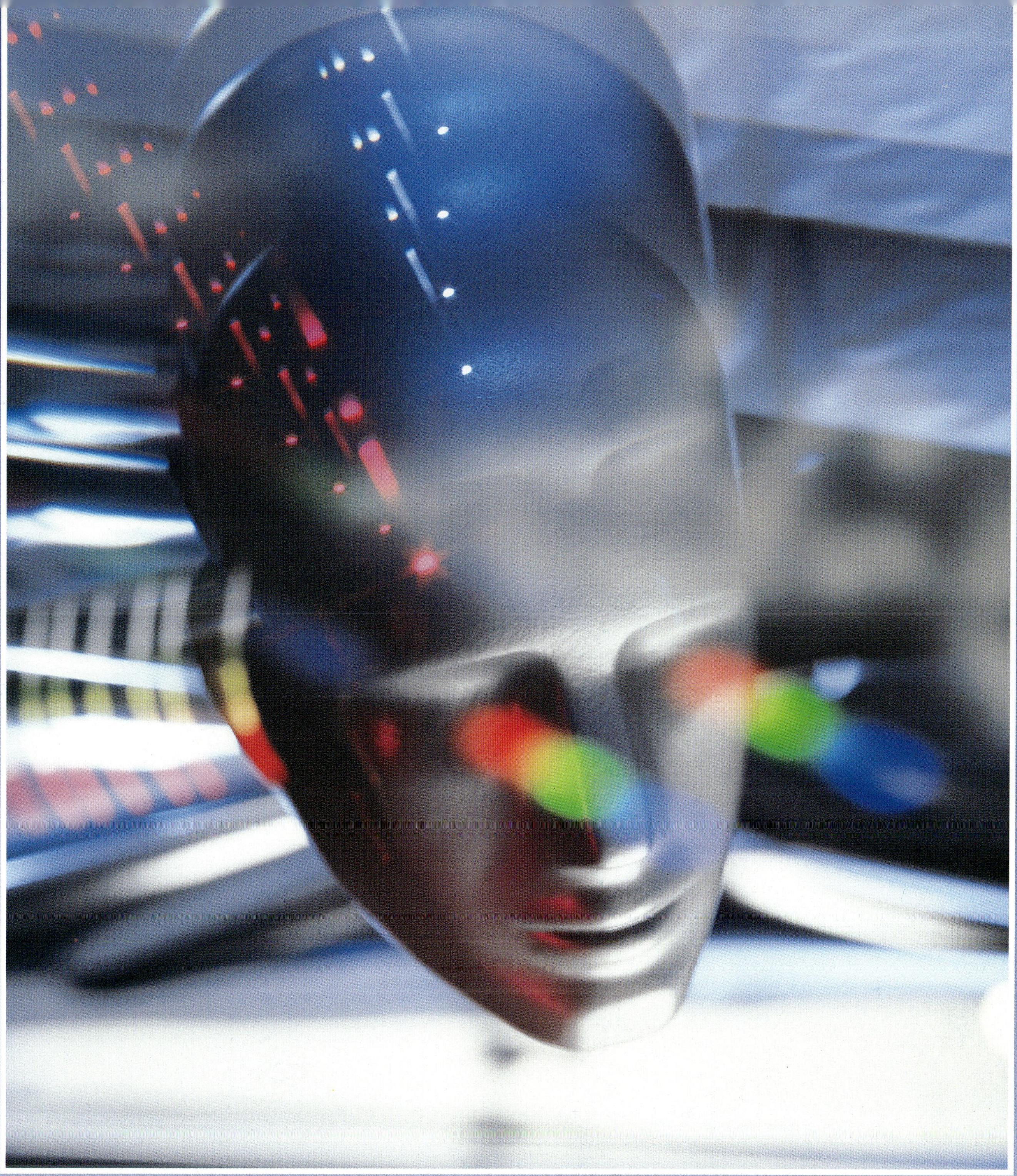

COMMUNICATION DESIGN

WITH THE FUTURE IN MIND

THE SOUTHAM AUDIO VISUAL GROUP
SYSTEMS DIVISION

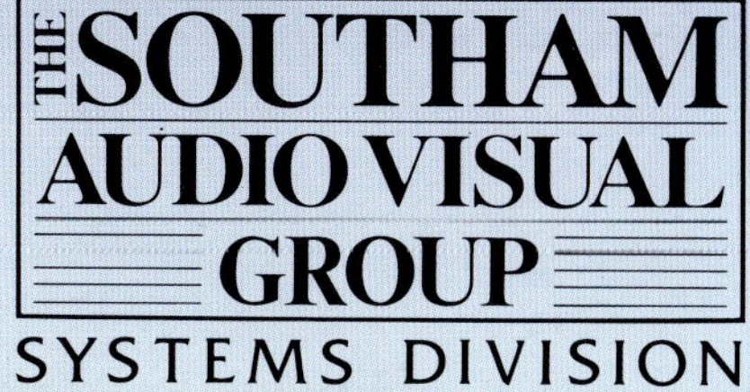

SYSTEMS DIVISION

Creating a lasting impression is everything when it comes to business presentations.

That's why the design of today's boardrooms and meeting areas demands a first-rate strategy for effective audio visual communications.

The Southam Systems Division is your best choice for a communication system that will integrate smoothly into the design of your project and meet your special AV requirements.

By working in conjunction with interior designers, architects, and general contractors we can ensure that the compatability and capability of our systems will meet the challenges prepared for an aesthetically pleasing environment. Our complete follow-through of every job guarantees expert communication design and efficient equipment installation.

To our many satisfied clients, the Systems Division is more than a source of outstanding sound and video equipment. It is the first step towards effective business communications from one of the largest systems companies in the world.

△
Today's presentations require the sophistication of computer data projection. Proper interfacing is a key challenge for an audio visual system.

▷
Training and conference facilities require flexibility and ease of use to accommodate a wide variety of users.

▷▷
A boardroom audio visual facility must be effective while being unobtrusive in a carefully appointed environment.

▽
Careful design planning by
our in-house staff is essential
early on in the construction
of any audio visual facility.
   Liaison between Southam
personnel and all parties
involved in planning and
construction ensure a timely,
cost effective result in the
finished product.

COMMUNICATION SYSTEMS

FOR ALL DESIGN PROJECTS

The Southam Systems Division has made an impact in large corporate projects, public presentation facilities and other design undertakings. Why not plan your communications strategy with the professionals at the Systems Division of The Southam Audio Visual Group.

For more information contact:

189 Dufferin Street
Toronto, Ontario
Canada M6K 1Y9
PHONE: (416) 533-6511
FAX: (416) 534-8469

960 Howe Street
Vancouver, B.C.
Canada V6Z 1N9
PHONE: (604) 685-7723
FAX: (604) 685-6673

Or dial toll free at 1-800-387-0373

Interior Design Choice 5 © The Southam Audio Visual Group
Printed in Hong Kong

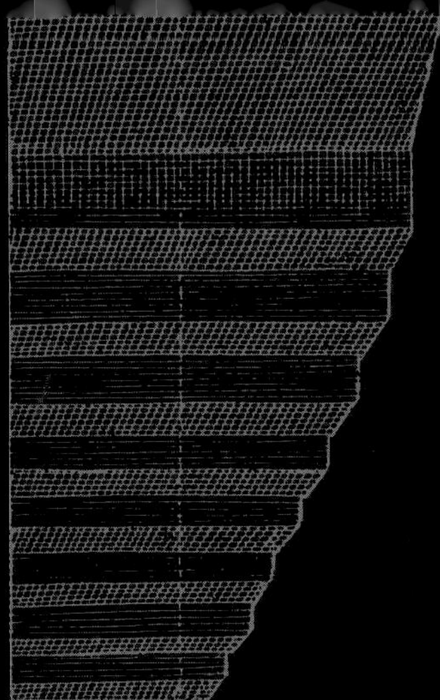

The setting is an historic mansion, steps from Toronto's Yorkville shopping complex, close to The Four Seasons Hotel.

The Gallery offers 18th and 19th Century furniture, English and Continental works of art, Japanese Cloisonné and Satsuma as well as Bronzes, Glass and Silver.

Step back in time to an era of elegance while shopping for that unusual acquisition or gift.

Oil on panel 26" × 33" in period frame
Signed: ANDRÉ PATROFF
Second half 19th Century. Subject to prior sale.

AVENUE ANTIQUES
THE AVENUE ANTIQUE CENTRE

Two Elgin Avenue (at Avenue Road)
Toronto, Ontario M5R 1G6
Telephone (416) 960-5913

Customer parking on the premises.
Hours: 10:00 am to 6:00 pm
Monday to Saturday or by appointment.

DESIGN COLLECTIONS INC.

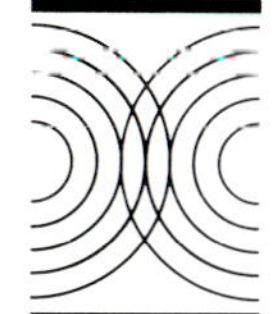

Design Collections Inc.
366 King Street East
Toronto, Ontario M5A 1K9
(416) 360-7015

Eleanor Grant
President

Always Appropriate

Professionals at Design Collections Inc. co-ordinate and design special projects for corporate clients.
Our mandate is to combine innovative ideas with dynamic style to create a memorable end result.

- Fine Art Consulting
- Design Consultation
- Special Functions/Major Events
- Incentive & Recognition Programs
- Corporate Gift Selection

Shorcan International Brokers Ltd.
Toronto, Ontario
1. Lounge – Dorothy Macina
2. Reception – Ronald Boaks

Advance Business Environments
Kitchener, Ontario
3. Inner Office – Lynn Campbell
4. Library – John Howlin
5. Boardroom – Stephen Bailey
6. Reception – Carol Summers

SHELLEY LAMBE FINE ART

2 Matilda Street, Toronto, Ontario M4M 1L9   (416) 778-0700
Gallery ▪ Art Consultation ▪ Custom Framing ▪ Professional Installation ▪ Rental and Sale of Original Art

Interior Design Choice 5 © Shelley Lambe Fine Art

exclusives
PROGRESSIVE EDITIONS

Original Acrylic on Paper
48 x 36

Monoprint Intaglio
22 x 30¾

Irises Serigraph
47½ x 35½

Marblehead Intaglio
38 x 24

HOBART

FORSYTHE

Monoprint Mixed Media Intaglio
41½ x 30¼

West of Eden Serigraph
38 x 24

Monoprint Mixed Media Intaglio
29 x 32

Generation to Generation Serigraph
26¼ x 15½

DIMITROV

HERCHENRADER

Original Collage
35½ x 31
Twilight, Key River Serigraph
34¼ x 24½
Original Collage
35½ x 31
Dawn, Lingham Lake Serigraph
34¼ x 24½
CERJ
ROLSTON
Design by 20/20 Designers and Consultants Inc., Toronto © 1989. Cover: original painting by Catherine Hobart. Printed in Hong Kong
Progressive Editions Ltd. Showroom: 418 Queen Street East, Toronto, Ontario M5A 1T4 (416) 860-0983

Art is essential in creating a stimulating environment or
in continuing the harmony in a residential setting. Valenart invites you to use
our professional service customized to suit your clients' surroundings.

1. T. Fenton
Bau-Xi Gallery

2. G. Berteig
Bonnie Kagan Gallery

3. R. Boaks
Marianne Friedland Gallery

4. D. Wright

Client:
Peelco Industries Inc.

Interior Designer:
Edwards Kirsh
Designers/Planners

Greta Valen, art consultant
238 Davenport Road
Toronto, Ontario
M5R 1J6
(mailing address only)
(416) 860-1733

VALENART
& ASSOCIATES INC.

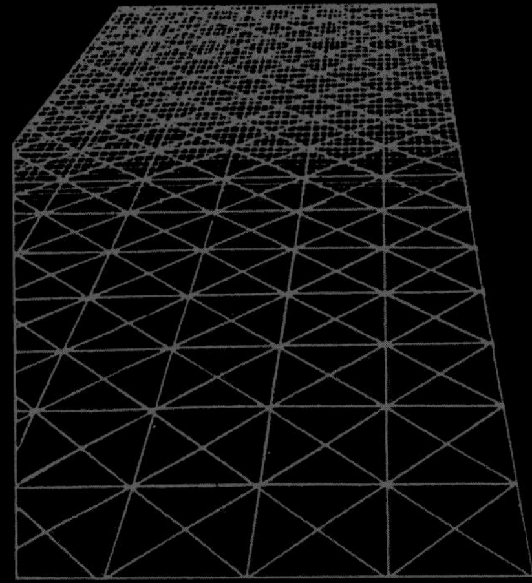

K E O G H
R E N D E R I N G

ARCHITECTURAL AND INTERIOR DESIGN RENDERING • PAUL KEOGH • TORONTO • (416) 423-2412

MORELLO DESIGN STUDIOS INC.

2 Gibson Avenue (rear)

Toronto, Ontario

M5R 1T5

Tel. (416) 963-4315

Fax (416) 964-2060

Architectural and

Interior rendering

in water-colour

Architectural Renderings
Presentation Renderings
Murals
Interior Renderings
CONTACT:
James Sweetland
The Render Group Inc.
277 MacPherson Avenue
Toronto Canada
M4V 1A4
Telephone: (416) 960 0028
(416) 424 2101
Fax: (416) 323 0018
Photograph of James
Sweetland by Ivor Sharp.
THE RENDER GROUP

DESIGN
ARCHIVE

Scollozi & Watt Architects
– 1881 Yonge Street

276 Carlaw Ave.
Suite 219
Toronto, Ontario
M4M 3L1
(416) 466-0211

Robert Burley
André Beneteau

Specializing in Architectural and
Interior Design photography.

1. Moriyama & Teshima Architects
 – Bay-Bloor Radio
2. Christopher Hanna of FHW Design
 – Lime Rickey's Restaurant
3. Peter Prangnell Architect
 – Rhapsody Restaurant

276 Carlaw Ave.
Suite 219
Toronto, Ontario
M4M 3L1
(416) 466-0211

Rounthwaite, Dick & Hadley Architects

IKEA / C.D.A.

TMT Marble

Marble Trend

Rounthwaite, Dick & Hadley Architects

Gadi
Hoz
Photographics
Inc.

Gadi Hoz • Amir Gavriely

416•665-2233
105 Dolomite Drive
Downsview, Ont. M3J 2N1

ELAINE KILBURN PHOTOGRAPHY

Elaine Kilburn

US Gypsum — National Gallery of Canada

353 Eastern Avenue
Suite 104
Toronto, Canada
M4M 1B7
(416) 466-9270

Corporate Offices
Retail
Hospitality
Residential
Special Assignments

A strong image

is your most

effective publicity.

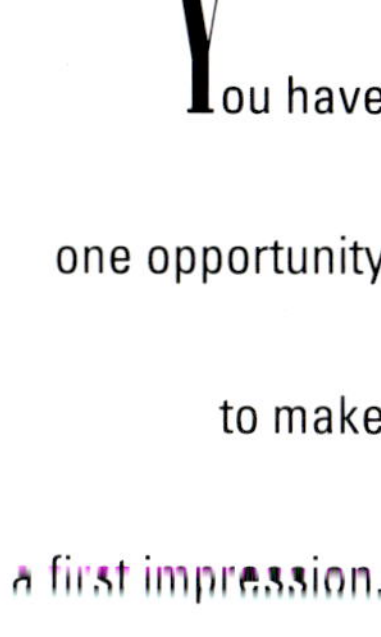

You have

one opportunity

to make

a first impression.

Let us show you

in your best light.

Make your

first impressions

last.

PHOTOGRAPHY

Toronto Life Homes - Residence of Randy Knox

LIGHTWORKS
photography

ROY OOMS

715 - 4A ST. N.E.

CALGARY, ALBERTA

T2E 3W1

403-276-4321

RAY VAN DUSEN PHOTOGRAPHY

Specializing in Architectural and
Interior Design Photography

...for the corporate, industrial,
commercial and design communities

IDOMO - ALEXIS NIHON

CARRE DOMINION

B D I

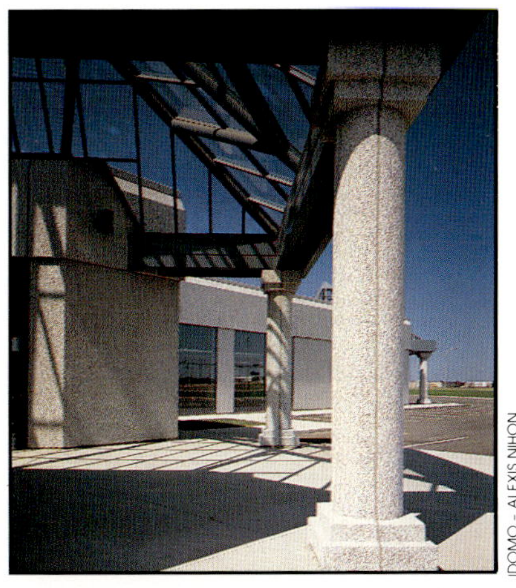

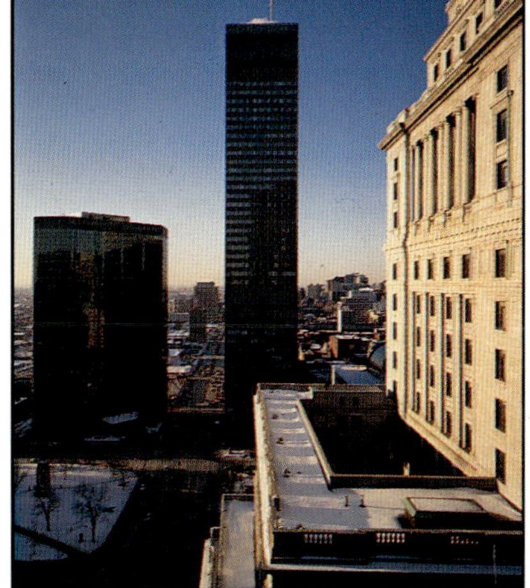

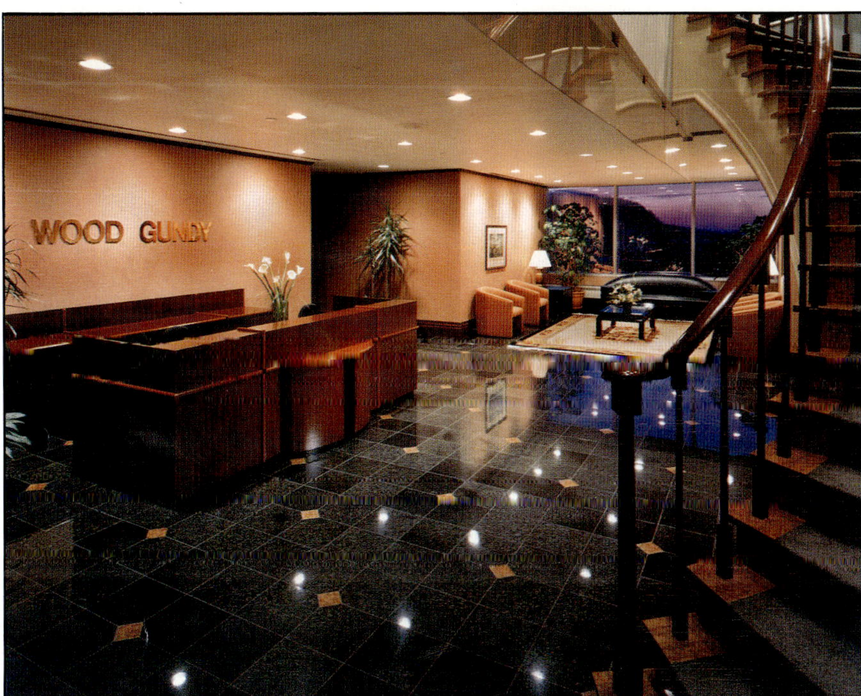

Partial Client List:
Alexis Nihon Corp.
Buro Decor Inc.
Beaver Design Build
Canderel
Gad Shaanan Design
Gavin Affleck, arch.
Groupe Mercille

L'ORCHIDEE DE CHINE

HOLT RENFREW - NAOMI LEFF & ASSOCIATES

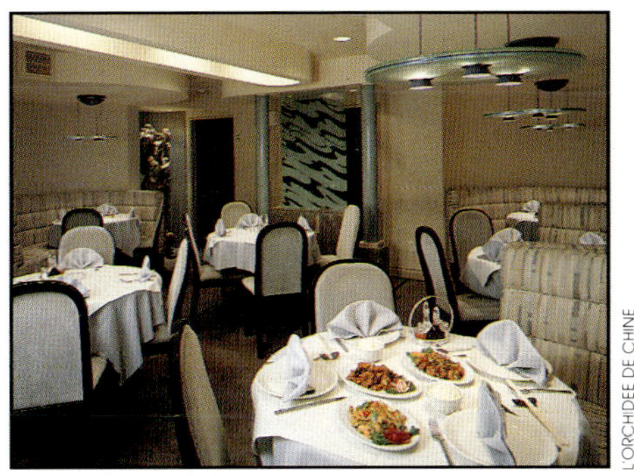

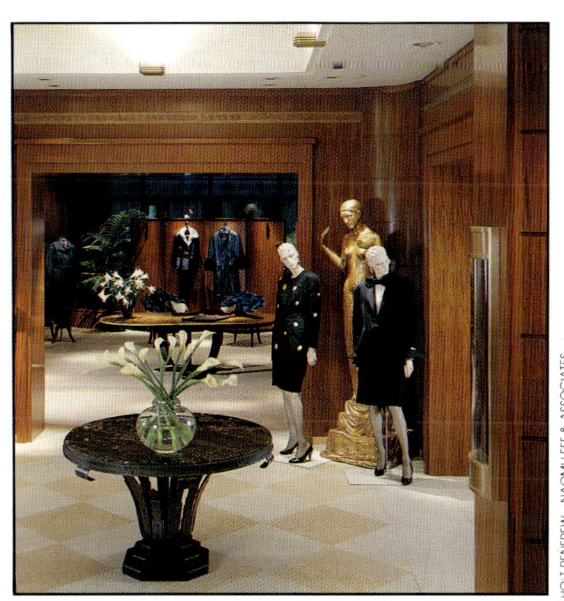

MONTREAL, CANADA (514) 486-5054

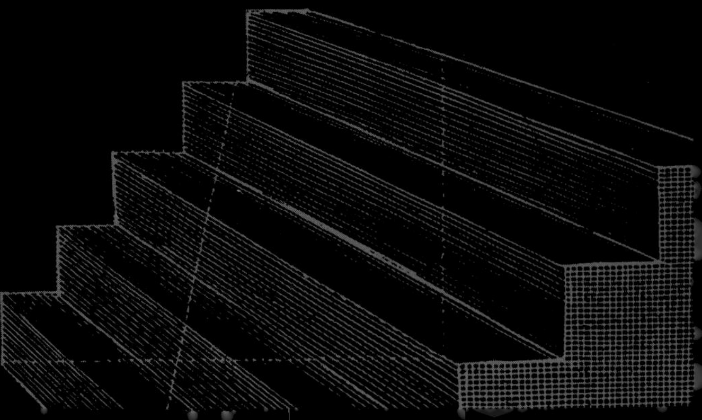

ARTOPEX INC.

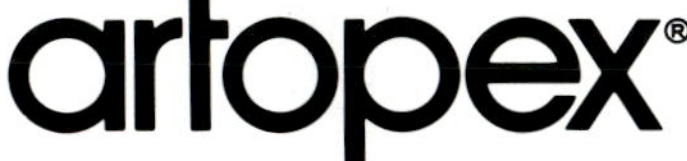

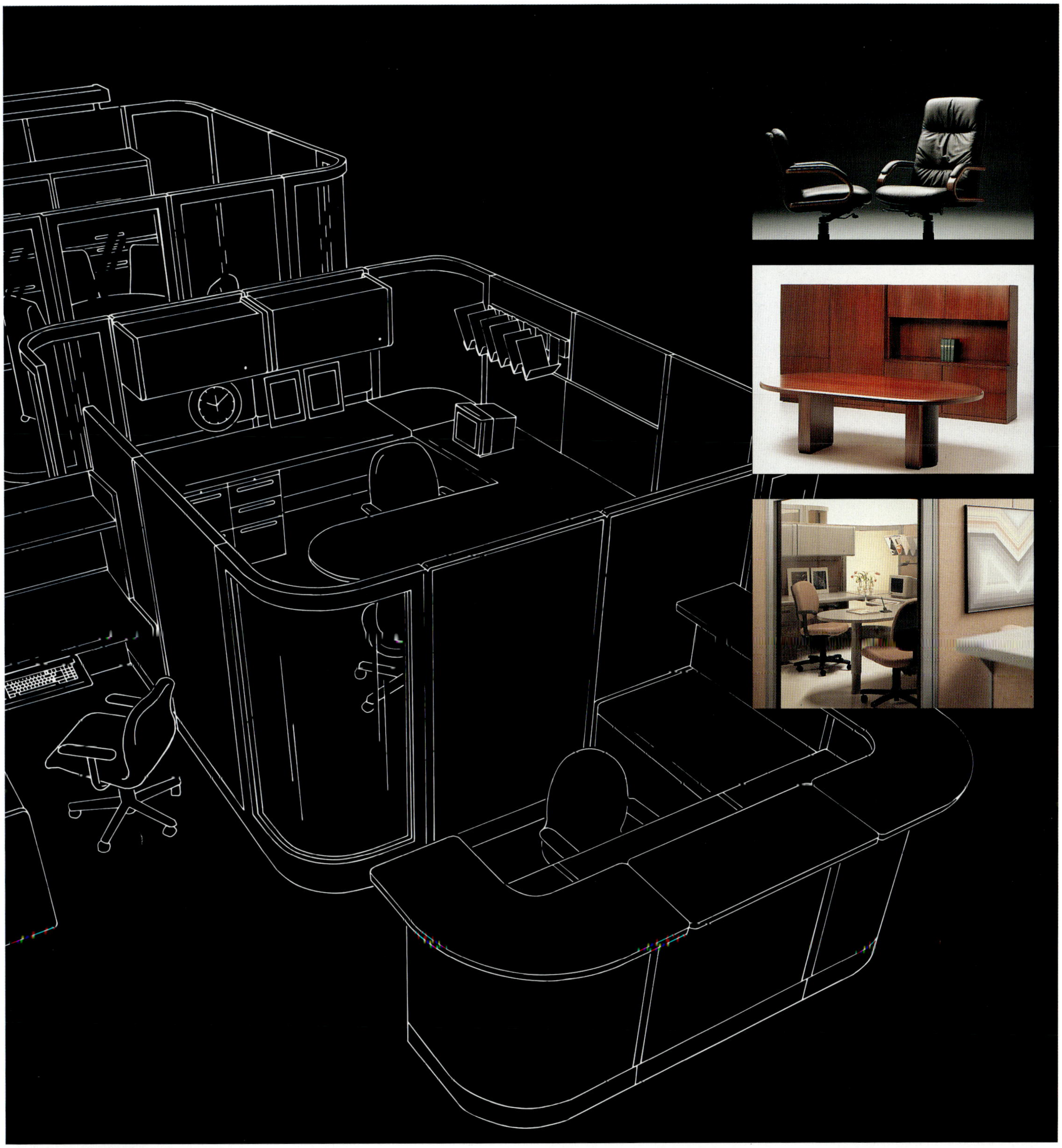

artopex®

Montréal:
2121, rue Berlier
Laval, Québec
Canada H7L 3M9
(514) 332-4420
Fax: (514) 688-5171

Toronto:
10 Lower Spadina Avenue
Suite 201
Toronto, Ontario
Canada M5V 2Z2
(416) 593-0111
Fax: (416) 593-5525

Artopex has been manufacturing quality office furniture and meeting the needs of the ever changing workplace for more than 30 years. Moreover, Artopex is one of the few companies that can offer a completely integrated range of products: seating, wood lines, metal filing cabinets and modular office systems. Artopex means one-stop shopping.

We also know that it takes more than just good products to make satisfied customers. We are committed to meeting customer needs for sophisticated products and fast delivery. You can count on us for service and technical support.

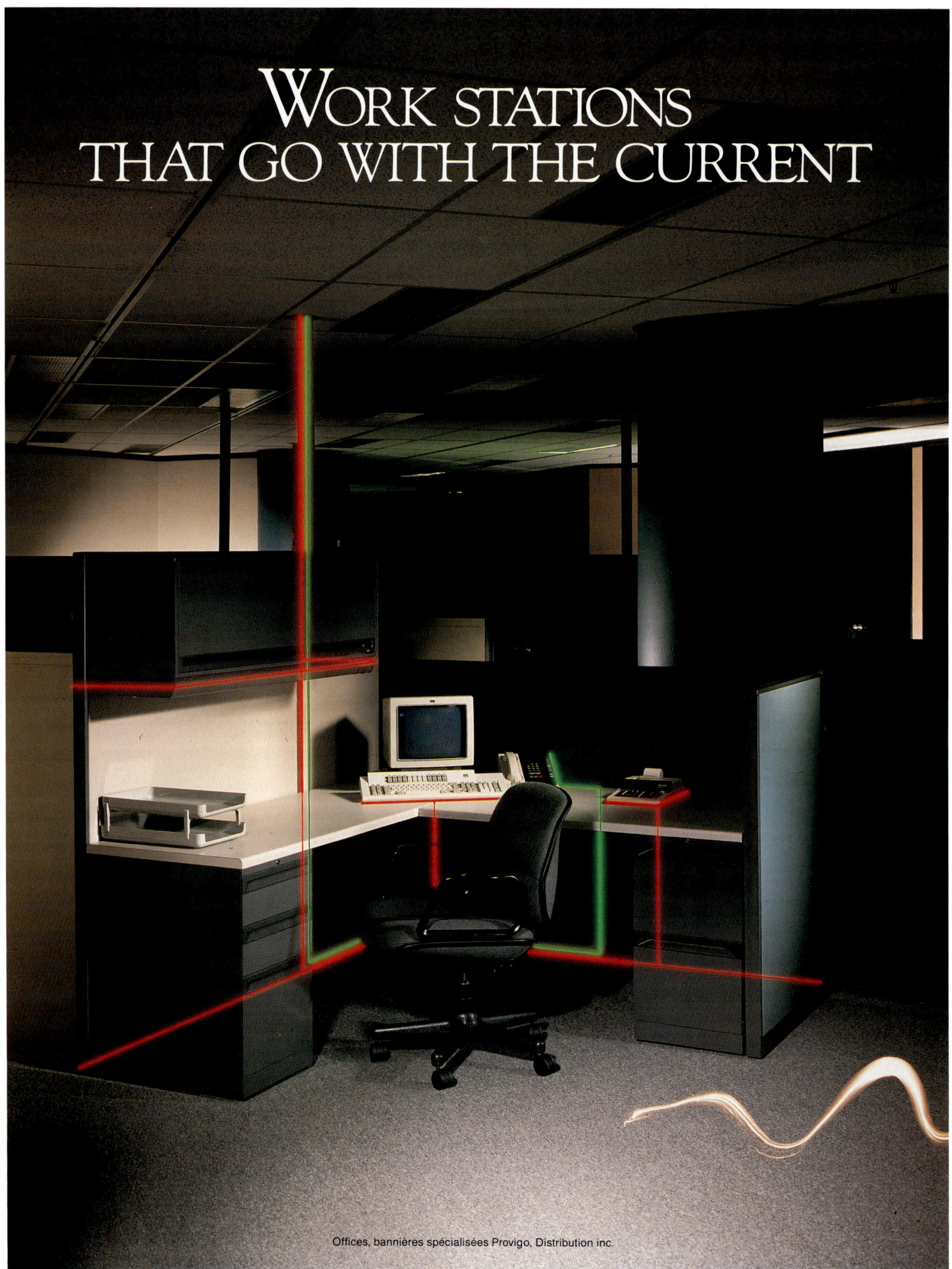

Offices, bannières spécialisées Provigo, Distribution inc.

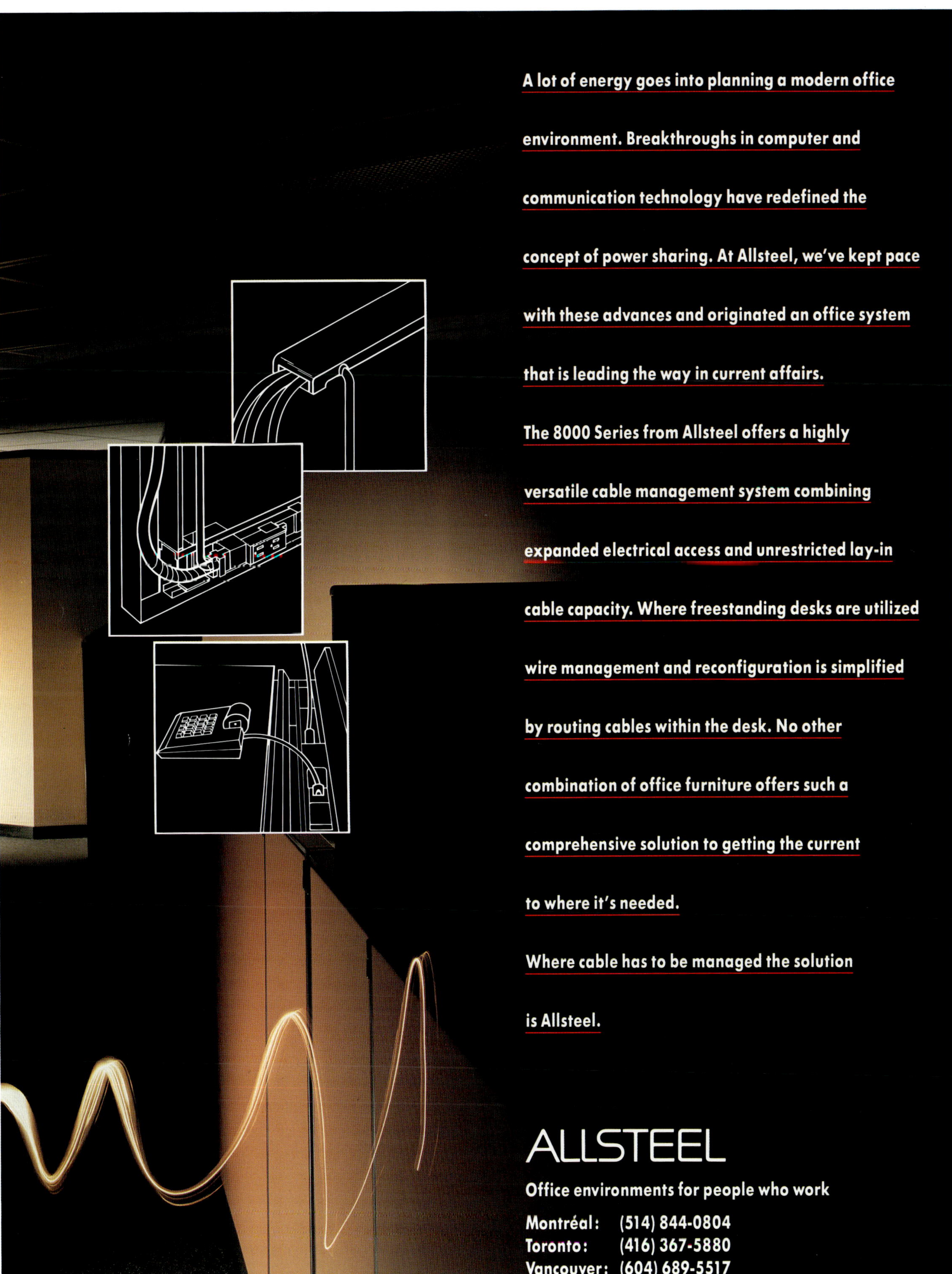
A lot of energy goes into planning a modern office environment. Breakthroughs in computer and communication technology have redefined the concept of power sharing. At Allsteel, we've kept pace with these advances and originated an office system that is leading the way in current affairs.

The 8000 Series from Allsteel offers a highly versatile cable management system combining expanded electrical access and unrestricted lay-in cable capacity. Where freestanding desks are utilized wire management and reconfiguration is simplified by routing cables within the desk. No other combination of office furniture offers such a comprehensive solution to getting the current to where it's needed.

Where cable has to be managed the solution is Allsteel.

ALLSTEEL
Office environments for people who work
Montréal: (514) 844-0804
Toronto: (416) 367-5880
Vancouver: (604) 689-5517

25 WATLINE AVENUE, MISSISSAUGA, ONTARIO L4Z 2Z1 TEL. (416) 568-0200   FAX. (416) 890-9397   BY APPOINTMENT ONLY

SORMANI   ■   UNIFOR   ■   POLTRONA FRAU   ■   MOLTENI & C.   ■
IMPORTERS AND DISTRIBUTORS OF FINE ITALIAN FURNITURE

BNI
One source total office environment!
MARQUIS
Versatility, combined with style and uncompromising attention to detail, are the hallmarks of Marquis. This warm executive setting demonstrates the opulence of Marquis.
10251, boul. Ray Lawson
Montréal, Québec, Canada
H1J 1L7
Telephone (514) 352-7770
Telex 05-828560
Fax (514) 351-5216

BONAVENTURE FURNITURE INDUSTRIES LIMITED

Design: STANLEY JAY FRIEDMAN

B
BONAVENTURE

894 Bloomfield,
Montreal, Quebec
H2V 3S6
(514) 270-7311

Fax: (514) 270-7978

146 Dupont Street
Toronto, Ontario
M5R 1V2
(416) 961-5900

Fax: (416) 961-2714

COLLIER/C FURNITURE LTD.

CONSPEC– VIACRAFT

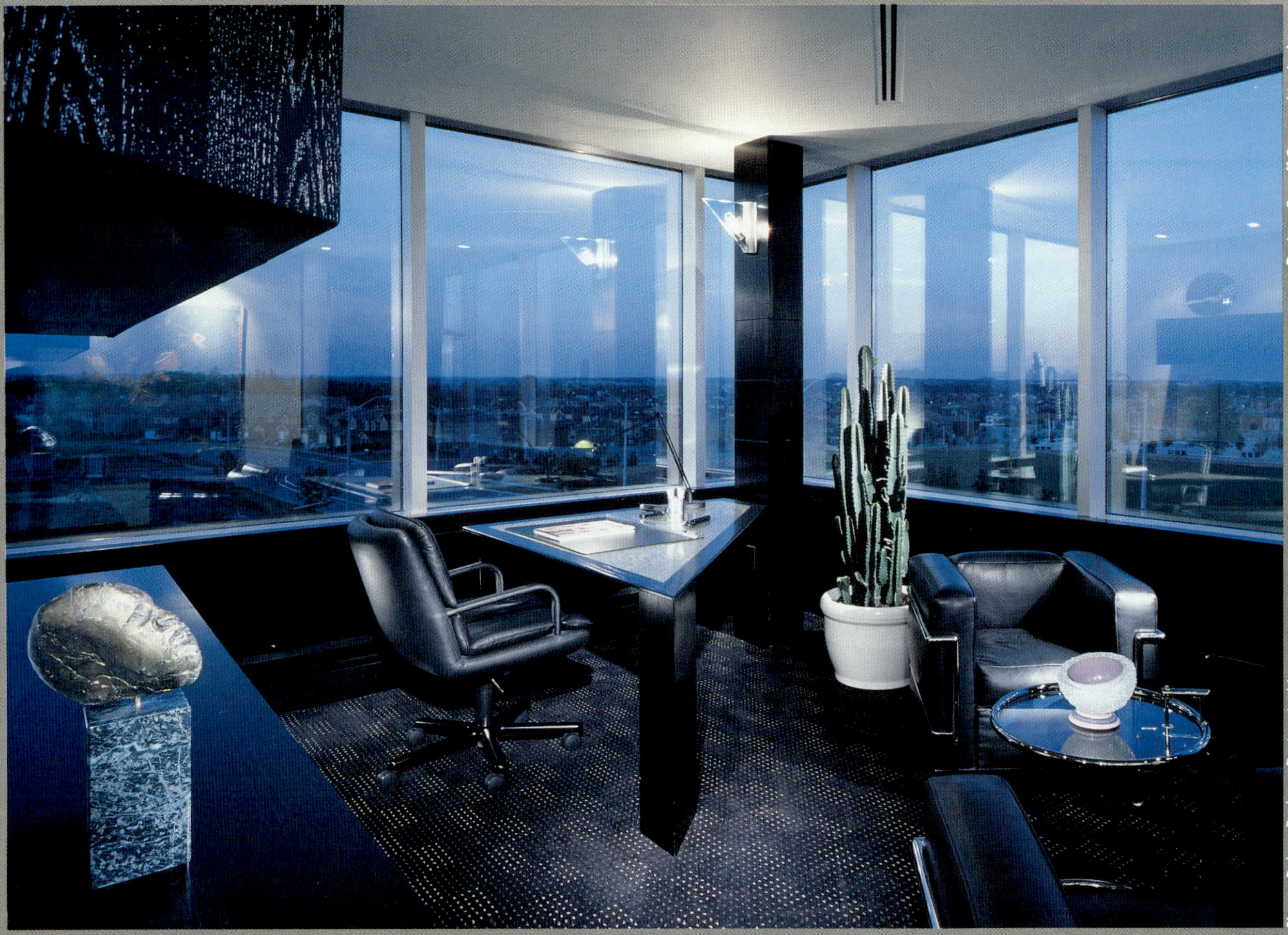

Design: Petroff Partnership Architects

Photo: Robert Burley – Design Archive

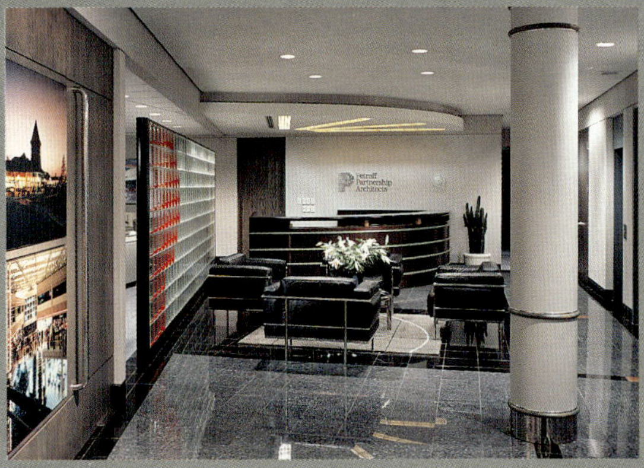

Photo: Robert Burley – Design Archive

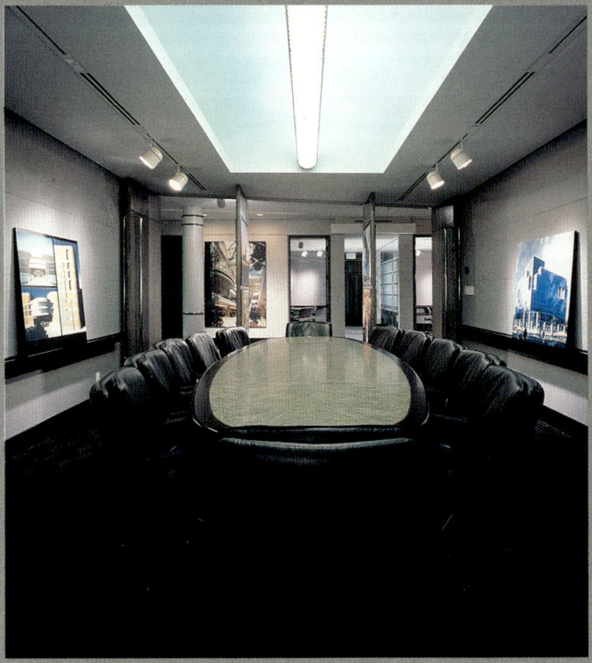

Photo: David Whittaker

CONSPEC

Contract Furniture Built to Specification

146 Laird Drive
Suite 203
Toronto, Ontario
M4G 3V7
(416) 429-5206
Fax: (416) 429-1314

Conspec – Viacraft products and services available through leading architects, designers, dealers and specifiers.

DECA INTERIORS LTD.

Boardroom of Porter, Wright, Morris & Arthur (Cleveland)

Designed by Oliver Design Group (Cleveland)

SERVING THE DESIGN COMMUNITY FOR 30 YEARS
with
FINE CUSTOM CRAFTED EXECUTIVE OFFICE FURNITURE

LES INTÉRIEURS DECA LTÉE

617 St-RÉMI, MONTRÉAL, QUÉBEC H4C 3G7
TEL.: (514) 933-8307   FAX: (514) 933-8918

DECA INTERIORS LTD.

MONTREAL · TORONTO · NEW YORK · BOSTON · PHILADELPHIA · WASHINGTON, D.C. · PITTSBURGH · CHICAGO · ATLANTA

From The Classics.....
GLOBAL
Sovereign
560 Supertest Road, Downsview, Ontario, Canada M3J 2M6 (416)661-3660 Telex: 06-22448 Fax: (416)661-4300

THE HARTER GROUP

*The Harter Wallaby, designed by Australia's Robinson & Alexander, is
a commanding presence in any corporate setting.
From this position of authority the future can be set in motion.*

TORONTO, ONTARIO 416.363.0303 GUELPH, ONTARIO 519.824.2850

INTARC LIMITED

INTARC – The designer's choice for exclusive quality products since 1974

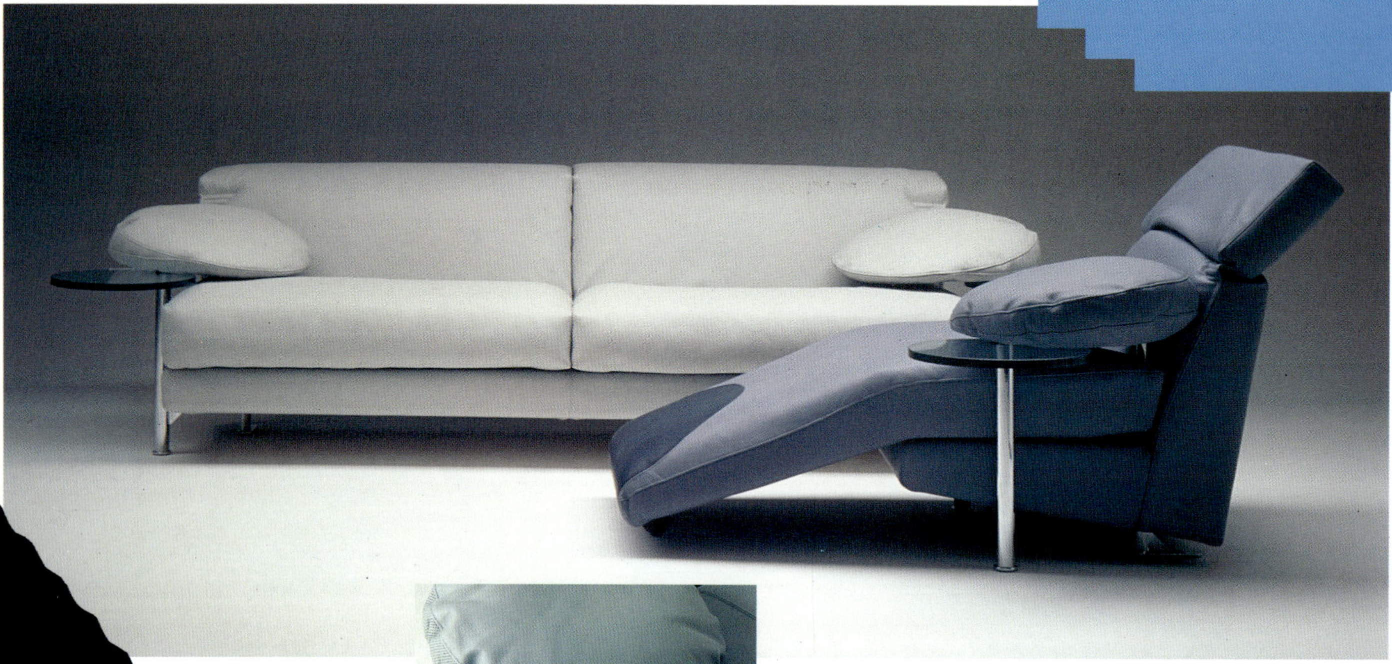

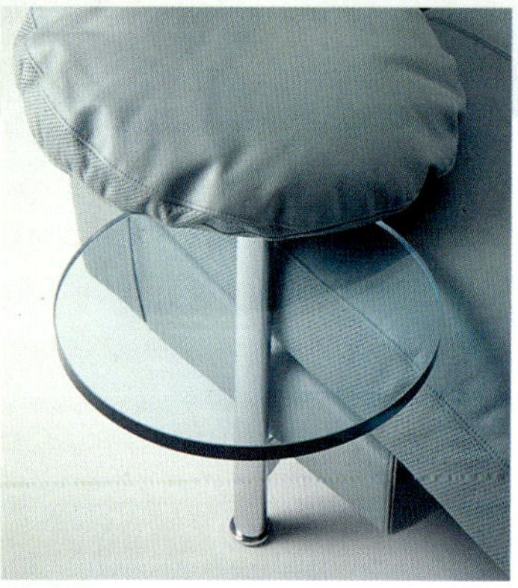

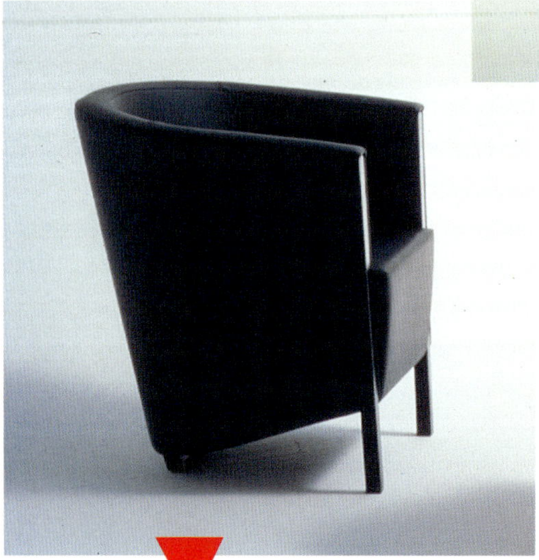

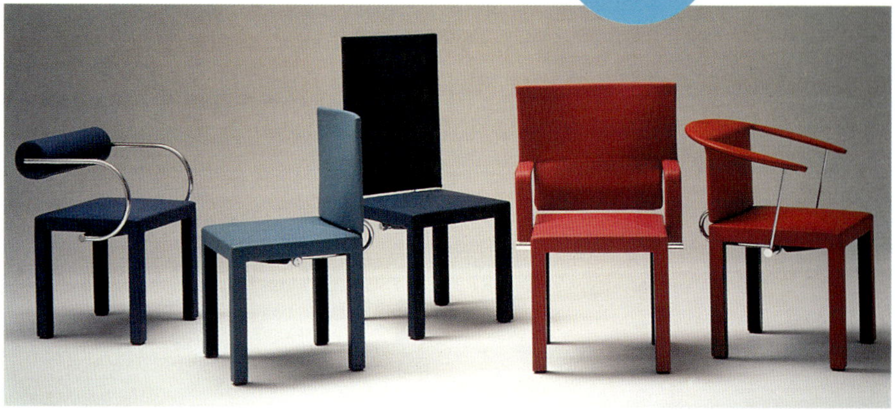

intarc

147 Davenport Road
Toronto, Ontario M5R 1J1
Tel: (416) 924-7111
Fax: (416) 924-0534

B&B ITALIA

cidue

MOROSO

cattelan italia

Jeffrey-Craig

763 Warden Avenue
Scarborough, Ontario M1L 4B7
(416) 757-4153
Fax: (416) 757-5461

Exciting is the word to describe the range of colours and textures available in laminate furniture from Jeffrey-Craig. Its durability and versatility make it the ideal solution for today's office environment. Plus, our custom production process allows you to alter sizes and change functions – an important feature that sets us apart from standard production furniture. For your next project, don't simply make do. Make a statement.

KRUG

Krug Furniture Inc.
P.O. Box 9035
421 Manitou Drive
Kitchener, Ontario
Canada N2G 4J3
(519) 748-5100

Fax
(519) 748-5177

Showroom
4th Floor
260 King Street East
Toronto, Ontario
Canada M5A 1K3
(416) 366-7246

Fax
(416) 366-4914

The Oval Series features slim oval shaped members of solid oak which are steam bent into fluid curves. Four different arm chairs and complementing desk tilter chairs provide a comprehensive family of graceful seating.
KRUG has been providing quality wood office environments since 1880.

Avantgarde
Desk
by Leitner
Donau Desk by Sottsass
by Sottsass
Donau TV

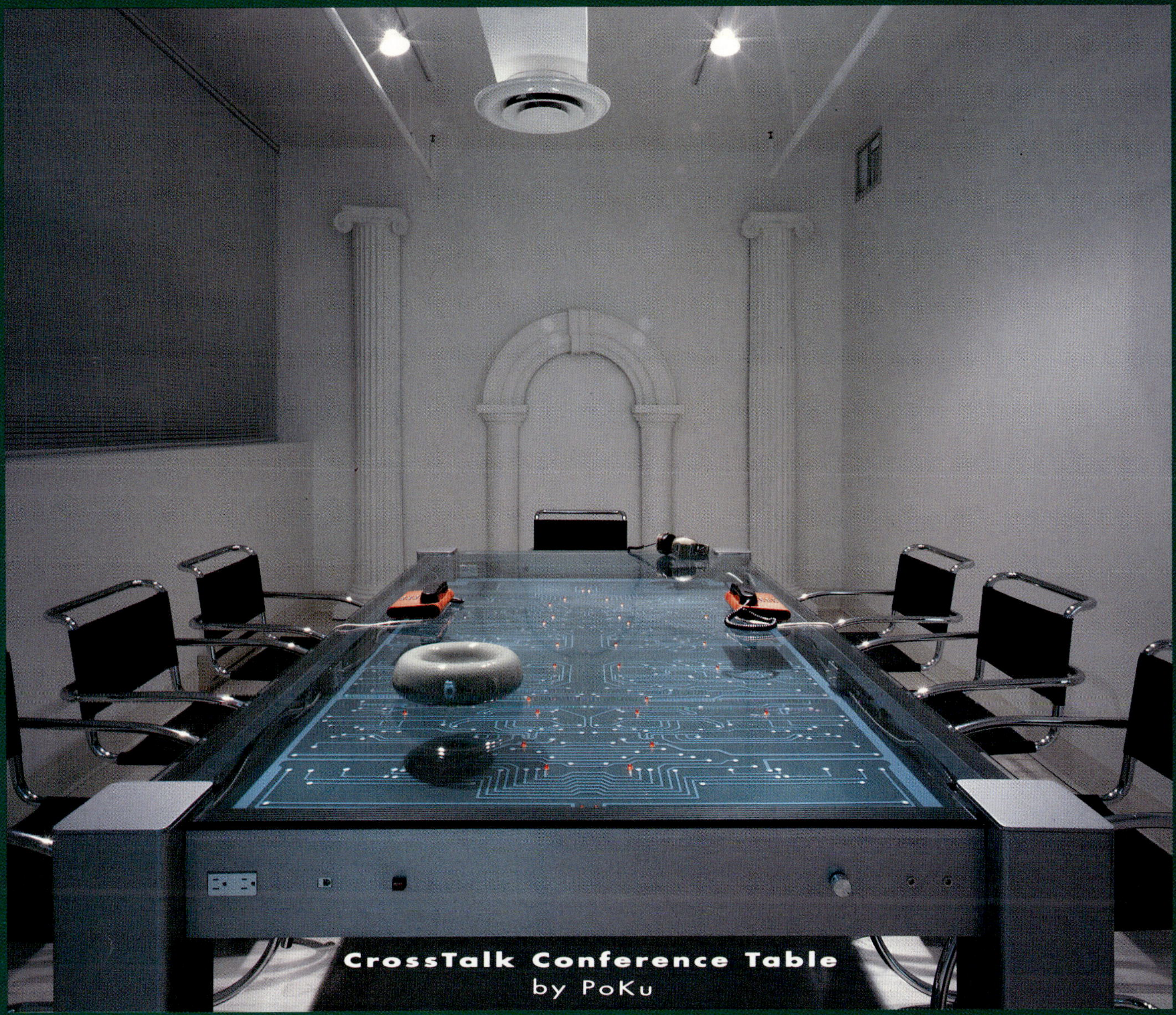

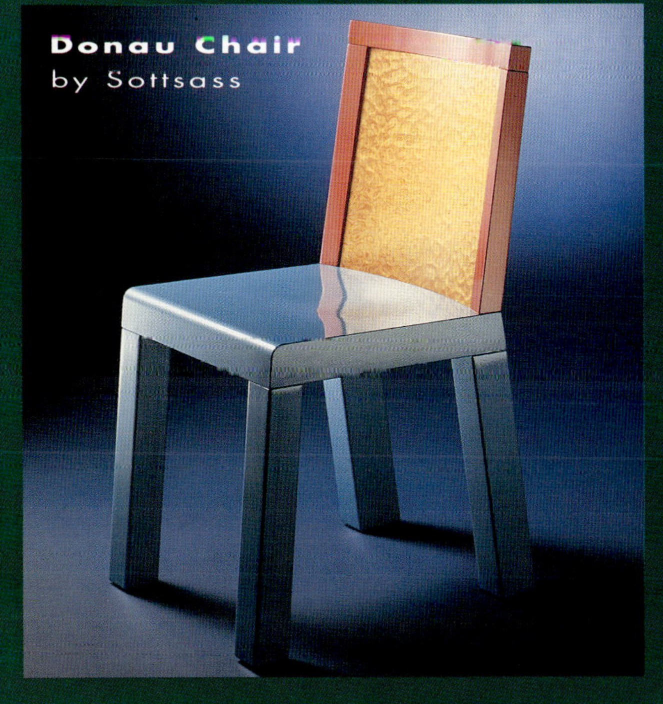

CrossTalk Conference Table
by PoKu

The Quess Showroom features exquisitely crafted furniture for commercial and residential use. Exclusive in Canada — The Donau Collection, designed by Ettore Sottsass and Marco Zanini, reflecting Memphis cultural initiative in design; the Avantgarde Collection — 40's and 50's revival pieces, and the Ritual series by Borek Sipek. Also furniture designed by Canadian Architect PoKu and manufactured by Quess.

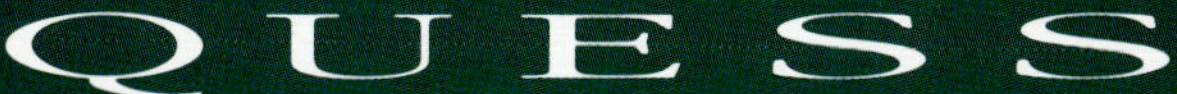

QUESS

Ontario Design Centre
157 Princess Street, 2nd Floor
Toronto On M5A 4M4
Tel.: 416-366-4744
Fax.: 416-366-4461

Donau Chair
by Sottsass

A W A R D S

- 1983 I.B.D. award
- 1987 Roscoe award
- Two 1987 ARIDO awards
- 1988 ARIDO award

PRECISION

Precision Mfg Inc

2200, 52nd Avenue (Lachine)

Montreal, Quebec

Canada H8T 2Y6

(514) 631-2120

Fax: (514) 631-5811

ERGODATA®

Ergodata was introduced to North American business in 1983, and gained immediate acceptance as the essential complement to the technology-oriented office of the present. Within the intervening period, Ergodata has evolved into a Total Ergonomic Modular Desk System.

Ergodata provides an alternative structural opportunity that accomodates the diversity of human anatomical requirements and fulfills the need for individual privacy on a selective basis.

Precision's written unlimited time period warranty, the most generous in the industry, is the measure of our firm's confidence in the quality and merits of Ergodata.

Stow&Davis

A Division of Steelcase
The Office Environment Company

P.O. Box 9, Don Mills, Ontario

M3C 2R7

(416) 475-6333

One of *The Financial Post*
100 BEST
COMPANIES TO WORK FOR IN CANADA

Clients can be hard to figure.

They want to be the same, but different. They want a look appropriate to their business, but still different from the guy across the street. Or across the hall.

Enter Neo System, with flying colours.

Neo is a single wood-and-steel furniture system that lets you customize, creatively and flexibly, in a variety of different ways. Neo gives you multiple surfaces, fabrics, tones – so the resulting options can be as limitless as your imagination.

And every Neo System comes complete with the Steelcase heritage of quality and service, plus the Stow & Davis reputation for wood craftsmanship. All built right in.

So bring out your client's true colours ...all across the business spectrum.

SNYDER FURNITURE LIMITED

snyder

SNYDER FURNITURE LIMITED
87 COLVILLE ROAD, TORONTO, ONTARIO, CANADA M6M 2Y6
TELEPHONE: (416) 247-6285   TELEX: 06-969659   FAX: (416) 247-5738

HOUSTON DALLAS MINNEAPOLIS BUFFALO WASHINGTON NEW YORK HALIFAX MONCTON MONTREAL WINNIPEG CALGARY EDMONTON VANCOUVER

THE TEKNION

TELLA SYSTEMS INC.

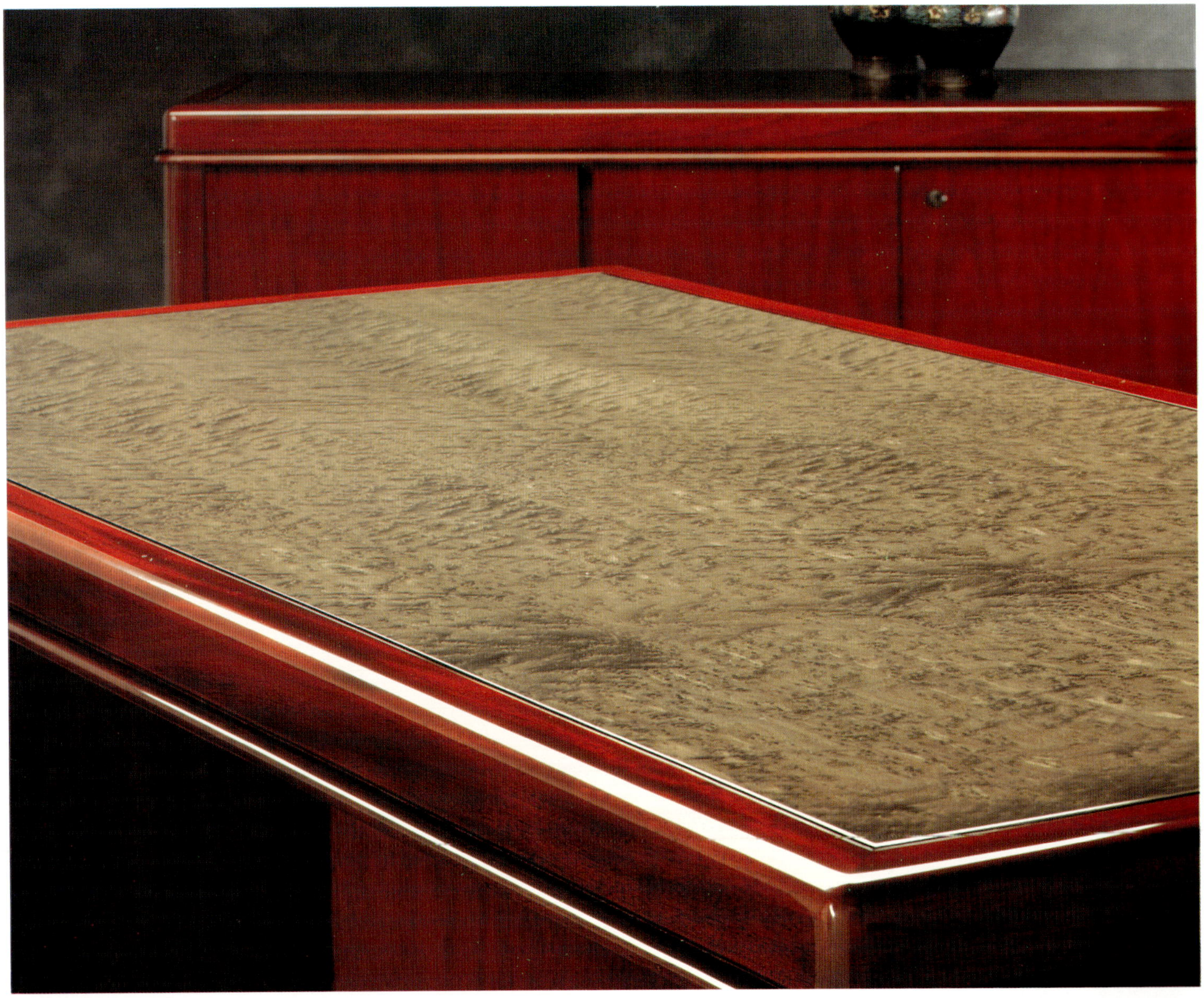

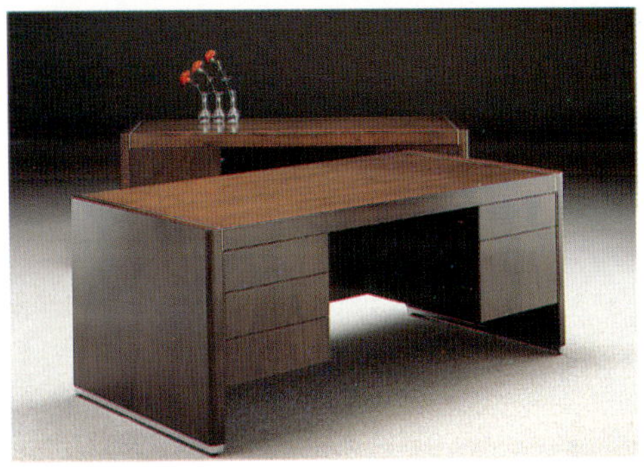

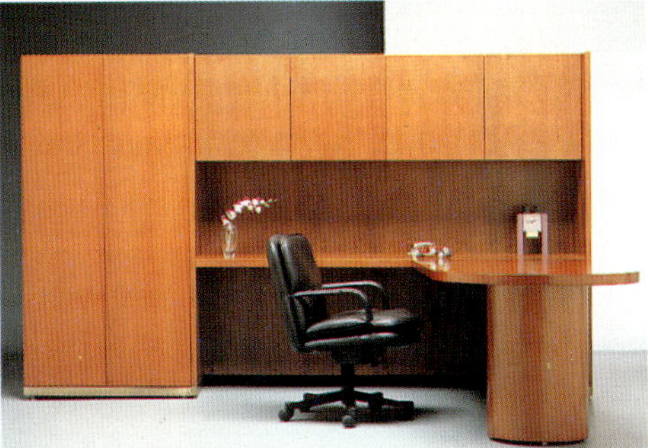

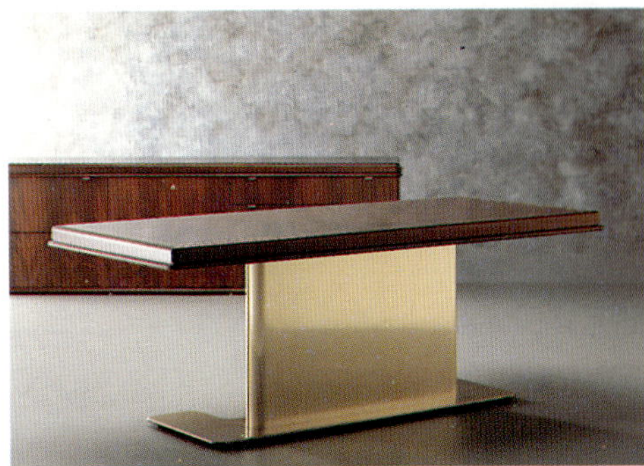

TELLA®

TELLA SYSTEMS INC.
Division of Patella Industries Inc.

Head office:
161 Stirling Avenue
LaSalle, Quebec
Canada H8R 3P3
Tel.: (514) 364-0511
Fax: (514) 364-4177
Showrooms in Montreal, Toronto and Los Angeles

Manufacturer of executive environments and custom furniture.

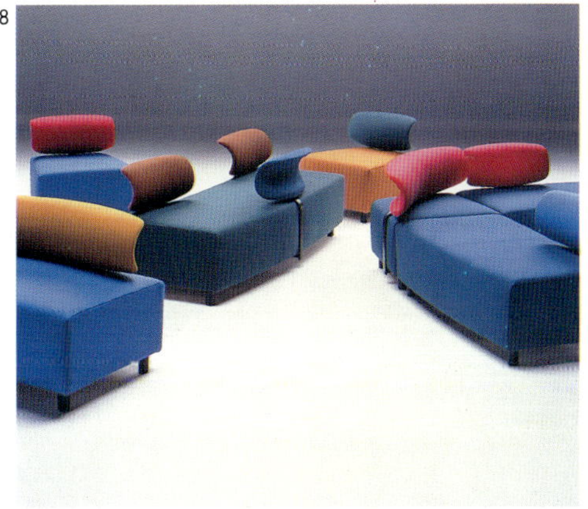

264 The Esplanade
Toronto, Ont., Canada   M5A 4J6
Telephone: (416) 361-1555
Telex: 06-217562   Fax: 361-3568

Importer & Distributor of:

ARCO	chairs & tables (Holland)
ARKETIPO	seating (Italy)
IMAT	tables (Spain)
LEOLUX	seating & tables (Holland)
MARKA ITALIA	chairs (Italy)
METAFORM	chairs (Holland)
PEROBELL	seating (Spain)
RIMADESIO	tables & showcases (Italy)
SALA	tables (Italy)
SEGIS	chairs (Italy)

1. **HELSINOOR** armchair
   Design: A. Lievore, J. Pensi
2. **CRONO** table
   Design: Armando Selva
3. **MOVE** chair
   Design: Arnold Merckx
4. **HORUS** sofa
   Design: Alberto Lievore
5. **DIVI DIVI** armchair
   Design: Mark van Tilburg
6. **COLIBRI** seating
   Design: Jan Armgardt
7. **WALDORF** seating
   Design: Jorge Pensi
8. **VIS A VIS** seating
   Design: Dillon, Wheeler, V.D. Broecke
9. **SCARABEE** sofa
   Design: Axel Enthoven

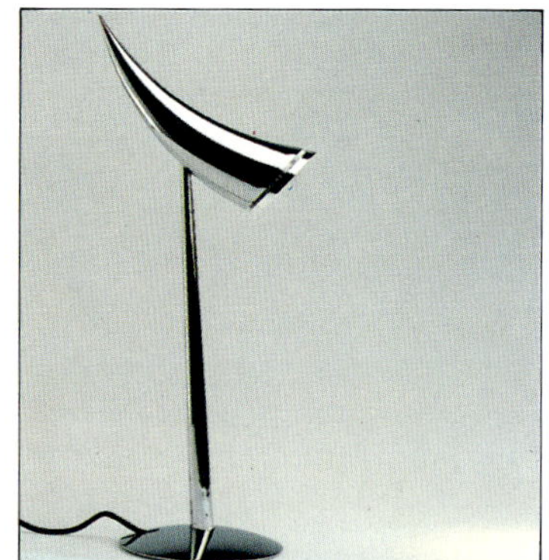

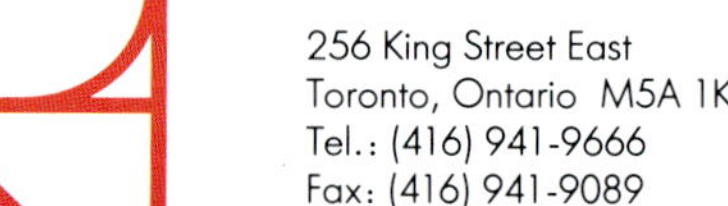

TRIEDE
DESIGN

Triede Design Inc.
460 McGill
Montréal, Québec H2Y 2H2
Tel.: (514) 398-0602
Fax: (514) 398-9009
Telex: 055-61888

256 King Street East
Toronto, Ontario M5A 1K3
Tel.: (416) 941-9666
Fax: (416) 941-9089

Triede Design Inc. agencies:
Winnipeg: (204) 956-1214
Calgary: (403) 290-0900 (all)
  (403) 233-7366 (lighting only)
Vancouver: (604) 687-6454

Exclusive Canadian importer and distributor, TRIEDE DESIGN displays masterpieces of contemporary design by world-renowned architects and designers in its Montreal and Toronto showrooms and in agency showrooms in Winnipeg, Calgary and Vancouver: enlightening advances in office, contract and residential furniture; track, task, outdoor and all-purpose lighting; office, contract, hotel, restaurant and home accessories; and area rugs by ALESSI, ARFLEX, ARTELUCE, BD EDICIONES, CARLO MORETTI, CASIGLIANI, DANESE, DRIADE, FLOS, FONTANA ARTE (furniture and accessories), FRITZ HANSEN, GOPPION, SWID-POWELL, TOULEMONDE-BOCHART, WITTMANN and ZANOTTA, all prestigious firms dedicated to an approach that incorporates both distinctive design and unsurpassed function. Architects and designers AULENTI, BRANDT, CASTIGLIONI, GRAVES, HOLL, HOLLEIN, HOFFMANN, JACOBSEN, KING & MIRANDA, MACINTOSH, MARI, MEIER, MENDINI, PIVA, PORTOGHESI, PUTMAN, ROSSI, SAARINEN, SAPPER, SCARPA, SOTTSASS, STARCK, TIGERMAN, TUSQUETS, VENTURI, VIGNELLI and VOGTHERR congregate in the 3-binder ''TRIEDE THREE'' Catalogue with designs capable of satisfying the toughest requirements. For the discerning specifier and dealer, the exclusive, inexhaustible Canadian source: TRIEDE.

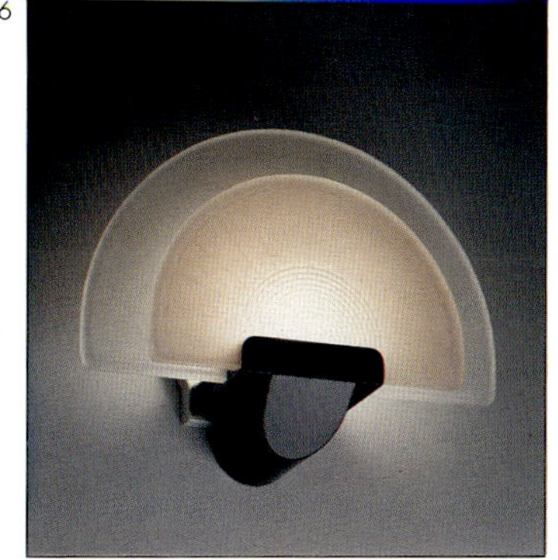

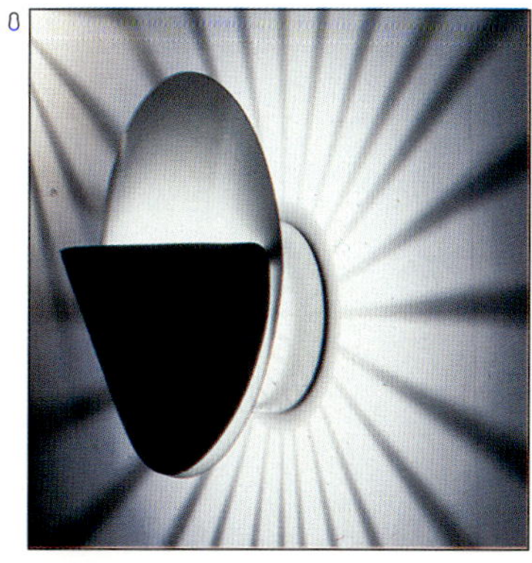

1. "WALL" Halogen Wall Sconce
   Design: King, Miranda, Arnaldi, 1979
2. "AURORA" Halogen Hanging Lamp
   Design: King & Miranda, 1983
3. "ARA" Halogen Table Lamp
   Design: Philippe Starck, 1988
4. "EXPANDED LINE" Halogen Hanging
   Track Lighting System
   Design: King & Miranda, 1983
5. "FRISBI" Hanging Lamp
   Design: Achille Castiglioni, 1978
6. "DIVA" Wall Sconce
   Design: Ezio Didone, 1987
7. "ZEFIRO/3" Hanging Lamp
   Design: P.G. Ramella, 1987
8. "GIOVI" Halogen Wall Sconce
   Design: Achille Castiglioni, 1982
9. "VARANA" MARKABIA Chair
   Design: Oscar Tusquets, 1988
10. "MINITONDA" Armchair
    Design: Burkhard Vogtherr, 1988
11. "COSTES" Aluminum
    Indoor/Outdoor Chair
    Design: Philippe Starck, 1988
12. "T-LINE" Armchair
    Design: Burkhard Vogtherr, 1984
13. "SLIDE" Gliding Armchair
    Design: Burkhard Vogtherr, 1985
14. "ANT" Stackable Chair
    Design: Arne Jacobsen, 1952
15. "CHAIR 44" Pull-up Chair
    Design: Phillipe Starck, 1987
16. "DUPLEX TRICOLOR" Stool
    Design: Javier Mariscal, 1983
17. "ONDA" Sofa Series
    Design: De Pas, D'Urbino, Lomazzi,
    1985
18. "AURA" Sofa Series
    Design: Paolo Piva
19. "MEETING" Office Series
    with "TA" Chairs
    Design: Roberto Pamio & Tito Agnoli
20. "EUROPA" Fully Adjustable
    Sofa Series
    Design: Gualtierotti & M. Delle Stelle,
    1988
21. "ALVA" Glass Cabinet &
    Display Case Series
    Design: Goppion, 1977
22. "VILLA GALLIA" Armchair
    Design: Josef Hoffmann, 1913
23. "HOB" Sofa Series
    Design: Toshiyuki Kita, 1989
24. "STAGE" Auditorium Seating Series
    Design: Jesse Marsh, 1987
25. "1932" Side Table
    Design: Fontana Arte, 1932
26. "METAFORA" Coffee Table
    Design: Massimo & Lella Vignelli
27. "TRASIMENE BLANC" Area Rug
    Design: Andrée Putman

For any additional info, contact:
Paul Papineau, (416) 941-9666

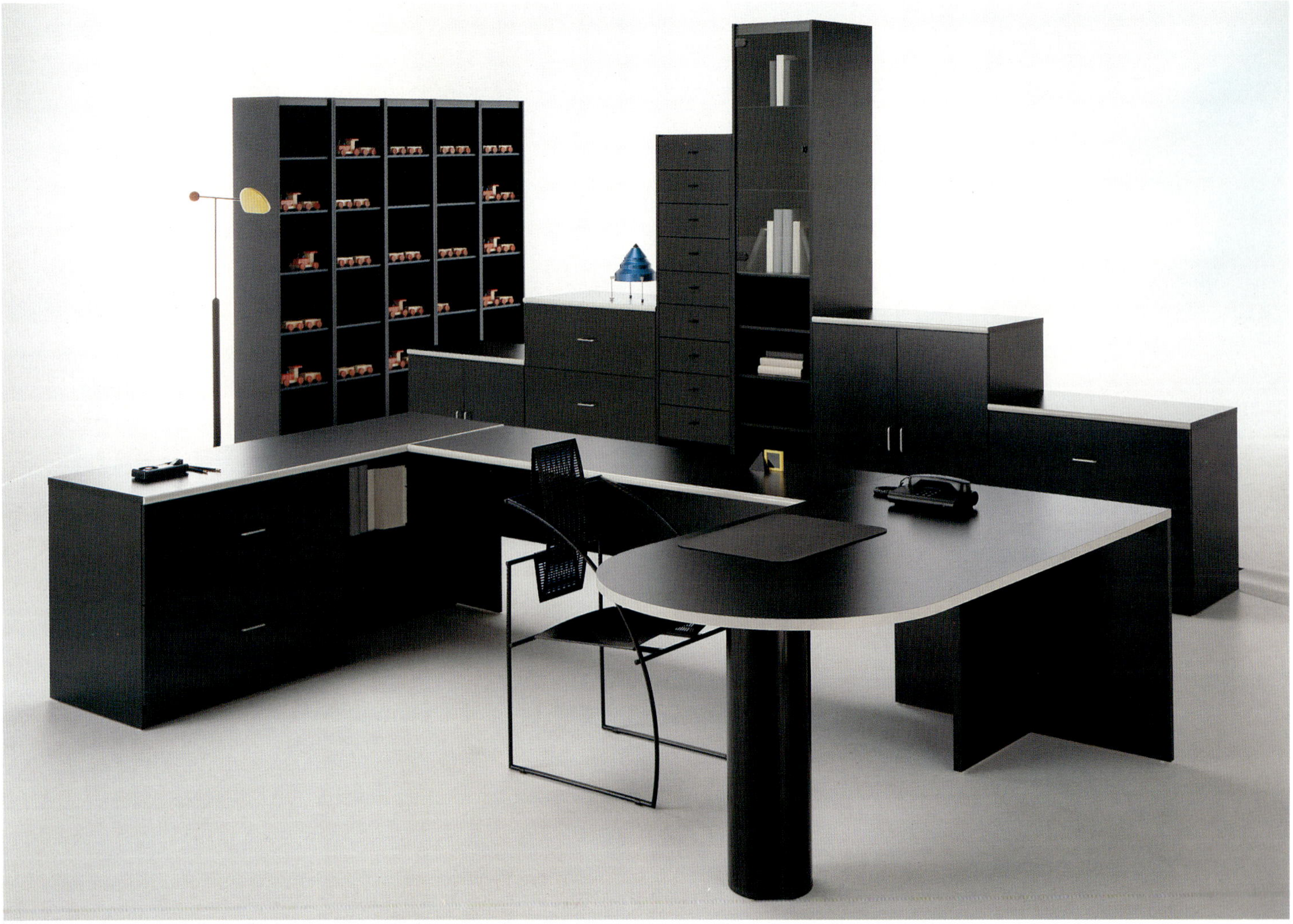

Three H Manufacturing Ltd.
Radley Hill Road,
New Liskeard, Ont.
Canada P0J 1P0
Tel. : 705 / 647-4323
Fax : 705 / 647-5705

Montreal
514 / 655-8145
Toronto
416 / 674-6533
Vancouver
604 / 922-1501
Winnipeg
204 / 943-4778

3H FUNCTION
The THREE H concept is to adapt the style
and comfort of the modern home environment
to the workplace.
In its implementation, the inherent needs
of the office of tomorrow for efficiency and
productivity have been respected.

- The Genie Awards are commissioned yearly for the Academy of Canadian Cinema and Television. They are individually cast in solid brass, gold plated and hand polished to a mirror finish.

- High precision sheet metal work by one of a diversified team of talented artisans and technicians. Soheil Mosun Limited can be relied upon for masterful implementation and timely, efficient project management.

- Our craftsmen work with the most advanced technology in acid etching and chemical milling. Architectural applications include elevator cab interiors and doors, signage and decorative ceiling panels.

Soheil Mosun Limited is manned by a team of toolmakers, machinists, welders, cabinetmakers, modelmakers, etching

artists and industrial designers — working from 30,000 square feet of well-equipped production and office facilities.

There are brake, sheer, welding and bending tools. Milling machines, lathes and a woodworking shop, as

well as the state of art etching facilities. Acid etching of brass, bronze and stainless steel sheets up to four feet by

nine feet. Laminating, silk screening, spray painting equipment and more.

These tools and the collective talents of the artisans at **Soheil Mosun Limited** are being increasingly called

upon for architectural metalwork, for acid etching, for the interior fabrication of elevator cabs, for labelled and

unlabelled door entrances and signage of every description.

Together they can be your tool, and instrumental in implementing your ideas: **Soheil Mosun Limited**.

Where craftsmanship is an art, a science and an attitude that nothing but the best will do.

• **A custom made table base, constructed and finished to exacting specifications. Working with architects and designers worldwide, we will implement your custom fabrication requirements in metal, wood, plastic and glass.**

• **The prototype development of a new elevator cab interior for Olympia & York's First Canadian Place In Toronto. We specialize in the manufacturing and interior finishing of elevator cabs...from concept to installation.**

Soheil Mosun Limited

Soheil Mosun Limited
Custom Fabricators

34 Greensboro Drive
Rexdale, Canada
M9W 1E1

AID 2000 INC.

AID 2000 Inc.
101 Freshway Drive
Unit 66D
Concord, Ontario
L9K 1R9
(416) 661-6433

V. Flander
B.A. Architecture,
Interior Design,
P.G. Furniture Design

B. Papernick
Design Consultant

Transitional lighting-designer V. Flander, 1988–1989

Unique lighting and tables, each drawing on architectural style and detail for its design.

A large selection of colour and material to create beautifully co-ordinated interiors.

* Custom colour and materials to the trade.

AU COURANT

Function, form, design… *au courant*

Designers Walk
354 Davenport Road
Toronto, Ontario
M5R 1K6
(416) 922·5611
Fax: 922·3834

Low voltage track lighting
by Reggiani – Milano (Italy)

Table lamp custom design
by Sigma L2 – Firenze (Italy)

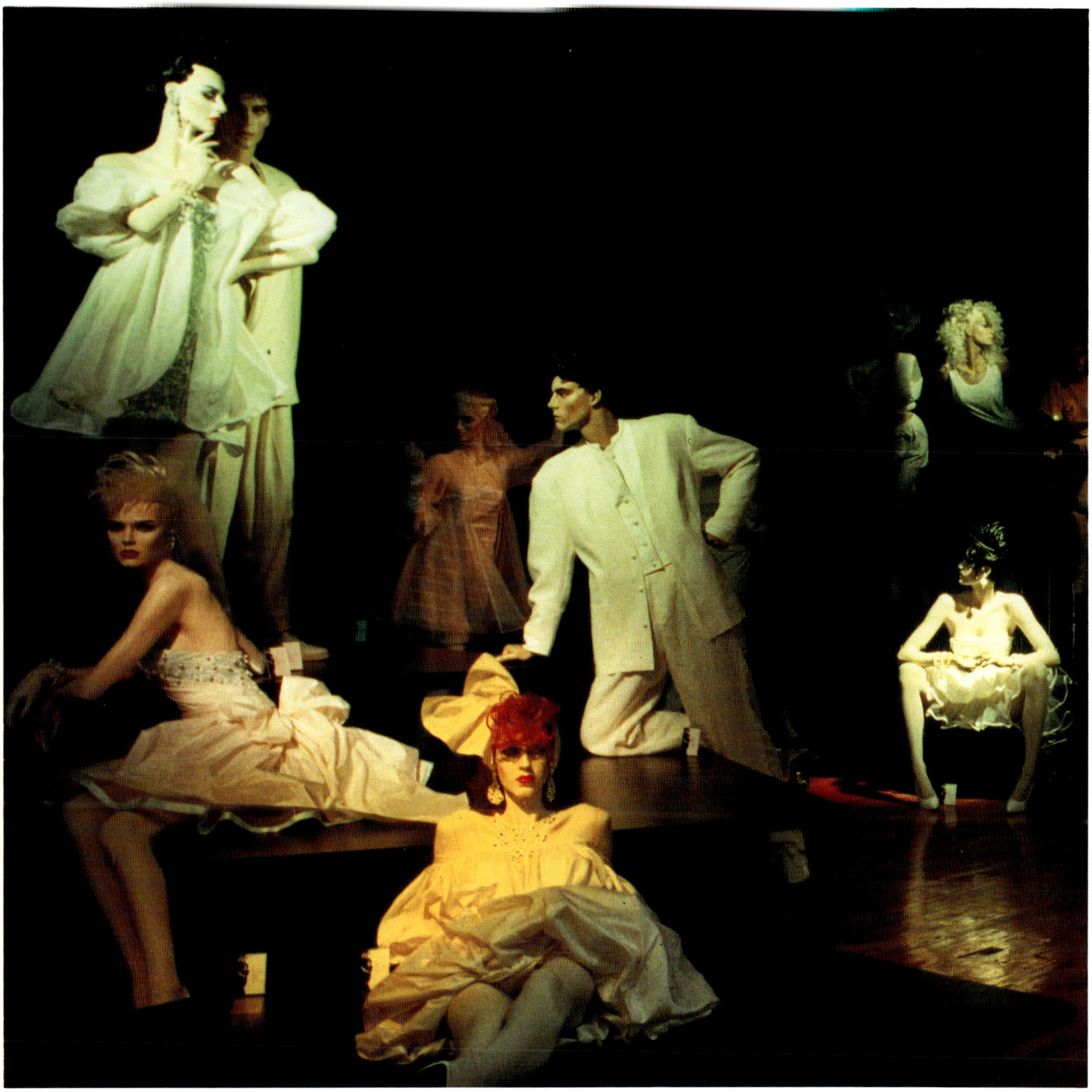

Credit: Profile Mannequins, Montreal, Quebec. Photography: Donigan Cumming, Montreal, Quebec.

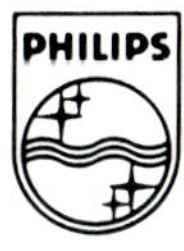

The art of lighting to sell, to stop shopper traffic, calls for the unique Philips WHITE SON lamps.
They are unsurpassed in their ability to bring the vibrant touch of life to mannequins and merchandise.

Energy efficient, cool, flexible, brilliant and precise! Try WHITE SON. You'll find there is a real difference with Philips.

Philips Lighting

PHILIPS

PHILIPS

Marquésa® Lana
leading the way

A-1-86

The complete interior yarn is…Marquesa Lana.
Create that perfect combination of carpet, contract upholstery, and wall covering from one yarn system. The color options are unlimited, from popular solids to sophisticated blends. It's beautiful, It's tough…Choose the Star Performer Marquesa Lana.

Amoco Fabrics and Fibers Ltd. makes fibers and yarn, not finished carpet, upholstery or wall covering fabrics.

Marquesa' Lana is the registered trademark for bulked continuous filament olefin yarn produced by Amoco Fabrics and Fibers Ltd.

Amoco Fabrics and Fibers Ltd.,
Tissus et Fibres D'Amoco Ltée,
955 St. John Road,
Pointe Claire, Que. H9R 5K3

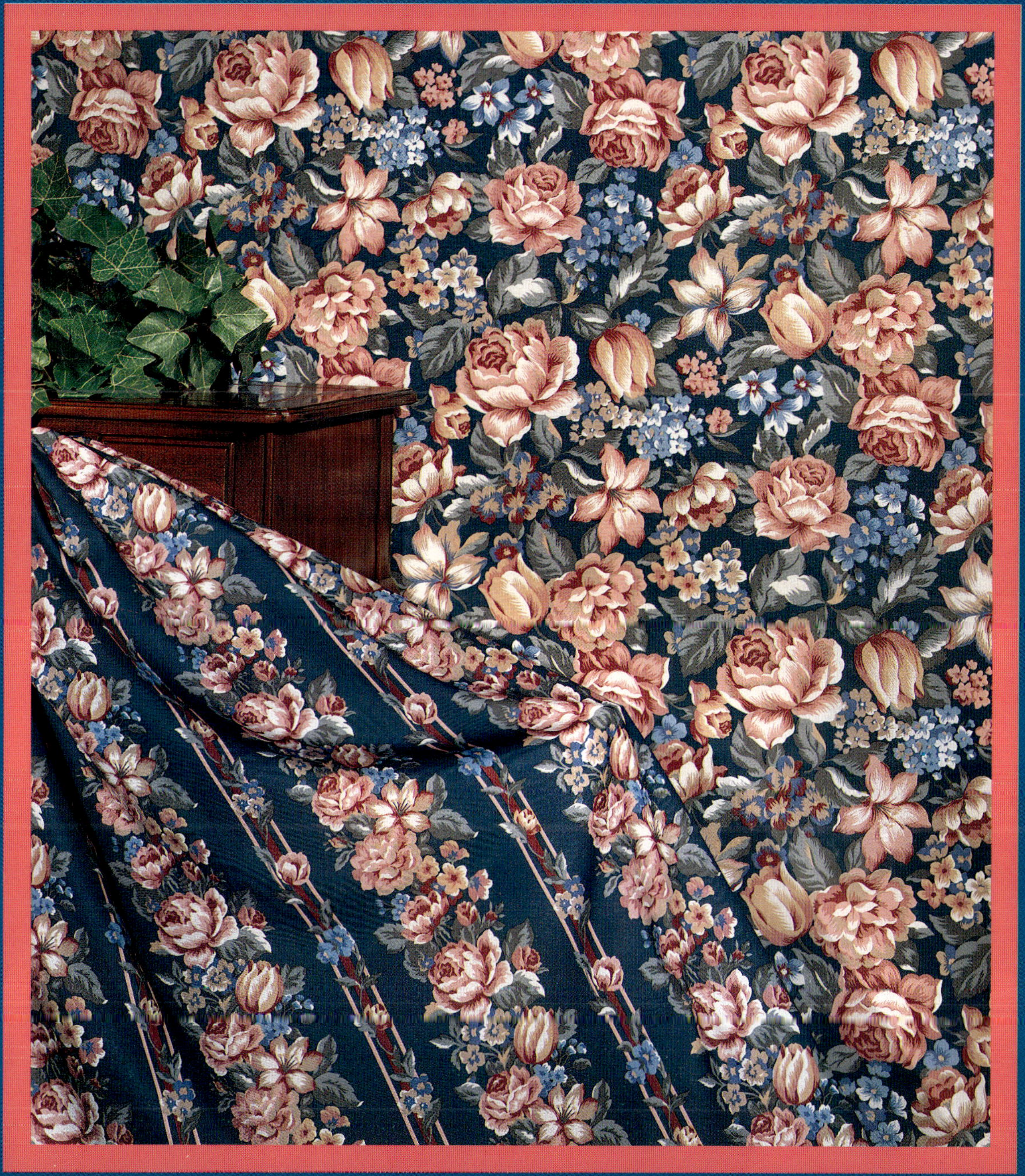

100% Trevira® – Inherently Flame Resistant

The excitement of
leather, softness
and colour...
European hides
processed to
perfection by
professionals for
professionals!
Over 180 colours
in stock!
Custom matching to
Designers' and
Architects'
specifications also
available.

Inter-Leather
Marketing Services Ltd.
131 Brunel Road
Mississauga, Ontario
L4Z 1X3
(416) 890-5505
Fax: (416) 890-5770
Telex: 06960403

Contract & Designers Division:
Tissus AVANT-GARDE
Fabrics Ltd.
7955, rue Alfred
Ville d'Anjou, Québec H1J 1J3
Télex: 05829561
Fax: (514) 351-9440
Montréal (514) 355-2890
Maritimes, Ontario, Quebec:
1-800-361-8886
Manitoba, Saskatchewan,
Alberta, British Columbia
1-800-361-8064

ELMO
AMERICAN LEATHER
PASUBIO

The Perfect Balance
of colour and texture.

RODGERS
WALLCOVERINGS LIMITED

10-415 Horner Avenue, Toronto, Ontario M8W 2A5   (416) 253-1600

85 Rue St. Paul Ouest, S3, Montréal, Québec H2Y 3V4 (514) 844-6666

Vancouver
Calgary
Edmonton

Winnipeg
Toronto
Ottawa

Montreal
Moncton
Halifax

CUSTOM ACOUSTICAL INTERIOR FINISHES
Meeting your acoustical and aesthetic requirements
with a wide variety of custom shapes, sizes, finishes,
edge details, and performance features.
Armstrong
SONOTROL DIVISION
ARMSTRONG WORLD INDUSTRIES CANADA LTD.
4 Kenview Boulevard
Brampton, Ontario L6T 5E4
Phone: (416) 458-5337   Fax: (416) 458-4789

Design: Tudhope Associates Inc.   Illustration: Simon Ng

THE FAMILY OF ANTRON® NYLON FIBRES

Du Pont Canada Flooring Systems is dedicated to providing technological solutions that help great designs to work and endure.

We have made a commitment to manufacture the best fibres and yarns for the commercial carpet market and to provide comprehensive support programmes that help to make commercial carpets better and easier to specify.

For more than two decades Du Pont ANTRON nylon has been the fibre of choice for specifiers everywhere. The reasons are simple: beauty, performance, versatility, reliability. No other fibre offers the same range of colours, patterns, textures and meaningful user benefits. And the family of ANTRON nylon fibres is expanding with new products that offer additional features and enhanced performance for the most demanding commercial installations.

And now commercial carpets of ANTRON nylon fibres are certified by Du Pont to meet strict quality standards. More than ever, carpets of Du Pont ANTRON nylon can be specified with confidence.

FLOORING SYSTEMS

®Registered trademark of E.I. du Pont de Nemours and Company. Du Pont Canada Inc. is a registered user.

For more information write: Du Pont Canada Inc., Commercial Carpet Fibres, P.O. Box 2200 — Streetsville, Mississauga, Ontario L5M 2H3

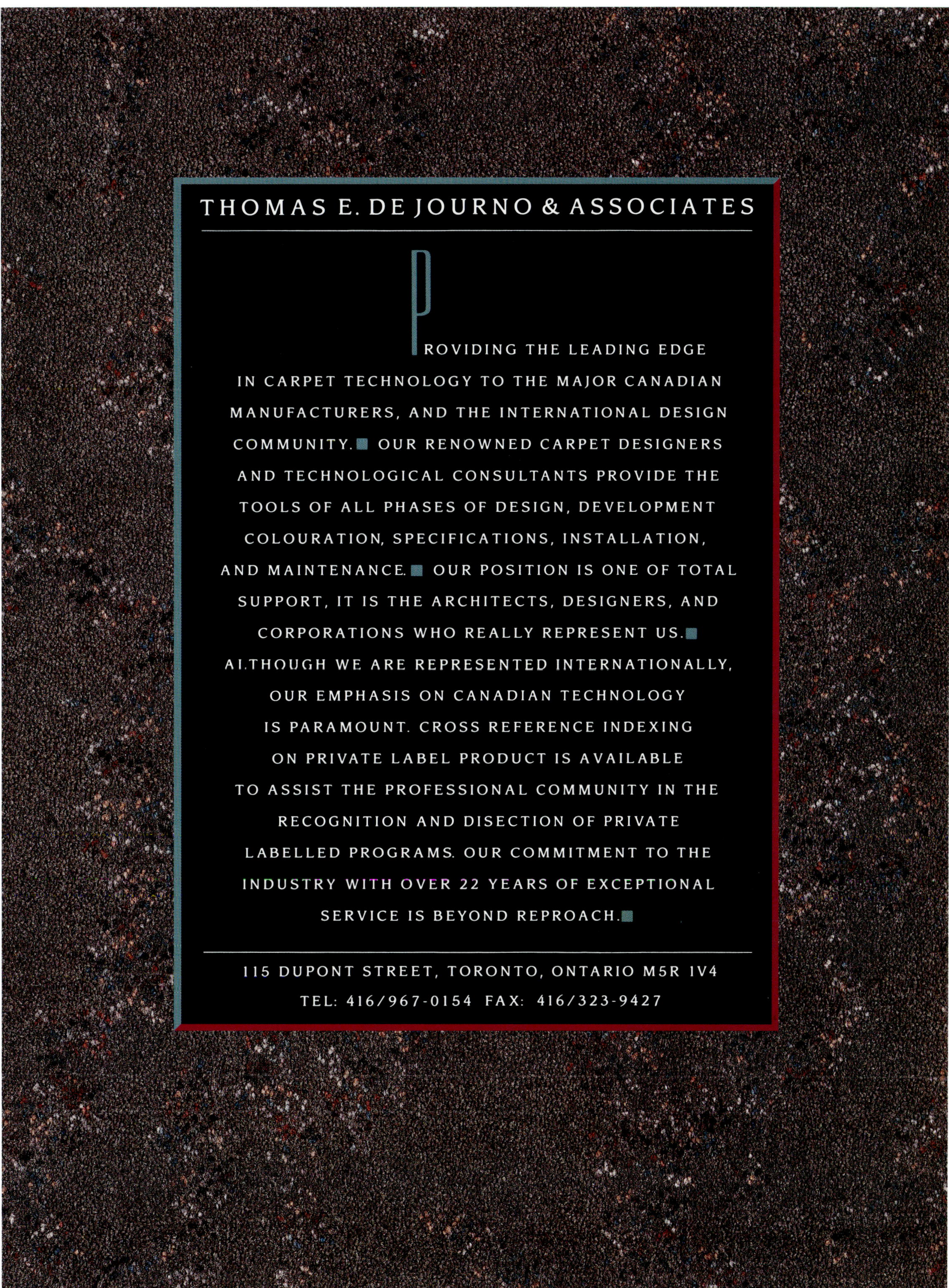

THOMAS E. DE JOURNO & ASSOCIATES

PROVIDING THE LEADING EDGE IN CARPET TECHNOLOGY TO THE MAJOR CANADIAN MANUFACTURERS, AND THE INTERNATIONAL DESIGN COMMUNITY. OUR RENOWNED CARPET DESIGNERS AND TECHNOLOGICAL CONSULTANTS PROVIDE THE TOOLS OF ALL PHASES OF DESIGN, DEVELOPMENT COLOURATION, SPECIFICATIONS, INSTALLATION, AND MAINTENANCE. OUR POSITION IS ONE OF TOTAL SUPPORT, IT IS THE ARCHITECTS, DESIGNERS, AND CORPORATIONS WHO REALLY REPRESENT US. ALTHOUGH WE ARE REPRESENTED INTERNATIONALLY, OUR EMPHASIS ON CANADIAN TECHNOLOGY IS PARAMOUNT. CROSS REFERENCE INDEXING ON PRIVATE LABEL PRODUCT IS AVAILABLE TO ASSIST THE PROFESSIONAL COMMUNITY IN THE RECOGNITION AND DISECTION OF PRIVATE LABELLED PROGRAMS. OUR COMMITMENT TO THE INDUSTRY WITH OVER 22 YEARS OF EXCEPTIONAL SERVICE IS BEYOND REPROACH.

115 DUPONT STREET, TORONTO, ONTARIO M5R 1V4
TEL: 416/967-0154 FAX: 416/323-9427

Gallery
of
MILL

Milliken Design Showroom
Toronto Design Centre
416-323-3328
Modular Carpet Systems

1-800-267-9410 (East)
1-800-267-0955 (West)

Design by 20/20 Designers and Consultants Inc. Toronto • 1988

Modular

Art.

PEERLESS
The commercial carpet specialists

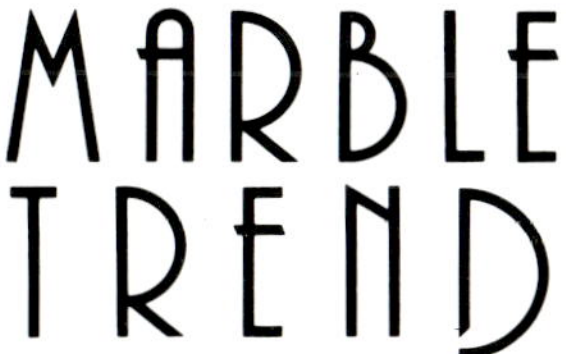

Photography: Gadi Hoz Photographics Inc.

MARBLE TREND

710 Rowntree Dairy Road
Woodbridge, Ontario
L4L 5T7
(416) 738-0400
Telex: 06-964759

The classic beauty and durability of marble ensures its timeless appeal and makes it an investment of lasting value in any project.
Marble Trend imports an impressive selection of marble tiles and slabs; also ''designer'' products from all over the world that can add a note of luxurious simplicity to any interior. Our tiles are carefully selected and available for immediate delivery from our modern warehouse facility.

So, whether you are a Designer, Architect, Builder or Specifier you will value the extensive selection and knowledgeable, experienced team to coordinate your needs.
A constantly changing display of traditional and up-to-date products (tables, executive desks, furnishings and accessories) awaits your inspection in our showroom – ''where imagination comes to life''. We invite you to visit our showroom or call one of our regional representatives.

1. Installation:
   Gem Campbell Terrazzo & Tile
2. Installation: General Tiling
3. Design: Descon
   Installation: Accurate Ceramics and Marble
4. Design: Marble Trend

Jacob Boutique

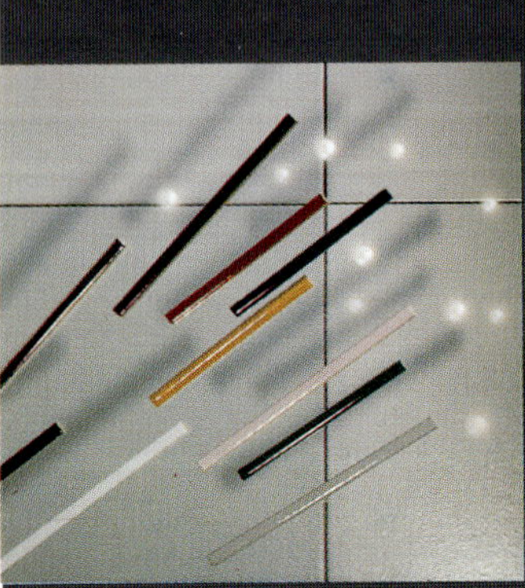

Design Visuel, D plus inc.

Ramca is the designer's edge.

For over 20 years, Ramca has offered the finest selection of original wall and floor tiles for those seeking the extraordinary. Ramca features three superlative collections imported from over 15 countries, RAMCA PLUS… a grand collection of marbles, granites, slates and more. CONTEMPO… Ramca's well known avant-garde ceramic tiles. GALLERIA… hand crafted tiles with town and country charm. No matter how large or small your project may be, our expert design consultants are ready to assist. Visit one of our convenient showrooms today and get the designer's edge.

Ramca Tiles Ltd.

Toronto
Downtown showroom
Designers Walk
354 Davenport Road
(416) 781-5521

Northwest showroom
170 Tycos Dr.
(416) 781-5521
Toll free: 1-800-268-1846
Fax: (416) 781-2368

Montreal
1085, Ave Van Horne
(514) 270-9192
Toll free: 1-800-361-7836
Fax: (514) 270-5897

Ottawa
515 Industrial Ave
(613) 523-4758
Toll free: 1-800-267-6333
Fax: (613) 523-5519

Quebec
1240 boul. Charest O.
(418) 683-2987
Toll free: 1-800-463-2690
Fax: (418) 683-0258

The Queen Elizabeth Hotel

North York Civic Center

Molson's Brewery

TMT MARBLE SUPPLY LTD.

TMT Marble Supply Ltd.
900 Keele Street
Toronto, Ontario
M6N 3E7
(416) 653-6111
Telex: 06-969638

Photography: Gadi Hoz Photographics Inc.

QUARELLA

135 EAST BEAVER CREEK ROAD
RICHMOND HILL, ONTARIO, CANADA
L4B 1E2
(416) 764-0141
TELEFAX (416) 764-2643

THROUGHOUT THE WORLD, DEVELOPERS
AND ARCHITECTS ARE DISCOVERING
THE INHERENT QUALITIES OF QUARELLA,
A PREMIERE AGGLOMERATE MARBLE.
QUARELLA IS A COMPOSITE OF CAREFULLY
SELECTED MARBLE AGGREGATES AND A
RESIN BONDING THAT PRODUCE A PRODUCT
WITH ALL THE AESTHETIC QUALITIES OF
MARBLE, BUT WITHOUT MARBLE'S
FRAGILITY AND COST.

Interior Design Choice 5 © Quarella Inc.

MULTIFLEK PAINT SYSTEMS INC.

Multiflek Paint Systems Inc.
111 Granton Dr., Unit 410
Richmond Hill, Ontario
L4B 1L5 Tel. 886-9733

HERE IS JUST A TASTE OF THE NEW COLORFLEK
RANGE OF MULTICOLOUR PAINTS.
IT INCLUDES PORTAFLEK WITH ITS STRONG, BOLD FLECKS,
AND PORTATONE, A SOFT, FINE FLECKED PAINT.
WE NOW HAVE 92 VIBRANT SHADES IN THE RANGE.

Photo: Didier Dorval   Architectural Elements by : Iconoplast

Photos: Design Archive

2001 COLOURS

AND COUNTING...

POLOMYX®

A CREATIVELY
EXCITING
INTERIOR FINISH
FOR WALL
SURFACES
INCLUDING
DRY WALL
PLASTER CONCRETE
CONCRETE BLOCK
METAL AND
PREVIOUSLY
PAINTED
SURFACES

Classic Architectural Coatings
Premises – Toronto

CLASSIC
ARCHITECTURAL COATINGS

2700 DUFFERIN STREET, UNIT 23, TORONTO, ONTARIO M6B 3R1
TEL.:(416)789-7887 FAX.:(416)789-0420
CALL FOR YOUR CATALOGUE

COST CONSCIENTIOUS

AND CLASSIC...

POLOMYX

A POLYCHROMATIC SPRAY-ON COATING OFFERING AESTHETIC APPEAL OF VINYL WALLCOVERING AT A LIFE CYCLE COST LOWER THAN LATEX PAINT.

Photos: Design Archive

Headquarters Entertainment Corp.
Toronto

Pink Pearl Restaurant
Queen's Quay – Toronto

CLASSIC
ARCHITECTURAL COATINGS

2700 DUFFERIN STREET, UNIT 23, TORONTO, ONTARIO M6B 3R1
TEL.: (416) 789-7887 FAX.: (416) 789-0420

CALL FOR YOUR CATALOGUE

Lipton's Fairview Mall, Toronto. *A large entrance is filled with tempered bi-fold doors and transom, leaving a very open feeling.*

Making Design Something to be Proud of!

*Fine workmanship
is the foundation
of good design.*

Workmanship is critical, and if absent, even the most innovative design looses the special ingredient that makes it stand apart.

Alpha Glass has a tremendous support staff including artists, design and technical consultants, and knowledgeable sales staff, backing-up their expert installation crews.

Alpha Glass has some of the best craftsmen in the industry, a fact recognized by designers, contractors, and other glaziers. Craftsmen with

Park Avenue Restaurant, Toronto. *Sand blasted motif adds style and privacy.*

the experience, the knowledge and the support to make the most innovative designs something to be proud of ■

The possibilities of glass can excite the imagination...

Sandblasting, Back Painting, Watercutting, Chemical treatments, Coloured Laminates, Patterned Glass...

Glass is just now coming to the forefront of design in North America. Designs can be simple or incredibly ornate. Glass can open an area but still offer privacy; can be the centre of the design or the finishing touch.

When you need to know more, Alpha Glass can supply the answers ■

The Leading Edge of Technology

With the introduction of new technology and better production controls, the quality is now better than ever before.

Top to bottom: *1/2'' clear glass with an O.G. edge, 1/2'' clear glass with a polished edge, 3/4'' clear glass with a decorative 1/2'' mitre, and 3/8'' clear glass with an 1-1/4'' bevel.*

All polished edges are not the same. Some are done with a belt by hand, others by regular edge-polishing machine and fewer still are done by machine using an agent called Cerium Oxide.

Cerium Oxide provides a lubricant that enables the polishing wheels to produce a crystal clear finish – whether the glass has a polished edge, a bevelled edge, or an O.G. edge.

Presently, if a designer would like good edge work they specify a "high polish". Shortly they will be asking for a Cerium Oxide polish. With better made, higher speed machinery, higher quality is achieved for the same price as inferior edge work.

At Alpha Glass quality is never taken for granted. They continually

New resource library getting praise from design industry.

seek out high-tech machinery and advanced methods to remain the leaders in their industry ■

In addition to the recently renovated offices, Alpha Glass has created a 300 square feet Resource Library to be used by Architects, Interior Designers and their clients.

Intended to facilitate detail specifications and creative glass applications, the library will display samples of patterns, techniques, edge finishes, architectural fittings, and glass hardware. Additionally, books, drawings and information texts dealing with glass will be available. Samples may be "signed-out" from the library.

This resource centre is another appreciated area of service to the Architecture and Design community from Alpha Glass ■

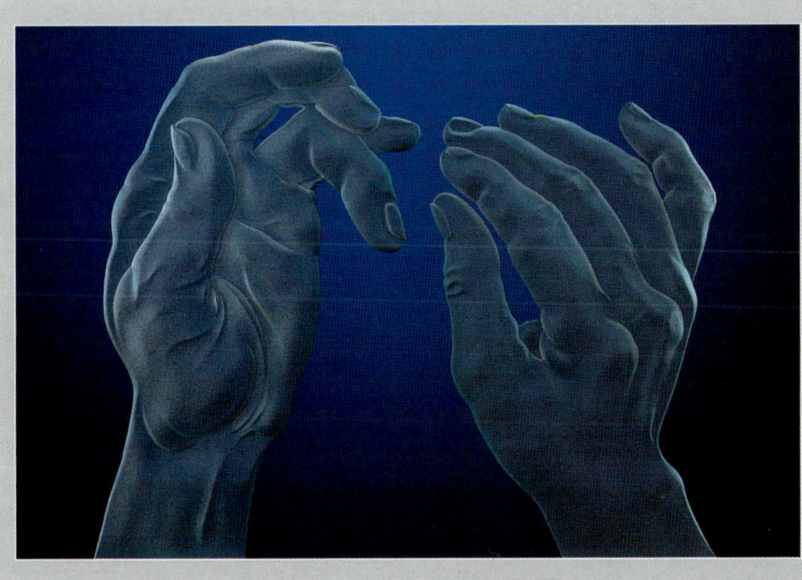

**JOEL BERMAN GLASS STUDIOS/
E.J.B. GLASSWORKS LTD.**
1-1244 Cartwright St.
Granville Island, Vancouver, B.C.
V6H 3R8

(604) 604-0332
Fax: (604) 684-8373

Joel Berman specializes in the
design and fabrication of successful
architectural glass art for commercial
interior space with emphasis on
corporate offices and building
lobbies. Our work includes most
forms of flat glass as well as indoor
and outdoor glass sculpture.

Our clients include:
Group 5 Design Associates
Musson Cattell Mackey Architects
City Interiors
Paul Merrick Architects
Campeau Corporation
BCE Development
Ferguson Gifford Law Office
Orpheum Theatre
Jim Pattison Group
Lignum Lumber
Merrill Lynch

GLASS MOSAIC:

Lobby: MSA BUILDING

Interior Design: City Interiors
Architect: Musson Cattell Mackey
        Architects
Photo: John Fulker – Associates

Designers
Artists
in Glass

Installations
of glass
mirror

and
related
materials

Fabricators
of art
walls
railings
ceilings
bridges
table tops
furnishings
store fronts

laminations
multilevel
bevelling
blasting
blowing
painting
etching

hands
on

DAG

clients
include

Air Canada
Rice Brydone
Labyrinth Design
Royal Bank Plaza
Pellow Architect
Adrienne Clarkson
Atlantis Films Limited

contact Rick Armstrong

Toronto, Canada (416) 963 9422

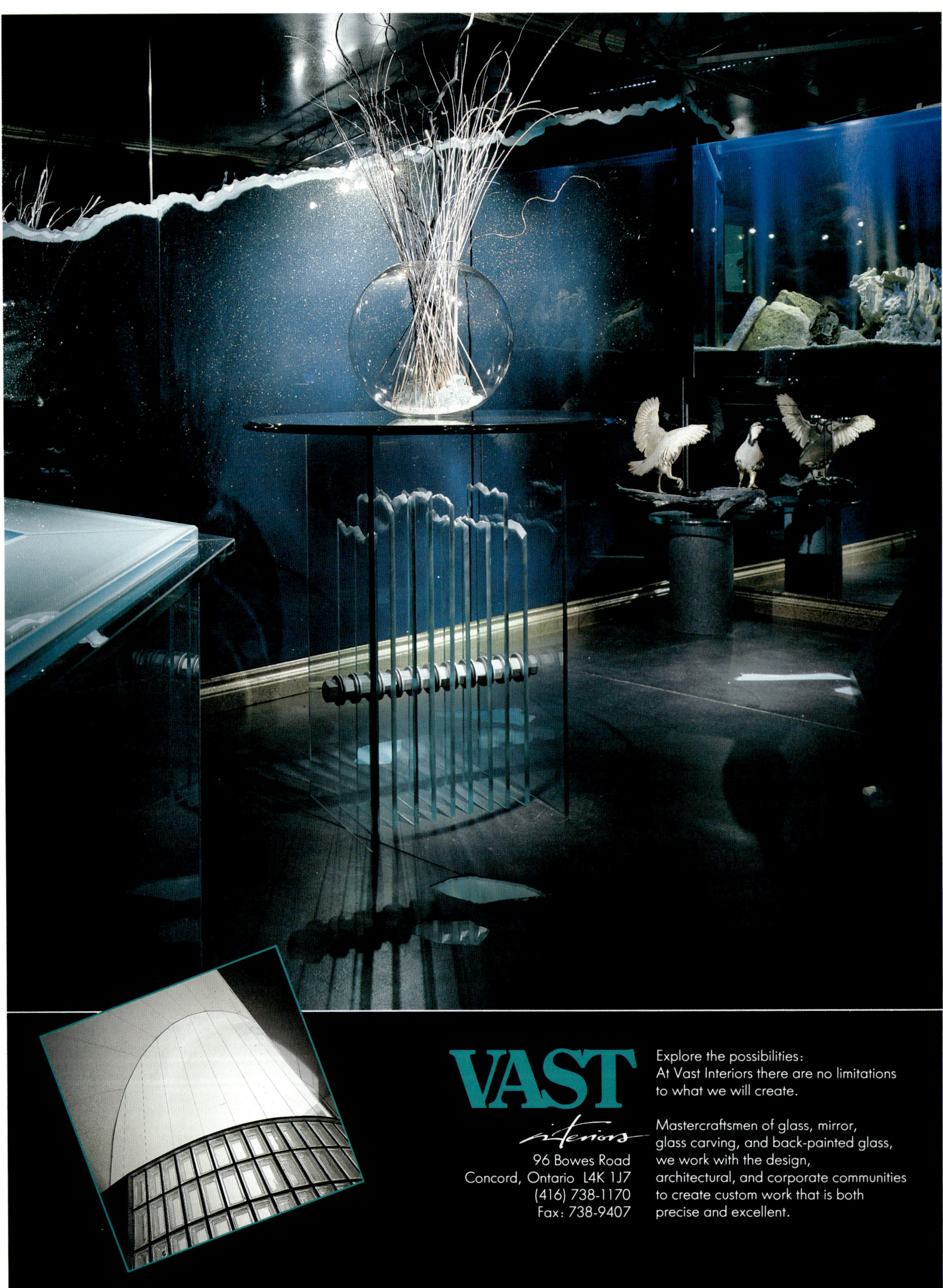

Interior Design Choice 5 © Vast Interiors Limited

VAST INTERIORS LIMITED

We do what no other company does. We provide custom glass and mirror to your exact specifications, then advise and modify. From mirror installations free of clips and mouldings, to distressed edged and back-painted glass, all of our work is executed, completed, and inspected by us. And we are constantly innovating to provide for even the most difficult of design requests.

Examine the potential for quality, creativity and excellence. Before making your next design decision, see what a Vast difference we can make.

GENERAL WOODS & VENEERS LTD.

Design: Cecconi Eppstadt Simone Inc.　　　Photo: Shin Sugino

**General Woods &
Veneers Ltd.
Group of Companies**

P.O. Box 1059, Station A
Montreal, Quebec
H3C 2X6
(514) 674-4957
Fax: (514) 674-3494
Telex: 055-60593

6625 Kestrel Road
Mississauga, Ontario
L5T 1P4
(416) 670-2763
Fax: (416) 670-8561

4305 – 75th Avenue S.E.
Calgary, Alberta
T2C 2K8
(403) 236-3511
Fax: (403) 236-0494

Specialists in domestic and exotic species of wood veneers, logs, and lumber, with commercial activities in North and South America, Africa and Asia.

Interior Design Choice 5 © Donn Canada Ltd. / Ltée

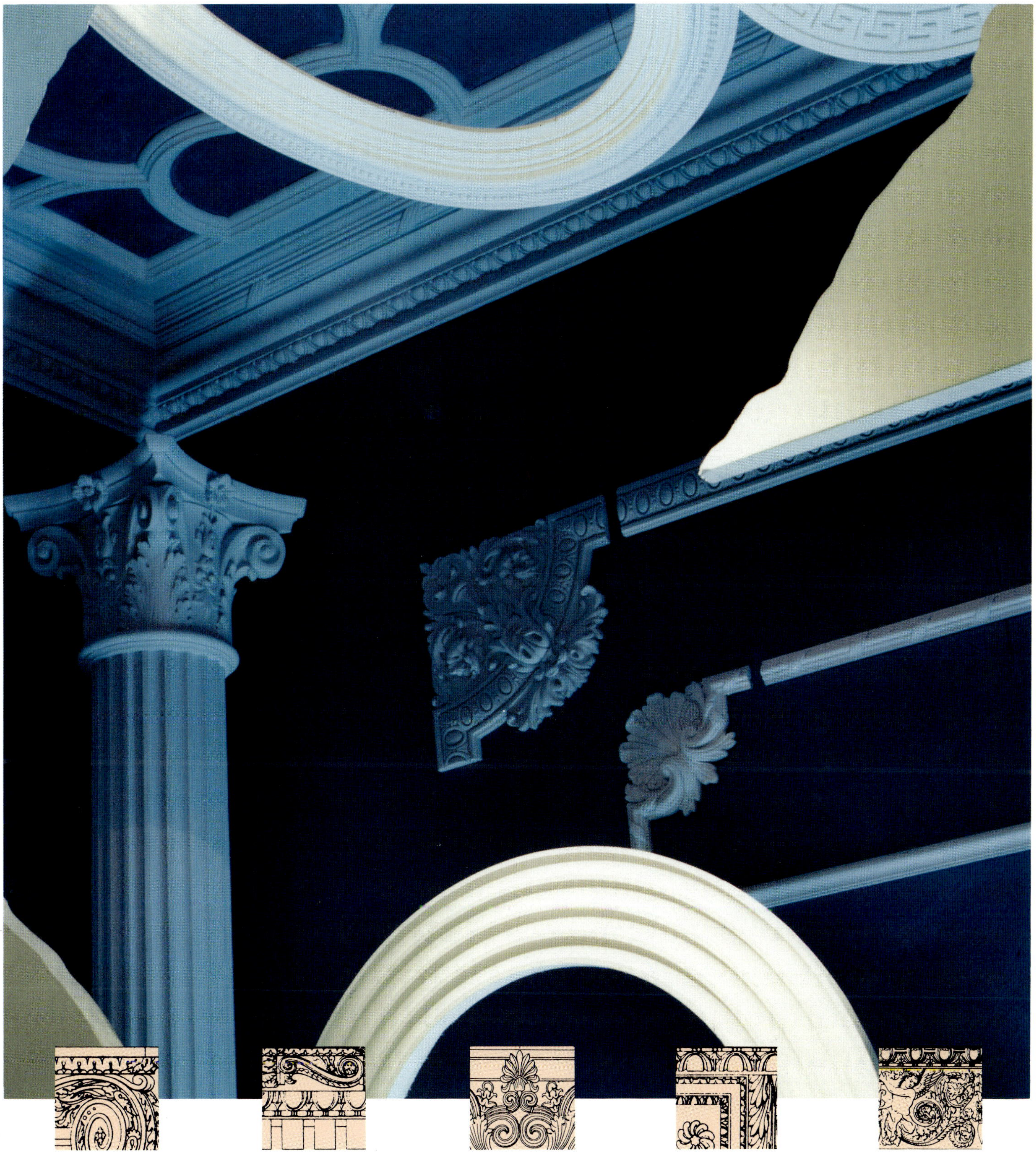

CLASSIC MOULDINGS INC.

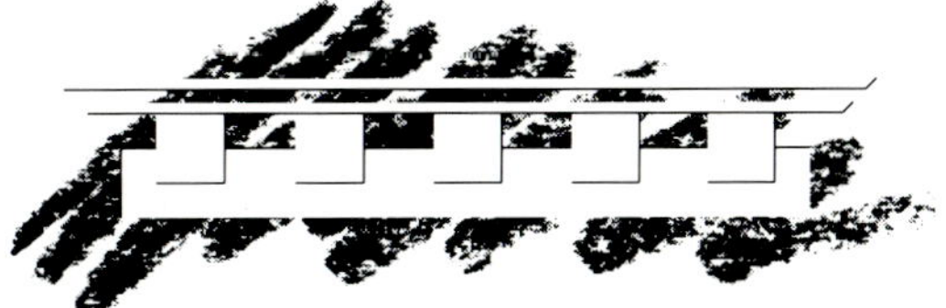

UNIT 1, 155 TORYORK DRIVE, WESTON, ONTARIO M9L 1X9 PHONE (416) 745-5560 FAX (416) 745-5566

QuarryCast®

QuarryCast® is a "Molded Stone" manufactured with glassfiber reinforced inorganic minerals.

The 5/16" thick standard "Veneer" panels (16" & 24" × 48" long) are manufactured in 4 popular colors. Colored throughout, they can be field cut by carpenters (with regular tools) to suit site conditions and being lightweight can be adhered to almost any type of substrate.

As part of the complete wall system, we supply corners, baseboards, moldings, lightsconces, etc. For sizeable projects a variety of interior elements can be custom made in special colors.

QuarryCast is dimensionally stable with a flame spread rating of "0", but is not suitable for exterior applications or floors.

Formglas Interiors Inc.
250 Rayette Road, Unit 4
Concord, Ontario
L4K 2G6   (416) 669-5111

Formglas Inc.
1015 Timothy Street
San Jose, CA
95133   (408) 288-1444

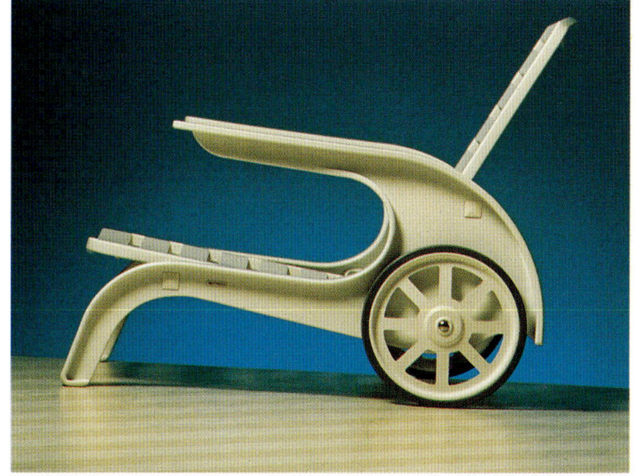

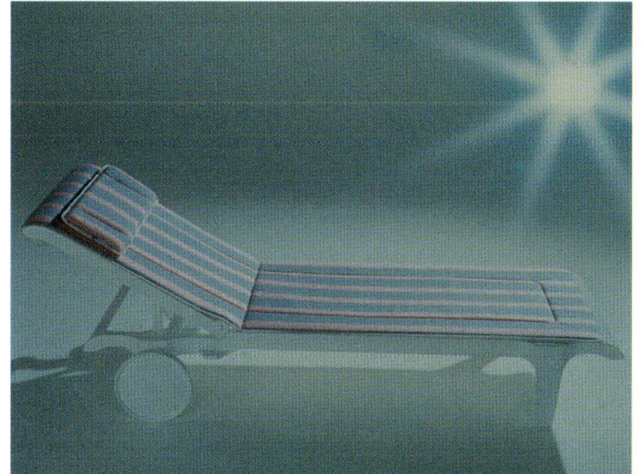

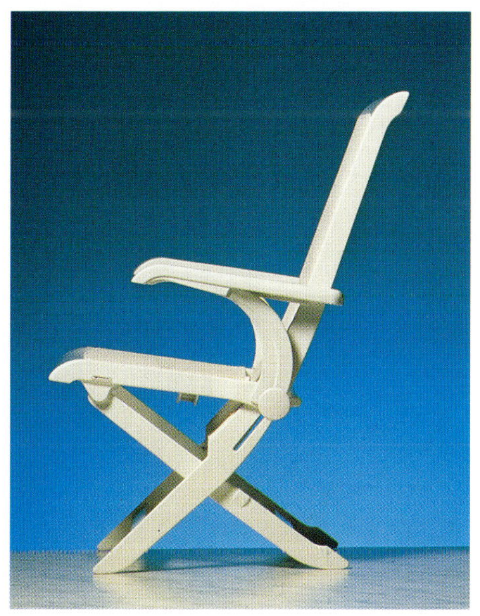

TRICONFORT

MORE THAN GARDEN FURNITURE

Showrooms:

165 Montée de Liesse
St-Laurent, Québec H4T 1T9
(514) 735-6255
Fax: (514) 342-1769

Ontario Design Centre
260 King Street East
Toronto, Ontario M5A 1K3
(416) 360-7949
Fax: (416) 360-6214

210-1080 Mainland
Vancouver, B.C. V6B 2T4
(604) 683-7696
Fax: (604) 683-2799

TRICONFORT furniture is made with the greatest care, skill and flare to bring to you the ultimate in leisure living, luxury and pleasure. Weather-resistant and maintenance-free, our complete range of furniture is as seductive on a private penthouse terrace as around a hotel pool-side.

ALLIBERT –TRICONFORT
THE WIDEST SELECTION
EVER AVAILABLE!
• Seats
• Loungers
• Tables
• Parasols

Imported and distributed by ALLIBERT HABITAT CANADA INC.

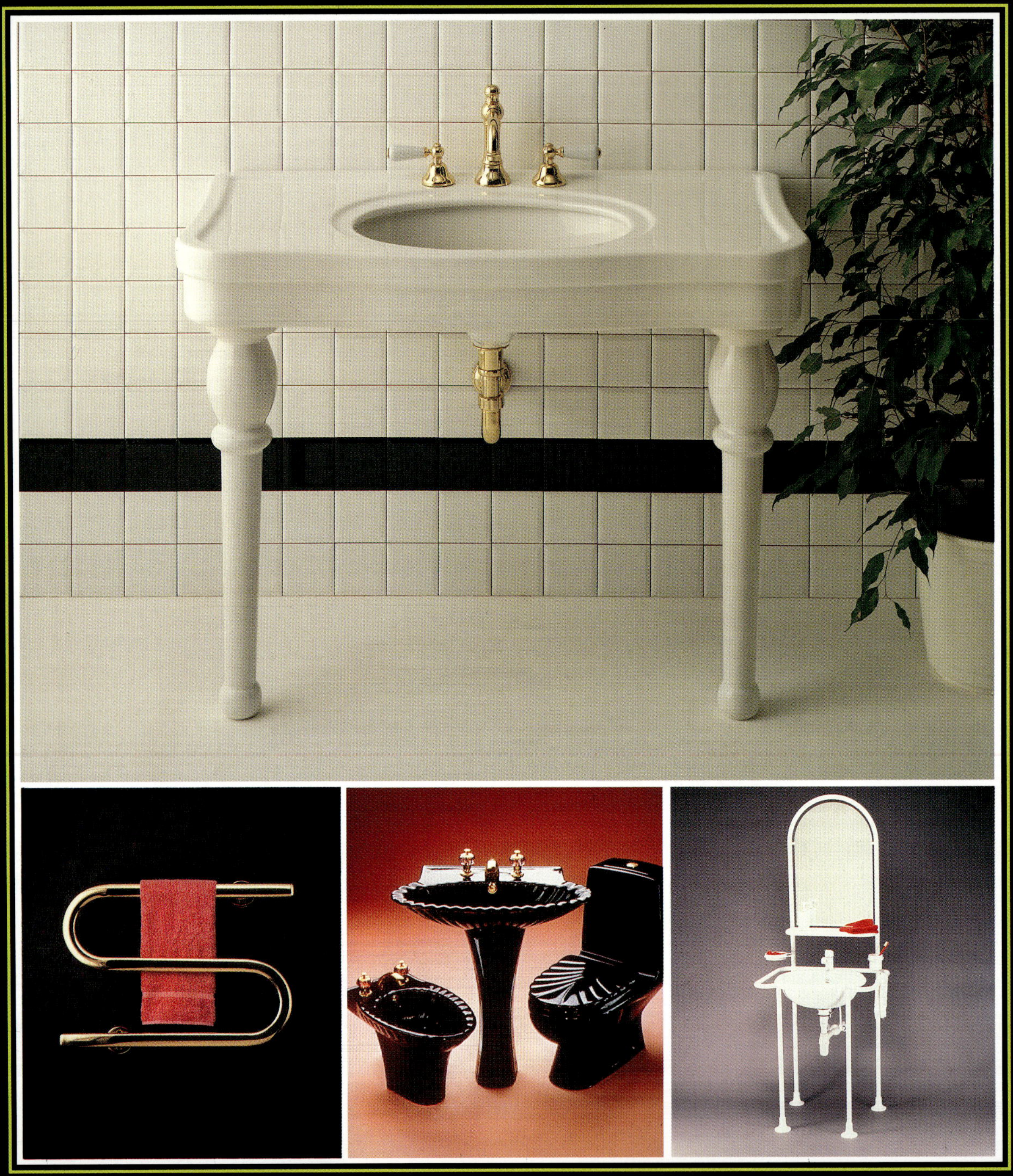

Ginger's Bathrooms

The largest selection of the finest European and North American bathroom and kitchen fixtures, hardware and accessories.

GINGER'S BATHROOMS

945 Eglinton Ave. East at Brentcliffe, Toronto, Ontario (416) 429-3444

THE FINAL TOUCH

The "Designer Series" was specifically created for professional and commercial environments.

Your clients image is important to you and to us.

We are committed to manufacturing superior quality silk plants and trees to satisfy the most discriminating customer.

Photography by Henry Feather

FINAL TOUCH

DESIGN

CONCEPT

Manufacturers of Quality Silk Plants and Trees

Designer Series

HEAD OFFICE
12 ONTARIO STREET
ORILLIA, ONTARIO
L3V 6H1

TORONTO
(416) 472-0726

Silk Design

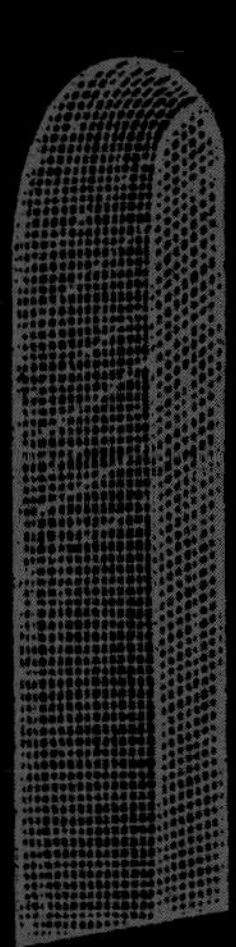

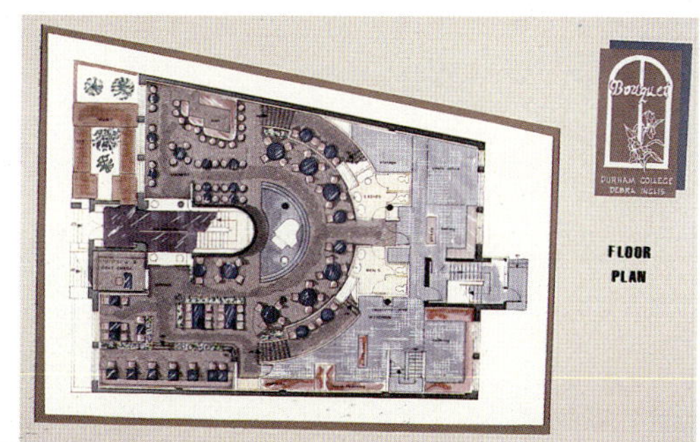

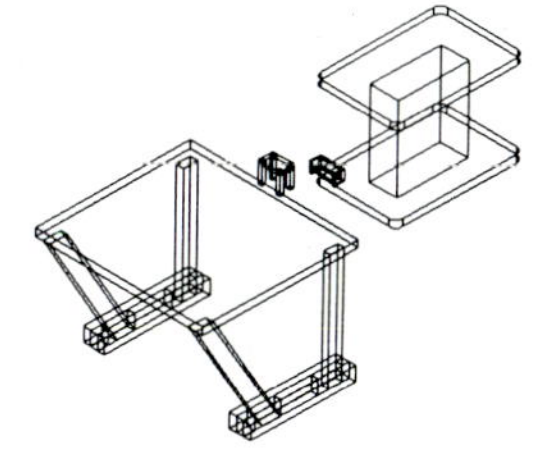

The five essentials of professional interior design....

- ***The Process***
- ***The Rationale***
- ***Technical Knowledge***
- ***Technique***
- ***Craftsmanship***

We strive to provide all of these in our three year interior design program.

We pride ourselves in producing interior designers who will make a valuable contribution to the profession.

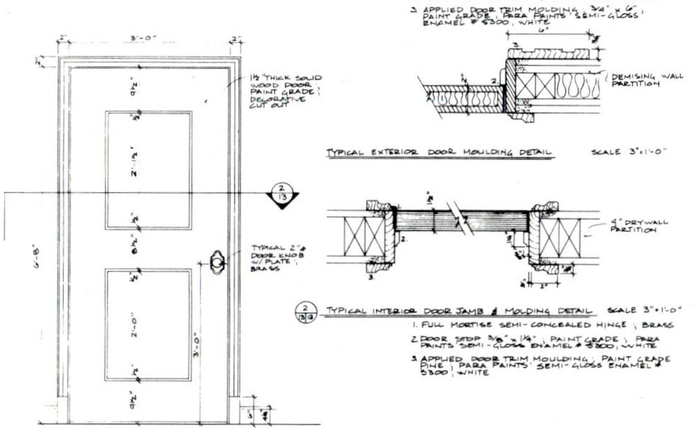

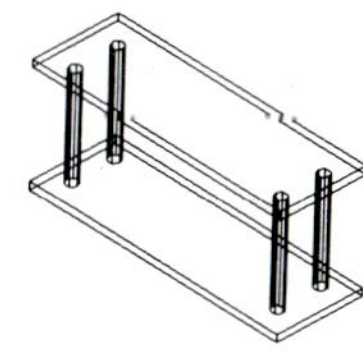

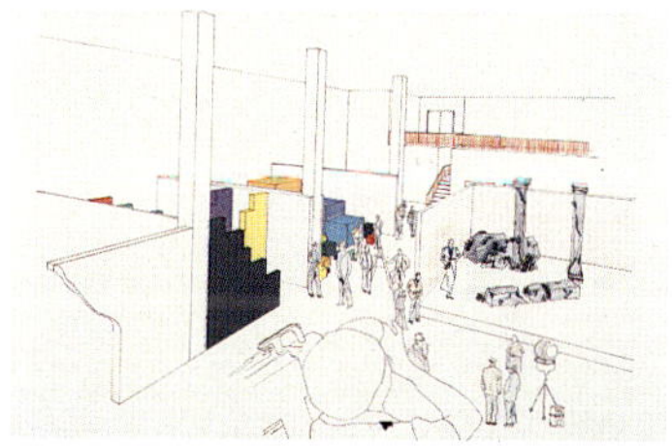

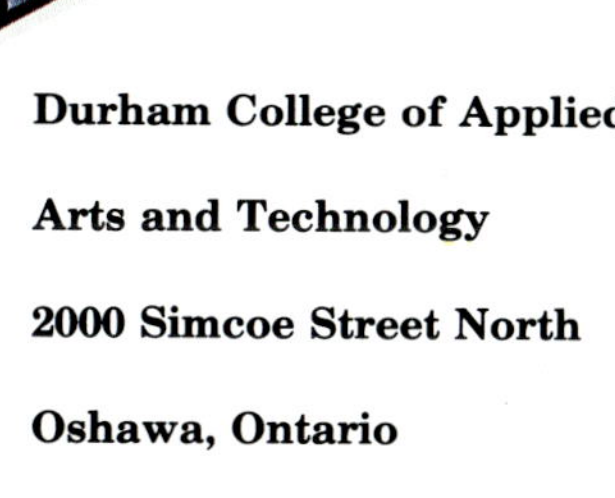

Durham College of Applied

Arts and Technology

2000 Simcoe Street North

Oshawa, Ontario

L1H 7L7

Tel. (416) 576-0210

Studio 4 · Final Project · J. Martenstyn

Studio 2
Island Symposium
C. Jarvis

Studio 2 · Island Symposium Model · C. Huffman

Studio 2 · Collage · M. Theodosiu

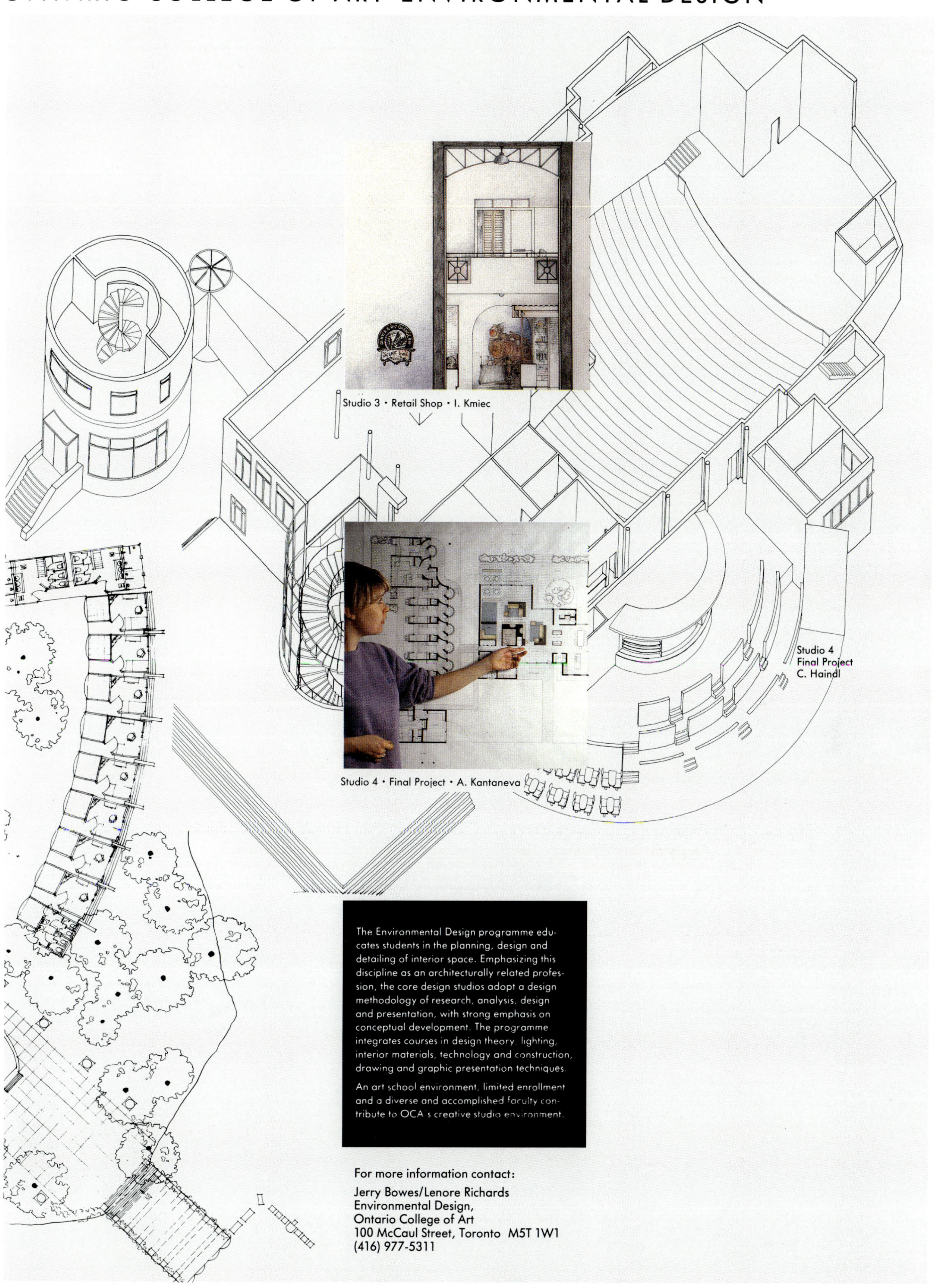

Studio 3 · Retail Shop · I. Kmiec

Studio 4 · Final Project · A. Kantaneva

Studio 4
Final Project
C. Haindl

The Environmental Design programme educates students in the planning, design and detailing of interior space. Emphasizing this discipline as an architecturally related profession, the core design studios adopt a design methodology of research, analysis, design and presentation, with strong emphasis on conceptual development. The programme integrates courses in design theory, lighting, interior materials, technology and construction, drawing and graphic presentation techniques.

An art school environment, limited enrollment and a diverse and accomplished faculty contribute to OCA's creative studio environment.

For more information contact:

Jerry Bowes/Lenore Richards
Environmental Design,
Ontario College of Art
100 McCaul Street, Toronto M5T 1W1
(416) 977-5311

If an "interior designer" does not use the initials I.D.C. (Interior Designers of Canada) after their name, they are probably not a registered member of any provincial interior design association in Canada. The I.D.C. designation is for the exclusive use of professional/registered members of one of these eight provincial interior design associations. Now numbering 1600 members the Interior Designers of Canada represents a group of practising professionals dedicated to encouraging excellence in interior design in the public interest.
They assist the interior design educational institutions in the development of future interior designers and encourage the practitioner with his/her continuing education. They assist the provincial associations with research in support of accreditation and entry examinations through active participation at the executive level of international accreditation bodies, whose standards maintain strength, relevance, and currentness in the demands of today's high standards of excellence. They uphold a code of ethics in professional practice.

Public recognition through legislation has been achieved in eight provinces. This means that members of I.D.C. are assuring the necessary enforcement of high standards of practice and discipline and upholding the satisfaction of the public interest. Now, all applicants for the professional/registered category must write a stringent entry exam following a set minimum for education and practical experience. This exam is used throughout North America. While legislation does not prohibit the practice of interior design, it does by law prohibit the false claim to membership.

If you are in need of the services of an interior designer, it would be in your interest to retain a member of the Interior Designers of Canada, as this is the strongest signal of professional interior design excellence in Canada.

Institute of Interior Designers
of British Columbia
745 Clark Drive
Vancouver, British Columbia
V5L 3J3
(604) 251-5343

Interior Designers of Saskatchewan
c/o Leku Interior Design Ltd.
2356 Scarth Street
Regina Saskatchewan
S4P 2J7
(306) 757-9399

Interior Designers of Alberta
7515 142A Street
Edmonton, Alberta
T5R 0N5
(403) 486-7821

Professional Interior Designers
Institute of Manitoba
100 Osborne Street South
Winnipeg, Manitoba
R3L 1Y5
(204) 453-6718

Association of Registered
Interior Designers of Ontario
168 Bedford Road
Toronto, Ontario
M5R 2K9
(416) 921-2127

Association of Interior Designers
of New Brunswick
P.O. Box 1541
Fredericton, New Brunswick
E3B 5G2
(506) 458-9043

Société de Décorateurs-Ensembliers
du Québec
85, rue St-Paul ouest, Suite B3
Montréal, Québec
H2Y 3V4
(514) 288-9046

Association of Interior Designers
of Nova Scotia
P.O. Box 2042
Station M
Halifax, Nova Scotia
B3J 3B4
(902) 469-8190

160 PEARS AVE.
SUITE 207
TORONTO, ONTARIO
M5R 1T2
(416) 964-0906

► **NEW BRUNSWICK**

Edmunston

OUELLET–CASTONGUAY
746 CANADA ROAD
EDMUNSTON, NEW BRUNSWICK E3V 3K5
(506) 739-7743

Fredericton

FELLOWS & COMPANY
P.O. BOX 1284
FREDERICTON, NEW BRUNSWICK E3B 5C8
(506) 458-9043

HOMEWORKS INC.
201 ABERDEEN STREET
FREDERICTON, NEW BRUNSWICK E3B 1R6
(506) 457-1922

Moncton

MARWIN INTERIORS
26 TRITES ROAD
MONCTON, NEW BRUNSWICK E1B 2V6
(506) 387-7055

► **NEWFOUNDLAND**

St. John's

**BUTT, JUDY
INTERIOR DESIGN CONSULTANT**
28 CRAIGMILLAR AVENUE
ST. JOHN'S, NFLD. A1E 1Z8
(709) 579-6424

MURPHY, LINDA INTERIOR DESIGN LTD.
16 GILLETT PLACE
MOUNT PEARL, NFLD. A1N 2V3
(709) 368-0780

PARAB & ASSOCIATES LTD.
36 PIPPY PLACE
ST. JOHN'S, NFLD. A1B 3X4
(709) 726-9701

► **NOVA SCOTIA**

Bedford

CORPORATE DESIGNS
18 KING'S COURT
BEDFORD, NOVA SCOTIA B4A 3K6
(902) 835-3500

Dartmouth

SEAMAN CROSS
46 WRIGHT AVENUE
DARTMOUTH, NOVA SCOTIA B2Y 4B2
(902) 469-8190

SPERRY MACLENNAN
14 WENTWORTH STREET
DARTMOUTH, NOVA SCOTIA B2Y 2S5
(902) 469-9000

Halifax

A.R.P. DESIGN
1819 GRANVILLE STREET
HALIFAX, NOVA SCOTIA B3J 1Y1
(902) 421-1975

BERARDINELLI DESIGN LTD.
P.O. BOX 801, ARMDALE
HALIFAX, NOVA SCOTIA B3L 4K5
(902) 477-7706

CONCEPT DESIGN
5162 DUKE STREET
HALIFAX, NOVA SCOTIA B3J 1N7
(902) 425-2066

CONTRACT DESIGN INCORPORATED
1791 BARRINGTON STREET
HALIFAX, NOVA SCOTIA B3J 3K9
(902) 429-3311

D'ARCY DENNEHY INTERIOR DESIGN
1690 ROBIE STREET
HALIFAX, NOVA SCOTIA B3H 3E7
(902) 429-9105

KAD DESIGNS
2223 CREIGHTON STREET
HALIFAX, NOVA SCOTIA B3K 3R5
(902) 454-9889

KEDDY, GEOFF & ASSOCIATES LIMITED
1225 QUEEN STREET
HALIFAX, NOVA SCOTIA B3J 2H3
(902) 425-2068

MATTINSON-WHITE INTERIORS
1259 BARRINGTON STREET
HALIFAX, NOVA SCOTIA B3J 1Y2
(902) 422-2275

ROBERTSON MACLEAN DESIGN
P.O. BOX 375, STATION "M"
HALIFAX, NOVA SCOTIA B3J 2R7
(902) 466-5511

TROUP, SUSAN DESIGN
1567 ARGYLE STREET
HALIFAX, NOVA SCOTIA B3J 2B2
(902) 425-4959

WINSTON POWER DESIGN INC.
5162 DUKE STREET
HALIFAX, NOVA SCOTIA B3J 1N7
(902) 425-2068

► **QUEBEC**

Hull

OFFICE EQUIPMENT CO. OF CANADA
75, RUE ST-RAYMOND
HULL, QUEBEC J8Y 1S4
(819) 770-0275

Montreal

ADD DESIGN INC.(LE GROUPE)
1255, BOULEVARD LAIRD
MONTREAL, QUEBEC H3P 2T1
(514) 733-5305

• **AMENAGEMENT COMMERCIAL
ET DESIGN SIMPSON**
P.O. BOX 1133, PLACE BONAVENTURE
MONTREAL, QUEBEC H5A 1G4
(514) 866-9991 **Pg. 144, 145**

ARBOUR, MADELEINE ET ASSOCIES
266, RUE ST-PAUL EST
MONTREAL, QUEBEC H2Y 1G9
(514) 878-3846

ATELIER GAUTHIER, L'
1463, RUE PREFONTAINE
MONTREAL, QUEBEC H1W 2N6
(514) 523-1623

AVGARD / 129142-CANADA INC.
845 RUE ST-CATHERINE EST
MONTREAL, QUEBEC H2L 4N4
(514) 288-8105

BELANGER, JACQUES GROUPE DESIGN
2200, BOULEVARD LE CORBUSIER
LAVAL, QUEBEC H7S 2C9
(514) 337-7074

BERNARD, CLAUDE DESIGN LTEE
451, RUE ST-SULPICE
MONTREAL, QUEBEC H2Y 2V9
(514) 287-9716

BLOCH, CARL DESIGN CONSULTANT
6630, RUE SHERBROOKE OUEST
MONTREAL, QUEBEC H4B 1N7
(514) 481-5748

BOLTE, GABRIELLE DESIGN
112, RUE ST-PAUL OUEST
MONTREAL, QUEBEC H2Y 1Z3
(514) 287-1461

BRAM GROUPE DESIGN INC.
1421, RUE MICHELIN
LAVAL, QUEBEC H7L 4S2
(514) 667-1421

BRISSET-DES-NOS, FRANCINE
5055, AVENUE GATINEAU
MONTREAL, QUEBEC H3V 1E4
(514) 342-2496

BDI GROUP
2000 McGILL COLLEGE AVENUE
MONTREAL, QUEBEC H3A 3H3
(514) 842-9223

BUROPLAN INC.
7945 ROUTE TRANSCANADIENNE
MONTREAL, QUEBEC H4S 1L3
(514) 337-6170

• **CAMDI INTERNATIONAL**
711, RUE DE LA COMMUNE OUEST
MONTREAL, QUEBEC H3C 1X6
(514) 874-1234 **Pg. 103**

CARRE TROIS
3906 RUE CLARK
MONTREAL, QUEBEC H2W 1W6
(514) 842-1364

**CARSLEY, JEAN INTERIEURS
& ASSOCIES**
1226, RUE BISHOP
MONTREAL, QUEBEC H3G 2E3
(514) 871-1643

CASAREMO DESIGN
1550, AVENUE DOCTEUR PENFIELD
MONTREAL, QUEBEC H3G 1C2
(514) 933-3076

• **CHAMPALIMAUD, ALEXANDRA
ET ASSOCIES INC.**
1420, RUE SHERBROOKE OUEST
MONTREAL, QUEBEC H3G 1K5
(514) 845-9532 **Pg. 32**

CONCEPTS IWA, LES
721, RUE IRENE
MONTREAL, QUEBEC H4C 2P2
(514) 932-4637

CONTINUUM DESIGN INC.
1303, AVENUE GREEN
WESTMOUNT, QUEBEC H3Z 2A7
(514) 939-2300

CORRIVEAU, JACQUES DESIGNER INC.
438, RUE ST-PIERRE
MONTREAL, QUEBEC H2Y 2M5
(514) 845-3233

DAGENAIS, PHILIPPE DESIGN INC.
1600, RUE SHERBROOKE OUEST
MONTREAL, QUEBEC H3H 1C9
(514) 931-7294

DESIGN D.A.C. LTEE
6830, RUE JARRY EST
ST-LEONARD, QUEBEC H1R 1W6
(514) 329-2006

• **DESIGN FORREST, LE GROUPE**
1155, BOULEVARD LEVESQUE OUEST
MONTREAL, QUEBEC H3B 1R2
(514) 875-8507 **Pg. 45-48**

DESIGN NOVY INC.
1610, RUE SHERBROOKE OUEST
MONTREAL, QUEBEC H3H 1E1
(514) 932-7870

DESIGN & PLANIFICATION PLUS INC.
5402, RUE RENTY
ST-LEONARD, QUEBEC H1R 1N7
(514) 324-6953

DESIGN 125
1255, RUE UNIVERSITY
MONTREAL, QUEBEC
(514) 866-9206

DESJARDINS, BERNARD DESIGN LTEE
1134, RUE STE-CATHERINE OUEST
MONTREAL, QUEBEC H3B 1H4
(514) 879-1345

DIMENSIONS MJM INC.
5021, AVENUE GROSVENOR
MONTREAL, QUEBEC H3W 2M2
(514) 342-6121

• **DUBOIS, ANDRE & ASSOCIES
DESIGNERS INC.**
1550 RUE DOCTEUR PENFIELD
MONTREAL, QUEBEC H3G 1C2
(514) 935-9303 **Pg. 41-44**

DUCHARME, BENOIT & ASSOCIES INC.
65, RUE DE CASTELNAU OUEST
MONTREAL, QUEBEC H2R 2W3
(514) 495-1719

FOTI + DROUIN DESIGNERS
273, AVENUE LAURIER OUEST
MONTREAL, QUEBEC H2V 2K1
(514) 273-5625

G S M DESIGN
317, PLACE D'YOUVILLE
MONTREAL, QUEBEC H2Y 2B5
(514) 288-4233 **Pg. 52, 53**

GOYETTE DUPLESSIS DESIGN
750, BOULEVARD LAURENTIEN
MONTREAL, QUEBEC H4M 2M4
(514) 744-4714

GROUPE PLANI DESIGN INC.
1996, BOULEVARD ST-JOSEPH EST
MONTREAL, QUEBEC H2H 1E3
(514) 527-1393

HAYART OUIMET & ASSOCIES
5150, RUE CHARLEROI
MONTREAL, QUEBEC H1G 3A1
(514) 327-3151

HICKS DESIGN
4800, AVENUE DU PARC
MONTREAL, QUEBEC H2V 4E6
(514) 271-1108

HINTON, CLAUDE INC.
912, AVENUE McEACHRAN
MONTREAL, QUEBEC H2V 3E2
(514) 277-7401

IDEE ENVIRONMENT INC.
218, RUE ST-PAUL OUEST
MONTREAL, QUEBEC H2Y 1Z9
(514) 849-3205

INNOVA DESIGN INC.
1030, RUE ST-ALEXANDRE
MONTREAL, QUEBEC H2Z 1P3
(514) 875-5655

INTERIEURS BELAIR PAGNETTI INC.
4807 VICTORIA AVENUE
MONTREAL, QUEBEC H3W 2M9
(514) 486-2643

IRON CAT INC.
1225, AVENUE GREENE
MONTREAL, QUEBEC H3Z 2A4
(514) 933-1149

JOLY INTERNATIONAL
511, PLACE D'ARMES
MONTREAL, QUEBEC H2Y 2W7
(514) 843-8662

KINTOL ASSOCIATES INC.
5165, CHEMIN QUEEN MARY
MONTREAL, QUEBEC H3W 1X7
(514) 489-3245

LAMBERT & BONNEAU
1261, BOULEVARD ST-JOSEPH EST
MONTREAL, QUEBEC H2J 1L9
(514) 521-1633

• **LEOPOLD ARCHITECTURAL DESIGN INC.**
1180, RUE DRUMMOND
MONTREAL, QUEBEC H3G 2S1
(514) 393-1636 **PG. 79-82**

LE CHASSEUR BRUCE CHARBONEAU
1000, RUE ST-ANTOINE OUEST
MONTREAL, QUEBEC H3C 3R7
(514) 875-5115

• **LERCH, MICHAEL INTERIORS INC.**
1448 RUE SHERBROOKE OUEST
MONTREAL, QUEBEC H3G 1K4
(514) 287-0851 **Pg. 116, 136**

LE STUDIO
740, RUE WILLIAMS
MONTREAL, QUEBEC H3C 1P1
(514) 878-9222

MAGNUS DESIGNS LTD.
5165, CHEMIN QUEEN MARY
MONTREAL, QUEBEC H3W 1X7
(514) 489-5578

MARGAR INTERIORS
373, PLACE D'YOUVILLE
MONTREAL, QUEBEC H2Y 2B7
(514) 844-3575

• **MARSHALL/MOORE/GOYETTE DESIGN INC.**
CENTRE MANUVIE-2000 MANSFIELD
MONTREAL, QUEBEC H3A 3A3
(514) 875-8696 **Pg. 62**

• **McCLINTOCK, PATRICIA ASSOCIES INC.**
4040-A, CHEMIN TRAFALGAR
MONTREAL, QUEBEC H3Y 1R2
(514) 932-1860 **Pg. 63**

• **MOUREAUX HAUSPY DESIGN INC.**
2140, RUE ST-MATHIEU
MONTREAL, QUEBEC H3H 2J4
(514) 935-4321 **Pg. 69-72**

OSTROFF, LEONARD DESIGN ASSOCIES
1200, RUE DE LOUVAIN OUEST
MONTREAL, QUEBEC H4N 1G5
(514) 382-0571

OUIMET, ROBERT DESIGN INC.
7393, 18e AVENUE
MONTREAL, QUEBEC H2A 2N4
(514) 376-1880

• **OVE DESIGN INTERIORS INC.**
356, RUE LE MOYNE
MONTREAL, QUEBEC H2Y 1Y3
(514) 844-8421 **Pg. 74, 75**

PAGE, PIERRE ET ASSOCIES
354, RUE NOTRE DAME OUEST
MONTREAL, QUEBEC H2Y 1T9
(514) 849-8101

REED, KATE DESIGNS INC.
5101, BOULEVARD DE MAISONNEUVE OUEST
MONTREAL, QUEBEC H4A 1Z1
(514) 486-4292

**ROBILLARD, SENECAL HOUDE
DESIGNERS ENR.**
3575, BOULEVARD ST-LAURENT
MONTREAL, QUEBEC H2X 2T6
(514) 281-0088

RODRIGUE, MARC DESIGNER INC.
6650, RUE METIVIER
MONTREAL, QUEBEC H4K 2L1
(514) 335-1233

**ROY, JAQUES & ASSOCIES
DESIGNER INC.**
306, PLACE D'YOUVILLE
MONTREAL, QUEBEC H2Y 2B6
(514) 845-4587

- **RUBIN, SHULIM DESIGN INC.**
400, RUE McGILL
MONTREAL, QUEBEC H2Y 2G1
(514) 393-1862 **Pg. 112**

SHERIF DESIGN ASSOCIES
3704, RUE ST-DENNIS
MONTREAL, QUEBEC H2X 3L7
(514) 849-2864

SODEPLAN INC.
1180, RUE DRUMMOND
MONTREAL, QUEBEC H3G 2S1
(514) 871-8833

STUDIO MARQUIS AUCLAIR
3620, RUE JEAN-TALON EST
MONTREAL, QUEBEC H2A 1W1
(514) 725-6661

- **TDI ASSOCIATES DESIGN INC.**
303, RUE ST-SULPICE
MONTREAL, QUEBEC H2Y 3W2
(514) 288-8303 **Pg. 118**

- **ROBERT VACHON DESIGN INC.
LE GROUPE**
360 ST-FRANCOIS XAVIER
MONTREAL, QUEBEC H2Y 2S8
(514) 843-3505 **Pg. 85-88**

- **VAILLANCOURT, GILLES-ANDREE INC.**
1621, RUE SHERBROOKE OUEST
MONTREAL, QUEBEC H3H 1E2
(514) 989-9413 **Pg. 134**

YUEN, PHILLIS CONCEPTS
229, PLACE LE MANS
ST-LAMBERT, QUEBEC J4S 1X9
(514) 671-1809

Quebec City

ATELIER AVANT-GARDE INC., L'
2646, CH. STE-FOY
STE-FOY, QUEBEC G1V 1V2
(418) 651-1616

BELLEY FORTIN & ASSOCIES INC.
908-2200, AVENUE CHAPDELAINE
STE-FOY, QUEBEC G1V 4G8
(418) 653-7248

BOUCHARD LAROCHELLE ET ASSOCIES
245 49ᵉ RUE OUEST
CHARLESBOURG, QUEBEC G1H 5E3
(418) 623-7293

GROUPE CONCEPT ENR.
269, RUE ST-PAUL
QUEBEC CITY, QUEBEC G1K 3W6
(418) 692-0516

GROUPE PLANI-DESIGN INC.
140, COTE DAMBOURGES
QUEBEC CITY, QUEBEC G1K 8L5
(418) 694-1021

HOUDE GUAY GYSLAINE
253, RUE ST-PAUL
QUEBEC CITY, QUEBEC G1K 8C1
(418) 692-3668

INTERIEUR DESIGN J L D INC.
51, 81ᵉ RUE OUEST
CHALRLESBOURG, QUEBEC G1C 3B3
(418) 626-8315

**LAPLANTE, YVON ET ASSOCIES
DESIGNERS**
1745, CHEMIN DU FLEUVE
QUEBEC CITY, QUEBEC G6W 1Z6
(418) 839-1748

NORMAND JACQUES DESIGNER INC.
8180, RUE BOYER
CHARLESBOURG, QUEBEC G2Q 1S9
(418) 623-4004

SIMARD, PAUL DESIGNER INC.
130, RUE SAUNDERS
QUEBEC CITY, QUEBEC G1R 2R3
(418) 523-0398

▶ ONTARIO

Ajax

CHIROMMATOS, TONY
29 KIPLING CRESCENT
AJAX, ONTARIO L1S 5A7
(416) 428-1467

Brampton

ISOMETRIC DESIGN GROUP
3 CONESTOGA DRIVE
BRAMPTON, ONTARIO L6Z 4N5
(416) 846-8675

NELSON HOFER ASSOC. INC.
1 BARTLEY BULL PKWY.
BRAMPTON, ONTARIO L6W 3T7
(416) 459-7263

OADBE ASSOCIATES LTD.
32 REGAN ROAD
BRAMPTON, ONTARIO L7A 1A7
(416) 846-5001

Burlington

- **DESIGNS WEST**
855HARRINGTON COURT
BURLINGTON, ONTARIO L7N 3P3
(416) 639-7474 **Pg. 147**

Guelph

GUYMARK PALMER DESIGN GROUP
41 LEWIS ROAD
GUELPH, ONTARIO N1H 1E9
(519) 821-9730

Hamilton

BECK, A.W. DESIGN
921 SCENIC DRIVE
HAMILTON, ONTARIO L9C 1H7
(416) 383-5557

COOPER'S THE OFFICE PEOPLE
673 KING STREET EAST
HAMILTON, ONTARIO L8M 1A1
(416) 522-7651

CREATIVE DESIGN CONSULTANTS
775 KING STREET WEST
HAMILTON, ONTARIO L8S 1K2
(416) 525-4140

DAVIS, PATRICIA PLANNING & DESIGN
52 HAROLD COURT
HAMILTON, ONTARIO L8S 2R8
(416) 525-2238

FENNELL DESIGN
718 MAIN STREET EAST
HAMILTON, ONTARIO L8M 1K9
(416) 547-6046

NIEUWLAND ASSOCIATES INC.
187 HERKIMER STREET
HAMILTON, ONTARIO L8P 2H7
(416) 523-5945

SOBEL HARVEY / AUGUSTA HOUSE
283 MAIN STREET WEST
HAMILTON, ONTARIO L8P 1J7
(416) 528-7973

Kingston

- **SIMPSONS
COMMERCIAL INTERIORS & DESIGNS**
791 BLACKBURN MEWS WEST
TAYLOR-KIDD BOULEVARD
KINGSTON, ONTARIO K7P 1Y5
(613) 389-5750 **Pg. 144, 145**

STONE, DAVID & ASSOCIATES LTD.
24 CHATHAM STREET
KINGSTON, ONTARIO K7K 4G5
(613) 546-0207

London

AD HOC DESIGN
189 COLLEGE AVENUE
LONDON, ONTARIO N6A 1X9
(519) 663-9048

BROWN, THORNTON K. INTERIORS INC.
131 WYCHWOOD PLACE
LONDON, ONTARIO N6G 1S7
(519) 473-9566

COMMON MARKET, THE
339 TALBOT STREET
LONDON, ONTARIO N6A 2R5
(519) 679-0390

- **DAWSON, R.C. COMPANY LTD.
DAWSON GROUP DESIGN**
544 EGERTON STREET
LONDON, ONTARIO N5W 3Z8
(519) 451-1980 **Pg. 142**

DECISION PLANNING ASSOCIATES
627 CENTRAL AVENUE
LONDON, ONTARIO N5W 3P7
(519) 438-9967

GIELEN DESIGN LINES INC.
116 MILL STREET
LONDON, ONTARIO N6A 1P6
(519) 432-2238

GILL, DOUGLAS LIMITED
479 RICHMOND STREET
LONDON, ONTARIO N6A 3E4
(519) 672-6001

HAY OFFICE ENVIRONMENTS
1950 OXFORD STREET EAST
LONDON ONTARIO N6A 4J3
(519) 455-055

INNERSPACE BUSINESS INTERIORS
200 QUEENS AVENUE
LONDON, ONTARIO N6A 1J3
(519) 679-0165

INTERIO OF LONDON LTD.
240 RICHMOND STREET
LONDON, ONTARIO N6B 2H6
(519) 433-5113

LONDON BUSINESS INTERIORS INC.
200 QUEENS AVENUE
LONDON, ONTARIO N6A 1J3
(519) 438-2324

• **SIMPSONS**
COMMERCIAL INTERIORS & DESIGN
400 YORK STREET
LONDON, ONTARIO N6B 3N2
(519) 679-4811 **Pg. 144, 145**

TODAY'S BUSINESS INTERIORS
317 ADELAIDE STREET SOUTH
LONDON, ONTARIO N5Z 3L3
(519) 681-8585

Oakville

ANGELA, BARBARA INTERIORS
114 LAKESHORE ROAD EAST
OAKVILLE, ONTARIO L6J 6N2
(416) 842-2103

HELLER, F. DESIGN SERVICES
1570 BAYVIEW ROAD
OAKVILLE, ONTARIO L6L 1A1
(416) 827-6882

SIL AND ASSOCIATES
333 WYECROFT ROAD
OAKVILLE, ONTARIO L6K 2H2
(416) 842-5183

Orillia

HAMILTON, DOUGLAS DESIGN
11 COLDWATER STREET EAST
ORILLIA, ONTARIO L3V 1W4
(705) 325-4545

SUTHERLAND, WENDY INTERIORS
15 BRANT STREET EAST
ORILLIA, ONTARIO L3V 1Y7
(705) 325-6230

Ottawa

ACCENTS INCORPORATED
338 SOMERSET WEST
OTTAWA, ONTARIO K2P 0J9
(613) 233-7435

ATELIER D'OR, L'
487 LEWIS STREET
OTTAWA, ONTARIO K2P 0T2
(613) 563-3343

• **ATKINSON McKEE DESIGN**
360 ALBERT STREET
OTTAWA, ONTARIO K1R 7X7
(613) 563-3797 **Pg. 27**

BOBROW FIELDMAN GROUP INC., THE
46 ELGIN STREET
OTTAWA, ONTARIO K1P 5K8
(613) 238-4091

BUSINESS ENVIRONMENTS FURNITURE LTD.
130 ALBERT STREET
OTTAWA, ONTARIO K1P 5G4
(613) 238-7651

CAPITAL OFFICE INTERIORS LTD.
17 AURIGA DRIVE
NEPEAN, ONTARIO K2E 7T9
(613) 723-2000

CLAUDE DESIGN & ASSOCIATES
1312 BANK STREET
OTTAWA, ONTARIO K1S 5H7
(613) 523-6707

CORUSH LAROCQUE SUNDERLAND & PARTNERS LTD.
15 AURIGA DRIVE
NEPEAN, ONTARIO K2E 7T9
(613) 723-1611

COURDIN, MICHAEL DESIGN
45 BLACKBURN AVENUE
OTTAWA, ONTARIO K1N 8A4
(613) 233-3570

CREATIVE DESIGN ALTERNATIVES
77 METCALFE STREET
OTTAWA, ONTARIO K1P 5L6
(613) 230-5622

DG INTERIORS
28 MEADOWBANK DRIVE
NEPEAN, ONTARIO K2G 0N9
(613) 820-7202

DESIGN ASSOCIATES LTD., THE
332 SOMERSET STREET WEST
OTTAWA, ONTARIO K2P 0J9
(613) 230-3850

DISEGNO INTERIORS LTD.
75 ALBERT STREET
OTTAWA, ONTARIO K1P 5E7
(613) 232-2449

ELITE DESIGN STUDIOS INC.
323 SOMERSET STREET WEST
OTTAWA, ONTARIO K2P 0J8
(613) 238-7979

• **FORREST DESIGN GROUP**
130 ALBERT STREET
OTTAWA, ONTARIO K1P 5G4
(613) 236-9473 **Pg. 45-48**

GABRIEL DESIGN
109 MURRAY STREET
OTTAWA, ONTARIO K1N 5M5
(613) 230-1822

HALLMARK INTERIORS
325 DALHOUSIE STREET
OTTAWA, ONTARIO K1N 7G1
(613) 230-5666

KALIL, ANITA DESIGNS INC.
53 QUEEN STREET
OTTAWA, ONTARIO K1P 5C5
(613) 238-2565

KOMAR DESIGNS
2581 HOBSON ROAD
OTTAWA, ONTARIO K1V 8M7
(613) 738-4479

LOATES, W. & ASSOCIATES
260 HEARST WAY
KANATA, ONTARIO K2L 3H1
(613) 592-3153

MOBILIA LTD.
1723 CARLING AVENUE
OTTAWA, ONTARIO K3A 1C8
(613) 729-9100

NOLAN, LINDA INTERIORS
190 BRONSON AVENUE
OTTAWA, ONTARIO K1R 6H4
(613) 238-4447

OBI DESIGN GROUP
146 COLONNADE ROAD
NEPEAN, ONTARIO K2E 7Y1
(613) 727-9966

OTTAWA CABINET CO. LTD.
24 FLORENCE STREET
OTTAWA, ONTARIO K2P 0W7
(613) 234-0552

PRESTON
1741 WOODWARD AVENE
OTTAWA, ONTARIO K2C 0P9
(613) 723-3111

REISMAN, CARIN C. DESIGN
146 ROGER ROAD
OTTAWA, ONTARIO K1H 5C8
(613) 733-5441

ROLLIN, MICHEL INTERIORS
5 ARLINGTON AVENUE
OTTAWA, ONTARIO K2P 1C1
(613) 233-3408

S & H PLANNING ASSOCIATES LTD.
148 BANK STREET
OTTAWA, ONTARIO K1P 5N8
(613) 235-1165

**SAUNDERS-McFARLANE
DESIGN CONSULTANTS INC.**
157 GILMOUR STREET
OTTAWA, ONTARIO K2P 0N8
(613) 237-4481

• **SIMPSONS
COMMERCIAL INTERIORS & DESIGN**
275 SLATER STREET
OTTAWA, ONTARIO K1P 5H9
(613) 236-6200 **Pg. 144, 145**

SPACESCAPES INTERIORS INC.
53 QUEEN STREET
OTTAWA, ONTARIO K1P 5C5
(613) 235-4677

**SMIT-BOURTON CORPORATE DESIGN
& PLANNING LTD.**
379 METCALFE STREET
OTTAWA, ONTARIO K2P 1S7
(613) 233-1945

TAYLOR-IRVING & ASSOCIATES
325 DALHOUSIE STREET
OTTAWA, ONTARIO K1N 7G2
(613) 236-7702

THATCHER, CARROLL DESIGN INC.
311 RICHMOND ROAD
OTTAWA, ONTARIO K1Z 6X3
(613) 729-2646

TIMM ROBINSON INTERIORS
193 BANK STREET
OTTAWA, ONTARIO K2P 1W7
(613) 232-2649

TREASURES DECORATIVE ARTS STUDIO
145 YORK STREET
OTTAWA, ONTARIO K1N 5Y3
(613) 235-3015

VAN LEUWEN BOOMKAMP LTD.
430 HIGHWAY 7
KANATA, ONTARIO K2L 1T9
(613) 836-1400

VILLENEUVE, MICHELE INTERIOR DESIGN
50 FLORENCE STREET
OTTAWA, ONTARIO K2P 0W7
(613) 234-4323

WOZNIAK, J. DESIGN INC.
98 LEOPOLDS DRIVE
OTTAWA, ONTARIO K1V 7E3
(613) 233-9379

Pickering

HOLMES & BRAKEL LIMITED
830 BROCK ROAD SOUTH
PICKERING, ONTARIO L1W 2Z8
(416) 683-6222

JPN PLANNING ASSOCIATES LTD.
824 ELVIRA COURT SOUTH
PICKERING, ONTARIO L1W 2L1
(416) 839-7557

OMNIPLAN DESIGN GROUP LIMITED
92 CHURCH STREET SOUTH
AJAX, ONTARIO L1S 6B4
(416) 427-2902

St. Catharines

**PARKER, LEX DESIGN
CONSULTANTS LTD.**
32 ST. PAUL STREET WEST
ST. CATHARINES, ONTARIO L2S 2C2
(416) 641-2112

Stratford

BROCK, JOHN ARCHITECTS
151 NILE STREET
STRATFORD, ONTARIO N5A 4E1
(519) 271-4603

WAYSIDE INTERIORS
150 HURON STREET
STRATFORD, ONTARIO N5A 5S8
(519) 273-0880

Sudbury

CALLINGHAM CONTRACT INTERIORS
1535 PARIS STREET
SUDBURY, ONTARIO P3E 3B7
(705) 522-5227

MANOR HOUSE INTERIOR DESIGNS
251 ELM STREET WEST
SUDBURY, ONTARIO P3C 1V5
(705) 673-1773

PARAMOUNT HOME FURNISHINGS LTD.
327 ELM STREET WEST
SUDBURY, ONTARIO P3C 1V7
(705) 674-6427

• **SIMPSONS
COMMERCIAL INTERIORS & DESIGN**
96 LARCH STREET
SUDBURY, ONTARIO P3E 1C1
(705) 673-4181 **Pg. 144, 145**

Metro Toronto

Including: Concord, Don Mills, Etobicoke,
Islington, Markham, Mississauga, Rexdale,
Richmond Hill, Scarborough, Thornhill,
Toronto, Weston, Woodbridge.

• **AID 2000 INC.**
101 FRESHWAY DRIVE
CONCORD, ONTARIO L9K 1R9
(416) 661-6433 **Pg. 235**

ACCETTE, GUY INTERIORS LTD.
55 YORK STREET
TORONTO, ONTARIO M5J 1R7
(416) 368-9287

• **ACORN DESIGN**
67 MOWAT AVENUE
TORONTO, ONTARIO M6K 3E3
(416) 537-0090 **Pg. 26**

ADAMS, LEONARD INC.
65 HIGH PARK AVENUE
TORONTO, ONTARIO M6P 2R7
(416) 769-2814

ADAMS, RON S.
283 MACPHERSON AVENUE
TORONTO, ONTARIO M4V 1A1
(416) 928-0593

AGENDA LTD.
1125B LESLIE STREET
DON MILLS, ONTARIO M3C 2J6
(416) 445-7429

AGNELLI-ORSINI DESIGN INC.
626 KING STREET WEST
TORONTO, ONTARIO M5V 1M7
(416) 866-7454

ALBERTINE DESIGN
225 MACPHERSON AVENUE
TORONTO, ONTARIO M4V 1A1
(416) 964-0600

ALLEN, BEVERLEY INTERIORS
160 BEDFORD ROAD
TORONTO, ONTARIO M5R 2K9
(416) 927-8720

**ALLEN, PATRICK JOHN
INTERIOR DESIGN**
53 BEACHVIEW CRESCENT
TORONTO, ONTARIO M4E 2L6
(416) 699-0273

AMES, DOROTHY DESIGN STUDIO LTD.
160 PEARS AVENUE
TORONTO, ONTARIO M5R 1T2
(416) 922-4769

ARCHITECTURAL INTERIORS
162 PARLIAMENT STREET
TORONTO, ONTARIO M3C 1W2
(416) 367-9144

ART SHOPPE
2131 YONGE STREET
TORONTO, ONTARIO M4S 2A6
(416) 487-3211

**ATKINSON McLEOD DESIGN
CONSULTANTS LTD.**
211 YONGE STREET
TORONTO, ONTARIO M5B 1M4
(416) 362-2311

ATWOOD'S EXECUTIVE OFFICE INTERIORS
110 BLOOR STREET WEST
TORONTO, ONTARIO M5S 2W7
(416) 968-0820

AULD DESIGN INC.
112 MERTON STREET
TORONTO, ONTARIO   M4S 2Z7
(416) 482-5597

AYLWIN, E.D.
83 HOWLAND AVENUE
TORONTO, ONTARIO M5R 3B2
(416) 925-6295

• **B & H INTERIOR DESIGN**
481 UNIVERSITY AVENUE
TORONTO, ONTARIO M5G 2H4
(416) 596-2299   **Pg. 30, 31**

BABCOCK ZANNER INCORPORATED
118 AVENUE ROAD
TORONTO, ONTARIO M5R 2H4
(416) 920-8162

BAKER, LAURA INTERIOR DESIGN
95 THORNCLIFFE PARK DRIVE
TORONTO, ONTARIO M4H 1L6
(416) 425-0016

BANCLIFFE INTERIORS
2014 QUEEN STREET EAST
TORONTO, ONTARIO M4L 1J3
(416) 694-3423

BANGAY, SONIA
INTERIOR DESIGN CONSULTANT
165 KINGSWOOD ROAD
TORONTO, ONTARIO M4E 3N4
(416) 698-3159

BANRI NAKAMURA ASSOCIATES LTD.
173 MARGUERETTA STREET
TORONTO, ONTARIO M6H 3S4
(416) 535-5933

BARONE, MICHAEL & ASSOCIATES
393 NUGGET AVENUE
TORONTO, ONTARIO M1S 4G3
(416) 299-1090

BARTELLO'S
2 BERNARD AVENUE
TORONTO, ONTARIO M5R 1R2
(416) 967-6311

• **BARTLETT, INGER & ASSOCIATES**
2-A GIBSON AVENUE
TORONTO, ONTARIO M5R 1T5
(416) 926-8247   **Pg. 28, 29**

BAYLEY, STEPHEN R., CONSULTANTS
1132 BAY STREET
TORONTO, ONTARIO M5S 2Z4
(416) 924-4240

BELL, LEE INTERIORS LTD.
47 THORNCLIFFE PARK DRIVE
TORONTO, ONTARIO M4H 1J5
(416) 421-0825

BENITZ & BENITZ LTD.
120 CARLTON STREET
TORONTO, ONTARIO M5A 4K2
(416) 962-1632

BERLONI DESIGN ASSOCIATES
1778 WESTON ROAD
TORONTO, ONTARIO M9N 1V8
(416) 241-6408

BERNARD & ASSOCIATES
144 FRONT STREET WEST
TORONTO, ONTARIO M5J 1G2
(416) 979-1100

BIDINI, JOANNE
368 KING STREET EAST
TORONTO, ONTARIO M5A 1K9
(416) 362-8075

BIGIO, JOSEPH INTERIOR DESIGN INC.
1041 AVENUE ROAD
TORONTO, ONTARIO M5N 2L5
(416) 481-5423

• **BJARNASON + ASSOCIATES**
11 CHURCH STREET
TORONTO, ONTARIO M5E 1W1
(416) 368-4040   **Pg. 94**

BLEAKLEY LABBETT LTD.
25 HAYDEN STREET
TORONTO, ONTARIO M4Y 2P2
(416) 923-2442

BOULEVARD COMMUNICATION LTD.
260 KING STREET EAST
TORONTO, ONTARIO M5A 1K3
(416) 860-0605

BRADMAN, DON ASSOCIATES
56 THE ESPLANADE
TORONTO, ONTARIO M5E 1A6
(416) 368-0054

BRAEM & MINNETTI INTERIORS
1262 YONGE STREET
TORONTO, ONTARIO M4T 1W5
(416) 923-7437

BRAY, HAROLD INTERIORS LTD.
1790 ALBION ROAD
REXDALE, ONTARIO M9V 4J8
(416) 749-7811

BRISBIN BROOK BEYNON ARCHITECTS
20 DUNCAN STREET
TORONTO, ONTARIO M5H 3G8
(416) 591-8999

BRISLAND, WILLIAM DESIGN INC.
843 GERRARD STREET EAST
TORONTO, ONTARIO M4M 1Y8
(416) 469-5208

• **BRITACAN BUSINESS INTERIORS LTD.**
505 CONSUMMERS ROAD
WILLOWDALE, ONTARIO M2J 4V8
(416) 494-2007   **Pg. 33-36**

BROCK, JOHN C.
81A FRONT STREET EAST
TORONTO, ONTARIO M5E 1B8
(416) 366-1333

BURANDT INTERIORS LTD.
63 BERKELEY STREET
TORONTO, ONTARIO M5A 2W5
(416) 864-1331

• **BURKE, KATHERINE**
DESIGN CONSULTANT
72 BALMORAL AVENUE
TORONTO, ONTARIO M4V 1J4
(416) 923-6562   **Pg. 120**

BURNELL, DAVID/BY DESIGN ONLY
3015 QUEEN STREET EAST
SCARBOROUGH, ONTARIO M1N 1A5
(416) 699-0352

BURO DECOR INC.
3 CHURCH STREET
TORONTO, ONTARIO M5E 1M2
(416) 860-1400

BUSAT DESIGN ASSOCIATES
298 MERTON STREET
TORONTO, ONTARIO M4S 1A9
(416) 487-4191

CBL DESIGN GROUP LTD.
1523 HURONTARIO STREET
MISSISSAUGA, ONTARIO L5G 3H7
(416) 274-1325

CWD INTERIORS & CONSULTANTS LTD.
151 CARLINGVIEW DRIVE
REXDALE, ONTARIO M9W 5S4
(416) 675-2225

CABRERA, RAFAELL INTERNATIONAL
914 YONGE STREET
TORONTO, ONTARIO M4W 3C8
(416) 964-6947

CABRETTA DESIGN
1591 GERRARD STREET EAST
TORONTO, ONTARIO M4E 2A9
(416) 698-6747

CAMPAIS DESIGN
77 PROGRESS AVENUE
SCARBOROUGH, ONTARIO M1P 2Y7
(416) 298-0320

CAMPBELL – ALLEN DESIGN
2300 YONGE STREET
TORONTO, ONTARIO M4P 1E4
(416) 482-5292

CAVILLA DESIGNS INC.
23 ROSEMONT AVENUE
THORNHILL, ONTARIO L3T 6E5
(416) 889-8896

• **CECCONI EPPSTADT SIMONE INC.**
663 QUEEN STREET EAST
TORONTO, ONTARIO M4M 1G4
(416) 462-1445   **Pg. 37-40**

CHABAN, ROBERT J. AND ASSOCIATES
268 LAKESHORE ROAD EAST
MISSISSAUGA, ONTARIO L5G 1H1
(416) 274-1510

CHAMI DESIGN ASSOCIATES
264 SPRING GARDEN AVENUE
WILLOWDALE, ONTARIO M2N 3G9
(416) 222-4198

● **CHAPMAN, ALEX DESIGN LTD.**
49 SPADINA AVENUE
TORONTO, ONTARIO M5V 2J1
(416) 597-1576 **Pg. 121-124**

CHENIER, D. ASSOCIATES LTD.
1027 YONGE STREET
TORONTO, ONTARIO M4W 2K9
(416) 964-1545

CHENG, JOSEPH INTERIOR DESIGN INC.
22 KIMLOCH CRESCENT
DON MILLS, ONTARIO M3B 2J6
(416) 449-0380

CHRISTENSEN, RANDY & ASSOCIATES LTD.
229 MACPHERSON AVENUE
TORONTO, ONTARIO M4V 1A1
(416) 928-9024

● **CHUNG DESIGNS**
722 KING STREET WEST
TORONTO, ONTARIO M6J 1E6
(416) 862-8282 **Pg. 104, 105**

CITIWORKS DESIGN INC.
296 RICHMOND STREET WEST
TORONTO, ONTARIO M5V 1X2
(416) 503-5827

CLAUDE, PIERRETTE, DESIGN INC.
346 DAVENPORT ROAD
TORONTO, ONTARIO M5R 1K6
(416) 921-9772

COLLINS DESIGN GROUP INTERNATIONAL
550 ALDEN ROAD
MARKHAM, ONTARIO L3R 6A8
(416) 479-4919

COMMERCESPACE DESIGN LTD.
85 EGLINTON AVENUE EAST
TORONTO, ONTARIO M4P 1H5
(416) 489-6936

COMMERCIAL DESIGN GROUP
505 EGLINTON AVENUE WEST
TORONTO, ONTARIO M5N 3A2
(416) 488-7554

COOPERSLIPPER, PAT DESIGN INC.
77 MOWAT AVENUE
TORONTO, ONTARIO M6K 3E3
(416) 538-3203

CORPORATE BUSINESS INTERIORS
562 EGLINTON AVENUE EAST
TORONTO, ONTARIO M4P 1B6
(416) 485-5111

CONCEPTS INTERIOR DESIGN
117 MANVILLE ROAD
SCARBOROUGH, ONTARIO M1L 4J7
(416) 752-4559

CONNOISSEUR, THE
194 DAVENPORT ROAD
TORONTO, ONTARIO M5R 1J2
(416) 925-1020

CORE DESIGN SERVICES
24 BISHOP TUTU BOULEVARD
TORONTO, ONTARIO M5U 2Z7
(416) 340-0295

CORPLAN DESIGN INC.
11 SOHO STREET
TORONTO, ONTARIO M5T 1Z6
(416) 340-1588

CORPORATE OFFICE DESIGN INC.
1903 LESLIE STREET
TORONTO, ONTARIO M3B 2M3
(416) 447-8507

COTTON, PETER C. INC
56 THE ESPLANADE
TORONTO, ONTARIO M5E 1A7
(416) 863-6743

CURR DESIGN CORPORATION
464 KING STREET EAST
TORONTO, ONTARIO M5A 1L7
(416) 366-2234

DI DESIGN AND DEVELOPMENT CONSULTANTS LTD.
110 BOND STREET
TORONTO, ONTARIO M5B 1X8
(416) 595-9598

DANA CONSULTANTS LTD.
19 YORKVILLE
TORONTO, ONTARIO M4W 1L1
(416) 924-8453

DALQUEN GRIMETT INTERIOR DESIGN
1179A KING STREET WEST
TORONTO, ONTARIO M6K 3C5
(416) 537-1179

DANN DUNN DESIGNS INC.
3240A YONGE STREET
TORONTO, ONTARIO M4N 2L4
(416) 483-0629

DARRAGH DESIGN ASSOCIATES LTD.
77 MOWAT AVENUE
TORONTO, ONTARIO M6K 3E3
(416) 534-7519

DEBRA'S DESIGN INTERIORS
66 HOWLAND AVENUE
TORONTO, ONTARIO M5R 2B3
(416) 537-2631

DESICON PLUS
146 WEST BEAVER CREEK ROAD
RICHMOND HILL, ONTARIO L4B 1C2
(416) 731-7151

DESIGN CANADA
1290 SOUTHALDO DRIVE
MISSISSAUGA, ONTARIO L5H 3E6
(416) 271-4010

DESIGN GROUP CONSULTANTS LTD.
2 GLOUCESTER STREET
TORONTO, ONTARIO M4Y 1L5
(416) 967-1500

DESIGN OPTIONS
363A DAVENPORT ROAD
TORONTO, ONTARIO M5R 1K5
(416) 964-7385

DESIGN PLANNING ASSOCIATES
322 KING STREET WEST
TORONTO, ONTARIO M5V 1J2
(416) 977-2355

DESIGNCORP LTD.
48 SHERBOURNE STREET
TORONTO, ONTARIO M5A 2P7
(416) 263-4622

DESMOND INTERIORS
79 HAZELTON AVENUE
TORONTO, ONTARIO M5R 2E3
(416) 922-8087

DESTAR DESIGN LTD.
284 KING STREET WEST
TORONTO, ONTARIO M5V 1J2
(416) 596-0486

DIBOW KOROKNAY BREHN
366 ADELAIDE STREET EAST
TORONTO, ONTARIO M5A 3X9
(416) 368-5700

DIMENNA, FLORA DESIGNS INC.
1111 FINCH AVENUE WEST
DOWNSVIEW, ONTARIO M3J 2E5
(416) 665-8994

DIRSTEIN ROBERTSON LTD.
77 YORKVILLE AVENUE
TORONTO, ONTARIO M5R 1C1
(416) 961-6211

DIRSTEIN & WEALE INTERIORS LTD.
369 EGLINTON AVENUE WEST
TORONTO, ONTARIO M5N 1A2
(416) 481-1155

DOWNTON, JOHN INTERIORS LTD.
50 PRINCE ARTHUR AVENUE
TORONTO, ONTARIO M5R 1B5
(416) 964-8819

DOWNER, ERIC INTERIORS LTD.
116 PURVIS CRESCENT
SCARBOROUGH, ONTARIO M1B 1H9
(416) 291-3155

DUNCAN, CHERYL L. AND ASOCIATES
60 ST. CLAIR AVENUE WEST
TORONTO, ONTARIO M4V 1M7
(416) 967-6090

DZYNE QUARTERS
517 WELLINGTON STREET WEST
TORONTO, ONTARIO M5V 1G1
(416) 340-0572

EDWARDS KIRSH INC.
610 OSTER LANE
CONCORD, ONTARIO L4K 2C1
(416) 738-6855

ELLMAN BONIC DESIGN CONSULTANTS LTD.
67 MOWAT AVENUE
TORONTO, ONTARIO M6K 3E3
(416) 531-3569

ERDOS-POLLAK DESIGN CONSULTANTS
194 WILSON AVENUE
TORONTO, ONTARIO M5M 3A7
(416) 489-5128

**FACILITIES PLANNING
& DESIGN CONSULTANTS**
3461 DIXIE ROAD
MISSISSAUGA, ONTARIO L4Y 3X4
(416) 238-5949

• **FIELDING & ASSOCIATES**
300 NORTH QUEEN STREET
ETOBICOKE, ONTARIO M9C 5K4
(416) 626-6727 **Pg. 49**

**FLETCHER, SHEILAGH
DESIGN CONSULTANTS**
431 RICHMOND STREET EAST
TORONTO, ONTARIO M5A 1R1
(416) 864-9146

• **FORREST DESIGN GROUP**
439 UNIVERSITY AVENUE
TORONTO, ONTARIO M5G 1Y8
(416) 598-2965 **Pg. 45-48**

• **FRANKLAND RUSZNYAK
ASSOCIATES LTD.**
228 GERRARD STREET EAST
TORONTO, ONTARIO M5A 2E8
(416) 928-7422 **Pg. 50**

FRECKLES AND CO.
18 BELMONT STREET
TORONTO, ONTARIO M5R 1P8
(416) 920-2763

**FREUND, FRANCES R.
DESIGN CONSULTANTS**
94 CUMBERLAND STREET
TORONTO, ONTARIO M5R 1A3
(416) 964-6540

GALEA, ELLIS CONSULTANTS LTD.
225 RICHMOND STREET WEST
TORONTO, ONTARIO M5V 1W2
(416) 971-8880

**GEDDES, ELISABETH
DESIGN CONSULTANT**
79 BERKELEY STREET
TORONTO, ONTARIO M5A 2W7
(416) 364-1260

GIANNA DESIGN ASSOCIATES
593 YONGE STREET
TORONTO, ONTARIO M4Y 1Z4
(416) 967-1761

GILES & ASSOCIATES
333 DENISON STREET
MARKHAM, ONTARIO L3R 2Z4
(416) 475-3986

GIO TAN DESIGN ASSOCIATES INC.
169 CARLTON STREET
TORONTO, ONTARIO M5A 2K3
(416) 926-1937

GIRARD ROGERS DESIGN
86 ROSELAWN AVENUE
TORONTO, ONTARIO M4R 1E6
(416) 534-7004

GLUCKSTEIN DESIGN PLANNING INC.
161 DUPONT STREET
TORONTO, ONTARIO M5R 1V5
(416) 928-2067

GUILD, JOHN INTERIOR DESIGN LTD.
310 DAVENPORT ROAD
TORONTO, ONTARIO M5R 1K6
(416) 922-3700

GUTHRIL, W.J. PLANNING ASSOCIATES
797 DON MILLS ROAD
DON MILLS, ONTARIO M3C 1V1
(416) 429-3230

**HAHN, D. ASSOCIATES
PLANNERS & DESIGNERS**
107 SCOLLARD STREET
TORONTO, ONTARIO M5R 1G4
(416) 967-3718

HANNA, DOROTHY DESIGN
25 PRICE STREET
TORONTO, ONTARIO M4W 1Z1
(416) 964-4821

**HARRISON / BLACK
PARTNERSHIP ARCHITECTS**
1681 BAYVIEW AVENUE
TORONTO, ONTARIO M4G 3C1
(416) 489-0893

• **HEFELE MAKOWKA INC.**
525 ADELAIDE STREET WEST
TORONTO, ONTARIO M5V 1T6
(416) 367-3666 **Pg. 54**

HELENA INTERIORS
10 WALKER AVENUE
TORONTO, ONTARIO M4V 1G9
(416) 323-0569

HERCZEGH, INGRID INC.
54 AUSTIN TERRACE
TORONTO, ONTARIO M5R 1Y6
(416) 533-7034

HERITAGE INTERIORS
224 DAVENPORT ROAD
TORONTO, ONTARIO M5R 1J7
(416) 922-6448

HEYBURN LIEBERMAN LTD.
40 KODIAK CRESCENT
DOWNSVIEW, ONTARIO M3J 3G5
(416) 633-9933

• **HIRSCHBERG, MARTIN
DESIGN ASSOCIATES LTD.**
334 QUEEN STREET EAST
TORONTO, ONTARIO M5A 1S8
(416) 868-1210 **Pg. 106, 115**

HOLMAN DESIGN
160 LESMILL ROAD
DON MILLS, ONTARIO M3B 2T7
(416) 441-1877

• **HOLMBERG ASSOCIATES INC.**
260 RICHMOND STREET EAST
TORONTO, ONTARIO M5A 1P4
(416) 364-2950 **Pg. 55**

HOUGHTON DESIGNS LTD.
81-A LOWTHER AVENUE
TORONTO, ONTARIO M5R 1C9
(416) 967-5246

• **HOWLETT DESIGN CONSULTANTS LTD.**
8 MARKET STREET
TORONTO, ONTARIO M5E 1M6
(416) 363-5281 **Pg. 54, 95**

HUI, ALBERT DESIGN ASSOCIATES
742 QUEEN STREET WEST
TORONTO, ONTARIO M6J 1E9
(416) 869-0894

**HYMAS, ALISON
DESIGN ASSOCIATES INC.**
322 KING STREET WEST,
TORONTO, ONTARIO M5V 1J2
(416) 977-8387

IDACA ARCHITECTURAL INTERIORS
270 AVENUE ROAD
TORONTO, ONTARIO M4V 2G7
(416) 964-6264

IDEA CONSULTANTS INC.
250 THE ESPLANADE
TORONTO, ONTARIO M5A 1J2
(416) 860-1679

IMAGIMAX DESIGN CORPORATION
2 BERKELEY STREET
TORONTO, ONTARIO M5A 2W3
(416) 362-7878

**IMPETUS INTERNATIONAL
CORPORATE DESIGN INC.**
430 KING STREET WEST
TORONTO, ONTARIO M5V 1L5
(416) 593-8844

INSPIRATION 2
959 KINGSTON ROAD
TORONTO, ONTARIO M4E 1S8
(416) 698-9774

• **INTEFAC INC. FACILITIES DESIGN GROUP**
25 MATHESON BOULEVARD WEST
MISSISSAUGA, ONTARIO L5R 3G3
(416) 890-3000 **Pg. 51**

INTER-DESIGN
30 RIDLEY GARDENS
TORONTO, ONTARIO M6R 2T8
(416) 532-9435

INTERCEDE FACILITY MANAGEMENT LTD.
1220 ELLESMERE ROAD
SCARBOROUGH, ONTARIO M1P 2X5
(416) 292-1997

INTERIORS BY OLGA MACLELLAN
14 VICTOR AVENUE
TORONTO, ONTARIO M4K 1A8
(416) 465-8824

INTERIOR PLUS INC.
50 GALAXY BOULEVARD
REXDALE, ONTARIO M9W 4Y4
(416) 675-7993

INTERNATIONAL DESIGN GROUP INC., THE
188 AVENUE ROAD
TORONTO, ONTARIO M5R 2J1
(416) 961-1811

INTERSPACE
151 NASHDENE ROAD
SCARBOROUGH, ONTARIO M1V 2T3
(416) 299-7788

IRVINE HERBERT & JULIE LOMBARD INTERIOR DESIGN
9 ROSEMARY LANE
TORONTO, ONTARIO M5P 3E7
(416) 781-7229

IVEY DESIGN CONCEPTS LTD.
139 SPRUCE STREET
TORONTO, ONTARIO M5A 2J6
(416) 961-7153

JC OFFICE PLANNING AND DESIGN CONSULTANTS
54 TWINBERRY CRESCENT
WOODBRIDGE, ONTARIO L4L 3X5
(416) 851-6270

JD DESIGN
263 DAVENPORT ROAD
TORONTO, ONTARIO M5R 1J9
(416) 928-6766

• **JEFFREY / BULLOCK DESIGN CONSULTANTS**
8 MARKET STREET
TORONTO, ONTARIO M5E 1M6
(416) 868-1616 **Pg. 55**

JOHNSTON DESIGN ASSOCIATES LTD.
29A LESLIE STREET
TORONTO, ONTARIO M4M 3C3
(416) 461-6394

JOHNSTON, ROBERT DESIGNS INC.
25 LIBERTY STREET
TORONTO, ONTARIO M6K 1A6
(416) 535-6077

JOLANDA INTERIORS
2368 BLOOR STREET WEST
TORONTO, ONTARIO M6S 1P5
(416) 762-9638

KEARNS MANCINI ARCHITECTS
191 NIAGARA STREET
TORONTO, ONTARIO M5V 1C9
(416) 360-6464

KETCHESON, DONALD LTD.
13 CLARENCE SQUARE
TORONTO, ONTARIO M5V 1H1
(416) 593-0744

KING, DALE K. INTERIOR DESIGN INC.
238 DAVENPORT ROAD
TORONTO, ONTARIO M4R 1J6
(416) 481-6001

• **KING, NORMA DESIGN INC.**
114A SACKVILLE STREET
TORONTO, ONTARIO M5A 3E7
(416) 862-9180 **Pg. 125-128**

KIRK, A.G. CONSULTANTS LTD.
205 RICHMOND STREET WEST
TORONTO, ONTARIO M5V 1V5
(416) 595-1737

KNAPP & ASSOCIATES
420 SACKVILLE STREET
TORONTO, ONTARIO M4X 1S9
(416) 922-4772

KNOX, RANDY INTERIOR DESIGN INC.
65 CASTLE FRANK ROAD
TORONTO, ONTARIO M4W 2Z9
(416) 961-7133

• **KUBIK-ZDOBINSKY & ASSOCIATES LTD.**
119 SPADINA AVENUE
TORONTO, ONTARIO M5V 2L1
(416) 977-4222 **Pg. 58**

KURTZ MANN DESIGN
390 DUPONT STREET
TORONTO, ONTARIO M5R 1V9
(416) 927-0353

KYRANIS, CHRIS & ASSOCIATES LTD.
5233 DUNDAS STREET WEST
ISLINGTON, ONTARIO M9B 1A6
(416) 239-0549

LAUMANN, GERRARD LTD.
154 DAVENPORT ROAD
TORONTO, ONTARIO M5R 1J2
(416) 964-2323

LAURENCE, ROBERT DESIGNS
267½ QUEEN STREET EAST
TORONTO, ONTARIO M5A 1S6
(416) 363-1157

• **LABYRINTH DESIGN AND DEVELOPMENT CONSULTANTS**
262 AVENUE ROAD
TORONTO, ONTARIO M4V 2G7
(416) 968-1750 **Pg. 97**

LAVENTHOL & HORWATH
20 QUEEN STREET WEST
TORONTO, ONTARIO M5H 3V7
(416) 977-2555

LEE, W. INTERIOR DESIGN INC.
523 THE QUEENSWAY
TORONTO, ONTARIO M8Y 1J7
(416) 252-7115

LEMISHKA BROOKS APIGIAN INC.
74 ST. CLAIR WEST
TORONTO, ONTARIO M4V 1M7
(416) 964-2603

• **L'IMAGE DESIGN**
7100 WARDEN AVENUE
MARKHAM, ONTARIO L3R 5M7
(416) 475-7703 **Pg. 59-61, 129-131**

LINDON, MICHAEL DESIGNS LTD.
14 COLLEGE STREET
TORONTO, ONTARIO M5G 1K2
(416) 923-2011

LINEATION LTD.
352 MELROSE AVENUE
TORONTO, ONTARIO M5M 1Z4
(416) 789-3232

LOVETT, DAVID DESIGN CONSULTANTS INC.
366 ADELAIDE STREET WEST
TORONTO, ONTARIO M5A 1X3
(416) 368-0072

• **LUNA PARK**
67 MOWAT AVENUE
TORONTO, ONTARIO M6K 3E3
(416) 536-3807 **Pg. 107**

MDI DESIGN CONSULTANTS INC.
72 FRASER AVENUE
TORONTO, ONTARIO M6K 3E1
(416) 533-4642

MJ DESIGN CONSULTANTS
373 QUEEN STREET EAST
TORONTO, ONTARIO M5A 1T2
(416) 364-0494

MANION, BURT INTERIOR DESIGN LTD.
283 MACPHERSON AVENUE
TORONTO, ONTARIO M4V 1A4
(416) 923-6611

• **MANOLIU, MARIA & ASSOCIATES DESIGN CONSULTANTS LTD.**
372 BAY STREET
TORONTO, ONTARIO M5H 2W9
(416) 860-1511 **Pg. 98, 99**

MARCUS, H.D. ENTERPRISES INC.
294 BERKELEY STREET
TORONTO, ONTARIO M5A 2X5
(416) 967-7617

MARGULIS, DAVID B. & ASSOCIATES INC.
413 DUNDAS STREET EAST
TORONTO, ONTARIO M5A 2A9
(416) 363-3303

MAROUHOS, SAM AND ASSOCIATES
17 ST. JOSEPH STREET
TORONTO, ONTARIO M4Y 1J8
(416) 923-4074

MARSHALL CUMMINGS & ASSOCIATES LTD.
43 DAVIES AVENUE
TORONTO, ONTARIO M4M 2A9
(416) 461-3563

MASTER DESIGN GROUP
550 ALDEN ROAD
MARKHAM, ONTARIO L3R 6A8
(416) 479-4466

MASTRANGELI, GINO & ASSOCIATES LTD.
28 OAKLEY BOULEVARD
SCARBOROUGH, ONTARIO M1P 3P3
(416) 755-9419

MATTHEW DESIGN ASSOCIATES
46 STEPHENSON AVENUE
TORONTO, ONTARIO M4C 1G1
(416) 699-6725

MAYHEW AND PETERSON INC.
64 PRINCE ARTHUR PLACE
DON MILLS, ONTARIO M3C 2H4
(416) 444-7315

- **McGREGOR CHARBONNEAU
  DESIGN CONSULTANTS**
  507 KING STREAT EAST
  TORONTO, ONTARIO M5A 1M3
  (416) 359-0002 **Pg. 64**

- **McWATT ANDERSON
  DESIGN CONSULTANTS INC.**
  28 ATLANTIC AVENUE
  TORONTO, ONTARIO M6K 1X8
  (416) 530-4800 **Pg. 65**

  MEICKLE, BETTY INTERIORS
  110 CONFEDERATION WAY
  THORNHILL, ONTARIO L3T 5R5
  (416) 881-2227

  **MEICKLEJOHN, ROBERT
  DESIGN ASSOCIATES**
  133 LOWTHER AVENUE
  TORONTO, ONTARIO M5R 1E4
  (416) 964-2081

- **MEYRICK-EASTICK, ANTHONY
  DESIGN GROUP INC.**
  430 KING STREET WEST
  TORONTO, ONTARIO M5V 1L5
  (416) 593-8844 **Pg. 66, 67**

  MINAKER, CAROL ASSOCIATES INC.
  16 McRAE DRIVE
  TORONTO, ONTARIO M4G 1R9
  (416) 489-7354

  MOFFET, HELEN ASSOCIATES LTD.
  45-A HAZELTON AVENUE
  TORONTO, ONTARIO M5R 2E3
  (416) 925-3831

- **MOLE WHITE & ASSOCIATES LTD.**
  260 KING STREET EAST
  TORONTO, ONTARIO M5A 1K3
  (416) 867-1414 **Pg. 68**

- **MOMENTUM**
  2533 YONGE STREET
  TORONTO, ONTARIO M4P 2H9
  (416) 485-3000 **Pg. 117**

- **MONIZ DESIGN GROUP INC.**
  473 QUEEN STREET EAST
  TORONTO, ONTARIO M5A 1T9
  (416) 941-9840 **Pg. 158**

  MOOREHEAD FLEMING CORBAN
  33 BRITAIN STREET
  TORONTO, ONTARIO M5A 1R7
  (416) 366-9238

  MORDEN, JACQUELINE INTERIORS LTD.
  4192 DUNDAS STREET WEST
  TORONTO, ONTARIO M8X 1X3
  (416) 233-3636

  MOREL INTERIORS
  162 CUMBERLAND STREET
  TORONTO, ONTARIO M5R 3N5
  (416) 961-3385

- **NEWS**
  121 AVENUE ROAD
  TORONTO, ONTARIO M5R 2G2
  (416) 925-6484 **Pg. 108, 109**

  NOAKES COHEN LTD.
  1250 BAY STREET
  TORONTO, ONTARIO M5R 2B1
  (416) 967-2800

  NOFFKE, EDGAR W. INTERIORS
  27 MACLENNAN AVENUE
  TORONTO, ONTARIO M4W 2Y5
  (416) 922-8366

  OLIVER, MURRAY W. LTD.
  19 EDGEWOOD CRESCENT
  TORONTO, ONTARIO M4W 3A8
  (416) 923-6240

  O.E. DESIGN GROUP
  525 DENISON STREET
  MARKHAM, ONTARIO L3R 1B8
  (416) 491-9330

  OMEGA DESIGN TEAM, THE
  11 C LAIDLAW ROAD
  MARKHAM, ONTARIO L3P 1W5
  (416) 294-3931

  OMNISPACE ENVIRONMENTS INC.
  260 RICHMOND STREET WEST
  TORONTO, ONTARIO M5V 1W5
  (416) 323-1645

- **OVE DESIGN INTERIORS INC.**
  219 DUFFERIN STREET
  TORONTO, ONTARIO M6K 1Y9
  (416) 588-9040 **Pg. 74, 75**

  PANACHE DESIGN LIMITED
  361 KING STREET EAST
  TORONTO, ONTARIO M5A 1L1
  (416) 369-0084

  POI BUSINESS INTERIORS
  120 VALLEYWOOD DRIVE
  MARKHAM, ONTARIO L3R 6A7
  (416) 479-1123

  PATTON, BRYON & ASSOCIATES LTD.
  160 PEARS AVENUE
  TORONTO, ONTARIO M5R 2T2
  (416) 960-6060

  PEGGIE-JOYCE INTERIORS LTD.
  1742 AVENUE ROAD
  TORONTO, ONTARIO M5N 2G7
  (416) 787-1100

  PETERS McKINNON & ASSOCIATES
  209 ADELAIDE STREET EAST
  TORONTO, ONTARIO M5A 1M8
  (416) 364-4548

  PLANNING HOUSE, THE
  67 MOWAT AVENUE
  TORONTO, ONTARIO M6K 3E3
  (416) 534-6244

- **PLUS 5 INTERIORS**
  1230 YONGE STREET
  TORONTO, ONTARIO M4T 1W3
  (416) 923-5231 **Pg. 137**

  PRESTON
  60 BLOOR STREET WEST
  TORONTO, ONTARIO M4W 3B8
  (416) 925-3341

  PRO CAN DESIGNERS
  593 YONGE STREET
  TORONTO, ONTARIO M4Y 1Z4
  (416) 925-9351

- **PULSANN**
  111 QUEEN STREET EAST
  TORONTO, ONTARIO M5C 1S2
  (416) 865-1196 **Pg. 76**

  QUADRUM DESIGN
  585 MIDDLEFIELD ROAD
  SCARBOROUGH, ONTARIO M1V 4Y5
  (416) 298-2613

  RDL DESIGN CONSULTANTS
  344 DUPONT STREET
  TORONTO, ONTARIO M5R 1V9
  (416) 968-0133

- **RAYMOND TIPPING CHIAPPETTA INC.**
  550 QUEEN STREET EAST
  TORONTO, ONTARIO M5A 1V2
  (416) 368-6819 **Pg. 77**

  RETAIL ENVIRONMENTS LTD.
  2382 DUNDAS STREET WEST
  TORONTO, ONTARIO M6P 1W9
  (416) 536-2204

  RICE, VALERIE & ASSOCIATES
  43 ALVIN AVENUE
  TORONTO, ONTARIO M4T 2A7
  (416) 323-9914

  RICE, WARREN ASSOCIATES LTD.
  77 MOWAT AVENUE
  TORONTO, ONTARIO M6K 3E3
  (416) 537-5597

  RICE BRYDONE LTD.
  512 KING STREET EAST
  TORONTO, ONTARIO M5A 1M2
  (416) 864-9094

  RIDPATH'S INTERIOR DESIGN
  906 YONGE STREET
  TORONTO, ONTARIO M4W 2J2
  (416) 920-4441

  RIDPATH, VIRGINIA DESIGN INC.
  260 KING STREET EAST
  TORONTO, ONTARIO M5A 1K3
  (416) 865-1760

  ROBINSON GROUP LTD., THE
  263 DAVENPORT ROAD
  TORONTO, ONTARIO M5R 1J9
  (416) 960-2444

  ROLLINS RAEBURN INTERIOR DESIGN INC.
  146 DAVENPORT ROAD
  TORONTO, ONTARIO M5S 1J1
  (416) 923-5676

  ROBB STEWART DESIGN INC.
  521 KING STREET WEST
  TORONTO, ONTARIO M5V 1K4
  (416) 596-8301

  ROWLAND JEFFERIES
  238 DAVENPORT ROAD
  TORONTO, ONTARIO M5R 1J6
  (416) 787-2631

RYAN, WILLIAM DESIGN ASSOCIATES
160 PEARS AVENUE
TORONTO, ONTARIO M5R 1T2
(416) 923-0015

SANKEY ASSOCIATES
172 KING STREET EAST
TORONTO, ONTARIO M5A 1J3
(416) 869-1222

SAVEIN, LORRAINE INTERIORS LTD.
191 HIGHBOURNE ROAD
TORONTO, ONTARIO M5P 2J8
(416) 486-3933

SCHOFIELD, MANUEL J. LTD.
74 HAZELTON AVENUE
TORONTO, ONTARIO M5R 2E2
(416) 962-3190

SDI CORPORATE INTERIOR DESIGN
172 KING STREET EAST
TORONTO, ONTARIO M5A 1J3
(416) 869-1222

SEARS & RUSSELL CONSULTANTS
147 DAVENPORT ROAD
TORONTO, ONTARIO M5R 1J1
(416) 926-8242

SHIRO/ROBERTS & ASSOCIATES
15 GERVAIS DRIVE
DON MILLS, ONTAIO M3C 1Y8
(416) 449-1529

• **SIMPSONS**
COMMERCIAL INTERIORS AND DESIGN
49 GERVAIS DRIVE
DON MILLS, ONTARIO M3C 1Y9
(416) 449-0110 **Pg. 144, 145**

SMALL, NEAL DESIGN LTD.
160 PEARS AVENUE
TORONTO, ONTARIO M5R 1T2
(416) 964-3396

SMITH GRIMLEY BERG INC.
411 RICHMOND STREET EAST
TORONTO, ONTARIO M5A 3S5
(416) 360-0488

• **G.L. SMITH PLANNING & DESIGN INC.**
260 KING STREET EAST
TORONTO, ONTARIO M5A 4L5
(416) 360-1158 **Pg. 113**

SOEGANDI, ADRIAN
DESIGN ASSOCIATES
338 DUNDAS STREET EAST
TORONTO, ONTARIO M5A 2A1
(416) 960-6193

SPACE TIME PLANNING
10 BRITAIN STREET
TORONTO, ONTARIO M5A 1R6
(416) 868-0111

STAHMER, MAIKE
INTERIOR DESIGN LTD.
178 CRESCENT ROAD
TORONTO, ONTARIO M4W 1V3
(416) 923-2364

STEIN, BETTY INTERIORS
19 GLENGROVE AVENUE EAST
TORONTO, ONTARIO M4N 1E6
(416) 487-9153

STERLING, M. DESIGN GROUP INC.
146 FRONT STREET WEST
TORONTO, ONTARIO M5J 1G2
(416) 596-1279

STEVENSON, JOHN INTERIORS LTD.
110 RICHMOND STREET EAST
TORONTO, ONTARIO M5C 2P9
(416) 860-0010

STICKS & STONES INCORPORATED
15 HILLSBORO AVENUE
TORONTO, ONTARIO M5R 1S6
(416) 928-0587

• **STOCKS, PAUL A. LTD.**
35 COLDWATER ROAD
DON MILLS, ONTARIO M3B 1Y8
(416) 449-9733 **Pg. 78**

STUDIO 85 INTERIOR PLANNING INC.
300 NORTH QUEEN STREET
ETOBICOKE, ONTARIO M9C 5K4
(416) 626-7277

SUITSO, J.E. DESIGN
740 BROADVIEW AVENUE
TORONTO, ONTARIO M4K 2P1
(416) 465-4008

SUTTON + VESKA INC.
1216 YONGE STREET
TORONTO, ONTARIO M4T 1W1
(416) 924-9295

SWAIN, ANNE
INTERIOR DESIGN INC.
202 MERTON STREET
TORONTO, ONTARIO M4S 1A1
(416) 485-0244

SWEENEY ASSOCIATES
5405 EGLINTON AVENUE WEST
TORONTO, ONTARIO M9C 5K6
(416) 622-7773

SYNKARYON DESIGN
78 LAIRD DRIVE
TORONTO, ONTARIO M4G 3V1
(416) 421-5227

• **TANNER HILL ASSOCIATES INC.**
73 LAIRD DRIVE
TORONTO, ONTARIO M4G 3T4
(416) 429-1600 **Pg. 132, 133**

TAYLOR, ARLENE ASSOCIATES
73 LAIRD DRIVE
TORONTO, ONTARIO M4G 3T4
(416) 422-4283

• **THOMAS, DAVID J.**
24 ADMIRAL ROAD
TORONTO, ONTARIO M5R 2L5
(416) 961-9949 **Pg. 138, 139**

TODAY'S BUSINESS INTERIORS
875 MIDDLEFIELD ROAD
SCARBOROUGH, ONTARIO M1V 4Z5
(416) 292-5155

TOMCZYK & ASSOCIATES LTD.
52 TALLWOOD DRIVE
TORONTO, ONTARIO M3B 2P5
(416) 443-8660

• **TORONTO BUSINESS INTERIORS LTD.**
250 BRITANNIA ROAD
MISSISSAUGA, ONTARIO L4Z 1S6
(416) 890-1580 **Pg. 146**

• **TOTAL ENVIRONMENTAL PLANNING**
265 HOOD ROAD
MARKHAM, ONTARIO L3R 4N3
(416) 474-0510 **Pg. 83**

URBAN SHOWCASE, THE
67 BRUNSWICK AVENUE
TORONTO, ONTARIO M5S 2C8
(416) 923-8965

WATSON, ROBERT INTERIORS
17 ROBIN HOOD ROAD
ISLINGTON, ONTARIO M9A 2W6
(416) 964-6682

WATSON, RUTH INTERIOR DESIGN
400 WALMER ROAD
TORONTO, ONTARIO M5P 2X7
(416) 923-8046

WELKER, EDWARD INTERIORS LTD.
1964 AVENUE ROAD
TORONTO, ONTARIO M5M 4A1
(416) 787-9531

WILLIAM BUSINESS INTERIORS
2465 CAWTHRA ROAD
MISSISSAUGA, ONTARIO L5A 3P2
(416) 277-1463

WILSON, DOROTHY INTERIOR DESIGN
53 BALMORAL AVENUE
TORONTO, ONTARIO M4V 1J5
(416) 923-6722

WILSON, MICHAEL INTERIOR DESIGN LTD.
8B LINDEN STREET
TORONTO, ONTARIO M4Y 1V6
(416) 968-3362

WINNICK, M.J. INTERIOR DESIGNERS LTD.
2 BLOOR STREET WEST
TORONTO, ONTARIO M4W 3E2
(416) 964-8808

WINTERS DESIGN PLANNING
1869 GERRARD STREET EAST
TORONTO, ONTARIO M4L 2B8
(416) 462-9384

WINTZEN, LUC DESIGN INC.
62 BELMONT STREET
TORONTO, ONTARIO M5R 1P8
(416) 961-3760

WINSTON, JACK DESIGNS INC.
12 LAWTON BOULEVARD
TORONTO, ONTARIO M4V 1Z4
(416) 968-6511

YABU PUSHELBERG
359 KING STREET EAST
TORONTO, ONTARIO M5A 1L1
(416) 362-1414

- **YEN, CHRIS DESIGNS INC.**
  120 CARLTON STREET
  TORONTO, ONTARIO M5A 4K2
  (416) 323-3888 **Pg. 84**

- **YOUNG, SUSAN DESIGN
  ASSOCIATES LTD.**
  113 DUPONT STREET
  TORONTO, ONTARIO M5R 1V4
  (416) 927-7411 **Pg. 140**

- **ZEIDLER ROBERTS INTERIORS LIMITED**
  315 QUEEN STREET WEST
  TORONTO, ONTARIO M5V 2X2
  (416) 596-8300 **Pg. 89-92**

ZULIANI, MARIO
124 PORTLAND STREET
TORONTO, ONTARIO M5V 2N5
(416) 368-7717

Windsor

**ARMADA, JAN
DESIGN CONSULTANTS**
3694 ASKIN BLVD.
WINDSOR, ONTARIO N9E 3J9
(519) 969-7313

BASIC TWO DESIGNS LIMITED
108 McDOUGALL STREET
WINDSOR, ONTARIO N9A 1K8
(519) 254-0880

BENNING INTERIORS LIMITED
3203 WALKER ROAD
WINDSOR, ONTARIO N8W 3B7
(519) 966-6226

BUCKNER, DOUGLAS W. LTD.
4769 WYANDOTTE STREET EAST
WINDSOR, ONTARIO N8Y 1H9
(519) 945-1951

**FONTANA, M.
DESIGNS & WOODWORK INC.**
5145 HALFORD STREET
RR NO. 1, WINDSOR, ONTARIO N9A 6J3
(519) 737-6550

INTEGRATED DESIGNS
2260 UNIVERSITY AVENUE WEST
WINDSOR, ONTARIO N9B 1B5
(519) 256-9061

JAMIESON, NEIL INTERIORS LTD.
322 PELISSIER STREET
WINDSOR, ONTARIO N9A 4K7
(519) 253-6670

McLEAN, GREGORY M.
5161 TECUMSEH ROAD EAST
WINDSOR, ONTARIO N8T 1C3
(519) 944-4744

O'NEILL, JAMES D. LTD.
1574 LINCOLN ROAD
WINDSOR, ONTARIO N8V 2J4
(519) 258-5501

RYAN, PETER K. LTD.
256 PELISSIER STREET
WINDSOR, ONTARIO N9A 4K2
(519) 253-7471

► M A N I T O B A

Winnipeg

ARNOTT & ASSOCIATES
115 BANNATYNE AVENUE
WINNIPEG, MANITOBA R3B 0R3
(204) 943-8844

**AUSTEN GERALD INTERIOR DESIGN
LTD.**
585 RIVER AVENUE
WINNIPEG, MANITOBA R2M 2R3
(204) 284-9964

BBC3 DESIGN INC.
221 McDERMOT AVENUE
WINNIPEG, MANITOBA R3B 0S2
(204) 943-3404

CALNITSKY HESHKA ASSOCIATES
110 OSBORNE STREET
WINNIPEG, MANITOBA R3L 1Y5
(204) 453-6441

COREY SMITH DESIGN LTD.
685 PEMBINA HWY.
WINNIPEG, MANITOBA R3M 2L6
(204) 453-7306

COUNTERPOINT DESIGN INC.
120 FORT STREET
WINNIPEG, MANITOBA R3C 1C7
(204) 956-0542

CUNNINGHAM BUSINESS INTERIORS
1680 ELLICE AVENUE
WINNIPEG, MANITOBA R3H 0Z2
(204) 774-1624

DC DESIGN CONCEPT
46 MONTCLAIR BAY
WINNIPEG, MANITOBA R3T 4B3
(204) 269-7253

DECOR 8
2 DONALD STREET
WINNIPEG, MANITOBA R3L 0K5
(204) 475-6193

DECORAGE
850 KEEWATIN STREET
WINNIPEG, MANITOBA R2R 0Z5
(204) 633-6085

DESIGN IDEAS INC.
932 ST. JONES STREET
WINNIPEG, MANITOBA R3H 0K3
(204) 775-2540

DESIGN MANITOBA
433 RIVER AVENUE
WINNIPEG, MANITOBA R3L 0C3
(204) 453-2390

DESIGN PROFILE
100 OSBORNE STREET
WINNIPEG, MANITOBA R3C 1V3
(204) 475-3588

DESIGNWORKS INC.
90 ALBERT STREET
WINNIPEG, MANITOBA R3B 1G2
(204) 942-2129

DOJACK, TOM DESIGN INC.
88 SPENCE STREET
WINNIPEG, MANITOBA R3C 1Y3
(204) 772-1600

ENVIRONMENTAL SPACE PLANNING
290 VAUGHAN STREET
WINNIPEG, MANITOBA R3B 2N8
(204) 944-9292

FINGOLD ENTERPRISES LTD.
93 LOMBARD AVENUE
WINNIPEG, MANITOBA R3B 3B1
(204) 942-5578

GIRLING, L.F. & ASSOCIATES
8 DONALD STREET
WINNIPEG, MANITOBA R3L 2T8
(204) 477-0218

GREGORY – CARTWRIGHT
812 WALL STREET
WINNIPEG, MANITOBA R3G 2T8
(204) 786-8601

INSITE DESIGN CONSULTANTS
240 GRAHAM AVENUE
WINNIPEG, MANITOBA R3C 0J7
(204) 942-3583

INTERPLANNING ASSOCIATES
93 LOMBARD AVENUE
WINNIPEG, MANITOBA R3B 3B1
(204) 942-5578

JAMES DUGUAY ASSOCIATES
930 – 360 MAIN STREET
WINNIPEG, MANITOBA R3C 3Z3
(204) 947-2843

**JOHNSON, STELLA
DESIGN CONSULTANTS**
67 MONTCLAIR BAY
WINNIPEG, MANITOBA R3T 4B4
(204) 261-7538

MARSHALL, GRANT INTERIORS
158 SPENCE STREET
WINNIPEG, MANITOBA R3C 1Y3
(204) 774-0211

McLACHLAN & McLACHLAN
130 SCOTT STREET
WINNIPEG, MANITOBA R3L 0K9
(204) 284-1860

MITCHELL, MARK & ASSOCIATES INC.
749 WALL STREET
WINNIPEG, MANITOBA R3G 2T6
(204) 775-1025

NUMBER TEN DESIGN GROUP
310-115 BANNATYNE AVENUE EAST
WINNIPEG, MANITOBA R3B 0R3
(204) 942-0981

PANACHE, THE LTD.
1129 EMPRESS STREET
WINNIPEG, MANITOBA R3E 3H1
(204) 786-1427

PARCOR LTD.
464 HARGRAVE STREET
WINNIPEG, MANITOBA R3A 0X5
(204) 943-3438

SMITH CARTER PARTNERS
1601 BUFFALO PLACE
WINNIPEG, MANITOBA R3T 3K7
(204) 477-1260

VEITCH, RONALD M.
57 MIDDLE GATE
WINNIPEG, MANITOBA R3C 2C5
(204) 783-1059

WIEBE, KAREN
513 HELMSDALE AVENUE
WINNIPEG, MANITOBA R2K 0W7
(204) 669-6914

YOUNG SNOW DESIGN ASSOCIATES
1183 MARKHAM ROAD
WINNIPEG, MANITOBA R3T 3Z9
(204) 269-0333

▶ S A S K A T C H E W A N

R e g i n a

ALFORD'S
1500 4TH AVENUE
REGINA, SASKATCHEWAN S4R 8G8
(306) 522-5651

**BOWERING CARBONNEAU &
ASSOCIATES LTD.**
2353 SMITH STREET
REGINA, SASKATCHEWAN S4P 2P7
(306) 757-0145

CITE DESIGN
1316 RAE STREET
REGINA, SASKATCHEWAN S4T 2C3
(306) 525-1991

INNER DIMENSIONS DESIGN ASSOCIATES
2347B CORNWALL STREET
REGINA, SASKATCHEWAN S4P 2L4
(306) 359-3101

KUPCHANKO DESIGN
312 McDONALD STREET
REGINA, SASKATCHEWAN S4N 5V9
(306) 924-0762

LEKU INTERIOR DESIGN LTD.
2356 SCARTH STREET
REGINA, SASKATCHEWAN S4P 2J7
(306) 757-9399

McDONALD, JANETTE INTERIORS
2398 SCARTH STREET
REGINA, SASKATCHEWAN S4P 2J7
(306) 757-6781

REGINA DESIGNWORKS LTD.
312 McDONALD
REGINA, SASKATCHEWAN S4N 6P6
(306) 924-0762

RELIABLE STATIONERS LTD.
106 LEONARD STREET NORTH
REGINA, SASKATCHEWAN S4N 5V7
(306) 924-0555

• **SIMPSONS
COMMERCIAL INTERIORS & DESIGN**
240 LEONARD STREET NORTH
REGINA, SASKATCHEWAN S4N 5V7
(306) 775-1955 **Pg. 144, 145**

SUPREME OFFICE PRODUCTS LTD.
1916 DEWDNEY AVENUE
REGINA, SASKATCHEWAN S4R 1G9
(306) 757-8651

TAYLOR PATERSON INTERIORS
2176 7TH AVENUE
REGINA, SASKATCHEWAN S4R 1C4
(306) 525-6161

ZURICH DESIGN CONSULTANTS
2500 – 13TH AVENUE
REGINA, SASKATCHEWAN S4P 0W2
(306) 757-2542

S a s k a t o o n

BONLI INTERIORS LTD.
GROSVENOR PARK SHOPPING CENTRE
SASKATOON, SASKATCHEWAN
(306) 373-3113

DAYS DESIGN CONSULTANTS
740 1ST AVENUE NORTH
SASKATOON, SASKATCHEWAN S7K 1Y1
(306) 244-6500

DESIGN SHOPE LTD.
2313 HANSELMAN PLACE
SASKATOON, SASKATCHEWAN S7L 6A9
(306) 653-3246

DUDDRIDGE INTERIOR DESIGN INC.
613 9TH STREET EAST
SASKATOON, SASKATCHEWAN S7H 0M4
(306) 652-1612

HOLLIDAY-SCOTT INTERIORS LTD.
1026 LOUISE AVENUE
SASKATOON, SASKATCHEWAN S7H 2P6
(306) 477-1556

PLANNED COMMERCIAL INTERIORS
626 BROADWAY AVENUE
SASKATOON, SASKATCHEWAN S7N 1A9
(306) 244-8314

• **SIMPSONS
COMMERCIAL INTERIORS & DESIGN**
3040 MINERS AVENUE NORTH
SASKATOON, SASKATCHEWAN S7K 5V1
(306) 933-4311 **Pg. 144, 145**

WELLS STUDIO OF DESIGN
617 MAIN STREET
SASKATOON, SASKATCHEWAN S7H 0J8
(306) 653-1012

WESTERN RETAIL INTERIORS LTD.
208 JESSOP AVENUE
SASKATOON, SASKATCHEWAN S7N 1Y4
(306) 477-2244

▶ A L B E R T A

C a l g a r y

• **ANGUS WRIGHT
DESIGN CONSULTANTS LTD.**
306 MOUNT ROYAL VILLAGE
1550 – 8TH STREET SW
CALGARY, ALBERTA T2R 1K1
(403) 229-2717 **Pg. 24, 25**

ASSOCIATED DESIGN GROUP
8947 BAYLOR CT. SW
CALGARY, ALBERTA T2V 3N5
(403) 281-6637

BALTZAN FURNISHINGS & INTERIORS
2115 4TH STREET SW
CALGARY, ALBERTA T2S 1W8
(403) 228-4682

BERGMEISTER B. & ASSOCIATES LTD.
2916 19TH STREET NE
CALGARY, ALBERTA T2E 6Y9
(403) 250-2807

BOND & MOGRIDGE ARCHITECTS LTD.
926 – 5TH AVENUE SW
CALGARY, ALBERTA T2P 0N7
(403) 228-4712

BONDAR INTERIORS
1451 14TH STREET SW
CALGARY, ALBERTA T3C 1C8
(403) 229-2005

**BRAND E.H. INTERIOR DESIGN
CONSULTANT LTD.**
2424 4TH STREET SW
CALGARY, ALBERTA T2S 2T4
(403) 228-0000

BURNS, ROBERT INTERIORS
1223, RANCHVIEW ROAD NW
CALGARY, ALBERTA T3G 2C2
(403) 238-6042

BUSBY KERRY INTERIOR DESIGNER
1802 BOWNESS ROAD NW
CALGARY, ALBERTA T2N 3K4
(403) 270-3767

BUSINESS INTERIORS LIMITED
926 5TH AVENUE SW
CALGARY, ALBERTA T2P 0N7
(403) 269-7303

CBL DESIGN GROUP LTD.
222 – 3RD STREET SW
CALGARY, ALBERTA T2P 1P9
(403) 233-2585

CWA INTERIOR SYSTEMS LTD.
2608 – 43RD STREET SE
CALGARY, ALBERTA T2B 1H7
(403) 235-2277

CALETO INTERIORS
1040 THORNEYCROFT DRIVE NW
CALGARY, ALBERTA T2K 3K8
(403) 274-1941

CAMPBELL, STEPHEN DESIGN LTD.
224 11TH AVENUE SW
CALGARY, ALBERTA T2R 0C3
(403) 262-7416

COHOS EVAMY PARTNERSHIP, THE
902 11TH AVENUE SW
CALGARY, ALBERTA T2R 0E7
(403) 245-5501

CONSTRUCTION CONCEPTS
1509 CENTRE STREET SW
CALGARY, ALBERTA T2G 2E6
(403) 232-6353

CULHAM PEDERSEN & VALENTINE ARCHITECTS
1011 GLENMORE TRAIL S.W.
CALGARY, ALBERTA T2V 4R6
(403) 253-6459

CRIDLAND, DOUGLAS INTERIOR DESIGN LTD.
908 17TH AVENUE SW
CALGARY, ALBERTA T2T 0A3
(403) 228-0636

CRKVENAC & ASSOCIATES INTERIOR DESIGN
831 7TH AVENUE SW
CALGARY, ALBERTA T2P 1A2
(403) 265-4427

DAVANTI CONTEMPORARY INTERIORS LTD.
708 11TH AVENUE SW
CALGARY, ALBERTA T2R 0E4
(403) 264-1316

DESIGN 28 LTD.
618 18TH AVENUE NW
CALGARY, ALBERTA T2M 0T8
(403) 289-7979

DESIGN TEXTURES LTD.
416 MERIDIAN ROAD SE
CALGARY, ALBERTA T2A 1X2
(403) 248-7770

DESIGN WORK
3932 EDMONTON TRAIL NE
CALGARY, ALBERTA T2E 3P6
(403) 230-9464

DEUCE INTERIOR & DESIGN INC.
1700 VARSITY ESTATES DR. NW
CALGARY, ALBERTA T3B 2W9
(403) 288-9297

DOBBYN SHELAGH INTERIOR DESIGN LTD.
10 MEADOWLARK CR. SW
CALGARY, ALBERTA T2V 1Z1
(403) 255-0464

DOMUS DESIGN GROUP LTD.
239 10TH AVENUE SE
CALGARY, ALBERTA T2G 0V9
(403) 234-9090

DRAWING BOARD
224 11TH AVENUE SW
CALGARY, ALBERTA T2R 0C3
(403) 233-8448

ETHAN ALLEN GALLERY
GLENMORE TRAIL & ELBOW DRIVE SW
CALGARY, ALBERTA
(403) 258-2346

FELDBERG DESIGNS LTD.
1815 BAYSHORE ROAD SW
CALGARY, ALBERTA T2V 3M2
(403) 281-0835

FINAL TOUCH INTERIORS
9203 MACLEOD TRAIL SW
CALGARY, ALBERTA T2H 0M2
(403) 258-2720

FISHMAN, ARTHUR & ASSOCIATES
2424 4TH STREET SW
CALGARY, ALBERTA T2S 2T4
(403) 229-3590

FORM 3 DESIGNS LTD.
2215 27TH AVENUE NE
CALGARY, ALBERTA T2E 7M4
(403) 250-1470

• **FORREST DESIGN GROUP**
602 11TH AVENUE SW
CALGARY, ALBERTA T2R 1J8
(403) 266-6612 **Pg. 45-48**

GRAHAM McCOURT ARCHITECTS
602 12TH AVENUE SW
CALGARY, ALBERTA T2R 0H5
(403) 264-7760

GREENWOOD, EV INTERIOR DESIGN
40 ABINGDON CR. NE
CALGARY, ALBERTA T2A 6S5
(403) 272-8192

HARDING & ASSOCIATES
808 4TH AVENUE SW
CALGARY, ALBERTA T2P 3E8
(403) 266-0811

HAYASHI & ASSOCIATES LTD.
404 6TH AVENUE SW
CALGARY, ALBERTA T2P 0R9
(403) 261-2601

HEMMING, JAMES DESIGN LTD.
1057 20TH AVENUE NW
CALGARY, ALBERTA T2M 1E7
(403) 284-3488

HOWELL ASSOCIATES INTERIOR DESIGN LTD.
116A 8TH AVENUE SE
CALGARY, ALBERTA T2G 0K6
(403) 269-8267

HUGHES, BABOUSHKIN & ASSOCIATES LTD.
309 2ND AVENUE SW
CALGARY, ALBERTA T2P 0C5
(403) 262-3930

HUTCHISON, KEN ARCHITECT LTD.
1518A 7TH STREET SW
CALGARY, ALBERTA T2R 1A7
(403) 228-9307

INTERIORS BY DM SIMONE MAC RAE & ASSOCIATES LTD.
CALGARY, ALBERTA
(403) 242-2994

INTERIOR EXPRESSIONS
908 17TH AVENUE SW
CALGARY, ALBERTA T2T 0A3
(403) 229-4484

IRELAND, SHIRLEY INNER-VISION DESIGN
3838 ELBOW DRIVE SW
CALGARY, ALBERTA T2S 2J8
(403) 243-0120

JACOBS, KATHLEEN DESIGN CONSULTANT
63 QUEEN ISABELLA CLOSE SE
CALGARY, ALBERTA T2J 3R2
(403) 278-1831

JANET DESIGN
300 17TH AVENUE SW
CALGARY, ALBERTA T2S 0A8
(403) 228-3029

KPL DESIGN ASSOCIATES LTD.
2835 19TH STREET NE
CALGARY, ALBERTA T2E 7A2
(403) 250-1411

KRAEMER, TAIPALE & ASSOCIATES LTD.
112 4TH AVENUE SW
CALGARY, ALBERTA T2P 0H3
(403) 237-7890

LOCKHART DESIGN LTD.
3707 54TH AVENUE SW
CALGARY, ALBERTA T3E 5H5
(403) 242-2644

MARSHALL CUMMINGS & ASSOCIATES LTD.
221 10TH AVENUE SW
CALGARY, ALBERTA T2R 0A4
(403) 233-8423

McARTHUR FINE FURNITURE
67 GLENBROOK PLACE SW
CALGARY, ALBERTA T3E 6W4
(403) 246-6266

McEVOY, MARY INTERIORS LTD.
614A 17TH AVENUE SW
CALGARY, ALBERTA T2S 0B4
(403) 228-1330

MARIHOF INTERIORS LTD.
CALGARY, ALBERTA
(403) 282-9516

MILLER, RON DESIGN CONSULTANT LTD.
639 5TH AVENUE SW
CALGARY, ALBERTA T2P 0M9
(403) 265-0974

MORTENSEN'S, KAI
1235 11TH AVENUE SW
CALGARY, ALBERTA T3C 0M5
(403) 245-5751

MACDONALD, NELSON DESIGN LTD.
2424 4TH STREET SW
CALGARY, ALBERTA T2S 2T4
(403) 228-9010

MOLYNEAUX INTERIORS LTD.
604 1ST STREET SW
CALGARY, ALBERTA T2P 1M7
(403) 264-8878

OBELISK INTERIOR DESIGN LTD.
1405 2ND STREET SW
CALGARY, ALBERTA T2R 0W7
(403) 265-3055

OLLIVER INTERIORS
188 BRACEWOOD ROAD SW
CALGARY, ALBERTA T2W 3C1
(403) 238-0559

PENTHOUSE
6020 2ND STREET SW
CALGARY, ALBERTA T2H 0H2
(403) 253-7835

PRESTUPA, NOPLE INTERIOR DESIGN LTD.
815 17TH AVENUE SW
CALGARY, ALBERTA T2T 0A1
(403) 229-2826

PROJECT INTERIORS
BOX 4484 STN. C
CALGARY, ALBERTA
(403) 277-3321

**RAINES, BARRET PARTNERSHIP
CONSULTANTS**
714 1ST STREET SE
CALGARY, ALBERTA T2G 2G8
(403) 269-4961

**RHODES RENTON
INTERIOR DESIGN CONSULTANTS LTD.**
321 10TH AVENUE SW
CALGARY, ALBERTA T2R 0A5
(403) 266-7222

RICE BRYDONE LIMITED
404 6TH AVENUE SW
CALGARY, ALBERA T2P 0R9
(403) 233-8865

**RICHARDSON HARRADANCE
ASSOCIATES LTD.**
237-8TH AVENUE SW
CALGARY, ALBERTA T2G 0L9
(403) 269-9290

SHOE STRINGS
312 WEST PALLISER SQUARE
CALGARY, ALBERTA T2P 2G8
(403) 271-0526

STAGE II INTERIORS LTD.
908 17TH AVENUE SW
CALGARY, ALBERTA T2T 0A3
(403) 245-5546

STEF DESIGN SOFT ART STUDIOS
2845 23RD STREET NE
CALGARY, ALBERTA T2E 7A4
(403) 250-5669

STYLEX INTERIORS LTD.
3504 66TH AVENUE SE
CALGARY, ALBERTA T2C 1P3
(403) 279-3739

**TAVENDER WARWICK INTERIOR DESIGN
CONSULTANTS LTD.**
709 11TH AVENUE SW
CALGARY, ALBERTA T2R 0E3
(403) 264-7400

TIMM ROBINSON INTERIORS LTD.
2500 4TH STREET SW
CALGARY, ALBERTA T2S 1X6
(403) 228-5644

TURNER, G.E. CONSULTING LTD.
3607 ELBOW DRIVE SW
CALGARY, ALBERTA T2S 2J6
(403) 243-8906

TURVEY, BOB DESIGN INC.
3016 19TH STREET NE
CALGARY, ALBERTA T2E 6Y9
(403) 250-1655

UNICA DESIGN STUDIO LTD.
75 GLENDEER DRIVE SW
CALGARY, ALBERTA T2H 2S8
(403) 259-4040

VAN BUREN DESIGN
6024 LEWIS DRIVE SE
CALGARY, ALBERTA T2E 5Z3
(403) 240-1119

VAN ELLENBERG DESIGNS LTD.
129 WOODFERN PLACE SW
CALGARY, ALBERTA T2W 4R7
(403) 281-1700

**WALLACE & ASSOCIATES
DESIGNERS & PLANNERS**
260 SCENIC WAY NW
CALGARY, ALBERTA T3L 1B8
(403) 239-2967

WILLIAMS, L.A. INTERIOR DESIGNER
1518 7TH STREET SW
CALGARY, ALBERTA T2R 1A7
(403) 229-0177

WINNICK, M.J. INTERIOR DESIGNERS LTD.
239 10TH AVENUE SE
CALGARY, ALBERTA T2G 0V9
(403) 265-7040

WOODBINE INTERIORS LTD.
1416 107TH AVENUE SW
CALGARY, ALBERTA T2W 0B9
(403) 258-2535

ZUL, BOGA ARCHITECT LTD.
338 15TH AVENUE SW
CALGARY, ALBERTA T2R 0P8
(403) 228-4177

Edmonton

ARCHIMAGE DESIGN GROUP INC.
10357 109TH STREET
EDMONTON, ALBERTA T5J 1N3
(403) 428-6120

ARDEN WHITE DESIGN GROUP
11221 79TH AVENUE
EDMONTON, ALBERTA T6G 0P2
(403) 437-7339

**ARRINGTON, SHELLY
DESIGN CONTRACTOR**
15221 104TH AVENUE
EDMONTON, ALBERTA T5P 0R6
(403) 489-7210

BALTZAN FURNISHINGS & INTERIORS
10815 103RD AVENUE
EDMONTON, ALBERTA T5J 0J4
(403) 424-7351

BARRIGAN FRANK – DESIGNS
5 WESTVIEW PLACE
ST. ALBERT, ALBERTA T8N 3J8
(403) 459-0423

BERNWARD DESIGN LTD.
10134 87TH STREET
EDMONTON, ALBERTA T5H 1N4
(403) 429-0392

**BILINSKE, KAREN DESIGN
& PROJECT CONSULTANTS LTD.**
9908 109TH STREET
EDMONTON, ALBERTA T5K 1H5
(403) 424-9666

**BRAND, EDITH H.
INTERIOR DESIGN CONSULTANT LTD.**
8525 ARGYLL ROAD
EDMONTON, ALBERTA T6C 4B2
(403) 468-4853

CAMERON INTERIORS
284 SADDLEBACK ROAD
EDMONTON, ALBERTA T6J 4R7
(403) 453-4357

CARTER, DONNA DESIGN CONSULTANT
10402 28A AVENUE
EDMONTON, ALBERTA T6J 4J6
(403) 438-4098

CHANCELLOR INTERIORS
14234 98TH AVENUE
EDMONTON, ALBERTA T5N 0C3
(403) 451-0441

CHERIDEA DESIGN CONSULTATION
6710 93RD STREET
EDMONTON, ALBERTA T6E 3B4
(403) 439-0611

COHOS, EVAMY PARTNERSHIP
10130 112TH STREET
EDMONTON, ALBERTA T5K 2K4
(403) 429-1580

**CORPORATE ENVIRONMENT
CONSULTANTS INC.**
9945 – 50TH STREET
CALGARY, ALBERTA T6A 3X5
(403) 468-2464

DESIGNER'S TOUCH
14107 58TH AVENUE
EDMONTON, ALBERTA T6H 1C8
(403) 437-3061

DINGMAN, ROBERT & ASSOCIATES LTD.
10050 117TH STREET
EDMONTON, ALBERTA T5K 1W7
(403) 482-6368

DOMA DESIGN CONSULTANTS LTD.
10235 101ST STREET
EDMONTON, ALBERTA T5J 3G1
(403) 424-2229

DUGGAN, B INTERIOR DESIGN LTD.
10345 – 133RD STREET
EDMONTON, ALBERTA T5N 1Z8
(403) 451-0696

ENVIROCORP DESIGN GROUP
10160 112TH STREET NW
EDMONTON, ALBERTA T5K 2L6
(403) 424-2832

FROST, EMILY & ASSOCIATES LTD.
10431 140TH STREET
EDMONTON, ALBERTA T5N 2L8
(403) 452-7603

GLENORA ANTIQUES & INTERIORS
12415 STONY PLAIN ROAD
EDMONTON, ALBERTA T5N 3N3
(403) 482-2266

GRUNDAU'S FURNITURE LTD.
9938 70TH AVENUE
EDMONTON, ALBERTA T6E 0V7
(403) 439-4618

HAHN, R.F. DESIGNS LIMITED
9327 74TH AVENUE
EDMONTON, ALBERTA T6E 1E3
(403) 433-7453

HOLZ-STRACHAN INTERIOR DESIGN LTD.
10110 107 STREET
EDMONTON, ALBERTA T5J 1J4
(403) 424-0911

**HUGH C. WENDY
INTERIOR DESIGN CONSULTANT LTD.**
14026 101A AVENUE
EDMONTON, ALBERTA T5N 0L2
(403) 453-3062

INNERTECH DESIGN CONSULTANTS
10711 181ST STREET
EDMONTON, ALBERTA T5S 1N3
(403) 489-4645

INTERFORM FURNITURE LTD.
6912 76TH AVENUE
EDMONTON, ALBERTA T6B 2R2
(403) 466-1269

INTERIORS BY JANE
10014 109TH STREET
EDMONTON, ALBERTA T5J 1M4
(403) 428-1323

INTERPLAN LTD.
10567 109TH STREET
EDMONTON, ALBERTA T5H 3B1
(403) 423-6785

JOSTAR INTERIORS LTD.
5204 86TH STREET
EDMONTON, ALBERTA T6E 5J6
(403) 468-1727

KASIAN DESIGN GROUP
9707 110TH STREET
EDMONTON, ALBERTA T5K 2L9
(403) 482-6912

LE BELLE ARTI
12722 ST. ALBERT TRAIL
EDMONTON, ALBERTA T5L 4S5
(403) 452-4111

McMURRAY STORE FIXTURES LTD.
11315 154TH STREET
EDMONTON, ALBERTA T5M 1X8
(403) 451-3476

MILLER OFFICE GROUP
4990 92ND AVENUE
EDMONTON, ALBERTA T6B 2S2
(403) 468-4990

**NOYCE, DOUG & ASSOCIATES
INTERIOR DESIGN LTD.**
11158 65TH STREET
EDMONTON, ALBERTA T5W 4K1
(403) 474-0473

OMNI DESIGN LIMITED
10852 97TH STREET
EDMONTON, ALBERTA T5H 2M5
(403) 421-4869

PALEY, ROBERT L. ARCHITECT
14448 118TH AVENUE
EDMONTON, ALBERTA T5L 2M5
(403) 453-6855

PLUS GROUP LTD., THE
10024 JASPER AVENUE
EDMONTON, ALBERTA T5J 1R9
(403) 420-1133

PROTZ, ALICE INTERIOR DESIGN
11220 99TH AVENUE
EDMONTON, ALBERTA T5K 2K6
(403) 488-9581

RGO OFFICE PRODUCTS LTD.
10733 104TH AVENUE
EDMONTON, ALBERTA T5J 3K1
(403) 426-6063

ROMAN INTERIOR DESIGN LTD.
1632 42ND STREET
EDMONTON, ALBERTA T6L 5P4
(403) 461-6117

SANDE'S INTERIOR DECORATING
14804 STONY PLAIN ROAD
EDMONTON, ALBERTA T5N 3S5
(403) 452-5246

SCOTT-CALVIN INTERIORS
9540 104TH AVENUE
EDMONTON, ALBERTA T5H 3X3
(403) 424-1233

SPRAGUE FURNITURE LTD.
9947 109TH STREET
EDMONTON, ALBERTA T5K 1H6
(403) 423-3196

SUROWIAK, J.I. INTERIOR DESIGNS
14120 80TH STREET
EDMONTON, ALBERTA T5C 1L6
(403) 476-9291

**TANNER & ASSOCIATES
INTERIOR DESIGN LTD.**
10822 – 123RD STREET
EDMONTON, ALBERTA T5M 0C6
(403) 452-9667

**UNIGROUP ARCHITECTS AND
INTERIOR DESIGNERS INC.**
10408 124TH STREET NW
EDMONTON, ALBERTA T5N 1R5
(403) 488-7271

**WALTERS & WRIGHT
DESIGN CONSULTANTS**
15968 – 109TH AVENUE
EDMONTON, ALBERTA T5P 1B7
(403) 489-5914

WILKIN, R.L. ARCHITECT
10545 87TH AVENUE
EDMONTON, ALBERTA T6E 2P6
(403) 432-7491

WOLSKI, M.B. INTERIOR DESIGN LTD.
10132 105TH STREET NW
EDMONTON, ALBERTA T5J 1C9
(403) 423-1811

WOODWARD STORES (ALBERTA) LTD.
SOUTHGATE SHOPPING CENTER
EDMONTON, ALBERTA T6H 4M6
(403) 435-0511

WOODWARD STORES (ALBERTA) LTD.
10205 101ST STREET
EDMONTON, ALBERTA T5J 3E8
(403) 424-0151

ZUBYK DESIGN SERVICES
10361 82ND AVENUE
EDMONTON, ALBERTA T6E 1Z8
(403) 461-6091

▶ BRITISH COLUMBIA

Burnaby

CITYSCAPE INTERIORS
4142 RUMBLE STREET
BURNABY, B.C. V5J 1Z8
(604) 434-7174

COLLINS FURNITURE GALLERY LTD.
4240 MANOR STREET
BURNABY, B.C. V5G 1B2
(604) 435-5566

GRAY, PATRICIA INTERIORS INC.
5801 MAYVIEW CIRCLE
BURNABY, B.C. V5E 4B7
(604) 522-9141

INTERPLAN DESIGN ASSOCIATES
4695 HASTINGS EAST
BURNABY, B.C. V5C 2K6
(604) 299-2324

Richmond

D & L DESIGN
7560 BRIDGE
RICHMOND, B.C. V6Y 2S7
(604) 273-4711

GERRARD DESIGNS INC.
132-3031 WILLIAMS
RICHMOND, B.C. V7E 4G1
(604) 272-5414

IPL INTEGRA PLANNING WESTERN
11140 MELLIS
RICHMOND, B.C. V6X 1L7
(604) 273-7197

PBI DESIGN CONSULTANTS LTD.
7520 RIVER ROAD
RICHMOND, B.C. V6X 1X6
(604) 278-0225

TANDA DESIGN GROUP
200 – 12640 BRIDGEPORT ROAD
RICHMOND, B.C. V6V 1J5
(604) 270-9958

WOODWARD'S
5300 NO. 3 ROAD
RICHMOND, B.C. V6X 2X9
(604) 270-3322

Vancouver

ABBA DESIGN LTD.
698 SEYMOUR STREET
VANCOUVER, B.C. V6B 3K6
(604) 669-6204

ARCHIPELAGO DESIGN LTD.
101 – 1290 HOMER STREET
VANCOUVER, B.C. V6B 2Y5
(604) 685-8011

ASHLEY – PRYCE, JOHN
32 – 1386 NICOLA STREET
VANCOUVER, B.C. V6G 2G2
(604) 685-2910

ATELIER DESIGN CONSULTANTS LTD.
202 – 1089 W. BROADWAY
VANCOUVER, B.C. V6H 1E2
(604) 738-7250

BBA DESIGN CONSULTANTS INC.
202 – 1168 HAMILTON STREET
VANCOUVER, B.C. V6B 2S2
(604) 688-4434

BEKKE DESIGN ASSOCIATES LTD.
1555 W. 7TH
VANCOUVER, B.C. V6J 1S1
(604) 732-7696

BERTUZZI, GEORGI DESIGNS LTD.
911 HOMER STREET
VANCOUVER, B.C. V6B 2W6
(604) 669-1846

BIKADI INTERIOR DESIGN LTD.
312 – 674 LEG IN BOOT SQUARE
VANCOUVER, B.C. V5Z 4B3
(604) 872-2431

BLUEBIRD INTERIORS LTD.
1718 MARINE
VANCOUVER, B.C. V7V 1J3
(604) 922-6968

CANWEST MARKETING SYSTEMS LTD.
1038 HOMER STREET
VANCOUVER, B.C. V6B 2W9
(604) 681-5070

CITY INTERIORS LTD.
535 THURLOW STREET
VANCOUVER, B.C. V6E 3L2
(604) 682-2489

CLOSE, SUSAN & ASSOCIATES LTD.
203 – 1836 W
VANCOUVER, B.C. V6J 1P3
(604) 733-2716

**COLLABORATIVE DESIGN
CONSULTANTS INC.**
301 – 1028 HAMILTON STREET
VANCOUVER, B.C. V6B 2R9
(604) 669-4606

COLLISON, ELLEN AND ASSOCIATES
1946 WEST 13TH AVENUE
VANCOUVER, B.C. V6J 2H6
(604) 736-6803

CO-ORDINATED HOTEL INTERIORS LTD.
626 BUTE STREET
VANCOUVER, B.C. V6E 3M1
(604) 688-8571

DESIGN 21
21 WATER STREET
VANCOUVER, B.C. V6B 1A1
(604) 682-6871

DESIGNCORP
405 – 550 BURRARD STREET
VANCOUVER, B.C. V6C 2J6
(604) 687-2888

DESIGN WEST INTERIORS
3396 MARINE DRIVE
WEST VANCOUVER, B.C. V7V 1M9
(604) 922-9550

EXECUTIVE OFFICE INTERIORS LTD.
500 – 73 WATER STREET
VANCOUVER, B.C. V6B 1A1
(604) 685-6331

GITTINS MASON INC.
308 – 1111 WEST GEORGIA STREET
VANCOUVER, B.C. V6E 3G7
(604) 682-0700

GLADWIN, ALIKI & ASSOCIATES INC.
12 WATER STREET
VANCOUVER, B.C. V6B 1A5
(604) 687-7411

GOLDENROD DESIGNS
1455 WEST 10TH AVENUE
VANCOUVER, B.C. V6H 1J8
(604) 734-8383

GROUP 5 DESIGN ASSOCIATES LTD.
1305 W. GEORGIA STREET
VANCOUVER, B.C. V6E 3K6
(604) 681-8155

H & S DESIGN
1672 WEST 2ND AVENUE
VANCOUVER, B.C. V6J 1H4
(604) 733-4818

HESKIA, LAZAR
1672 WEST 2ND AVENUE
VANCOUVER, B.C. V6J 1H4
(604) 926-0076

HIGGINS, DARRELL
1103 – 2077 NELSON STREET
VANCOUVER, B.C. V6G 2Y2
(604) 689-7032

**HOPPING KOVACH GRINNELL
DESIGN CONSULTANTS**
81 WEST CORDOVA STREET
VANCOUVER, B.C. V6B 1C8
(604) 684-6438

HUISH, DON & ASSOCIATES LTD.
946 MAIN STREET
VANCOUVER, B.C. V6A 2W3
(604) 684-7211

HURRELL, ROBIN ASSOCIATES LTD.
3561 DUVAL ROAD
VANCOUVER, B.C. V7J 3E8
(604) 734-8212

IDEAL INTERIORS LTD.
1036 MAINLAND STREET
VANCOUVER, B.C. V6B 2T4
(604) 685-4207

**IMPETUS INTERNATIONAL
CORPORATE DESIGN INC.**
1305 W. GEORGIA STREET
VANCOUVER, B.C. V6E 3K6
(604) 681-8155

**INTEGRATED DESIGN SERVICES
VANCOUVER LTD.**
353 WATER STREET
VANCOUVER, B.C. V6B 1B8
(604) 685-1719

JACOBSON DESIGN GROUP INC.
200 – 565 HORNBY STREET
VANCOUVER, B.C. V6C 2E8
(604) 683-3221

JONES, LYN T. & ASSOCIATES LTD.
P.O. BOX 46354, STATION G
VANCOUVER, B.C. V6R 4G6
(604) 327-8898

JORDANS INTERIORS LTD.
1470 WEST BROADWAY
VANCOUVER, B.C. V6H 1H4
(604) 733-1174

KBD ASSOCIATES
400 – 744 WEST HASTINGS STREET
VANCOUVER, B.C. V6C 1A5
(604) 688-3893

KAVANAUGH, DON & ASSOCIATES LTD.
2050 CARDINAL CRESCENT
DEEP COVE, B.C. V7G 1Y4
(604) 929-7623

KEATE & CO. DESIGNERS
2554 VINE STREET
VANCOUVER, B.C. V6K 3L1
(604) 736-5491

KENNEDY, PATRICK INTERIOR DESIGN
527 – 119 WEST PENDER STREET
VANCOUVER, B.C. V6B 1S4
(604) 682-2024

KIDDO WORKS DESIGN INC.
22 EAST 2ND AVENUE
VANCOUVER, B.C. V5T 1B1
(604) 874-3384

KOEMAN DESIGN CONSULTANTS LTD.
800 WEST PENDER STREET
VANCOUVER, B.C. V6C 2V6
(604) 688-9988

LECHTZIER, MERTON R. INC.
4675 HUDSON STREET
VANCOUVER, B.C. V6H 3B9
(604) 733-2873

LEDINGHAM, ROBERT M. INC.
125 – EAST 4TH AVENUE
VANCOUVER, B.C. V5T 1G4
(604) 874-4900

MCM INTERIORS LTD.
1793 NO. 3 BENTALL
P.O. BOX 49047
VANCOUVER, B.C. V7X 1C4
(604) 684-0159

**McCUTCHEON & ARNDT
DESIGN CONSULTANTS LTD.**
108 – 1365 HOWE STREET
VANCOUVER, B.C. V6Z 1R7
(604) 669-3211

MAGNUSON INTERIORS
6020 FLEMING STREET
VANCOUVER, B.C. V5P 3G6
(604) 327-6979

MAY, DENNIS INTERNATIONAL
4011 WEST 33RD AVENUE
VANCOUVER, B.C. V6N 2H9
(604) 224-7607

MIRICH, SHELLY DESIGN INC.
1290 HOMER STREET
VANCOUVER, B.C. V6B 2Y5
(604) 669-6939

NIELSEN DESIGN CONSULTANTS
1314 FULTON
WEST VANCOUVER, B.C. V7T 1N8
(604) 926-6801

NOVUS BUSINESS ENVIRONMENTS INC.
1108 HOMER STREET
VANCOUVER, B.C. V6B 2X6
(604) 688-2394

PARK ASSOCIATES
1141 WEST 8TH AVENUE
VANCOUVER, B.C. V6H 1C5
(604) 736-7664

• **PAVELEK & ASSOCIATES**
1101 WEST GEORGIA
VANCOUVER, B.C. V6E 3G4
(604) 687-4566 **Pg. 111**

PRESTON'S INTERIORS LTD.
2574 VINE STREET
VANCOUVER, B.C. V6K 3L1
(604) 733-8345

PURCELL & ASSOCIATES LTD.
1490 HORNBY STREET
VANCOUVER, B.C. V6Z 1X3
(604) 687-8544

R INTERIORS
4 – 1003 WOLFE AVENUE
VANCOUVER, B.C. V6H 1V6
(604) 734-1942

RAMSAY–MATTHEWS DESIGN GROUP
445 MOUNTAIN HWY
VANCOUVER, B.C. V7J 2L1
(604) 986-3331

RICHARDS, VIRGINIA & ASSOCIATES LTD.
1494 HORNBY STREET
VANCOUVER, B.C. V6Z 1X3
(604) 689-1885

RIDGEWOOD STUDIOS & ASSOCIATES LTD.
2199 GRANVILLE
VANCOUVER, B.C. V6H 3E9
(604) 733-9434

SALTER, RICHARD INTERIORS LTD.
863 HAMILTON STREET
VANCOUVER, B.C. V6B 2R7
(604) 688-2284

SASSAFRASS INTERIORS LTD.
3701 WEST 1ST AVENUE
VANCOUVER, B.C. V6R 1H3
(604) 228-9245

**SEETON SHINKEWSKI
DESIGN GROUP LTD.**
510 – 119 WEST PENDER STREET
VANCOUVER, B.C. V6B 1S4
(604) 685-4301

**SIMON ASSOCIATES
DESIGN GROUP INC.**
1328 SEYMOUR STREET
VANCOUVER, B.C. V6B 3P3
(604) 687-9548

SPIRO GROUP CONSULTANTS LTD., THE
1 WEST 7TH AVENUE
VANCOUVER, B.C. V5Y 1L5
(604) 875-9131

SYNCOR BUSINESS ENVIRONMENTS LTD.
601 – 889 WEST PENDER STREET
VANCOUVER, B.C. V6C 3B2
(604) 688-0052

TERRA FIRMA DESIGN LTD.
2358 WEST 41ST AVENUE
VANCOUVER, B.C. V6M 2A4
(604) 266-9718

TOTALPLAN INC.
806 – 750 WEST PENDER STREET
VANCOUVER, B.C. V6C 2T8
(604) 689-7241

UPTOWN DESIGN GROUP INC.
207 – 601 WEST CORDOVA STREET
VANCOUVER, B.C. V6B 1G1
(604) 669-7043

VANCOUVER DESIGN TEAM LTD.
503 – 321 WATER STREET
VANCOUVER, B.C. V6B 1B8
(604) 669-1125

WALKER REINHOLD DESIGN GROUP
310 – 675 WEST HASTINGS STREET
VANCOUVER, B.C. V6B 1N2
(604) 687-8470

WATTS, JOHN L. INTERIORS
1 – 252 EAST 1ST STREET
VANCOUVER, B.C. V7L 1B3
(604) 987-6214

**YOUNGREN, CATHERINE
INTERIOR DESIGNERS INC.**
2110 WEST 12TH AVENUE
VANCOUVER, B.C. V6K 2N2
(604) 734-3231

Victoria

BRISTO, BARBARA INTERIOR DESIGNER
2033 OAK BAY AVENUE
VICTORIA, B.C. V8R 1E5
(604) 598-9116

DEKORIS INTERIORS LTD.
2880 SEAVIEW ROAD
VICTORIA, B.C. V8N 1L1
(604) 477-2353

DESIGN ASSOCIATES
4699 AMBLEWOOD
VICTORIA, B.C. V8Y 1C4
(604) 658-1389

EGO INTERIORS
1028 FORT STREET
VICTORIA, B.C. V8V 3K4
(604) 382-3200

INTEREX CONTRACT INTERIORS INC.
3318 OAK STREET
VICTORIA, B.C. V8X 1R1
(604) 384-3033

INTERIORS BY HAROLD E. TWETEN
1608 FORT STREET
VICTORIA, B.C. V8R 1H9
(604) 598-2151

IVEY, S.E. IMPORTS LTD.
911 FORT STREET
VICTORIA, B.C. V8V 3K3
(604) 385-7111

LIESCH INTERIORS LTD.
2020 DOUGLAS STREET
VICTORIA, B.C. V8T 4L1
(604) 384-8321

NORTH PARK DESIGNS LTD.
1619 STORE STREET
VICTORIA, B.C. V8W 3K3
(604) 381-3422

SAGER'S
1802 GOVERNMENT STREET
VICTORIA, B.C. V8T 4N5
(604) 382-3200

▶ UNITED STATES

Denver

• **OOMS DESIGN INC.**
1415 LARIMER SQUARE
DENVER, COLORADO 80202
(303) 534-0444 **Pg. 73, 110**

▶ ATLANTIC CANADA

FOWLER BAULD & MITCHEL LTD.
1717 BARRINGTON
HALIFAX, NOVA SCOTIA
(902) 429-4100

LEE INTERIORS LTD.
39 DUNDAS
HALIFAX, NOVA SCOTIA
(902) 466-7536

LYNCH, LYNDON ASSOCIATES LTD.
1741 GRAFTON
HALIFAX, NOVA SCOTIA
(902) 422-1476

WEBER HARRINGTON WELD GROUP INC.
5409 RAINNIE DRIVE
HALIFAX, NOVA SCOTIA
(902) 429-5190

▶ QUEBEC

ABCO DESIGNS INC.
5005, RUE JEAN TALON OUEST
MONTREAL, QUEBEC H4P 1W7
(514) 731-9479

BRAM GROUPE DESIGN INC.
1421, RUE MICHELIN
LAVAL, QUEBEC H7L 4S2
(514) 667-1421

CONSORTIUM DESIGN INTERNATIONAL INC.
239, RUE ST-SACREMENT
MONTREAL, QUEBEC H2Y 1W9
(514) 845-8141

CONTINUUM DESIGN INC.
7881, BOULEVARD DECARIE
MONTREAL, QUEBEC H4P 2H2
(514) 739-7708

DALLAIRE MICHEL DESIGNERS INC.
2151-A, RUE DE LA MONTAGNE
MONTREAL, QUEBEC H3G 1Z8
(514) 282-9262

DALLEGRET FRANCOIS ARTORIUM INC.
353, AVENUE PRINCE ALBERT
MONTREAL, QUEBEC H3Z 2N9
(514) 486-1444

DESIGN & COMMUNICATION INC.
4465, RUE SHERBROOKE OUEST
MONTREAL, QUEBECH3Z 1E7
(514) 932-1428

DUCHARME, BENOIT & ASSOCIES INC.
65, RUE DE LA CASTELNAU OUEST
MONTREAL, QUEBEC H2R 2W3
(514) 495-1719

• **G.S.M. DESIGN INC.**
317, PLACE D'YOUVILLE
MONTREAL, QUEBEC H2Y 2B5
(514) 288-4233 **Pg. 52, 53**

JOLY JORISCH ET ASSOCIES
1463, RUE PREFONTAINE
MONTREAL, QUEBEC H1W 2N6
(514) 521-2541

LALANDE, PHILIPPE DESIGNERS INC.
370, RUE GUY
MONTREAL, QUEBEC H3J 1S6
(514) 932-8582

LAVAL BLUTEAU LEVESQUE
1648-C, RUE SHERBROOKE OUEST
MONTREAL, QUEBEC H3H 1C9
(514) 931-9249

LOCAS BERNARD DESIGNERS LTEE
391, RUE ST-JACQUES
MONTREAL, QUEBEC H2Y 1N9
(514) 284-2288

MORELLI MICHEL DESIGNERS INC.
1463, RUE PREFONTAINE
MONTREAL, QUEBEC H1W 2N6
(514) 521-9288

MORIN LESSARD McINNIS & ASSOCIES INC.
1840, RUE SHERBROOKE OUEST
MONTREAL, QUEBEC H3H 1E4
(514) 935-5409

MULTIFORME DESIGN INC.
8255, AVENUE MOUNTAIN SIGHTS
MONTREAL, QUEBEC H4P 2B3
(514) 342-6024

• **OVE DESIGN INTERIORS INC.**
356, RUE LE MOYNE
VIEUX-MONTREAL, QUEBEC H2Y 1Y3
(514) 844-8421 **Pg. 74, 75**

NORMAN SLATER INC.
4845, RUE SHERBROOKE OUEST
MONTREAL, QUEBEC H3Z 1G6
(514) 932-4164

PRODESIGN LTEE
296, RUE ST-PAUL OUEST
MONTREAL, QUEBEC H2Y 2A3
(514) 844-3349

SERI PLUS
304, RUE NOTRE DAME EST
MONTREAL, QUEBEC H2Y 1C7
(514) 861-2343

SODEPLAN INC.
1180, RUE DRUMMOND
MONTREAL, QUEBEC H3G 2S1
(514) 871-8833

UNILIGHT LTD.
4999, RUE ST-CATHERINE OUEST
MONTREAL, QUEBEC H3Z 1T3
(514) 482-1710

WELGOLAN DESIGN INC.
4846, RUE SHERBROOKE OUEST
MONTREAL, QUEBEC H3Z 1G8
(514) 483-5073

▶ ONTARIO

ADAMS, LEONARD INC.
65 HIGH PARK AVENUE
TORONTO, ONTARIO M6P 2R7
(416) 769-2814

ADAMSON INDUSTRIAL DESIGN
174 AVENUE ROAD
TORONTO, ONTARIO M5R 2J1
(416) 963-9356

ALMDESIGN
74 WALMER ROAD
TORONTO, ONTARIO M5R 2X7
(416) 923-4944

AMBIANT
247 DAVENPORT ROAD
TORONTO, ONTARIO M5R 1J9
(416) 921-1900

ARCONAS CORPORATION
580 ORWELL STREET
MISSISSAUGA, ONTARIO L5A 3V7
(416) 272-0727

A.R.E.A
334 KING STREET EAST
TORONTO, ONTARIO M5A 1K8
(416) 367-5850

ARNOTT DESIGN GROUP, THE
11 ONTARIO STREET
TORONTO, ONTARIO M5A 4L6
(416) 867-8686

AZIZ DESIGNS
493 DAVENPORT ROAD
TORONTO, ONTARIO M4V 1B7
(416) 921-3809

CHENIER, D. ASSOCIATES LTD.
1027 YONGE STREET
TORONTO, ONTARIO M4W 2K9
(416) 964-1545

• **CHUNG DESIGNS**
722 KING STREET WEST
TORONTO, ONTARIO M6J 1E6
(416) 862-8282 **Pg. 104, 105, 154, 155**

• **COLLIER FURNITURE LTD.**
1377 LAWRENCE AVENUE EAST
TORONTO, ONTARIO M3A 3M4
(416) 449-7655 **Pg. 209**

CRAFTWOOD PRODUCTS
191 FINCHDENE SQUARE
SCARBOROUGH, ONTARIO M1X 1E3
(416) 297-1100

DVF DESIGNS INTERNATIONAL INC.
P.O. BOX 895
OAKVILLE, ONTARIO L6J 5C5
(416) 827-1740

DALLAS
7370 WOODBINE AVENUE, UNIT 4
MARKHAM, ONTARIO L3R 1A7
(416) 477-6296

- **DESIGNWERKE**
52 POWER STREET
TORONTO, ONTARIO M5A 3A6
(416) 362-6000 **Pg. 149-152**

- **DESIGNWERKE**
52 POWER STREET
TORONTO, ONTARIO M5A 3A6
(416) 362-6000 **Pg. 149-152**

FORTUNE, MICHAEL
278A GLADSTONE AVENUE
TORONTO, ONTARIO M6J 3L6
(416) 532-4607

GROUP FOUR
25-5 CONNELL COURT
TORONTO, ONTARIO M8Z 1E8
(416) 251-1128

HARRIS, STEPHEN DESIGNS
35 BOOTH AVENUE
TORONTO, ONTARIO   M4M 2M3
(416) 466-5892

HATHAWAY DESIGN GROUP
471 JARVIS STREET
TORONTO, ONTARIO M4Y 2G8
(416) 925-4158

KEILHAUER INDUSTRIES LTD.
946 WARDEN AVENUE
TORONTO, ONTARIO M1L 4C9
(416) 759-5665

KINETICS FURNITURE
110 CARRIER DRIVE
REXDALE, ONTARIO M9W 5R1
(416) 675-4300

KURTZ MANN DESIGN
390 DUPONT STREET
TORONTO, ONTARIO M5R 1V9
(416) 927-0353

KAN LTD.
76 RICHMOND STREET EAST
TORONTO, ONTARIO M5C 1P1
(416) 362-7737

THOMAS L. LAMB
31 MARIETTA STREET
OXBRIDGE, ONTARIO L0C 1K0
(416) 852-6859

LESER DESIGN INC.
499 ADELAIDE STREET WEST
TORONTO, ONTARIO M5V 1T4
(416) 360-7432

- **MONIZ DESIGN GROUP INC.**
473 QUEEN STREET EAST
TORONTO, ONTARIO M5A 1T9
(416) 941-9840 **Pg. 158**

MULLER, KEITH LTD.
56 THE ESPLANADE
TORONTO, ONTARIO M5E 1A7
(416) 362-6446

NICHOLLS & GILL LIMITED
479 RICHMOND STREET
LONDON, ONTARIO N6A 3E4
(519) 672-6001

NIENKAMPER
415 FINCHDENE SQUARE
TORONTO, ONTARIO M1X 1B7
(416) 298-5700

- **OVE DESIGN INTERIORS INC.**
219 DUFFERIN STREET
TORONTO, ONTARIO M6K 1Y9
(416) 588-9040 **Pg. 74, 75**

PANACHE DESIGN LIMITED
361 KING STREET EAST
TORONTO, ONTARIO M5A 1L1
(416) 369-0084

PETERAN, GORDON
248 DUPONT STREET
TORONTO, ONTARIO M5R 1V7
(416) 925-5342

PICCALUGA, FRANCESCO & ALDO
21 PRICE STREET
TORONTO, ONTARIO M4W 1Z1
(416) 923-9582

PRESTON
60 BLOOR STREET WEST
TORONTO, ONTARIO M4W 3B8
(416) 598-3540

PRISMATIQUE DESIGNS LTD.
265 DAVENPORT ROAD
TORONTO, ONTARIO M5R 1J9
(416) 961-7333

- **OTTOMAN EMPIRE INC.**
11 DAVIES AVENUE
TORONTO, ONTARIO M4M 2A9
(416) 466-0872 **Pg. 153**

ROWLAND JEFFERIES
238 DAVENPORT ROAD
TORONTO, ONTARIO M5R 1J6
(416) 787-2631

- **SOHEIL MOSUN LTD.**
34 GREENSBORO DRIVE
REXDALE, ONTARIO M9W 1E1
(416) 243-1600 **Pg. 231-234**

- **SNYDER FURNITURE LTD.**
87 COLVILLE ROAD
TORONTO, ONTARIO M6M 2Y6
(416) 247-6285 **Pg. 222, 223**

STRATA
240 KING STREET EAST
TORONTO, ONTARIO M5A 1K1
(416) 366-5915

STUDIO INNOVA INC.
8 CLARENCE SQUARE
TORONTO, ONTARIO M5V 1H1
(416) 595-5991

SUNARHAUSERMAN LTD.
1 SUNSHINE AVENUE
WATERLOO, ONTARIO N2J 4K5
(519) 886-2000

WHITELEY, WM. LIMITED
320 DON PARK ROAD
MARKHAM, ONTARIO L3R 1J4
(416) 474-1735

▶ **W E S T E R N   C A N A D A**

J. BUDD & ASSOCIATES LTD.
1440 9TH STREET NW
CALGARY, ALBERTA T2M 3L2
(403) 284-3699

DESIGN SYSTEMS
1330 CHURCH AVENUE
WINNIPEG, MANITOBA R2X 1G4
(204) 632-0149

DESIN INC.
490 NIAGARA STREET
WINNIPEG, MANITOBA R3N 0V5
(204) 477-0619

ENVIRONMENTAL SPACE PLANNING LTD.
300-290 VAUGHAN
WINNIPEG, MANITOBA R3B 2N8
(204) 944-9272

HOSALUK, MICHAEL
RR NO. 2
SASKATOON, SASKATCHEWAN S7K 3J5
(306) 382-2380

KONAD, KELLY & ASSOCIATES
32 MOHAWK
ST-BONIFACE, MANITOBA
(204) 257-3794

MITCHELL, MARK & ASSOCIATES INC.
245 BELL
WINNIPEG, MANITOBA
(204) 477-0481

ZAIDMAN, PAUL DESIGNS LTD.
1647 ST. JAMES STREET
ST. JAS., MANITOBA
(204) 775-4455

▶ **B R I T I S H   C O L U M B I A**

ATELIER DESIGN CONSULTANTS LTD.
202 – 1089 W BROADWAY
VANCOUVER, B.C.
(604) 738-7250

B.C. RESEARCH
3650 WESBROOK MALL
VANCOUVER, B.C.
(604) 224-4331

BRADFORD DESIGN & ASSOCIATES
13270 – 87B AVENUE
SURREY, B.C.
(604) 594-5787

CITY INTERIORS LTD.
535 THURLOW STREET
VANCOUVER, B.C. V6E 3L2
(604) 682-2489

DESIGN ART
205-1089 W. BROADWAY
VANCOUVER, B.C.
(604) 733-5518

GEPPERT W.A. & ASSOCIATES INC.
1015 BURRARD
VANCOUVER, B.C.
(604) 684-3722

GROUP 5 DESIGN ASSOCIATES LTD.
1305 W. GEORGIA STREET
VANCOUVER, B.C. V6E 3K6
(604) 681-8155

**HOPPING KOVACH GRINNELL
DESIGN CONSULTANTS LTD.**
81 WEST CORDOVA STREET
VANCOUVER, B.C. V6B 1C8
(604) 684-6438

LEAR INDUSTRIAL DESIGN
A-1535 WEST 3RD STREET
VANCOUVER, B.C.
(604) 732-6581

LIONEL HOLT ASSOCIATES
337 EAST, 10TH STREET
N. VANCOUVER, B.C.
(604) 980-2361

PURCELL, C. & ASSOCIATES LTD.
1490 HORNBY STREET
VANCOUVER, BC.
(604) 687-8544

PROTO / ZOAN
P.O. BOX 34182, STATION D
VANCOUVER, B.C. V6J 4M4
(604) 682-3881

RAMSAY – MATTEWS DESIGN GROUP
445 MOUNTAIN
N. VANCOUVER, B.C.
(604) 986-3331

ROGERS INTER DESIGNS INC.
1164 HAMILTON
VANCOUVER, B.C.
(604) 687-4462

VANCOUVER DESIGN TEAM LTD.
503 – 321 WATER STREET
VANCOUVER, B.C. V6B 1B8
(604) 669-1125

▶ QUEBEC

AMENAGEMENT EXPOSITIONS TCD INC.
605, RUE DESLAURIERS
MONTREAL, QUEBEC
(514) 335-0820

ARCHEX LTEE
2630, RUE SABOURIN
MONTREAL, QUEBEC
(514) 334-1012

LA BOITE AU PINCEAU D'ARLEQUIN INC.
760, RUE ST-FELIX
MONTREAL, QUEBEC
(514) 939-1919

CONTINUUM DESIGN INC.
7881, DECARIE
MONTREAL, QUEBEC
(514) 739-2303

EXPO 4 INC.
2300, VICTORIA
LACHINE, QUEBEC
(514) 637-4625

EXPO GRAPHICS AND DISPLAYS
65, RUE ADRIEN ROBERTS
HULL, QUEBEC J8Y 3S3
(819) 770-5167

▶ ONTARIO

**ADAMSON INDUSTRIAL DESIGN
ASSOCIATES INC.**
174 AVENUE ROAD
TORONTO, ONTARIO M5R 2J1
(416) 963-9356

GILTSPUR TORONTO
120 CARRIER DRIVE
REXDALE, ONTARIO M9W 5R1
(416) 674 0845

BGM COLOUR LABORATORIES LTD.
497 KING STREET EAST
TORONTO, ONTARIO M5A 1L9
(416) 947-1325

C.D.A. INDUSTRIES
1430 BIRCHMOUNT
SCARBOROUGH, ONTARIO M1P 2E8
(416) 752-2301

C.E.S. EXHIBITS INC.
7 WABASH
TORONTO, ONTARIO M6R 1N1
(416) 530-4411

CANADIAN DESIGN CONSULTANTS
697 CRAWFORD
TORONTO, ONTARIO
(416) 536-2806

CLICK SYSTEMS
2600 MATHESON BOULEVARD EAST
MISSISSAUGA, ONTARIO L4W 4J1
(416) 624-8844

DANN DUNN DESIGNS INC.
3240A YONGE STREET
TORONTO, ONTARIO M4N 2L4
(416) 483-0629

• **DISPLAY ARTS OF TORONTO**
233 CARLAW AVENUE
TORONTO, ONTARIO M4M 2S1
(416) 461-2787 **Pg. 157**

• **DESIGNWERKE**
52 POWER STREET
TORONTO, ONTARIO M5A 3A6
(416) 362-6000 **Pg. 149-152**

EXHIBITS INTERNATIONAL
55 FIELDWAY ROAD
TORONTO, ONTARIO M8Z 3L4
(416) 231-2818

EXPOSYSTEMS CANADA LTD.
2161 MIDLAND AVENUE
SCARBOROUGH, ONTARIO M1P 4T3
(416) 291-2932

FIFTY-ONE DESIGN
101 AMBER STREET
MARKHAM, ONTARIO L3R 3J7
(416) 475-7795

GERON ASSOCIATES LTD.
20 PROGRESS AVENUE
SCARBOROUGH, ONTARIO M1P 2Y4
(416) 293-2441

GORING ASSOCIATES INC.
77 MOWAT AVENUE
TORONTO, ONTARIO
(416) 536-3509

HOLMAN DESIGN INC.
160 LESMILL ROAD
DON MILLS, ONTARIO M3B 2T7
(416) 441-1877

KEPAC CANADA
288 JUDSON
TORONTO, ONTARIO M8Z 5T6
(416) 252-3145

KAN LTD.
76 RICHMOND STREET EAST
TORONTO, ONTARIO
(416) 362-7737

**McMANUS & ASSOCIATES
DESIGN CONSULTANTS LTD.**
275 SPADINA ROAD
TORONTO, ONTARIO M5R 2B3
(416) 922-7661

• **MONIZ DESIGN GROUP INC.**
473 QUEEN STREET EAST
TORONTO, ONTARIO M5A 1T9
(416) 941-9840 **Pg. 158**

PIDDI DESIGN ASSOCIATES LTD.
1 BEAVERDALE ROAD
TORONTO, ONTARIO M8Y 1H5
(416) 259-3768

SEARS & RUSSELL CONSULTANTS
111 AVENUE ROAD
TORONTO, ONTARIO M5R 3J8
(416) 926-8242

SEVEN CONTINENTS ENTERPRISES INC.
1 ATLANTIC AVENUE
TORONTO, ONTARIO M6K 3E7
(416) 535-5101

SMYTH-FISHER LTD.
1596 BONHILL ROAD
MISSISSAUGA, ONTARIO L5T 1C8
(416) 677-0026

STARK, JAMES GARY
862 MANNING AVENUE
TORONTO, ONTARIO M6G 2W8
(416) 535-6357

• **TAYLOR & BROWNING
DESIGN ASSOCIATES**
10 PRICE STREET
TORONTO, ONTARIO M4W 1Z4
(416) 927-7094 **Pg. 100, 101, 160, 161**

**TAYLOR
MANUFACTURING INDUSTRIES INC.**
55 VANSCO ROAD
TORONTO, ONTARIO M8Z 5Z8
(416) 251-3155

**WIEGAND, ERIC
DESIGN / DIRECTION**
143 MADISON AVENUE
TORONTO, ONTARIO M5R 2S6
(416) 928-0790

WORDEN-WATSON LTD.
12 PROGRESS AVENUE
SCARBOROUGH, ONTARIO M1P 2Y4
(416) 291-3432

▶ MANITOBA

ECLIPSE–3 LTD.
300-66 KING
WINNIPEG, MANITOBA
(204) 943-7557

HORIZON DISPLAYS INC.
303 NAIRN
WINNIPEG, MANITOBA
(204) 667-7962

LOWE MARTIN PORTER LTD.
444 DUFFERIN
WINNIPEG, MANITOBA
(204) 775-8441

TETRAD DESIGN GROUP INC.
1691 ST. MATTHEWS
ST. JAS, MANITOBA
(204) 775-8441

▶ ALBERTA

ADDENDA STUDIOS LTD.
4414 97TH STREET
EDMONTON, ALBERTA
(403) 438-1156

BRANN, WERNER DESIGNS LTD.
643 MARYVALE NE
CALGARY, ALBERTA
(403) 273-4174

BY DESIGN LTD.
200-10361 82ND AVENUE
EDMONTON, ALBERTA
(403) 439-5015

CAMPBELL, STEPHEN DESIGN LTD.
224 11TH AVENUE SW
CALGARY, ALBERTA
(403) 262-7416

DANTRADE INTERNATIONAL LTD.
10708 181ST STREET
EDMONTON, ALBERTA
(403) 483-6395

DISPLAY DESIGN SYSTEMS LTD.
10608 172ND STREET
EDMONTON, ALBERTA
(403) 483-6355

DURA COM IMAGES LTD.
10710 176TH STREET
EDMONTON, ALBERTA
(403) 484-2291

I. TANK & ASSOCIATES DESIGN LTD.
405–10357 109TH STREET
EDMONTON, ALBERTA
(403) 423-0434

XIBITA LTD.
200–10361 82ND AVENUE
EDMONTON, ALBERTA
(403) 439-5015

▶ BRITISH COLUMBIA

ALDRICH PEARS ASSOCIATES
1573 EAST PENDER
VANCOUVER B.C.
(604) 253-1125

**D.D. DISPLAY & DESIGN
ASSOCIATES CO. LTD.**
1139 WEST 14TH
NORTH VANCOUVER, B.C.
(604) 987-3816

DHARMA DESIGN & CONSULTATION LTD.
504–134 ABBOTT
VANCOUVER, B.C.
(604) 687-7701

EXCLUSIVE DISPLAYS LTD.
302 WEST 2ND
VANCOUVER, B.C.
(604) 879-6936

EXPOSYSTEMS LTD. CANADA
955 HOMER STREET
VANCOUVER, B.C. V6B 2W6
(604) 681-9102

**HOPPING KOVACH GRINNELL
DESIGN CONSULTANTS LTD.**
81 WEST CORDOVA STREET
VANCOUVER, B.C. V6B 1C8
(604) 684-6438

VANCOUVER DESIGN TEAM LTD.
503 – 321 WATER STREET
VANCOUVER, B.C.
(604) 669-1125

ABITARE DESIGN INC.
51 FRONT STREET EAST
TORONTO, ONTARIO M5E 1B3
(416) 363-1667

ADAMS, JANE CUSTOM ACCESSORIES
1390 SHERBROOKE STREET WEST
MONTREAL, QUEBEC H3G 1J9
(514) 845-7592

ALEXANDER'S FINE FURNITURE
2300 HAINES ROAD
MISSISSAUGA, ONTARIO L4Y 1Y6
(416) 897-3455

A.R.E.A.
334 KING STREET EAST
TORONTO, ONTARIO M5A 1K8
(416) 367-5850

ARTISTIC GLASS CO. LTD.
2108 DUNDAS STREET WEST
TORONTO, ONTARIO M6R 1W9
(416) 531-4881

ASHTON'S
267 QUEEN STREET EAST
TORONTO, ONTARIO M5A 1S6
(416) 366-6846

ATWOOD'S EXECUTIVE OFFICE INTERIORS
110 BLOOR STREET WEST
TORONTO, ONTARIO M5S 2W7
(416) 968-0820

ATWOOD'S, AN ETHAN ALLEN GALLERY
2161 DUNDAS STREET WEST
MISSISSAUGA, ONTARIO L5K 1R6
(416) 828-2264

ATWOOD'S, AN ETHAN ALLEN GALLERY
8134 YONGE STREET
THORNHILL, ONTARIO L4J 1W4
(416) 889-7761

• **AU COURANT**
354 DAVENPORT ROAD
TORONTO, ONTARIO M5R 1K6
(416) 922-5611 **Pg. 236**

BALMER ARCHITECTURAL ART
9 CODECO COURT
DON MILLS, ONTARIO M3A 1A1
(416) 449-2155

• **BONAVENTURE FURNITURE INDUSTRIES LTD.**
894 BLOOMFIELD
MONTREAL, QUEBEC H2V 3S6
(514) 270-7311 **Pg. 206**

BUSINESS ACCESSORIES INC.
415 DUNDAS STREET
CAMBRIDGE, ONTARIO N1R 5Y2
(519) 622-2222

CANADIAN BRASS AND COPPER CO.
261 BOWES ROAD
CONCORD, ONTARIO L4K 1H8
(416) 736-0797

CODD AND COMPANY
160 PEARS AVENUE
TORONTO, ONTARIO M5R 1T2
(416) 923-0066

CONTEMPORA DESIGNS INT'L INC.
887 YONGE STREET
TORONTO, ONTARIO M4N 3N6
(416) 964-9295

DESIGN CONCEPTS
20 MURAL STREET
RICHMOND HILL, ONTARIO L4B 1K3
(416) 764-3737

DESIGNERS I
1226 BISHOP STREET
MONTREAL, QUEBEC H3G 2E3
(514) 871-3931

DOOR STORE, THE
118 SHERBOURNE STREET
TORONTO, ONTARIO M5A 2R2
(416) 863-1590

DOVER, ELEANOR IMPORTS LTD.
5/ COLVILLE ROAD
TORONTO, ONTARIO M6M 2Y2
(416) 245-7100

EILEY, JOAN & ASSOCIATES LTD.
326 DAVENPORT ROAD
TORONTO, ONTARIO M5R 1K6
(416) 968-0778

ELDON INDUSTRIES, INC.
500 ESNA PARK DRIVE
MARKHAM, ONTARIO L3R 1H5
(416) 475-9407

EXECUTIVE PRECEDENTS INC.
44 EAST BEAVER CREEK ROAD
RICHMOND HILL, ONTARIO L4B 1G8
(416) 889-4944

FERLEO IMPORT EXPORT CO. LTD.
315 HUMBERLINE DRIVE
REXDALE, ONTARIO M9W 5T6
(416) 675-0075

• **GINGER'S BATHROOMS**
945 EGLINTON AVENUE EAST
TORONTO, ONTARIO M4G 4B5
(416) 429-3444 **Pg. 272**

HERITAGE INTERIORS
224 DAVENPORT ROAD
TORONTO, ONTARIO M5R 1J6
(416) 922-6448

HEWI CANADA LIMITED
170 ESNA PARK DRIVE
MARKHAM, ONTARIO L3R 1E3
(416) 477-5990

HOLLAND, JOHN ARCHITECTURAL SCULPTURES & DESIGN
349½ ASHLAND AVENUE
LONDON, ONTARIO N5W 4E9
(519) 451-9365

ICONOPLAST DESIGNS INC.
122 VANDERHOOF AVENUE
TORONTO, ONTARIO M4G 4C1
(416) 467-8819

• **INTARC LTD.**
147 DAVENPORT ROAD
TORONTO, ONTARIO M5R 1J1
(416) 924-7111 **Pg. 214**

ITALIA DESIGN OF CANADA
10357–109TH STREET
EDMONTON, ALBERTA T5J 1N3
(403) 420-0270

ITALINTERIORS LTD.
359 KING STREET EAST
TORONTO, ONTARIO M5A 1L1
(416) 366-9540

JOHNSON, CRAIG & ASSOCIATES INC.
462 WELLINGTON STREET WEST
TORONTO, ONTARIO M5B 1E3
(416) 597-0733

KRAFT HARDWARE LTD.
160 PEARS AVENUE
TORONTO, ONTARIO M5R 1T2
(416) 968-6666

• **MARBLE TREND**
710 ROWNTREE DAIRY ROAD
WOODBRIDGE, ONTARIO L4L 5T7
(416) 738-0400 **Pg. 251**

MARCUS, H.D. ENTERPRISES INC.
294 BERKELEY STREET
TORONTO, ONTARIO M5A 2X5
(416) 967-7617

METROPOLITAN COLLECTION, THE
24 ADMIRAL ROAD
TORONTO, ONTARIO M5R 2L5
(416) 961-9949

MILNE & ASSOCIATES INC.
49 SPADINA AVENUE
TORONTO, ONTARIO M5V 2J1
(416) 591-9114

• **MOSUN, SOHEIL**
34 GREENSBORO DRIVE
REXDALE, ONTARIO M9W 1E1
(416) 243-1600 **Pg. 231-234**

NIENKAMPER
300 KING STREET EAST
TORONTO, ONTARIO M5A 1K4
(416) 298-5700

NORMAN CARRIERE AGENCIES INC.
478 QUEEN STREET EAST
TORONTO, ONTARIO M5A 1T7
(416) 363-1152

OLAN DESIGNS
700 BAY STREET
TORONTO, ONTARIO M5G 1Z6
(416) 979-2600

PRIMAVERA INTERIOR ACCESSORIES LTD.
160 PEARS AVENUE
TORONTO, ONTARIO M5R 1T2
(416) 921-3334

• **QUESS FURNITURE**
157 PRINCESS STREET
TORONTO, ONTARIO M5A 4M4
(416) 366-4744 **Pg. 218, 219**

QUINTESSENCE DESIGNS
1657 BAYVIEW AVENUE
TORONTO, ONTARIO M4G 3C1
(416) 482-1252

- **RAMCA TILES LTD.**
1085, AVENUE VAN HORNE
MONTREAL, QUEBEC H2V 1J6
(514) 270-9192 **Pg. 252**

ROCKFORD MARBLE CENTRE LTD.
160 PEARS AVENUE
TORONTO, ONTARIO M5R 1T2
(416) 922-6122

SHAW-PEZZO & ASSOCIATES INC.
146 DUPONT STREET
TORONTO, ONTARIO M5R 1V2
(416) 961-8213

SHELAGH'S OF CANADA
354 DAVENPORT ROAD
TORONTO, ONTARIO M5R 1K6
(416) 924-7331

**STUDIO AZZURO /
ITALIAN DESIGN INC.**
2533 YONGE STREET
TORONTO, ONTARIO M4P 2H9
(416) 485-3000

SUMMERHILL HARDWARE LTD.
24 BIRCH AVENUE
TORONTO, ONTARIO M4V 1C8
(416) 962-0471

SWITZER, W. & ASSOCIATES LTD.
291 EAST 2ND AVENUE
VANCOUVER, B.C. V5T 1B8
(604) 255-5911

- **TMT MARBLE SUPPLY LTD.**
900 KEELE STREET
TORONTO, ONTARIO M6N 3E7
(416) 653-6111 **Pg. 253**

- **TENDEX SILKO INC.**
264 THE ESPLANADE
TORONTO, ONTARIO M5A 4J6
(416) 361-1555 **Pg. 227**

- **TRIEDE DESIGN**
256 KING STREET EAST
TORONTO, ONTARIO M5A 1K3
(416) 367-0667 **Pg. 228, 229**

UPPER CANADA SPECIALTY HARDWARE
45 MURAL STREET
RICHMOND HILL, ONTARIO L4B 1J4
(416) 764- 2600

WATTS, DIANE INC.
160 PEARS AVENUE
TORONTO, ONTARIO M5R 1T2
(416) 961-2887

WYLIE, GLENN J. & ASSOCIATES LTD.
81 KELFIELD STREET
REXDALE, ONTARIO M9W 5A3
(416) 243-7770

WYERS, BRIAN DESIGN
2661 KINGSTON ROAD
SCARBOROUGH, ONTARIO M1M 1M3
(416) 265-4500

▶ QUEBEC

BANYO CANADA LTD.
5500 FULLUM STREET
MONTREAL, QUEBEC H2G 2H3
(514) 274-3646

CERATEC INC.
414, ST-SACREMENT
QUEBEC, QUEBEC G1N 3Y3
(418) 681-0101

CORANCO CORP. LTD.
2409–46TH AVENUE
LACHINE, QUEBEC H8T 3C9
(514) 636-4067

CRANE CANADA LTD.
5800 COTE DE LIESSE ROAD
MONTREAL, QUEBEC H4T 1B4
(514) 735-3592

DESIGN FOCUS INC.
1000, RUE DE LA MONTAGNE
MONTREAL, QUEBEC H3G 1Y7
(514) 866-1893

▶ ONTARIO

AMERICAN STANDARD
80 WARD STREET
TORONTO, ONTARIO M6H 4A7
(416) 536-1078

APSCO PRODUCTS LTD.
4075 GORDON BAKER ROAD
AGINCOURT, ONTARIO M1W 2P4
(416) 499-5600

AQUALINE PRODUCTS LTD.
1677 AIMCO BOULEVARD
MISSISSAUGA, ONTARIO L4H 1H7
(416) 625-9301

CANA ROMA
3200 STEELES AVENUE
CONCORD, ONTARIO L4Y 3B2
(416) 661-8679

CARPANO INTERIORS
80 HANLAN ROAD
WOODBRIDGE, ONTARIO L4L 3P6
(416) 851-5552

CERAMIC DECOR ONTARIO LTD.
4544 DUFFERIN STREET
DOWNSVIEW, ONTARIO M3H 5R9
(416) 665-8787

• **GINGER'S BATHROOMS**
945 EGLINTON AVENUE EAST
TORONTO, ONTARIO M4G 4B5
(416) 429-3444 **Pg. 272**

**SUNCITY TRADING CO. LTD./
KOHLER CENTRE**
1979 LESLIE STREET
DON MILLS, ONTARIO M3B 2M3
(416) 449-3171

▶ QUEBEC

DOR-VAL MFG. LTD.
2760, BOULEVARD LAURENTIAN
ST-LAURENT, QUEBEC H4K 2E1
(514) 336-7780

**STANDARD DESK
DIV. JOYCE BUSINESS FURNITURE**
1000 ST. MARTIN BOULEVARD
LAVAL, QUEBEC H7S1M7
(514) 663-3030

MULTIFORM KITCHENS LTD.
5525 UPPER LACHINE
MONTREAL, QUEBEC H4A 2A5
(514) 483-1800

▶ ONTARIO

ABBEY LANE KITCHEN
2042 AVENUE ROAD
TORONTO, ONTARIO M5M 4A6
(416) 481-9327

ALAR FURNITURE INC.
707 CLAYSON ROAD
WESTON, ONTARIO M9M 2H4
(416) 743-1925

BECKERMAN CUSTOM KITCHENS LTD.
44 OTONABEE DRIVE
KITCHENER, ONTARIO N2C 1L6
(519) 893-6280

CAMEO KITCHENS
90 NOLAN COURT
UNIONVILLE, ONTARIO L3R 4L9
(416) 475-1081

CARPANO INTERIORS
80 HANLAN ROAD
WOODBRIDGE, ONTARIO L4L 3P6
(416) 851-5552

HANOVER KITCHENS TORONTO LTD.
2725 YONGE STREET
TORONTO, ONTARIO M4N 2H8
(416) 485-7615

JOHN HAUSER IRON WORKS LTD.
148 BEDFORD ROAD
KITCHENER, ONTARIO N2G 3W9
(519) 744-1138

KNAPE & VOGT CANADA LTD.
340 CARLINGVIEW DRIVE
REXDALE, ONTARIO M9W 5G5
(416) 675-3451

LAURENTIDE KITCHENS
945 EGLINTON AVENUE EAST
TORONTO, ONTARIO M4G 4B5
(416) 429-4900

NEW WORLD KITCHENS
366 ADELAIDE STREET EAST
TORONTO, ONTARIO M5A 3X9
(416) 869-0300

NIMA KITCHENS
2060 STEELES AVENUE WEST
CONCORD, ONTARIO L4K 1A1
(416) 667-8910

NUHAUS KITCHENS
260 KING STREET EAST
TORONTO, ONTARIO M5A 1L5
(416) 360-5404

PARIS KITCHENS
160 PEARS AVENUE
TORONTO, ONTARIO M5R 1T2
(416) 925-5454

POGGENPOHL KITCHEN STUDIO
5200 DIXIE ROAD
MISSISSAUGA, ONTARIO L4W 1E4
(416) 625-8811

ROBINSON GROUP, THE
263 DAVENPORT ROAD
TORONTO, ONTARIO M5R 1J9
(416) 923-1333

SNAIDERO CANADA LTD.
481 HANLAN ROAD
WOODBRIDGE, ONTARIO L4L 3T1
(416) 851-7777

▶ QUEBEC

- **ARMSTRONG WORLD INDUSTRIES CANADA LTD.**
  6911 RUE DECARIE
  MONTREAL, QUEBEC H3W 3E5
  (514) 733-9981 **Pg. 243**

  HUNTER DOUGLAS ARCHITECTURAL PRODUCTS
  2501, ROUTE TRANSCANADIENNE
  POINTE CLAIRE, QUEBEC H9R 1B3
  (514) 695-1020

  MASONITE CANADA LTD.
  418 GOLF AVENUE
  GATINEAU, QUEBEC J8R 6K2
  (819) 633-5331

  TAYLOR EVANS LTD.
  4645, RUE DES GRANDES PRAIRIES
  MONTREAL, QUEBEC H1R 1A5
  (514) 325-7700

  VENAIR DISTRIBUTING INC.
  7950 ALFRED STREET
  ANJOU, QUEBEC H1J 1J1
  (514) 354-2230

▶ ONTARIO

- **ARMSTRONG WORLD INDUSTRIES CANADA LTD.**
  2233 ARGENTIA ROAD
  MISSISSAUGA, ONTARIO L5N 2X7
  (416) 826-4832 **Pg. 243**

  BALMER ARCHITECTURAL ART
  9 CODECO COURT
  DON MILLS, ONTARIO M3A 1A1
  (416) 449-2155

  CDA INDUSTRIES INC.
  1430 BIRCHMOUNT ROAD
  SCARBOROUGH, ONTARIO M1P 2E8
  (416) 752-2301

  CANADIAN GYPSUM CO. LTD.
  777 BAY STREET
  TORONTO, ONTARIO M5G 2C8
  (416) 595-8800

  CANWELL LTD.
  44 MEDULLA AVENUE
  TORONTO, ONTARIO M8Z 5P9
  (416) 236-1851

- **CLASSIC MOULDINGS INC.**
  155 TORYORK DRIVE
  WESTON, ONTARIO M9L 1X9
  (416) 745-5560 **Pg. 269**

  CREATIVE CEILING DESIGN
  404-406 ORMONT DRIVE
  TORONTO, ONTARIO M9G 1N9
  (416) 748-1462

  DAMPA INC.
  1285 MORNINGSIDE AVENUE
  SCARBOROUGH, ONT M1B 3W2
  (416) 286-3020

- **DONN CANADA LTD./LTEE**
  735 4TH LINE
  OAKVILLE, ONTARIO L6L 5B7
  (416) 845-3883 **Pg. 268**

  FIBERGLASS CANADA INC.
  3080 YONGE STREET
  TORONTO, ONTARIO M4N 3N1
  (416) 482-2836

- **FORMGLAS INC.**
  250 RAYETTE ROAD
  CONCORD, ONTARIO L4K 2G6
  (416) 669-5111 **Pg. 270**

  ICONOPLAST DESIGNS INC.
  122 VANDERHOOF AVENUE
  TORONTO, ONTARIO M4G 4C1
  (416) 467-8819

  MILNE & ASSOC. INC.
  170 ROSEWELL AVENUE
  TORONTO, ONTARIO M4R 2A6
  (416) 322-5533

  ONTARIO CORK CO. LTD.
  36 ASHWARREN ROAD
  TORONTO, ONTARIO M3J 1Z5
  (416) 630-9702

  ROHM & HAAS CAN. INC.
  2 MANSE ROAD
  WEST HILL, ONTARIO M1E 3T9
  (416) 284-4711

  SOUND SOLUTIONS
  6235 TOMKEN ROAD
  MISSISSAUGA, ONTARIO L5T 1K2
  (416) 678-6363

  WESTROC INDUSTRIES LTD.
  2650 LAKESHORE ROAD WEST
  MISSISSAUGA, ONTARIO L5J 1K4
  (416) 823-9881

DRAPERIES

▶ ATLANTIC CANADA

**ATLANTIC VENETIAN BLINDS
AND DRAPERIES LTD.**
22 WADDELL AVENUE
DARTMOUTH, NOVA SCOTIA B3B 1K3
(902) 463-2263

H.G. ROGERS LTD.
87 GERMAIN STREET
SAINT JOHN, N.B. E2L 4S3
(506) 657-8350

▶ QUEBEC

• **AMOCO FABRICS AND FIBERS LTD.**
955, BOULEVARD ST-JEAN
POINT CLAIRE, QUEBEC H9R 5K3
(514) 694-9860 **Pg. 238**

AVANT-GARDE FABRICS LTD.
7955, RUE ALFRED
ANJOU, QUEBEC H1J 1J3
1-(800) 361-8886

CLAIRE FABRICS INC.
5445 IBERVILLE STREET
MONTREAL, QUEBEC H2G 2B2
(514) 260-1227

COMMONWEALTH CURTAIN CO.
1100 PORT ROYAL STREET
MONTREAL, QUEBEC H2C 2B4
(514) 384-8920

**CONNAISSANCE FABRICS &
WALLCOVERING LTD.**
1632 SHERBROOKE STREET WEST
MONTREAL, QUEBEC H3H 2L4
(514) 931-2437

WALTER DEPPING INC.
3157, BOULEVARD ROBERT
MONTREAL, QUEBEC H1Z 1X9
(514) 728-3609

J.T. DILLON DECOR
555 CHABANEL
MONTREAL, QUEBEC H2N 2H8
(514) 384-7440

HAFNER FABRICS OF CANADA LTD.
1405 PEEL STREET
MONTREAL, QUEBEC H3A 1S5
(514) 842-8172

LAURA ASHLEY SHOPS LTD.
2110 CRESCENT STREET
MONTREAL, QUEBEC H3G 2B8
(514) 284-9225

ROSEDALE DRAPERIES INC.
1100 PORT ROYAL EAST
MONTREAL, QUEBEC H2C 2B4
(514) 384-8290

SALETEX FABRICS LTD.
4716 THIMENS BOULEVARD
ST-LAURENT, QUEBEC H4R 2B2
(514) 334-7533

TELIO & CIE.
1407, RUE DE LA MONTAGNE
MONTREAL, QUEBEC H3G 1Z3
(514) 842-9116

VAL ABEL TEXTILES LTD.
55 MT. ROYAL AVENUE WEST
MONTREAL, QUEBEC H2T 2S6
(514) 842-9503

VISION TEXTILES INC.
100 PORT ROYAL EAST
MONTREAL, QUEBEC H3L 1H7
(514) 381-5941

▶ ONTARIO

ACCESSORIES CANADA
P.O. BOX 1277
GUELPH, ONTARIO N1H 6N6
(519) 836-3283

ANTHONY FOSTER & SONS
297 CARLINGVIEW DRIVE
REXDALE, ONTARIO M9W 5G4
(416) 675-7000

APPEL LIMITED
321 DAVENPORT ROAD
TORONTO, ONTARIO M5R 1K5
(416) 922-3935

ARJAY TEXTILES LIMITED
221 ADVANCE BOULEVARD
BRAMPTON, ONTARIO L6T 4J2
(416) 454-0444

BAUMANN FABRICS LTD.
302 KING STREET EAST
TORONTO, ONTARIO M5A 1K6
(416) 869-1221

W.H. BILBROUGH & CO. LTD.
326 DAVENPORT ROAD
TORONTO, ONTARIO M5R 1K6
(416) 960-1611

BONGAERTS MARKETING INC.
224 BEDFORD ROAD
TORONTO, ONTARIO M5R 2K9
(416) 964-9363

H. BROWN SILK CO. LTD.
530 ADELAIDE STREET WEST
TORONTO, ONTARIO M5V 1T5
(416) 364-2377

BRUNSCHWIG & FILS
320 DAVENPORT ROAD
TORONTO, ONTARIO M5R 1K6
(416) 968-0699

CARAVAN FABRICS
345 BRUNEL ROAD
MISSISSAUGA, ONTARIO L4Z 1Z5
(416) 890-4668

CARLTON MANUFACTURING INC.
8 DARBY WAY
THORNHILL, ONTARIO L3T 5V1
(416) 886-1050

CAYA FABRICS LTD.
P.O. BOX 304, 130 WEBER STREET WEST
KITCHENER, ONTARIO N2G 3Z2
(519) 743-0623

COMMERCIAL DRAPERIES LTD.
3180A LAKESHORE BOULEVARD WEST
TORONTO, ONTARIO M8V 1L7
(416) 251-6568

CROWN WALLPAPER CO.
88 RONSON DRIVE
REXDALE, ONTARIO M9W 1B9
(416) 245-2900

DRAPERY CONTRACT SERVICES
334 LAUDER AVENUE
TORONTO, ONTARIO M6E 3H8
(416) 651-5757

D.C.S. DRAPERY LTD.
DRAPERY CONTRACT SERVICES
579 RICHMOND STREET WEST
TORONTO, ONTARIO M5V 1Y4
(416) 368-4855

• **FABRICS INTERNATIONAL**
1090 AEROWOOD DRIVE
MISSISSAUGA, ONTARIO L4W 1Y5
(416) 624-5104 **Pg. 239**

FINNISH DESIGN IMPORTS LTD.
92C SCOLLARD STREET
TORONTO, ONTARIO M5R 1G2
(416) 961-9858

GREEFF FABRICS INC.
170 BEDFORD ROAD
TORONTO, ONTARIO M5R 2K9
(416) 960-8222

HABERT ASSOCIATES LIMITED
321 DAVENPORT ROAD
TORONTO, ONTARIO M5R 1K5
(416) 960-5323

JEFF BROWN FINE FABRICS LTD.
1785 ARGENTIA ROAD
MISSISSAUGA, ONTARIO L5N 3A2
(416) 821-3666

• **JOANNE FABRICS CO. LTD.**
1090 AEROWOOD DRIVE
MISSISSAUGA, ONTARIO L4W 1Y5
(416) 624-5104 **Pg. 239**

JOHNSON, CRAIG & ASSOCIATES
110 DAVENPORT ROAD
TORONTO, ONTARIO M5R 1H7
(416) 975-1867

KOBE FABRICS LTD.
5380 SOUTH SERVICE RD., P.O. BOX 939
BURLINGTON, ONTARIO L7R 3Y7
(416) 639-2730

LAURII TEXTILES
326 DAVENPORT ROAD
TORONTO, ONTARIO M5R 1K6
(416) 922-5514

LIONS WALLCOVERINGS & FABRICS INC.
265 DAVENPORT ROAD
TORONTO, ONTARIO M5R 1K5
(416) 924-7779

MACUSHLA AGENCY
260 KING STREET EAST
TORONTO, ONTARIO M5A 1K3
(416) 947-9155

MODERN WINDOW SHADES LTD.
267 DAVENPORT ROAD
TORONTO, ONTARIO M5R 1J9
(416) 927-0292

NEESHAT FURNISHING FABRICS
170 WEST BEAVER CREEK ROAD
RICHMOND HILL, ONTARIO L4B 1L6
(416) 886-0404

ONTARIO WALLCOVERINGS
462 FRONT STREET WEST
TORONTO, ONTARIO M5V 1B6
(416) 593-4519

PANACHE DESIGN LIMITED
361 KING STREET EAST
TORONTO, ONTARIO M5A 1L1
(416) 369-0084

PRIDE OF PARIS FABRICS LTD.
WEST RIVER STREET, BOX 130
PARIS, ONTARIO N3L 3E9
(519) 443-6351

**PRIMAVERA
INTERIOR ACCESSORIES LTD.**
160 PEARS AVENUE
TORONTO, ONTARIO M5R 1T2
(416) 921-3334

ROBBIE TEXTILES
487 CHAMPAGNE DRIVE
DOWNSVIEW, ONTARIO M3J 2C6
(416) 630-2493

SAMO TEXTILES LTD.
67 ST. REGIS CRESCENT NORTH
DOWNSVIEW, ONTARIO M3J 1Y9
(416) 636-7273

SAMO INTERNATIONAL
320 DAVENPORT ROAD
TORONTO, ONTARIO M5R 1K6
(416) 920-3020

SANDERSON, A. & SONS LTD.
320 DAVENPORT ROAD
TORONTO, ONTARIO M5R 1K6
(416) 323-1168

SEWING ROOM, THE
170 BEDFORD ROAD
TORONTO, ONTARIO M5R 2K9
(416) 961-5536

SUREWAY TRADING ENTERPRISES
111 PETER STREET
TORONTO, ONTARIO M5V 2H1
(416) 596-1887

TELIO & CIE
113 DUPONT STREET
TORONTO, ONTARIO M5R 1V4
(416) 968-2020

UNIFAB LTD.
250 WYECROFT ROAD
OAKVILLE, ONTARIO L6K 3T7
(416) 844-7433

WALTER L. BROWN LTD.
17 VICKERS ROAD
TORONTO, ONTARIO M9B 1C2
(416) 231-4499

E. WOELLER FABRICS LTD.
38 FRANCIS STREET SOUTH, P.O. BOX 666
KITCHENER, ONTARIO N2G 4B8
(519) 578-7880

WOOL BUREAU CANADA LTD.
33 YONGE STREET
TORONTO, ONTARIO M5E 1G4
(416) 485-9491

▶ WESTERN CANADA

CRAWFORD DAWSON AGENCY
520 CORYDON AVENUE
WINNIPEG, MANITOBA R3L 0P1
(204) 453-4832

ITALIA DESIGN OF CANADA
10357–109TH STREET
EDMONTON, ALBERTA T5J 1N3
(403) 420-0270

UPHOLSTERY

▶ QUEBEC

• **AMOCO FABRICS AND FIBERS LTD.**
955, BOULEVARD ST-JEAN
POINT CLAIRE, QUEBEC H9R 5K3
(514) 694-9860 **Pg. 238**

AVANT-GARDE FABRICS LTD.
7955 RUE ALFRED
ANJOU, QUEBEC H1J 1J3
1-(800) 361-8886

**CONNAISSANCE FABRICS &
WALLCOVERINGS LTD**
1632, RUE SHERBROOKE OUEST
MONTREAL, QUEBEC H2H 2L4
(514) 931-2437

DIVA LTEE
360, AVENUE LAURIER OUEST
MONTREAL, QUEBEC H2V 2K7
(514) 277-3319

NOVAX WALLCOVERINGS
740 PLACE TRANS CANADA
LONGUEUIL, QUEBEC J4G 1P1
(514) 651-7120

TELIO & CIE.
1407, RUE DE LA MONTAGNE
MONTREAL, QUEBEC H3G 1Z3
(514) 842-9116

VAL ABEL TEXTILES LTD.
55 MT. ROYAL AVENUE WEST
MONTREAL, QUEBEC H2T 2S6
(514) 842-9503

▶ ONTARIO

ARJAY TEXTILES LIMITED
221 ADVANCE BOULEVARD
BRAMPTON, ONTARIO L6T 4J2
(416) 454-0444

ARREDOTEX INC.
321 DAVENPORT ROAD
TORONTO, ONTARIO M5R 1K5
(416) 323-9700

APPEL LIMITED
321 DAVENPORT ROAD
TORONTO, ONTARIO M5R 1K5
(416) 922-3935

BAUMANN FABRICS LTD.
302 KING STREET EAST
TORONTO, ONTARIO M5A 1K6
(416) 869-1221

W.H. BILBROUGH & CO. LTD.
326 DAVENPORT ROAD
TORONTO, ONTARIO M5R 1K6
(416) 960-1611

BONGAERTS MARKETING INC.
224 BEDFORD ROAD
TORONTO, ONTARIO M5R 2K9
(416) 964-9363

H. BROWN SILK CO. LTD.
530 ADELAIDE STREET WEST
TORONTO, ONTARIO M5V 1T5
(416) 364-2377

BRUNSCHWIG & FILS
320 DAVENPORT ROAD
TORONTO, ONTARIO M3R 1K6
(416) 968-0699

CAYA FABRICS LTD.
P.O. BOX 304, 130 WEBER STREET WEST
KITCHENER, ONTARIO N2G 3Z2
(519) 743-0623

COMMTEX
91 KELFIELD STREET
ETOBICOKE, ONTARIO M9W 5A3
(416) 247-2103

D.C.S. DRAPERY LTD.
DRAPERY CONTRACT SERVICES
334 LAUDER AVENUE
TORONTO, ONTARIO M6E 3H8
(416) 651-5757

DELUXE UPHOLSTERY INTERIORS
34 DONCASTER AVENUE
THORNHILL, ONTARIO L3T 4S1
(416) 881-0439

EGAN LAING LTD.
1067 WESTPORT CRESCENT
MISSISSAUGA, ONTARIO L5T 1E8
(416) 678-9131

• **FABRICS INTERNATIONAL**
1090 AEROWOOD DRIVE
MISSISSAUGA, ONTARIO L4W 1Y5
(416) 624-5104 **Pg. 239**

GENERAL FABRICS
100 CLAREMONT STREET
TORONTO, ONTARIO M6J 3R2
(416) 368-7684

GREEFF FABRICS INC.
170 BEDFORD ROAD
TORONTO, ONTARIO M5R 2K9
(416) 960-8222

HABERT ASSOCIATES LIMITED
321 DAVENPORT ROAD
TORONTO, ONTARIO M5R 1K5
(416) 960-5323

• **INTER-LEATHER MARKETING SERVICES**
131 BRUNEL ROAD
MISSISSAUGA, ONTARIO L4Z 1X3
(416) 890-5505 **Pg. 240**

JEFF BROWN FINE FABRICS LTD.
1785 ARGENTIA ROAD
MISSISSAUGA, ONTARIO L5N 3A2
(416) 821-3666

• **JOANNE FABRICS CO. LTD.**
1090 AEROWOOD DRIVE
MISSISSAUGA, ONTARIO L4W 1Y5
(416) 624-5104 **Pg. 239**

JOHNSON, CRAIG & ASSOCIATES
110 DAVENPORT ROAD
TORONTO, ONTARIO M5R 1H7
(416) 975-1867

KOBE FABRICS LTD.
5380 SOUTH SERVICE RD., P.O. BOX 939
BURLINGTON, ONTARIO L7R 3Y7
(416) 639-2730

LACKAWANNA LEATHER
633 EASTERN AVENUE
TORONTO, ONTARIO M4M 1E5
(416) 465-3545

LAURII TEXTILES
326 DAVENPORT ROAD
TORONTO, ONTARIO M5R 1K6
(416) 922-5514

LIONS WALLCOVERINGS & FABRICS INC.
265 DAVENPORT ROAD
TORONTO, ONTARIO M5R 1K5
(416) 924-7779

MAVERICK LEATHER SALES INC.
260 KING STREET EAST
TORONTO, ONTARIO M5A 1K3
(416) 767-2366

MORBERN INC.
80 BOUNDARY ROAD
CORNWALL, ONTARIO K6H 5V3
(613) 932-8811

NEESHAT FURNISHING FABRICS
170 WEST BEAVER CREEK ROAD
RICHMOND HILL, ONTARIO L4B 1L6
(416) 886-0404

PRIDE OF PARIS FABRICS LTD.
WEST RIVER STREET, BOX 130
PARIS, ONTARIO N3L 3E9
(519) 443-6351

PRIMAVERA
INTERIOR ACCESSORIES LTD.
160 PEARS AVENUE
TORONTO, ONTARIO M5R 1T2
(416) 921-3334

ROBBIE TEXTILES
487 CHAMPAGNE DRIVE
DOWNSVIEW, ONTARIO M3J 2C6
(416) 630-2493

RODA WALLCOVERINGS LTD.
80 TYCOS DRIVE
TORONTO, ONTARIO M6B 1V9
(416) 782-1168

SAMO TEXTILES LIMITED
67 ST. REGIS CRESCENT NORTH
DOWNSVIEW, ONTARIO M3J 1Y9
(416) 628-7171

SAMO INTERNATIONAL
320 DAVENPORT ROAD
TORONTO, ONTARIO M5R 1K6
(416) 920-3020

SANDERSON, A. & SONS LTD.
320 DAVENPORT ROAD
TORONTO, ONTARIO M5R 1K6
(416) 323-1168

SPINNEYBECK ENTERPRISES LTD.
RR NO. 4
STOUFFVILLE, ONTARIO L0H 1L0
(416) 888-1987

TANDEM FABRICS INC.
320 DAVENPORT ROAD
TORONTO, ONTARIO M5R 1K6
(416) 964-6744

TELIO & CIE
113 DUPONT STREET
TORONTO, ONTARIO M5R 1V4
(416) 968-2020

UNIFAB LTD.
250 WYECROFT ROAD
OAKVILLE, ONTARIO L6K 3T7
(416) 844-7433

WALTER L. BROWN LTD.
17 VICKERS ROAD
TORONTO, ONTARIO M9B 1C2
(416) 231-4499

E. WOELLER FABRICS LTD.
38 FRANCIS STREET SOUTH, P.O. BOX 666
KITCHENER, ONTARIO N2G 4B8
(519) 578-7880

▶ WESTERN CANADA

J. ENNIS FABRICS
12163–68TH STREET
EDMONTON, ALBERTA T5B 1P9
(403) 474-5414

ITALIA DESIGN OF CANADA
10357–109TH STREET
EDMONTON, ALBERTA T5J 1N3
(403) 420-0270

CARPETS & RUGS

▶ ATLANTIC CANADA

H.G. ROGERS LTD.
87 GERMAIN STREET
SAINT JOHN, N.B. E2L 4S3
(506) 657-8350

▶ QUEBEC

• **AMOCO FABRICS AND FIBERS LTD.**
955, BOULEVARD ST-JEAN
POINT CLAIRE, QUEBEC H9R 5K3
(514) 694-9860 **Pg. 238**

CARNIVAL RUGS LTD.
5151 SAVANE STREET
MONTREAL, QUEBEC H4P 1V1
(514) 735-1198

CELANESE CANADA INC.
800, BOULEVARD DORCHESTER OUEST
MONTREAL, QUEBEC H3B 1Z1
(514) 871-5511

CENTURY CARPET DISTRIBUTORS INC.
350 McCAFFREY STREET
ST. LAURENT, QUEBEC H4T 1N1
(514) 735-1356

• **PEERLESS CARPET CORPORATION**
P.O. BOX 944, PLACE BONAVENTURE
MONTREAL, QUEBEC H5A 1E8
(514) 878-6800 **Pg. 250**

**TANGI COLLECTION/
TECH-STYLE RUG G.A. INC.**
85, RUE ST-PAUL OUEST
MONTREAL, QUEBEC H2Y 3V4
(514) 842-9272

TAPIS LIPMAN CARPET
9450 L'ACADIE BOULEVARD
MONTREAL, QUEBEC H4N 1L7
(514) 381-7279

TAPIS PERFECTION LTEE
1244, RUE STE-CATHRINE OUEST
MONTREAL, QUEBEC H3G 1P1
(514) 395-2400

▶ ONTARIO

ANGLO ORIENTAL LTD.
68 PRINCE ANDREW PLACE
DON MILLS, ONTARIO M3C 2H4
(416) 445-8111

APPEL LIMITED
321 DAVENPORT ROAD
TORONTO, ONTARIO M5R 1K5
(416) 922-3935

ATLAS RUG CO. LTD.
1014-16 BATHURST STREET
TORONTO, ONTARIO
(416) 534-4300

• **BASF FIBRES INC.**
QUEEN'S QUAY TERMINAL, SUITE 410
207 QUEEN'S QUAY WEST – P.O. BOX 111
TORONTO, ONTARIO M5J 1A7
(416) 862-7762 **Pg. 244, 245**

BARRYMORE CARPET INC.
190 LIBERTY STREET
TORONTO, ONTARIO M6K 1G1
(416) 537-1201

W.H. BILBROUGH & CO. LTD.
326 DAVENPORT ROAD
TORONTO, ONTARIO M5R 1K6
(416) 960-1611

WALTER L. BROWN LTD.
17 VICKERS ROAD
TORONTO, ONTARIO M9B 1C2
(416) 232-2449

BONNELL COMMERCIAL CARPET INC.
65B WEST BEAVER CREEK ROAD
RICHMOND HILL, ONTARIO L4B 1K4
(416) 764-6104

CLASSIC INTERIOR DESIGNS LTD.
477 ELIZABETH STREET
BURLINGTON, ONTARIO L7R 2M3
(416) 823-2105

CONSTELLATION CARPETS
3688 NASHUA DRIVE
MISSISSAUGA, ONTARIO L4V 1M5
(416) 677-5623

CORONET CARPETS INC.
4000 NASHUA DRIVE
MALTON, ONTARIO L4V 1P8
(416) 678-9595

CREATIVE MATTERS INC.
173 KING STREET EAST
TORONTO, ONTARIO M5A 1S4
(416) 369-9771

CROSSLEY KARASTAN CARPETS LTD.
40 CONSTELLATION COURT
REXDALE, ONTARIO M9W 1K2
(416) 675-3030

• **DE JOURNO, THOMAS E.
& ASSOCIATES**
115 DUPONT STREET
TORONTO, ONTARIO M5R 1V4
(416) 967-0154 **Pg. 247**

DOMINION RUG INC.
3420 YONGE STREET
TORONTO, ONTARIO M4N 2M9
(416) 485-9488

• **DU PONT OF CANADA INC.**
P.O. BOX 2200, STREETSVILLE
MISSISSAUGA, ONTARIO L5M 2H3
(416) 821-5858 **Pg. 246**

ELTE CARPETS LTD.
69 MONTCALM AVENUE
TORONTO, ONTARIO M6E 4N9
(416) 785-7885

FRANCO-BELGIAN CO. LTD.
115 DUPONT STREET
TORONTO, ONTARIO M5R 1V4
(416) 967-0115

GILT EDGE CARPETS LTD.
3405 AMERICAN DRIVE
MISSISSAUGA, ONTARIO L4V 1T6
(416) 671-3434

H. & I. CARPET CORPORATION
162 BEDFORD ROAD
TORONTO, ONTARIO M5R 2K9
(416) 961-6891

HARDING CARPETS
85 MORRELL STREET
BRANTFORD, ONTARIO N3T 4J6
(519) 746-5241

**INTERFACE FLOORING SYSTEMS
CANADA**
P.O. BOX 1182 LAHR DRIVE
BELLEVILLE, ONTARIO K8N 5E8
(613) 966-8090

KRAUS CARPET MILLS LTD.
565 CONESTOGA ROAD
WATERLOO, ONTARIO N2L 4E1
(519) 884-2310

KUTNER KREMER LTD.
1460 WHITEHORSE ROAD
DOWNSVIEW, ONTARIO M3J 3A7
(416) 636-4700

3M CANADA LTD.
P.O. BOX 5757
LONDON, ONTARIO N6A 4T1
(519) 451-2500

• **MILLIKEN INDUSTRIES OF CANADA LTD.**
P.O. BOX 530, 70 DUNDAS STREET WEST
DESERONTO, ONTARIO K0K 1X0
(613) 396-3421 **Pg. 248, 249**

NEESHAT FURNISHING FABRICS
170 WEST BEAVER CREEK ROAD
RICHMOND HILL, ONTARIO L4B 1L6
(416) 886-0404

O'NEIL, MARY & ASSOC.
166 SECOND STREET
OTTAWA, ONTARIO
(613) 235-6634

OSHAWA GLASS FIBRE PRODUCTS
341 DURHAM STREET
OSHAWA, ONTARIO
(416) 579-1433

PAGE FLOORING ENTERPRISES INC.
50 PRODUCTION DRIVE
SCARBOROUGH, ONTARIO M1H 2X8
(416) 438-6750

PENNINSULA CARPET DESIGN INC.
406 KING STREET EAST
TORONTO, ONTARIO M5A 1L4
(416) 360-8467

PERFECTION RUG CO. LTD.
113 DUPONT STREET
TORONTO, ONTARIO M5R 1V4
(416) 920-5900

QUALITY COMMERCIAL CARPET CORP.
20 EAST BEAVER CREEK ROAD
RICHMOND HILL, ONTARIO L4B 1G6
(416) 223-9573

REEVES BROS. CANADA LTD.
415 EVANS AVENUE
TORONTO, ONTARIO M8W 2T2
(416) 259-8451

SANDS, GORDON T. LTD.
40 TORBAY ROAD
MARKHAM, ONTARIO L3R 1G6
(416) 495-6380

SUMMIT CARPET INDUSTRIES LTD.
1773 BAYLY STREET
PICKERING, ONTARIO L1W 2Y7
1-800-263-4620

**TANGI COLLECTION/
FRANCO-BELGIAN CO. LTD.**
115 DUPONT STREET
TORONTO, ONTARIO M5R 1V4
(416) 967-0115

TEMPLETON, P.L. ANTIQUE CARPETS LTD.
131 AVENUE ROAD
TORONTO, ONTARIO M5R 2H7
(416) 923-2147

WILDER, DENNIS ENTERPRISES LTD.
26 JUBILEE COURT
BRAMPTON, ONTARIO L6S 2H2
(416) 791-5633

WOOL BUREAU CANADA LTD.
33 YONGE STREET
TORONTO, ONTARIO M5E 1G4
(416) 485-9491

WYANT & CO. LTD.
2040 ELLESMERE ROAD
SCARBOROUGH, ONTARIO M1H 3A8
(416) 438-6140

▶ W E S T E R N   C A N A D A

CHRISTOPHER CARPETS
12520 ST. ALBERT TRAIL
EDMONTON, ALBERTA T5L 4H4
(403) 452-9011

▶ B R I T I S H   C O L U M B I A

CLIFFORD E. WILSON LTD.
1416 W 8TH AVENUE
VANCOUVER, B.C. V6H 1E1
(604) 736-8631

TILES

▶ Q U E B E C

AMERICAN BILTRITE (CANADA) LTD.
200 BANK STREET
SHERBROOKE, QUEBEC J1H 4K3
(819) 556-6660

AMTICO FLOORING
P.O. BOX 310
SHERBROOKE, QUEBEC J1H 5J1
(819) 556-6660

• **ARMSTRONG WORLD INDUSTRIES
CANADA LTD.**
6911, BOULEVARD DECARIE
MONTREAL, QUEBEC H3W 3E5
(514) 739-2796 **Pg. 243**

CIOT IMPORTATIONS LTEE
9151, RUE ST-LAURENT
MONTREAL, QUEBEC H2N 1N2
(514) 382-7330

CERATEC INC.
414, RUE ST-SACREMENT
QUEBEC, QUEBEC G1N 3Y3
(418) 681-0101

DOMCO INDUSTRIES LTD.
1001 YAMASKA EAST
FARMHAM, QUEBEC J2N 2R4
(514) 866-5461

ENTERPRISES TUILES MONGIAT
1972, AVENUE DE L'ESPLANADE
MONTREAL, QUEBEC H3L 2Y6
(514) 331-4761

MONDO RUBBER CANADA LTD.
2655, AVENUE FRANCIS-HUGHES
LAVAL, QUEBEC H7L 3S8
(514) 663-6260

• **RAMCA TILES LTD.**
1085, AVENUE VAN HORNE
MONTREAL, QUEBEC H2V 1J6
(514) 270-9192 **Pg. 252**

▶ O N T A R I O

• **ARMSTRONG WORLD INDUSTRIES
CANADA LTD.**
2233 ARGENTIA ROAD
MISSISSAUGA, ONTARIO L5N 2X7
(416) 826-4832 **Pg. 243**

CENTRAL SUPPLY CO.
53 APEX ROAD
TORONTO, ONTARIO M6A 2V6
(416) 785-5151

COUNTRY TILES
321 DAVENPORT ROAD
TORONTO, ONTARIO M5R 1K5
(416) 922-9214

CROSS-CAN AGENCIES INC.
238 GALAXY BOULEVARD
REXDALE, ONTARIO M9W 5R8
(416) 675-7565

FERLEO IMPORT EXPORT CO. LTD.
315 HUMBERLINE DRIVE
REXDALE, ONTARIO M9W 5T6
(416) 675-0075

• **MARBLE TREND LTD.**
710 ROWNTREE DAIRY ROAD
WOODBRIDGE, ONTARIO L4L 5T7
(416) 738-0040 **Pg. 251**

MILNE & ASSOC. LTD.
49 SPADINA AVENUE
TORONTO, ONTARIO M5V 2J1
(416) 591-9114

NEW ENGLAND SLATE
P.O. BOX 503
ST. CATHARINES, ONTARIO L2R 6V9
(416) 892-5793

OLYMPIA FLOOR & WALL TILE CO.
1000 LAWRENCE AVENUE WEST
TORONTO, ONTARIO M6B 4A8
(416) 789-4122

• **RAMCA TILES LTD.**
354 DAVENPORT ROAD
TORONTO, ONTARIO M5R 1K6
(416) 781-5521 **Pg. 252**

ROCKFORD MARBLE CENTRE LTD.
160 PEARS AVENUE
TORONTO, ONTARIO M5R 1T2
(416) 922-6122

SPINNEYBECK ENTERPRISES LTD.
RR NO. 4
STOUFVILLE, ONTARIO L0H 1L0
(416) 888-1987

• **T.M.T. MARBLE SUPPLY LTD.**
900 KEELE STREET
TORONTO, ONTARIO M6N 3E7
(416) 653-6111 **Pg. 253**

THAMES VALLEY BRICK & TILE
4801 KEELE STREET
DOWNSVIEW, ONTARIO M3J 3A4
(416) 667-0010

TIVOLI MARBLE & CERAMIC INC.
4801 KEELE STREET
DOWNSVIEW, ONTARIO M3J 3A4
(416) 667-0010

YORK MARBLE
41 COLVILLE ROAD
TORONTO, ONTARIO M6M 2Y2
(4 6) 235-0161

▶ W E S T E R N   C A N A D A

CERAMATILE LTD.
383 CHENTON AVENUE
WINNIPEG, MANITOBA R3G 0H3
(204) 339-0217

▶ B R I T I S H   C O L U M B I A

C & S CERAMIC TILE DISTRIBUTORS
2720 INGLETON AVENUE
BURNABY, B.C. V5C 5X4
(604) 435-4431

CORPORATE

▶ ATLANTIC CANADA

H.G. ROGERS LTD.
87 GERMAIN STREET
SAINT JOHN, N.B. E2L 4S3
(506) 657-8350

SEAMAN-CROSS LTD.
46 WRIGHT AVENUE
DARTMOUTH, NOVA SCOTIA B2Y 4B2
(902) 469-8190

▶ QUEBEC

AARKASH CHAIR CO. OF CANADA LTD.
1350 TELLIER STREET
LAVAL, QUEBEC H7C 2H2
(514) 661-1271

• **ALLSTEEL CANADA LTD.**
6505 TRANS CANADA HIGHWAY
ST-LAURENT, QUEBEC H4T 1S3
(514) 744-1120 **Pg. 202, 203**

ALPHA VICO CANADA LTD.
1035 MAGENTA BOULEVARD EAST
FARNHAM, QUEBEC J2N 1B9
(514) 293-5354

ANGLE INTERNATIONAL
296, RUE ST-PAUL OUEST
MONTREAL, QUEBEC H2Y 2A3
(514) 284-2619

• **ARTOPEX INC.**
2121, RUE BERLIER
LAVAL, QUEBEC H7L 3M9
(514) 332-4420 **Pg. 201**

**ATELIER D'ARCHITECTURE
DUROCHER + PRATT, L'**
3643, RUE ST-LAURENT
MONTREAL, QUEBEC H2X 2V5
(514) 289-9344

BAUHAUS DESIGNS LTD.
85, RUE ST-PAUL OUEST
MONTREAL, QUEBEC H2Y 3V4
(514) 844-8812

• **BILTRITE NIGHTINGALE INC.**
10251, BOULEVARD RAY LAWSON
MONTREAL, QUEBEC H1J 1L7
(514) 352-7770 **Pg. 205**

• **BONAVENTURE
FURNITURE INDUSTRIES LTD.**
894 BLOOMFIELD
MONTREAL, QUEBEC H2V 3S6
(514) 270-7311 **Pg. 206**

BURO DECOR INC.
2000 McGILL COLLEGE AVENUE
MONTREAL, QUEBEC H3A 3H3
(514) 842-9223

CODD & COMPANY
85, RUE ST-PAUL OUEST
MONTREAL, QUEBEC H2Y 3V4
(514) 844-6680

• **DECA INTERIORS LTD.**
617, RUE ST-REMI
MONTREAL, QUEBEC H4C 3G7
(514) 933-8307 **Pg. 211**

DECABOIS INC.
234, RUE ST-URBAIN
GRANBY, QUEBEC J2G 7T4
(514) 378-7976

FRASER CONTRACT FURNITURE INC.
8310 DEVONSHIRE ROAD
ST-LAURENT, QUEBEC H4P 2P7
(514) 737-6550

HAWORTH OFFICE SYSTEMS, LTD.
2000 McGILL COLLEGE AVENUE
MONTREAL, QUEBEC H3A 3H3
(514) 842-2622

**HENDERSON
DIV. LES MEUBLES RADISSON LTEE.**
199, AVENUE UPPER EDISON
ST-LAMBERT, QUEBEC J4R 2R3
(514) 671-7221

ISHI-MOBART
7490, AVENUE JEAN VALETS
MONTREAL, QUEBEC H1E 3A1
(514) 648-7477

KNOLL INTERNATIONAL
17400 TRANS CANADA HIGHWAY
KIRKLAND, QUEBEC H9J 2M5
(514) 695-9030

MEUBLES SITA INC., LES
8241, RUE ALFRED-BROSSEAU
MONTREAL, QUEBEC H1E 3H5
(514) 648-1115

NOVELLA
646, RUE GIFFARD
LONGUEUIL, QUEBEC J4G 1T8
(514) 651-9133

OE INC.
5990 COTE DE LIESSE
TOWN OF MOUNT ROYAL, QUEBEC H4T 1V7
(514) 342-5151

• **PRECISION MFG. INC.**
2200 – 52ND AVENUE
LACHINE, QUEBEC H8T 2Y6
(514) 631-2120 **Pg. 220**

ROUND OFFICE
480, RUE ST-JEAN
MONTREAL, QUEBEC H2Y 253
(514) 288-5486

SMED MANUFACTURING LTD.
650 – 32ND AVENUE LTD.
LACHINE, QUEBEC
(514) 634-7063

• **SNYDER FURNITURE LTD.**
640, ST-PAUL OUEST
MONTREAL, QUEBEC H3C 1L9
(514) 866-0417 **Pg. 222, 223**

**STANDARD DESK
DIV. JOYCE FURNITURE INC.**
1000, BOULEVARD ST-MARTIN OUEST
LAVAL, QUEBEC H7S 1M7

SUNARHAUSERMAN, LTD
2040, RUE PEEL
MONTREAL, QUEBEC H3A 1W5
(514) 849-7323

• **TEKNION FURNITURE SYSTEMS INC.**
425, PLACE JACQUES CARTIER
MONTREAL, QUEBEC H2Y 3B1
(514) 866-4331 **Pg. 224, 225**

• **TELLA SYSTEMS**
161 STERLING AVENUE
LA SALLE, QUEBEC H8R 3P3
(514) 364-0511 **Pg. 226**

TODAY'S QUEBEC INC.
1895 46e AVENUE
LACHINE, QUEBEC H8T 2N9
(514) 636-4606

• **TRIEDE DESIGN INC.**
460 McGILL STREET
MONTREAL, QUEBEC H2Y 2H2
(514) 398-0602 **Pg. 228, 229**

XCEPTION DESIGN LTD.
2875 INDUSTRIAL BOULEVARD
LAVAL, QUEBEC H7L 3Y8
(514) 668-0710

▶ ONTARIO

• **AID 2000**
101 FRESHWAY DRIVE
CONCORD, ONTARIO L9K 1R9
(416) 661-6433 **Pg. 235**

A.R.E.A.
334 KING STREET EAST
TORONTO, ONTARIO M5A 1K8
(416) 367-5850

ABITARE DESIGN INC.
51 FRONT STREET EAST
TORONTO, ONTARIO M5E 1B3
(416) 363-1667

ALEXANDER'S FINE FURNITURE
2300 HAINES ROAD
MISSISSAUGA, ONTARIO L4Y 1Y6
(416) 897-3455

• **ALLSTEEL CANADA**
207 QUEEN'S QUAY WEST
TORONTO, ONTARIO M5J 1A7
(416) 367-5880 **Pg. 202, 203**

AMBIANT SYSTEMS LTD.
247 DAVENPORT ROAD
TORONTO, ONTARIO M5R 1J9
(416) 921-1900

ARCONAS CORPORATION
580 ORWEL STREET
MISSISSAUGA, ONTARIO L5A 3V7
(416) 272-0727

ARTMET
550 QUEEN STREET EAST
TORONTO, ONTARIO M5A 1V2
(416) 890-1999

ART SHOPPE
2131 YONGE STREET
TORONTO, ONTARIO M4S 2A6
(416) 487-3211

ARTOPEX INC.
10 LOWER SPADINA AVENUE
TORONTO, ONTARIO M5V 2Z2
(416) 593-0111 **Pg. 201**

ATELIER D'OR, LE
487 LEWIS STREET
OTTAWA, ONTARIO K2P 0T2
(613) 563-3343

**ATWOOD'S
EXECUTIVE OFFICE INTERIORS**
110 BLOOR STREET WEST
TORONTO, ONTARIO M5S 2W7
(416) 968-0820

• **AXIS INTERIORS**
25 WATLINE ROAD
MISSISSAUGA, ONTARIO L4Z 2Z1
(416) 568-0200 **Pg. 204**

BBF OFFICE INTERIORS
4362 CHESSWOOD DRIVE
DOWNSVIEW, ONTARIO M3J 2B9
(416) 636-9311

• **BILTRITE NIGHTINGALE INC.**
2501 DIXIE ROAD
MISSISSAUGA, ONTARIO L4Y 1Z9
(416) 896-3434 **Pg. 205**

• **BONAVENTURE
FURNITURE INDUSTRIES LIMITED**
146 DUPONT STREET
TORONTO, ONTARIO M5R 1V2
(416) 961-5900 **Pg. 206**

BRUNSWICK MANUFACTURING CO. LTD.
25 CURITY AVENUE
TORONTO, ONTARIO M4B 3M2
(416) 755-3388

BRAYTON INTERNATIONAL
65 FRONT STREET WEST
TORONTO, ONTARIO M5J 1E6
(416) 283-2615

BURO DECOR
3 CHURCH STREET
TORONTO, ONTARIO M5E 1M2
(416) 860-1400

BUSINESS ACCESSORIES INC.
415 DUNDAS STREET
CAMBRIDGE, ONTARIO N1R 5Y2
(519) 622-2222

CAPITAL OFFICE INTERIORS
17 AURIGA DRIVE
NEPEAN, ONTARIO K2E 7T9
(613) 723-2000

CHARVOZ CANADA
151 TELSON ROAD
MARKHAM, ONTARIO L3R 1E7
(416) 449-4101

CODD AND COMPANY
160 PEARS AVENUE
TORONTO, ONTARIO M5R 1T2
(416) 923-0066

CONCEPT B DESIGN GROUP
388 CARLAW AVENUE
TORONTO, ONTARIO M4M 2T4
(416) 462-1700

**CONTRACT FURNITURE
REFURNISHING LTD.**
431 ALDEN ROAD
MARKHAM, ONTARIO L3R 3R4
(416) 475-3666

CORPORATE BUSINESS INTERIORS
562 EGLINTON AVENUE EAST
TORONTO, ONTARIO M4P 1B9
(416) 485-5111

• **COLLIER FURNITURE LTD.**
1377 LAWRENCE AVENUE EAST
DON MILLS, ONTARIO M3A 3M4
(416) 449-7655 **Pg. 209**

• **CON•SPEC**
146 LAIRD DRIVE
TORONTO, ONTARIO M4G 3V7
(416) 429-5206 **Pg. 210**

CRAFTWOOD PRODUCTS
191 FINCHDENE SQUARE
SCARBOROUGH, ONTARIO M1X 1E3
(416) 297-1100

CREATIVE CUSTOM FURNISHINGS INC.
134 OAKDALE ROAD
DOWNSVIEW, ONTARIO M3N 1V9
(416) 742-7450

CROYDON FURNITURE SYSTEMS INC.
160 PEARS AVENUE
TORONTO, ONTARIO M5R 1T2
(416) 967-3526

CTI BUSINESS FURNISHINGS
5805 KENNEDY ROAD
MISSISSAUGA, ONTARIO L4Z 2G3
(416) 890-1999

CURTIS PRODUCTS LTD.
495 BALL STREET
COBOURG, ONTARIO K9A 4P9
(416) 372-2184

DACOTA INC.
175 TORYORK DRIVE
WESTON, ONTARIO M9L 1X9
(416) 747-6282

DAVID HUMPHREY INC.
411 RICHMOND STREET EAST
TORONTO, ONTARIO M5A 3S5
(416) 364-3887

DESIGN CASE INTERNATIONAL LTD.
2280 DREW ROAD
MISSISSAUGA, ONTARIO L5S 1B8
(416) 673-3363

DESIGN FORUM
260 RICHMOND STREET WEST
TORONTO, ONTARIO M5V 1W5
(416) 977-0987

FAIR LINE PRODUCTS LTD.
55 WOODLAWN AVENUE
MISSISSAUGA, ONTARIO L5G 3K7
(416) 274-3616

• **INTEFAC INC.**
255 MATHESON BOULEVARD WEST
MISSISSAUGA, ONTARIO L4R 3G3
(416) 890-3000 **Pg. 143**

GEIGER INTERNATIONAL LTD.
180 NORELCO DRIVE
WESTON, ONTARIO M9L 1S4
(416) 745-4000

GEMINI FURNITURE SALES LTD.
29–1 CONNELL COURT
TORONTO, ONTARIO M8Z 5T7
(416) 252-4656

• **GLOBAL UPHOLSTERY CO. LTD.**
560 SUPERTEST ROAD
DOWNSVIEW, ONTARIO M3J 2M6
(416) 661-3660 **Pg. 212**

GROUP FOUR FURNITURE INC.
25–5 CONNELL COURT
TORONTO, ONTARIO M8Z 1E8
(416) 251-1128

GUILDHALL CABINET SHOPS LTD.
11 JUTLAND ROAD
TORONTO, ONTARIO M8Z 2G6
(416) 255-3425

• **HARTER FURNITURE**
536 IMPERIAL ROAD
GUELPH, ONTARIO N1H 6L5
(519) 824-2850 **Pg. 213**

HAWORTH OFFICE SYSTEMS, LTD.
33 YONGE STREET
TORONTO, ONTARIO M5E 1G4
(416) 363-0702

HAUSERMAN LTD.
125 BETHRIDGE ROAD
REXDALE, ONTARIO M9W 1N4
(416) 743-3211

HAY OFFICE ENVIRONMENTS
1950 OXFORD STREET EAST
LONDON, ONTARIO N5V 2Z8
(519) 455-0055

HELKO SYSTEMS FURNITURE INC.
260 KING STREET EAST
TORONTO, ONTARIO M5A 1K3
(416) 362-5478

HERITAGE INTERIORS
244 DAVENPORT ROAD
TORONTO, ONTARIO M5R 1J7
(416) 922-6448

HERMAN MILLER CANADA, INC.
11 ADELAIDE STREET WEST
TORONTO, ONTARIO M5H 3Y2
(416) 366-3300

BRIAN G. HOLMES LTD.
81 McPHERSON STREET
MARKHAM, ONTARIO L3R 3L3
(416) 475-0166

HOLMES & BRAKEL LTD.
955 BROCK ROAD SOUTH
PICKERING, ONTARIO L1W 2X9
(416) 683-6222

• **INTARC LIMITED**
147 DAVENPORT ROAD
TORONTO, ONTARIO M5R 1J1
(416) 924-7111 **Pg. 214**

INTERIORS PLUS
50 GALAXY BOULEVARD
REXDALE, ONTARIO M9W 4Y5
(416) 675-7993

• **INTERNA FURNITURE DESIGN LTD.**
76 SIGNET DRIVE
WESTON, ONTARIO M9L 1T2
(416) 741-4211 **Pg. 215**

IRWIN SEATING CANADA LTD.
21 BELMONT STREET
TORONTO, ONTARIO M5R 1P9
(416) 929-3371

ITALINTERIORS LIMITED
359 KING STREET EAST
TORONTO, ONTARIO M5A 1L1
(416) 366-9540

• **JEFFREY-CRAIG LTD.**
763 WARDEN AVENUE, UNIT 2A
SCARBOROUGH, ONTARIO M1L 4B7
(416) 757-4153 **Pg. 216**

KARL GUTMANN INC.
P.O. BOX 1569
CORNWALL, ONTARIO K6H 5V6
(613) 932-0108

KEILHAUER INDUSTRIES LTD.
946 WARDEN AVENUE
TORONTO, ONTARIO M1L 4C9
(416) 759-5665

KINETICS FURNITURE
110 CARRIER DRIVE
REXDALE, ONTARIO M9W 5R1
(416) 675-4300

KNOLL INTERNATIONAL
160 PEARS AVENUE
TORONTO, ONTARIO M5R 1T2
(416) 960-9819

• **KRUG FURNITURE INC.**
421 MANITOU DRIVE, P.O. BOX 9035
KITCHENER, ONTARIO N2G 4J3
(519) 893-1100 **Pg. 217**

LEIF JACOBSEN LTD
15 RIVIERA DRIVE
MARKHAM, ONTARIO L3R 8N4
(416) 470-0010

LOOMIS & TOLES CO. LTD.
214 ADELAIDE STREET WEST
TORONTO, ONTARIO M5H 1W7
(416) 977-8877

MAYHEW AND PETERSON INC.
64 PRINCE ANDREW PLACE
DON MILLS, ONTARIO M3C 2S2
(416) 444-7315

METALSMITHS COMPANY LTD.
431 ALDEN ROAD
MARKHAM, ONTARIO L3R 3R4
(416) 475-3380

METROPOLITAN COLLECTION, THE
24 ADMIRAL ROAD
TORONTO, ONTARIO M5R 2L5
(416) 961-9949

MICHAEL HAAS AGENCIES
507 KING STREET EAST
TORONTO, ONTARIO M5A 1M3
(416) 923-7359

NKR ENVIRONMENTS LTD.
1045 MATHESON BOULEVARD
MISSISSAUGA, ONTARIO L4W 3P1
(416) 624-1657

SVEND NIELSEN LTD.
280 SIGNET DRIVE
WESTON, ONTARIO M9L 1V2
(416) 749-0131

NIENKAMPER
300 KING STREET EAST
TORONTO, ONTARIO M5A 1K4
(416) 298-5700

NORMAN CARRIERE AGENCIES INC.
478 QUEEN STREET EAST
TORONTO, ONTARIO M5A 1T7
(416) 363-1152

OE INC.
525 DENISON STREET
MARKHAM, ONTARIO L3R 1B8
(416) 491-9330

OFFICE SPECIALTY
322 KING STREET WEST
TORONTO, ONTARIO M5V 1J2
(416) 977-6007

O'NEAL, MARY & ASSOCIATES
166 SECOND STREET
OTTAWA, ONTARIO
(613) 235-6634

OTTAWA BUSINESS INTERIORS
183 COLONNADE ROAD
OTTAWA, ONTARIO K2E 7J4
(613) 226-4090

PALAZZETTI
431 CARLINGVIEW DRIVE
TORONTO, ONTARIO M9V 5G7
(416) 674-2599

POI BUSINESS INTERIORS
120 VALLEYWOOD DRIVE
MARKHAM, ONTARIO L3R 6A7
(416) 479-1123

PRESTON
60 BLOOR STREET WEST
TORONTO, ONTARIO M4W 3B8
(416) 925-3341

PRESTON
1741 WOODWARD AVENUE
OTTAWA, ONTARIO K2C 0P9
(613) 723-3111

PRISMATIQUE DESIGNS LTD.
265 DAVENPORT ROAD
TORONTO, ONTARIO M5R 1J9
(416) 961-7333

• **QUESS FURNITURE**
157 PRINCESS STREET
TORONTO, ONTARIO M5A 4M4
(416) 366-4744 **Pg. 218, 219**

RRL DESIGNS LTD.
3414 FONTENAY COURT
OTTAWA, ONTARIO K1V 7S9
(613) 521-9130

REFF INCORPORATED
1000 ARROW ROAD
WESTON, ONTARIO M9M 2Y7
(416) 741-5453

ROCHNOR FURNITURE LTD.
80 HANLAN ROAD
WOODBRIDGE, ONTARIO L4L 3R7
(416) 851-1567

ROVO CHAIR OF CANADA LTD.
3200 14TH AVENUE
MARKHAM, ONTARIO L3R 2L6
(416) 479-1970

SALIX SYSTEMS LTD.
1220 ELLESMERE ROAD
SCARBOROUGH, ONTARIO M1P 2X5
(416) 292-0090

SAVOIA CHAIR FRAMES LTD.
65 DENSLEY AVENUE
TORONTO, ONTARIO M6M 4Z2
(416) 244-4900

SCHAT IMPORT AGENCIES
P.O. BOX 202, STATION M
TORONTO, ONTARIO M6S 4T3
(416) 769-0812

SHAW-PEZZO & ASSOCIATES INC.
146 DUPONT STREET
TORONTO, ONTARIO M5R 1V2
(416) 961-8213

SIMMONS LTD.
6900 AIRPORT ROAD
MISSISSAUGA, ONTARIO L4V 1E8
(416) 671-1033

• **SIMPSONS
COMMERCIAL INTERIORS & DESIGN**
49 GERVAIS DRIVE
DON MILLS, ONTARIO M3C 1Y9
(416) 449-0110 **Pg. 144, 145**

SMED MANUFACTURING LTD.
478 QUEEN STREET WEST
TORONTO, ONTARIO M5A 1T7
(416) 363-3486

• **SNYDER FURNITURE LTD.**
87 COLVILLE ROAD
TORONTO, ONTARIO M6M 2Y6
(416) 247-6285 **Pg. 222, 223**

STEELCASE CANADA LTD.
P.O. BOX 9
DON MILLS, ONTARIO M3C 2R7
1-800-268 1121

STORWAL INTERNATIONAL INC.
156 FRONT STREET WEST
TORONTO, ONTARIO M5J 2L6
(416) 598-0716

• **STOW & DAVIS**
P.O. BOX 9
DON MILLS, ONTARIO M3C 2R7
1-800-268-1121 **Pg. 221**

SUNARHAUSERMAN, LTD.
1 SUNSHINE AVENUE
WATERLOO, ONTARIO N2J 4K5
(416) 886-2000

• **TEKNION FURNITURE SYSTEMS INC.**
1150 FLINT ROAD
DOWNSVIEW, ONTARIO M3J 2J5
(416) 661-3370 **Pg. 224, 225**

• **TELLA SYSTEMS INC.**
124 BERMONDSEY ROAD
TORONTO, ONTARIO M5A 1X5
(416) 752-7750 **Pg. 226**

• **TENDEX SILKO INC.**
264 THE ESPLANADE
TORONTO, ONTARIO M5A 4J6
(416) 361-1515 **Pg. 227**

TODAY'S BUSINESS PRODUCTS LTD.
875 MIDDLEFIELD ROAD
SCARBOROUGH, ONTARIO M1V 4Z5
(416) 292-5155

• **TRIEDE DESIGN INC.**
256 KING STREET EAST
TORONTO, ONTARIO M5A 1K3
(416) 367-0667 **Pg. 228, 229**

• **TORONTO BUSINESS INTERIORS LTD.**
250 BRITANNIA ROAD
MISSISSAUGA, ONTARIO L4Z 1S6
(416) 890-1580 **Pg. 146**

• **ULTIMATE SOURCE GROUP, THE**
855 HARRINGTON COURT
BURLINGTON, ONTARIO L7N 3P3
(416) 639-7474 **Pg. 147**

WALLWOOD FURNITURE
65 WEST BEAVER CREEK ROAD
RICHMOND HILL, ONTARIO L4B 1K4
(416) 889-8607

WILLIAMS BUSINESS INTERIORS
2465 CAWTHRA ROAD
MISSISSAUGA, ONTARIO L5A 3P2
(416) 277-1463

ZIGGURAT CONCEPT INC.
254 KING STREET EAST
TORONTO, ONTARIO M5A 1K3
(416) 362-5900

▶ W E S T E R N   C A N A D A

ARTMET
15935 114TH AVENUE
EDMONTON, ALBERTA T5M 2Z3
(403) 452-7522

GREGORY CARTWRIGHT
812 WALL STREET
WINNIPEG, MANITOBA R3G 2T8
(204) 786-8601

ITALIA DESIGN OF CANADA
10357 – 109TH STREET
EDMONTON, ALBERTA T5J 1N3
(403) 420-0270

K.P. MANUFACTURERS LTD.
7403 – 30TH STREET SE
CALGARY, ALBERTA T2C 1N6
(403) 279-7727

SIMO DOW MFG. LTD.
3526 – 26TH STREET NE
CALGARY, ALBERTA T1Y 4T7
(403) 291-1133

SMED MANUFACTURING INC.
4315 54TH STREET SE
CALGARY, ALBERTA T2C 2A2
(403) 279-1400

WESCAB INDUSTRIES LTD.
8910 YELLOWHEAD TRAIL
EDMONTON, ALBERTA T5B 1G2
(403) 474-6461

WESTNOFA OF CANADA LTD.
691 GOLSPIE STREET
WINNIPEG, MANITOBA R2K 2V3
(204) 677-7106

▶ B R I T I S H   C O L U M B I A

DANICA IMPORTS LTD.
22 EAST 2ND AVENUE
VANCOUVER, B.C. V5T 1B1
(604) 872-0277

INFORM INTERIORS INC.
97 WATER STREET
VANCOUVER, B.C. V6B 1A1
(604) 682-3868

**SCALI DURANTE
FURNITURE MANUFACTURERS LTD.**
5371 REGENT STREET
BURNABY, B.C. V5C 4H4
(604) 291-7551

SWITZER, W. & ASSOCIATES LTD.
291 EAST 2ND AVENUE
VANCOUVER, B.C. V5T 1B6
(604) 255-5911

COMMERCIAL INSTITUTIONAL

▶ A T L A N T I C   C A N A D A

ATLANTIC STORES FIXTURES LTD.
105 HENRI DUNANT STREET
MONCTON, N.B. E1C 9J1
(506) 855-5530

DOMINION CHAIR CO.
MAPLE AVENUE
BASS RIVER, NOVA SCOTIA B0M 1B0
(902) 353-2883

▶ Q U E B E C

**AARKASH CHAIR
CO. OF CANADA LTD.**
1350, RUE TELLIER
LAVAL, QUEBEC H7C 2H2
(514) 661-1271

• **ALLIBERT LEISURE FURNITURE**
165 MONTE DE LIESSE
ST-LAURENT, QUEBEC H4T 1T9
(514) 735-6255 **Pg. 271**

• **ALLSTEEL CANADA LTD.**
6505 TRANS CANADA HIGHWAY
ST-LAURENT, QUEBEC H4T 1S3
(514) 744-1120 **Pg. 202, 203**

ALPHA VICO CANADA LTD.
1035, BOULEVARD MAGENTA EST
FARNHAM, QUEBEC J2N 1B9
(514) 293-5354

ANGLE INTERNATIONAL
296, RUE ST-PAUL OUEST
MONTREAL, QUEBEC H2Y 2A3
(514) 284-2619

ARTEMIDE LTD.
2408, RUE DE LA PROVINCE
LONGUEUIL, QUEBEC J4G 1G1
(514) 679-3717

• **ARTOPEX INC.**
2121, RUE BERLIER
LAVAL, QUEBEC H7L 3M9
(514) 332-4420 **Pg. 201**

**ATELIER D'ARCHITECTURE
DUROCHER + PRATT, L'**
3643, RUE ST-LAURENT
MONTREAL, QUEBEC H2X 2V5
(514) 289-9348

BAUHAUS DESIGNS LTD.
85, RUE ST-PAUL OUEST
MONTREAL, QUEBEC H2Y 3V4
(514) 844-8812

• **BONAVENTURE
FURNITURE INDUSTRIES LTD.**
894 BLOOMFIELD
MONTREAL, QUEBEC H2V 3S6
(514) 270-7311 **Pg. 206**

CODD & COMPANY
85, RUE ST-PAUL OUEST
MONTREAL, QUEBEC H2Y 3V4
(514) 844-6680

• **DECA INTERIORS LTD.**
617 ST-REMI
MONTREAL, QUEBEC H4C 3G7
(514) 933-6360 **Pg. 211**

INTERNATIONAL CONTRACT FURNITURE
260 KING STREET EAST
TORONTO, ONTARIO M5A 1K3
(416) 362-2838

ISHI-MOBART
7490, AVENUE JEAN VALETS
MONTREAL, QUEBEC H1E 3A1
(514) 648-7477

INTERNATIONAL UPHOLSTERY
5005, RUE BUCHAN
MONTREAL, QUEBEC H4P 1S4
(514) 735-1501

LEACO FURNITURE LTD.
4960, RUE BOURG
ST-LAURENT, QUEBEC H4T 1J2
(514) 731-7501

MEUBLES SITA INC., LES
8421, RUE ALFRED BROSSEAU
MONTREAL, QUEBEC H1E 3H5
(514) 648-1115

NOVELLA
646, RUE GIFFARD
LONGUEUIL, QUEBEC J4G 1T8
(514) 651-9133

• **PRECISION MFG. INC.**
2200-52ND AVENUE
LACHINE, QUEBEC H8T 2Y6
(514) 631-2120 **Pg. 220**

PROULX FURNITURE
10367, AVENUE ARMAND-LAVERGNE
MONTREAL, QUEBEC H1H 3N8
(514) 322-8010

• **SNYDER FURNITURE LTD.**
640, ST-PAUL OUEST
MONTREAL, QUEBEC H3C 1L9
(514) 866-0417 **Pg. 222,223**

• **TRIEDE DESIGN INC.**
460 McGILL STREET
MONTREAL, QUEBEC H2Y 2H2
(514) 398-0602 **Pg. 228, 229**

YU-GO FURNITURE CO.
331 ST. MARC STREET
LOUISEVILLE, QUEBEC J5Y 2G2
(819) 228-5546

▶ O N T A R I O

ABITARE DESIGN INC.
51 FRONT STREET EAST
TORONTO, ONTARIO M5E 1B3
(416) 363-1667

ABSTRACTA SYSTEMS INC.
30 MALLEY ROAD
SCARBOROUGH, ONTARIO M1L 2E3
(416) 751-2717

ALAR FURNITURE INC.
707 CLAYSON ROAD
WESTON, ONTARIO M9M 2H4
(416) 743-1925

• **ALLIBERT LEISURE FURNITURE**
260 KING STREET EAST
TORONTO, ONTARIO M5A 1K3
(416) 360-7989 **Pg. 271**

• **ALLSTEEL CANADA LTD.**
207 QUEEN'S QUAY WEST
TORONTO, ONTARIO M5J 1A7
(416) 367-5880 **Pg. 202, 203**

AMBIANT SYSTEMS LTD.
247 DAVENPORT ROAD
TORONTO, ONTARIO M5R 1J9
(416) 921-1900

AMERICAN FIXTURE CO. LTD.
370 MAIN STREET EAST
HAMILTON, ONTARIO L8N 1J6
(416) 522-1257

ARCONAS CORPORATION
580 ORWELL STREET
MISSISSAUGA, ONTARIO L5A 3V7
(416) 272-0727

ARTEMIDE CANADA LTD.
160 PEARS AVENUE
TORONTO, ONTARIO M5R 1T2
(416) 960-3022

ATWOOD'S EXECUTIVE OFFICE INTERIORS
110 BLOOR STREET WEST
TORONTO, ONTARIO M5S 2W7
(417) 968-0820

AVENGER DESIGNS
1121 INVICTA DRIVE
OAKVILLE, ONTARIO L6J 5C1
(416) 845-3338

BAUHAUS DESIGNS LTD.
40 DENISON ROAD EAST
TORONTO, ONTARIO M9N 3T7
(416) 244-2592

BEAUTILINE SYSTEMS LTD.
420 EDDYSTONE AVENUE
DOWNSVIEW, ONTARIO M3N 1H7
(416) 742-5360

BRODA ENTERPRISES INC.
72 VICTORIA STREET SOUTH
KITCHENER, ONTARIO N2G 2A9
(416) 578-9630

CARPANO INTERIORS
80 HANLAN ROAD
WOODBRIDGE, ONTARIO L4L 3P6
(416) 851-5552

CENTRAC INDUSTRIES LTD.
2650 ST. CLAIR AVENUE WEST
TORONTO, ONTARIO M6N 1M2
(416) 763-4551

CHARVOZ CANADA
151 TELSON ROAD
MARKHAM, ONTARIO L5R 1E7
(416) 479-4101

CODD AND COMPANY
160 PEARS AVENUE
TORONTO, ONTARIO M5R 1T2
(416) 923-0066

• **COLLIER FURNITURE LTD.**
1377 LAWRENCE AVENUE EAST
DON MILLS, ONTARIO M3A 3M4
(416) 449-7655 **Pg. 209**

CONTEMPORA DESIGNS INT'L INC.
887 YONGE STREET
TORONTO, ONTARIO M4W 2H2
(416) 964-9295

CRAFTWOOD PRODUCTS
191 FINCHDENE SQUARE
SCARBOROUGH, ONTARIO M1X 1E3
(416) 297-1100

CREATIVE CUSTOM FURNISHINGS INC.
134 OAKDALE ROAD
DOWNSVIEW, ONTARIO M3N 1V9
(416) 742-7450

CURTIS PRODUCTS LTD.
495 BALL STREET
COBOURG, ONTARIO K9A 4P9
(416) 372-2184

DAVID HUMPHREY INC.
411 RICHMOND STREET EAST
TORONTO, ONTARIO M5A 3S5
(416) 364-3887

DESIGN BASICS FURNITURE LTD.
409 QUEEN STREET
OTTAWA, ONTARIO K1R 5A6
(613) 235-7177

DESIGN FORUM
260 RICHMOND STREET WEST
TORONTO, ONTARIO M5V 1W5
(416) 977-0987

DUBARRY FURNITURE LTD.
23 CONNELL COURT
TORONTO, ONTARIO M8Z 1E8
(416) 251-2295

THE EMPORIUM
12 BIRCH AVENUE
TORONTO, ONTARIO M5V 1C8
(416) 923-0485

EPOCA INTERIORS
28 ATLANTIC AVENUE
TORONTO, ONTARIO M6K 1X8
(416) 530-4140

FAIR LINE PRODUCTS LTD.
551 WOODLAWN AVENUE
MISSISSAUGA, ONTARIO L5G 3K7
(416) 274-3616

FREEMAN MFG. LTD.
477 ELLESMERE ROAD
SCARBOROUGH, ONTARIO M1R 4E5
(416) 751-9633

GLOBALCARE
325 LIMESTONE CRESCENT
DOWNSVIEW, ONTARIO M3J 2R1
(416) 736-8700

• **GLOBAL UPHOLSTERY CO. LTD.**
560 SUPERTEST ROAD
DOWNSVIEW, ONTARIO M3J 2M6
(416) 661-3660 **Pg. 212**

GROUP FOUR FURNITURE INC.
25–5 CONNELL COURT
TORONTO, ONTARIO M8Z 1E8
(416) 251-1128

GUILDHALL CABINET SHOPS LTD.
11 JUTLAND ROAD
TORONTO, ONTARIO M8Z 2G6
(416) 255-3425

• **HARTER FURNITURE LTD.**
536 IMPERIAL ROAD
GUELPH, ONTARIO N1H 6L5
(519) 824-2850 **Pg. 213**

JOHN HAUSER IRON WORKS LTD.
148 BEDFORD ROAD
KITCHENER, ONTARIO N2G 3W9
(519) 744-1138

HERMAN MILLER CANADA, INC.
11 ADELAIDE STREET WEST
TORONTO, ONTARIO M5H 3Y4
(416) 366-3300

**INTERHOME
INTERNATIONAL FURNITURE**
8400 WOODBINE AVENUE
UNIONVILLE, ONTARIO
(416) 475-0705

INTERIORS PLUS
50 GALAXY BOULEVARD
REXDALE, ONTARIO M9W 4Y5
(416) 675-7993

• **JEFFREY-CRAIG LTD.**
763 WARDEN AVENUE
SCARBOROUGH, ONTARIO M1L 4B7
(416) 757-4154 **Pg. 216**

KEILHAUER INDUSTRIES LTD.
946 WARDEN AVENUE
TORONTO, ONTARIO M1L 4C9
(416) 759-5665

KINETICS FURNITURE
110 CARRIER DRIVE
REXDALE, ONTARIO M9W 5R1
(416) 675-4300

KNAPE & VOGT CANADA LTD.
340 CARLINGVIEW DRIVE
REXDALE, ONTARIO M9W 5G5
(416) 675-3451

• **KRUG FURNITURE INC.**
421 MANITOU DRIVE, P.O. BOX 9035
KITCHENER, ONTARIO N2G 4J3
(519) 893-1100 **Pg. 217**

LMJ EXECUTIVE FURNISHING LTD.
254 GARYRAY DRIVE
WESTON, ONTARIO M9L 1P1
(416) 746-1410

LOUIS INTERIORS INC.
120 ORFUS ROAD
TORONTO, ONTARIO M6A 1L9
(416) 785-9909

LUNDIA LTD.
209 MINETS POINT ROAD
BARRIE, ONTARIO L4N 4C2
(705) 737-5222

METALSMITHS COMPANY LTD.
431 ALDEN ROAD
MARKHAM, ONTARIO L3R 3R4
(416) 475-3380

MILNE & ASSOC. INC.
49 SPADINA AVENUE
TORONTO, ONTARIO M5V 2J1
(416) 591-9114

NICHOLLS & GILL LIMITED
479 RICHMOND STREET
LONDON, ONTARIO N6A 3E4
(519) 672-6001

SVEND NIELSEN LTD.
280 SIGNET DRIVE
WESTON, ONTARIO M9L 1V2
(416) 749-0131

NIENKAMPER
300 KING STREET EAST
TORONTO, ONTARIO M5A 1K4
(416) 362-3434

NORMAN CARRIERE AGENCIES INC.
478 QUEEN STREET EAST
TORONTO, ONTARIO M5A 1T7
(416) 363-1152

OFFICE SPECIALTY
322 KING STREET WEST
TORONTO, ONTARIO M5V 1J2
(416) 977-6007

PRISMATIQUE DESIGNS LTD.
265 DAVENPORT ROAD
TORONTO, ONTARIO M5R 1J9
(416) 961-7333

SCHAT IMPORT AGENCIES
P.O. BOX 202, STATION M
TORONTO, ONTARIO M6S 4T3
(416) 769-0812

SHAW-PEZZO & ASSOCIATES INC.
146 DUPONT ROAD
TORONTO, ONTARIO M5R 1V2
(416) 961-8213

SHEPHERD PRODUCTS LTD.
57 ESNA PARK DRIVE
MARKHAM, ONTARIO L3R 1C9
(416) 475-6454

• **SNYDER FURNITURE LTD.**
87 COLVILLE ROAD
TORONTO, ONTARIO M6M 2Y6
(416) 247-6285 **Pg. 222, 223**

STUDIO PLASTICS
329 DEERHIDE CRESCENT
TORONTO, ONTARIO M9M 2Z2
(416) 741-2119

• **TENDEX SILKO INC.**
264 THE ESPLANADE
TORONTO, ONTARIO M5A 4J6
(416) 361-1555 **Pg. 227**

THAMES VALLEY ANTIQUES
260 SPADINA AVENUE
TORONTO, ONTARIO M5T 2E4
(416) 596-8898

• **TRIEDE DESIGN INC.**
256 KING STREET EAST
TORONTO, ONTARIO M5A 1K3
(416) 367-0667 **Pg. 228, 229**

WESTNOFA OF CANADA LTD.
260 KING STREET EAST
TORONTO, ONTARIO M5A 1K3
(416) 362-5478

WOODRITES LTD.
940 QUEEN STREET WEST
TORONTO, ONTARIO M6J 1G8
(416) 532-9621

ZEST FURNITURE INDUSTRIES LTD.
75 BROWN'S LINE
TORONTO, ONTARIO M8W 3S5
(416) 255-2324

ZIGGURAT CONCEPT INC.
254 KING STREET EAST
TORONTO, ONTARIO M5A 1K3
(416) 362-5900

▶ WESTERN CANADA

ITALIA DESIGN OF CANADA
10357 – 109TH STREET
EDMONTON, AMLBERTA T5J 1N3
(403) 420-0270

• **K.P. MANUFACTURERS LTD.**
7403 30TH STREET SE
CALGARY, ALBERTA T2C 1N6
(403) 279-7727

SIMO DOW MANUFACTURING LTD.
3526 26TH STREET NE
CALGARY, ALBERTA T1Y 4T7
(403) 291-1133

WESTNOFA OF CANADA LTD.
691 GOLSPIE STREET
WINNIPEG, MANITOBA R2K 2V3
(204) 677-7106

▶ BRITISH COLUMBIA

INFORM INTERIORS INC.
97 WATER STREET
VANCOUVER, B.C. V6B 1A1
(604) 682-3868

LEE IMPORTERS LTD.
21 WATER STREET
VANCOUVER, B.C. V6B 1A1
(604) 681-5371

**SCALI DURANTE
FURNITURE MANUFACTURERS LTD.**
5371 REGENT STREET
BURNABY, B.C. V5C 4H4
(604) 291-7551

SWITZER, W. & ASSOCIATES LTD.
291 EAST 2ND AVENUE
VANCOUVER, B.C. V5T 1B6
(604) 255-5911

RESIDENTIAL

▶ QUEBEC

**AARKASH CHAIR
CO. OF CANADA LTD.**
1350 TELLIER STREET
LAVAL, QUEBEC H7C 2H2
(514) 661-1271

• **ALLIBERT LEISURE FURNITURE**
165, MONTE DE LIESSE
MONTREAL, QUEBEC H46 1T9
(514) 735-6255 **Pg. 271**

ALPHA VICO CAN. LTD.
1035 MAGENTA BOULEVARD EAST
MONTREAL, QUEBEC J2N 1B9
(514) 293-5354

ARTEMIDE LTD.
2408, RUE DE LA PROVINCE
LONGUEUIL, QUEBEC J4G 1G1
(514) 679-3717

**ATELIERS D'ARCHITECTURE
DUROCHER + PRATT, L'**
3643, RUE ST-LAURENT
MONTREAL, QUEBEC H2X 2V5
(514) 289-9348

BAUHAUS DESIGNS LTD.
85, RUE ST-PAUL OUEST
MONTREAL, QUEBEC H2Y 3V4
(514) 844-8812

• **BONAVENTURE
FURNITURE INDUSTRIES LTD.**
894 BLOOMFIELD
MONTREAL, QUEBEC H2V 3S6
(514) 270-7311 **Pg. 206**

CAMO FURNITURE INC.
3155 HOWARD
ST-HUBERT, QUEBEC J3Y 4Z5
(514) 676-8469

**CARREFOUR INTERNATIONAL
DU DESIGN**
4801, AVENUE DU PARC
MONTREAL, QUEBEC H2V 4E7
(514) 273-7222

CHATEAU D'AUJOURD'HUI, LE
1828, BOULEVARD LE CORBUSIER
LAVAL, QUEBEC H7S 2K1
(514) 382-4710

CODD & COMPANY
85, RUE ST-PAUL OUEST
MONTREAL, QUEBEC H2Y 3V4
(514) 844-6680

DOR-VAL MFG. LTD.
2760, BOULEVARD LAURENTIAN
ST-LAURENT, QUEBEC H4K 2E1
(514) 336-7780

EL RAN FURNITURE LTD.
8315 PLACE LORRAINE
VILLE D'ANJOU, QUEBEC H1J 1E5
(514) 354-1220

INTERNATIONAL UPHOLSTERY
5005 BUCHAN STREET
MONTREAL, QUEBEC H4P 1A1
(514) 735-1501

MAISON CORBEIL
5692-5700, RUE JEAN TALON EST
MONTREAL, QUEBEC H1S 1M2
(514) 254-9951

MEUBLES SITA INC., LES
8421 ALFRED BROSSEAU
MONTREAL, QUEBEC H1E 3H5
(514) 648-1115

MOBILIER FORME D INC.
346, RUE HAMFORD
LACHUTE, QUEBEC J8H 3Y1
(514) 562-5245

NOVELLA
646, RUE GIFFARD
LONGUEUIL, QUEBEC J4G 1T8
(514) 651-9133

PROULX FURNITURE
10367 ARMAND LAVERGNE
MONTREAL NORD, QUEBEC H1H 3N8
(514) 322-8010

• **SNYDER FURNITURE LTD.**
640, ST-PAUL OUEST
MONTREAL, QUEBEC H3C 1L9
(514) 866-0417 **Pg. 222, 223**

• **TRIEDE DESIGN INC.**
460 McGILL STREET
MONTREAL, QUEBEC H2Y 2H2
(514) 398-0602 **Pg. 228, 229**

▶ ONTARIO

• **ALLIBERT LEISURE FURNITURE**
260 KING STREET EAST
TORONTO, ONTARIO M5A 1K3
(416) 360-7949 **Pg. 271**

A.R.E.A
334 KING STREET EAST
TORONTO, ONTARIO M5A 1K8
(416) 367-5850

ABITARE DESIGN INC.
51 FRONT STREET EAST
TORONTO, ONTARIO M5E 1B3
(416) 363-1667

ALEXANDER'S FINE FURNITURE
2300 HAINES ROAD
MISSISSAUGA, ONTARIO L4Y 1Y6
(416) 987-3455

AMBIANT SYSTEMS LTD.
247 DAVENPORT ROAD
TORONTO, ONTARIO M5R 1J9
(416) 921-1900

ART SHOPPE
2131 YONGE STREET
TORONTO, ONTARIO M4S 2A6
(416) 487-3211

ARTEMIDE CANADA LTD.
160 PEARS AVENUE
TORONTO, ONTARIO M5R 1T2
(416) 960-3022

ATELIER D'OR, L'
487 LEWIS STREET
OTTAWA, ONTARIO K2P 0T2
(613) 563-3343

**ATWOOD'S,
AN ETHAN ALLEN GALLERY**
2161 DUNDAS STREET WEST
TORONTO, ONTARIO L5K 1R2
(416) 828-2264

BARRYMORE FURNITURE CO.
1137 KING STREET WEST
TORONTO, ONTARIO M6K 1E2
(416) 532-2891

BAUHAUS DESIGNS LTD.
895 FENMAR DRIVE
WESTON, ONTARIO M9L 1C8
(416) 742-5185

• **BONAVENTURE
FURNITURE INDUSTRIES LIMITED**
146 DUPONT STREET
TORONTO, ONTARIO M5R 1V2
(416) 961-5900 **Pg. 206**

BRUNSWICK MANUFACTURING CO. LTD.
25 CURITY AVENUE
TORONTO, ONTARIO M4B 3M2
(416) 755-3388

• **CHUNG DESIGNS**
722 QUEEN STREET WEST
TORONTO, ONTARIO M6J 1E6
(416) 862-8282 **Pg. 154, 155**

CODD AND COMPANY
160 PEARS AVENUE
TORONTO, ONTARIO M5R 1T2
(416) 923-0066

• **COLLIER FURNITURE LTD.**
1377 LAWRENCE AVENUE EAST
DON MILLS, ONTARIO M3A 3M4
(416) 449-7655 **Pg. 204**

CONCEPT B
388 CARLAW AVENUE
TORONTO, ONTARIO M4M 2T4
(416) 462-1700

CONTEMPORA DESIGNS INT'L INC.
887 YONGE STREET
TORONTO, ONTARIO M4W 2H2
(416) 964-9295

CRAFTWOOD PRODUCTS
191 FINCHDENE SQUARE
SCARBOROUGH, ONTARIO M1X 1E9
(416) 297-1100

CREATIVE CUSTOM FURNISHINGS INC.
134 OAKDALE ROAD
DOWNSVIEW, ONTARIO M3N 1V9
(416) 742-7450

DESIGN CONCEPTS INC.
20 MURAL STREET
RICHMOND HILL, ONTARIO L4B 1K3
(416) 764-3737

DESIGN COOPERATIVE, THE
135 TECUMSETH STREET
TORONTO, ONTARIO M6J 2H2
(416) 947-1684

DUBARRY FURNITURE LTD.
23 CONNELL COURT
TORONTO, ONTARIO M8Z 1E8
(416) 251-2295

EILEY, JOAN & ASSOCIATES LTD.
326 DAVENPORT ROAD
TORONTO, ONTARIO M5R 1K6
(416) 968-0778

EPOCA INTERIORS
28 ATLANTIC AVENUE
TORONTO, ONTARIO M6K 1X8
(416) 530-4140

GROUP FOUR FURNITURE INC.
25–5 CONNELL COURT
TORONTO, ONTARIO M8Z 1E8
(416) 251-1128

GUILDHALL CABINET SHOPS LTD.
11 JUTLAND ROAD
TORONTO, ONTARIO M8Z 2G6
(416) 255-3425

HABERT ASSOCIATES LTD.
321 DAVENPORT ROAD
TORONTO, ONTARIO M5R 1K5
(416) 960-5325

HERITAGE INTERIORS
244 DAVENPORT ROAD
TORONTO, ONTARIO M5R 1J7
(416) 922-6448

• **INTARC LIMITED**
147 DAVENPORT ROAD
TORONTO, ONTARIO M5R 1J1
(416) 924-7111 **Pg. 214**

• **INTERNA FURNITURE DESIGN LTD.**
76 SIGNET DRIVE
WESTON, ONTARIO M9L 1T2
(416) 741-4211 **Pg. 215**

ITALIA DESIGN OF CANADA
260 KING STREET EAST
TORONTO, ONTARIO M5A 1K3
(416) 365-7969

ITALINTERIORS LIMITED
359 KING STREET EAST
TORONTO, ONTARIO M5A 1L1
(416) 366-9540

• **JEFFREY-CRAIG LTD.**
763 WARDEN AVENUE
SCARBOROUGH, ONTARIO M1L 4B7
(416) 757-4153 **Pg. 216**

KAUFMAN OF COLLINGWOOD
190 BALSAM STREET
COLLINGWOOD, ONTARIO L9Y 3Y6
(705) 445-6000

KEILHAUER INDUSTRIES LTD.
946 WARDEN AVENUE
TORONTO, ONTARIO M1L 4C9
(416) 759-5665

• **KRUG FURNITURE INC.**
421 MANITOU DRIVE, P.O. BOX 9035
KITCHENER, ONTARIO N2G 4J3
(519) 893-1100 **Pg. 217**

LAQUE MARTIN
115 DUPONT STREET
TORONTO, ONTARIO M5R 1V4
(416) 967-0115

LOUIS INTERIORS INC.
120 ORFUS ROAD
TORONTO, ONTARIO M6A 1L9
(416) 789-9909

MARCUS, H.D. ENTERPRISES INC.
294 BERKELEY STREET
TORONTO, ONTARIO M5A 2X5
(416) 967-7617

METROPOLITAN COLLECTION, THE
24 ADMIRAL ROAD
TORONTO, ONTARIO M5R 2L5
(416) 961-9949

NICHOLLS & GILL LIMITED
479 RICHMOND STREET
LONDON, ONTARIO N6A 3E4
(519) 672-6001

NIENKAMPER
300 KING STREET EAST
TORONTO, ONTARIO M5A 1K4
(416) 362-3434

PALMA BRAVA
3050 YONGE STREET
TORONTO, ONTARIO M4N 2K4
(416) 488-5636

PRISMATIQUE DESIGNS LTD.
265 DAVENPORT ROAD
TORONTO, ONTARIO M5R 1J9
(416) 961-7333

RENAISSANCE INC.
146 DUPONT STREET
TORONTO, ONTARIO M5R 1V2
(416) 927-0126

ROCHNOR FURNITURE LTD.
80 HANLAN ROAD
WOODBRIDGE, ONTARIO L4L 3R7
(416) 851-1567

SAVOIA CHAIR FRAMES
P.O. BOX 189, STATION W
TORONTO, ONTARIO M6M 4Z2
(416) 244-4900

**SEBASTIAN DEL LORENZIS
CUSTOM FURNITURE LTD.**
505 HESPELER ROAD
CAMBRIDGE, ONTARIO N1R 6J2
(519) 623-0210

SHAW-PEZZO & ASSOCIATES INC.
146 DUPONT ROAD
TORONTO, ONTARIO M5R 1V2
(416) 961-8213

SHELAGH'S OF CANADA LTD.
354 DAVENPORT ROAD
TORONTO, ONTARIO M5R 1K6
(416) 924-7331

• **SNYDER FURNITURE LTD.**
87 COLVILLE ROAD
TORONTO, ONTARIO M6M 2Y6
(416) 247-6285 **Pg. 222, 223**

SUNARHAUSERMAN, LTD.
1 SUNSHINE AVENUE
WATERLOO, ONTARIO N2J 4K5
(519) 886-2000

SUPERIOR FINE FURNITURE
321 DAVENPORT ROAD
TORONTO, ONTARIO M5R 1K5
(416) 964-7227

• **TENDEX SILKO**
264 THE ESPLANADE
TORONTO, ONTARIO M5A 4J6
(416) 361-1555 **Pg. 227**

THAMES VALLEY ANTIQUES
260 SPADINA AVENUE
TORONTO, ONTARIO M5T 2E4
(416) 596-8898

• **TRIEDE DESIGN INC.**
256 KING STREET EAST
TORONTO, ONTARIO M5A 1K3
(416) 367-6667 **Pg. 228, 229**

VAN LEEUWEN BOOMKAMP LTD.
430 HAZELDEAN ROAD
KANATA, ONTARIO K2L 1T9
(613) 836-1400

WATTS, DIANE LTD.
160 PEARS AVENUE
TORONTO, ONTARIO M5R 1T2
(416) 961-2887

WINDSOR HOUSE COLLECTION
1311 ALNESS STREET
CONCORD, ONTARIO L4K 1E8
(416) 665-9300

ZIGGURAT CONCEPT INC.
254 KING STREET EAST
TORONTO, ONTARIO M5A 1K3
(416) 362-5900

▶ W E S T E R N   C A N A D A

ITALIA DESIGN OF CANADA
10357 – 109TH STREET
EDMONTON, ALBERTA T5J 1N3
(403) 420-0270

WESTNOFA OF CANADA LTD.
691 GOLSPIE STREET
WINNIPEG, MANITOBA R2K 2V3
(204) 677-7106

▶ B R I T I S H   C O L U M B I A

W. SWITZER & ASSOCIATES LTD.
291 EAST 2ND AVENUE
VANCOUVER, B.C. V5T 1B6
(604) 255-5911

LEATHER

ABITARE DESIGN INC.
51 FRONT STREET EAST
TORONTO, ONTARIO M5E 1B3
(416) 363-1667

ARCONAS CORPORATION
580 ORWELL STREET
MISSISSAUGA, ONTARIO L5A 3V7
(416) 272-0727

ART SHOPPE
2131 YONGE STREET
TORONTO, ONTARIO M4S 2A6
(416) 487-3211

ATWOOD'S EXECUTIVE OFFICE INTERIORS
110 BLOOR STREET WEST
TORONTO, ONTARIO M5S 2W7
(416) 968-0820

**ATWOOD'S
AN ETHAN ALLEN GALLERY**
2161 DUNDAS STREET WEST
TORONTO, ONTARIO L5K 1R2
(416) 828-2264

**ATWOOD'S
AN ETHAN ALLEN GALLERY**
8134 YONGE STREET
THORNHILL, ONTARIO L4J 1W4
(416) 889-7761

- **BONAVENTURE
FURNITURE INDUSTRIES INC.**
894 BLOOMFIELD
MONTREAL, QUEBEC H2V 3S6
(514) 270-7311 **Pg. 206**

CHATEAU D'AUJOURD'HUI, LE
1828, BOULEVARD LE CORBUSIER
LAVAL, QUEBEC H7S 2K1
(514) 382-4710

- **COLLIER FURNITURE LTD.**
1377 LAVRENCE AVENUE EAST
DON MILLS, ONTARIO M3A 3M4
(416) 449-7655 **Pg. 209**

**CONTEMPORA DESIGNS
INTERNATIONAL INC.**
887 YONGE STREET
TORONTO, ONTARIO M4W 2H2
(416) 964-9295

FRASER CONTRACT FURNITURE INC.
5525 COTE DE LIESSE
MONTREAL, QUEBEC H4P 1A1
(514) 748-7306

- **HARTER FURNITURE LTD.**
536 IMPERIAL ROAD
GUELPH, ONTARIO N1H 6L5
(519) 824-2850 **Pg. 213**

- **INTARC LTD.**
147 DAVENPORT ROAD
TORONTO, ONTARIO M5R 1J1
(416) 924-7111 **Pg. 214**

- **INTERNA FURNITURE DESIGN LTD.**
76 SIGNET DRIVE
WESTON, ONTARIO M9L 1T2
(416) 741-4211 **Pg. 215**

ITALIA DESIGN OF CANADA
10357 – 109 STREET
EDMONTON, ALBERTA T5J 1N3
(403) 420-0270

ITALINTERIORS LIMITED
359 KING STREET EAST
TORONTO, ONTARIO M5A 1L1
(416) 366-9540

KEILHAUER INDUSTRIES LTD.
946 WARDEN AVENUE
TORONTO, ONTARIO M1L 4C9
(416) 759-5665

METALSMITHS COMPANY LTD.
431 ALDEN ROAD
MARKHAM, ONTARIO L3R 3R4
(416) 475-3380

METROPOLITAN COLLECTION, THE
24 ADMIRAL ROAD
TORONTO, ONTARIO M5R 2L5
(416) 961-9949

NIENKAMPER
300 KING STREET EAST
TORONTO, ONTARIO M5A 1K4
(416) 362-3434

PRISMATIQUE DESIGNS LTD.
265 DAVENPORT ROAD
TORONTO, ONTARIO M5R 1J9
(416) 961-7333

REFF INCORPORATED
1000 ARROW ROAD
WESTON, ONTARIO M9M 2Y7
(416) 741-5453

ROCHNOR FURNITURE LTD.
80 HANLAN ROAD
WOODBRIDGE, ONTARIO L4L 3R7
(416) 851-1567

- **SNYDER FURNITURE LTD.**
87 COLVILLE ROAD
TORONTO, ONTARIO M6M 2Y6
(416) 247-6285 **Pg. 222, 223**

SUNARHAUSERMAN
1 SUNSHINE AVENUE
WATERLOO, ONTARIO N2J 4K5
(519) 886-2000

SWITZER, W. & ASSOCIATES LTD.
291 EAST 2ND AVENUE
VANCOUVER, B.C. V5T 1B6
(604) 872-7611

- **TENDEX SILKO INC.**
264 THE ESPLANADE
TORONTO, ONTARIO M5A 4J6
(416) 361-1555 **Pg. 227**

ZIGGURAT CONCEPT INC.
254 KING STREET EAST
TORONTO, ONTARIO M5A 1K3
(416) 362-5900

METAL

ABITARE DESIGN INC.
51 FRONT STREET EAST
TORONTO, ONTARIO M5E 1B3
(416) 363-1667

- **ALLSTEEL CANADA LTD.**
6505 TRANS CANADA HIGHWAY
ST. LAURENT, QUEBEC H4T 1S3
(514) 744-1120 **Pg. 202, 203**

AMBIANT SYSTEMS LTD.
247 DAVENPORT ROAD
TORONTO, ONTARIO M5R 1J9
(416) 921-1900

- **ARTOPEX INC.**
2121 BERLIER
LAVAL, QUEBEC H7L 3M9
(514) 332-4420 **Pg. 201**

ARTEMIDE LIMITED
2408 RUE DE LA PROVINCE
LONGUEUIL, QUEBEC J4G 1G1
(514) 679-3717

- **BILTRITE NIGHTINGALE INC.**
10251, BOULEVARD RAY LAWSON
MONTREAL, QUEBEC H1J 1L7
(514) 352-7770 **Pg. 205**

BUSINESS ACCESSORIES INC.
415 DUNDAS STREET
CAMBRIDGE, ONTARIO M4W 2H2
(416) 964-9295

**CONTRACT FURNITURE
REFINISHING LTD.**
431 ALDEN ROAD
MARKHAM, ONTARIO L3R 3R4
(416) 475-3666

ITALIA DESIGN OF CANADA
10357 – 109TH STREET
EDMONTON, ALBERTA T5J 1N3
(403) 420-0270

ITALINTERIORS LIMITED
359 KING STREET EAST
TORONTO, ONTARIO M5A 1L1
(416) 366-9540

METALSMITHS COMPANY LTD.
431 ALDEN ROAD
MARKHAM, ONTARIO L3R 3R4
(416) 475-3380

OFFICE SPECIALTY
322 KING STREET WEST
TORONTO, ONTARIO M5V 1J2
(416) 366-9540

STORWALL INTERNATIONAL INC.
156 FRONT STREET WEST
TORONTO, ONTARIO M5J 2L6
(416) 598-0716

- **TENDEX SILKO INC.**
264 THE ESPLANADE
TORONTO, ONTARIO M5A 4J6
(416) 361-1555 **Pg. 227**

- **TRIEDE DESIGN INC.**
460 McGILL STREET
MONTREAL, QUEBEC H2Y 2H2
(514) 398-0602 **Pg. 228, 229**

▶ ATLANTIC CANADA

LIGHTOLIER CANADA INC.
174 AMARANTH CRESCENT
DARTMOUTH, NOVA SCOTIA B2W 4B9
(902) 434-4520

H.G. ROGERS LTD.
87 GERMAIN STREET
SAINT JOHN, N.B. E2L 4S3
(506) 657-8350

▶ QUEBEC

ACTUEL 5 IMPORT DESIGN
550 SHERBROOKE WEST
MONTREAL, QUEBEC H3A 1B9
(514) 288-4833

• **ALLSTEEL CANADA LTD.**
6505 TRANS CANADA HIGHWAY
ST. LAURENT, QUEBEC H4T 1S3
(514) 744-1120   **Pg. 202, 203**

ANGLE INTERNATIONAL
296, ST. PAUL STREET
MONTREAL, QUEBEC H2Y 2A3
(514) 284-2619

APPELLO SALES & MARKETING INC.
13 LAKESIDE ROAD
KNOWLTON, QUEBEC J0E 1V0
(514) 534-3334

APRES L'EDEN
5201, RUE ST-DENIS
MONTREAL, QUEBEC H2J 2K9
(514) 844-0350

ARTEMIDE LTD.
2408 DE LA PROVINCE
LONGUEUIL, QUEBEC J4G 1G1
(514) 679-3717

BEACON LUMINAIRES INC.
4075 BOULEVARD ST-LAURENT
MONTREAL, QUEBEC H2W 1X7
(514) 845-0136

• **BONAVENTURE
FURNITURE INDUSTRIES LTD.**
894 BLOOMFIELD
MONTREAL, QUEBEC H2V 3S6
(514) 270-7311   **Pg. 206**

BILUMEN-LUTREX
1557, RUE BEGIN
VILLE ST-LAURENT, QUEBEC H4R 1W9
(514) 745-1085

CHATEAU D'AUJOURD'HUI, LE
1828, BOULEVARD LE CORBUSIER
LAVAL, QUEBEC H7S 2K1
(514) 382-4710

DANESCO OF CANADA LTD.
7200 ROUTE TRANSCANADIENNE
MONTREAL, QUEBEC H4T 1A3
(514) 735-5757

DESIGN FOCUS INC.
1000, RUE DE LA MONTAGNE
MONTREAL, QUEBEC H3G 1Y7
(514) 866-1893

DESIGNER'S I
1226 BISHOP STREET
MONTREAL, QUEBEC H3G 2E3
(514) 871-3931

LA GALERIE DE NEON
5042 ST-LAURENT
MONTREAL, QUEBEC H2T 1R7
(514) 276-6984

IMPORTATIONS VOLT, LES
283 LAURIER OUEST
MONTREAL, QUEBEC H2V 2K1
(514) 279-8478

INTALITE INC.
9855 MEILEUR STREET
MONTREAL, QUEBEC H3L 3J6
(514) 382-2793

JOHNSON-LAZARE (CANADA) LTD.
7310 MT. SIGHTS AVENUE
MONTREAL, QUEBEC H4P 2A6
(514) 731-3763

LIGHTOLIER CANADA LTD.
3015 LOUIS A. AMOS
LACHINE, QUEBEC H8T 1C4
(514) 636-0670

**L'IMAGE, A DIVISION OF
CLEVEMONT INDUSTRIES LTD.**
8155 LARRY STREET
VILLE D'ANJOU, QUEBEC H1J 2L5
(514) 353-8762

LUCI LIGHTING LTD.
646 GIFFARD STREET
LONGUEUIL, QUEBEC J4G 1T8
(514) 651-9192

LUMEC INC.
618, BOULEVARD CURE BOIVIN
BOISBRIAND, QUEBEC J7G 2A7
(514) 430-7040

LUMICAN INC.
BOX 266
KNOWLTON, QUEBEC J0E 1V0
(514) 243-6854

LUTREX
204 LAURIER OUEST
MONTREAL, QUEBEC H2T 2N8
(514) 270-5133

LUXO LAMP LTD.
P.O. BOX 460
STE-THERESE, QUEBEC J7E 4J9
(514) 435-1971

MAISON CORBEIL
5692-5700, RUE JEAN TALON EST
MONTREAL, QUEBEC H1S 1M2
(514) 254-9951

NOVELLA
646, RUE GIFFARD
LONGUEUIL, QUEBEC J4G 1T8
(514) 651-9133

PRECISION MFG. INC.
2200 – 52ND AVENUE
LACHINE, QUEBEC H8T 2Y6
(514) 631-2120

QUARTZ
5103, RUE ST-LAURENT
MONTREAL, QUEBEC H2T 1R9
(514) 270-7532

SCANGIFT LTD.
10245 COTE DE LIESSE
DORVAL, QUEBEC H9P 1A3
(514) 631-6703

S. THAU INC.
4537 DROLET STREET
MONTREAL, QUEBEC H2T 2G3
(514) 845-1186

• **TRIEDE DESIGN INC.**
460 McGILL STREET
MONTREAL, QUEBEC H2Y 2H2
(514) 288-0063   **Pg. 228, 229**

VENAIR DISTRIBUTING INC.
7950 ALFRED STREET
ANJOU, QUEBEC H1J 1J1
(514) 354-2230

VOLT ERE
281, AVENUE LAURIER OUEST
MONTREAL, QUEBEC H2V 2K1
(514) 279-8477

▶ ONTARIO

ABITARE DESIGN INC.
51 FRONT STREET EAST
TORONTO, ONTARIO M5E 1B3
(416) 363-1667

• **AID 2000**
101 FRESHWAY DRIVE
CONCORD, ONTARIO L9K 1R9
(416) 661-6433   **Pg. 235**

• **ALLSTEEL CANADA LTD.**
207 QUEEN'S QUAY WEST
TORONTO, ONTARIO M5J 1A7
(416) 367-5880   **Pg. 202,203**

ARTEMIDE LTD.
160 PEARS AVENUE
TORONTO, ONTARIO M5R 1T2
(416) 960 3022

ATELIER D'OR, L'
487 LEWIS STREET
OTTAWA, ONTARIO K2P 0T2
(613) 563-3343

**ATWOOD'S
EXECUTIVE OFFICE INTERIORS**
110 BLOOR STREET WEST
TORONTO, ONTARIO M5S 2W7
(416) 968-0820

**ATWOOD'S,
AN ETHAN ALLEN GALLERY**
2161 DUNDAS STREET WEST
TORONTO, ONTARIO L5K 1R2
(416) 828-2264

ATWOOD'S,
AN ETHAN ALLEN GALLERY
8134 YONGE STREET
THORNHILL, ONTARIO L4J 1W4
(416) 889-7761

• **AU COURANT**
354 DAVENPORT ROAD
TORONTO, ONTARIO M5R 1K6
(416) 922-5611 **Pg. 236**

• **AXIS INTERIORS**
25 WATLINE AVENUE
MISSISSAUGA, ONTARIO L4Z 2Z1
(416) 568-0200 **Pg. 204**

C & M PRODUCTS LTD.
189 BULLOCK DRIVE
MARKHAM, ONTARIO L3P 1W4
(416) 294-9570

CANADIAN GENERAL ELECTRIC
2300 MEADOWVALE BOULEVARD
MISSISSAUGA, ONTARIO L5N 5P9
(416) 858-5390

CAN LYTE CENTRE
160 PEARS AVENUE
TORONTO, ONTARIO M5R 1T2
(416) 960-1400

CONTEMPORA DESIGNS INTL. INC.
887 YONGE STREET
TORONTO, ONTARIO M4N 3N6
(416) 964-9295

DAVID HUMPHREY INC.
411 RICHMOND STREET EAST
TORONTO, ONTARIO M5A 3S5
(416) 364-3887

DESIGN CONCEPTS INC.
20 MURAL STREET
RICHMOND HILL, ONTARIO L4B 1K3
(416) 764-3737

ENGELITE LIGHTING
777 RICHMOND STREET WEST
TORONTO, ONTARIO M6J 1C8
(416) 366-2843

• **INTEFAC INC.**
255 MATHESON BOULEVARD
MISSISSAUGA, ONTARIO L5R 3G3
(416) 624-6700 **Pg. 143**

GALAXY LIGHTING
110 JARDIN DRIVE, UNIT 4
CONCORD, ONTARIO L4K 2T7
(416) 669-6990

JOHN HAUSER IRON WORKS LTD.
148 BEDFORD ROAD
KITCHENER, ONTARIO N2G 3W9
(519) 744-1138

HOLOPHANE
1620 STEELES AVENUE EAST
BRAMPTON, ONTARIO L6T 1A5
(416) 793-3111

• **INTARC LTD.**
147 DAVENPORT ROAD
TORONTO, ONTARIO M5R 1J1
(416) 924-7111 **Pg. 214**

INTEGRATED A.V. & LIGHTING
132 BERKELEY STREET
TORONTO, ONTARIO M4H 1J9
(416) 477-2275

ITALIA DESIGN OF CANADA
260 KING STREET EAST
TORONTO, ONTARIO M5A 1K3
(416) 365-7969

ITALINTERIORS LIMITED
359 KING STREET EAST
TORONTO, ONTARIO M5A 1L1
(416) 366-9540

JOHNSON, CRAIG & ASSOCIATES INC.
110 DAVENPORT ROAD
TORONTO, ONTARIO M5R 1H7
(416) 975-1867

LIGHTOLIER CANADA INC.
488 COLONNADE ROAD
NEPEAN, ONTARIO K2K 7S6
(613) 828-8899

LOOMIS & TOLES CO. LTD.
214 ADELAIDE STREET WEST
TORONTO, ONTARIO M5H 1W7
(416) 977-8877

MILNE & ASSOCIATES
49 SPADINA AVENUE
TORONTO, ONTARIO M5V 2J1
(416) 591-9114

NIENKAMPER
300 KING STREET EAST
TORONTO, ONTARIO M5A 1K4
(416) 298-5700

PHASE THREE AUDIO & LIGHTING
358 QUEEN STREET EAST
TORONTO, ONTARIO M5A 1T1
(416) 865-1161

• **PHILIPS ELECTRONICS LTD.**
601 MILNER AVENUE
SCARBOROUGH, ONTARIO M1B 1M8
(416) 691-7372 **Pg. 237**

PRIMAVERA
INTERIOR ACCESSORIES LTD.
160 PEARS AVENUE
TORONTO, ONTARIO M5R 1T2
(416) 921-3334

PRISMATIQUE DESIGNS LTD.
265 DAVENPORT STREET
TORONTO, ONTARIO M5R 1J9
(416) 961-7333

QUASI MODO
789 QUEEN STREET WEST
TORONTO, ONTARIO M6J 1G1
(416) 485-3000

QUINTESSENCE DESIGNS
1657 BAYVIEW AVENUE
TORONTO, ONTARIO M4G 3C1
(416) 482-1252

RAAK LIGHTING OF CANADA LTD.
147 CHURCH STREET
TORONTO, ONTARIO M5B 1Y4
(416) 863-1990

REVEL LUMINAIRES LTD.
381 RICHMOND STREET EAST
TORONTO, ONTARIO M5A 1P6
(416) 364-6500

SESCOLITE LIGHTING
1461 CASTLEFIELD AVENUE
TORONTO, ONTARIO M6M 1Y4
(416) 651-6570

SHAW – PEZZO & ASSOCIATES INC.
146 DUPONT STREET
TORONTO, ONTARIO M5R 1V2
(416) 961-8213

SINGER LIGHTING
201 CARLAW AVENUE
TORONTO, ONTARIO M4M 2S3
(416) 461-0291

STAFF LIGHTING INC.
381 RICHMOND STREET EAST
TORONTO, ONTARIO M5A 1P6
(416) 364-6501

STUDIO AZZURRO
2533 YONGE STREET
TORONTO, ONTARIO M4P 2H9
(416) 485-3000

SYSTEMA LUCE
6325 DIXIE ROAD
MISSISSAUGA, ONTARIO L5T 2E5
(416) 670-1322

SYSTEMALUX
251 KING STREET EAST
TORONTO, ONTARIO M5A 1K2
(416) 362-9611

• **TENDEX SILKO**
264 THE ESPLANADE
TORONTO, ONTARIO M5A 4J6
(416) 361-1555 **Pg. 227**

• **TRIEDE DESIGN INC.**
256 KING STREET EAST
TORONTO, ONTARIO M5A 1K3
(416) 941-9666 **Pg. 228, 229**

ZIGGURAT CONCEPT INC.
254 KING STREET EAST
TORONTO, ONTARIO M5A 1K3
(416) 362-5900

▶ W E S T E R N   C A N A D A

ITALIA DESIGN OF CANADA
10357 – 109 STREET
EDMONTON, ALBERTA T5J 1N3
(403) 420-0270

NON-NEON MAGIC
P.O. BOX 3136
WINNIPEG, MANITOBA R3C 4E6
(204) 452-8606

UNO DESIGN GROUP
850 – 16TH AVENUE SW
CALGARY, ALBERTA T2R 0S9
(403) 245-8663

INFORM INTERIORS INC.
97 WATER STREET
VANCOUVER, B.C. V6B 1A1
(604) 682-3668

LANE INDUSTRIES LTD.
5558 LANE
BURNABY, B.C.
(604) 437-4454

LEE IMPORTERS LTD.
21 STREET, 3RD FLOOR
VANCOUVER, B.C. V6B 1A1
(604) 681-5371

LIGHTINGLAND
551 WEST BROADWAY
VANCOUVER, B.C.
(604) 879-6377

LIGHTOLIER CANADA INC.
157 – 10551 SHELLBRIDGE WAY
RICHMOND, B.C.
(604) 273-7732

MAXILITE MANUFACTURING LTD.
3008 SPRING
PORT MOODY, B.C.
(604) 461-4747

NORBURN LIGHTING CENTER
4600 EAST HASTINGS
BURNABY, B.C.
(604) 299-0666

W. SWITZER & ASSOCIATES LTD.
291 EAST 2ND AVENUE
VANCOUVER, B.C. V5T 1B6
(604) 255-5911

▶ QUEBEC

- **ALLSTEEL CANADA LTD.**
  3500 COTE VERTU
  MONTREAL, QUEBEC H4R 1R1
  (514) 334-0150 **Pg. 202, 203**

  APPELLO SALES & MARKETING INC.
  103 LAKESIDE ROAD
  KNOWLTON, QUEBEC J0E 1V0
  (514) 534-3334

- **ARTOPEX INC.**
  2121, RUE BERLIER
  LAVAL, QUEBEC H7L 3M9
  (514) 332-4420 **Pg. 201**

- **BILTRITE NIGHTINGALE INC.**
  10251, BOULEVARD RAY LAWSON
  MONTREAL, QUEBEC H1J 1L7
  (514) 352-7770 **Pg. 205**

  HAWORTH OFFICE SYSTEMS, LTD.
  2000 McGILL COLLEGE AVENUE
  MONTREAL, QUEBEC H3A 3H3
  (514) 842-2622

  MASONITE CANADA LTD.
  418 GOLF AVENUE
  GATINEAU, QUEBEC J8R 6K2
  (819) 633-5331

  PRECISION MFG. INC.
  2200 – 52ND AVENUE
  LACHINE, QUEBEC H8T 2Y6
  (514) 631-2120

- **TELLA SYSTEMS**
  161 STERLING AVENUE
  LA SALLE, QUEBEC H8R 3P3
  (514) 364-0511 **Pg. 226**

▶ ONTARIO

- **ALLSTEEL CANADA LTD.**
  207 QUEEN'S QUAY WEST
  TORONTO, ONTARIO M5J 1A7
  (416) 367-5880 **Pg. 202, 203**

- **ARMSTRONG WORLD INDUSTRIES CANADA LTD.**
  2233 ARGENTIA ROAD
  MISSISSAUGA, ONTARIO L5N 2X7
  (416) 826-4832 **Pg. 243**

- **ARTOPEX INC.**
  10 LOWER SPADINA AVENUE
  TORONTO, ONTARIO M5V 2Z2
  (416) 593-0111 **Pg. 201**

- **BILTRITE NIGHTINGALE INC.**
  2301 DIXIE ROAD
  MISSISSAUGA, ONTARIO L4Y 1Z9
  (416) 896-3434 **Pg. 205**

  CANADIAN GYPSUM COMPANY LTD.
  777 BAY STREET
  TORONTO, ONTARIO M5W 1A7
  (416) 595-8800

COLE BUSINESS FURNITURE DIV. OF JOYCE FURNITURE INC.
1865 BIRCHMOUNT ROAD
SCARBOROUGH, ONTARIO M1P 2J5
(416) 293-8221

CONTRACT FURNITURE REFINISHING LTD.
431 ALDEN ROAD
MARKHAM, ONTARIO L3R 3R4
(416) 475-3666

GILLANDERS
33 ATOMIC AVENUE
ETOBICOKE, ONTARIO M8Z 5T2
(416) 259-5446

- **GLOBAL UPHOLSTERY CO. LTD.**
  560 SUPERTEST ROAD
  DOWNSVIEW, ONTARIO M3J 2M6
  (416) 661-3660 **Pg. 212**

- **HARTER FURNITURE**
  536 IMPERIAL ROAD
  GUELPH, ONTARIO N1H 6L5
  (519) 824-2850 **Pg. 213**

  HAWORTH OFFICE SYSTEMS, LTD.
  33 YONGE STREET
  TORONTO, ONTARIO M5E 1G4
  (416) 363-0702

  HERMAN MILLER CANADA, INC.
  11 ADELAIDE STREET W.
  TORONTO, ONTARIO M5H 3Y2
  (416) 366-3300

  DAMPA INC.
  1285 MORNINGSIDE AVENUE
  SCARBOROUGH, ONTARIO M1B 3W2
  (416) 438-9640

  INTERHOME INTERNATIONAL FURNITURE
  8400 WOODBINE AVENUE
  UNIONVILLE, ONTARIO
  (416) 475-0705

  GEIGER INTERNATIONAL LTD.
  180 NORELCO DRIVE
  WESTON, ONTARIO M9L 1S4
  (416) 745-4000

  KAUFMAN OF COLLINGWOOD
  190 BALSAM STREET
  COLLINGWOOD, ONTARIO L9Y 3Y6
  (416) 445-6000

- **KRUG FURNITURE INC.**
  421 MANITOU DRIVE, P.O. BOX 9035
  KITCHENER, ONTARIO N2G 4J3
  (519) 893-1100 **Pg. 217**

  RAM PARTITION, DIV. INDAL LTD.
  350 CLAYSON
  WESTON, ONTARIO M9M 2G5
  (416) 745-2244

  REFF INCORPORATED
  1000 ARROW ROAD
  WESTON, ONTARIO M9M 2Y7
  (416) 741-5453

STEELCASE CANADA LTD.
7200 WOODBINE AVENUE
MARKHAM, ONTARIO L3R 1A2
(416) 475-6333

- **STRETCHWALL + CANADA LTD.**
  2215 MIDLAND AVENUE
  SCARBOROUGH, ONTAIO M1P 3E7
  (416) 297-8672 **Pg. 242**

  SUNARHAUSERMAN
  1 SUNSHINE AVENUE
  WATERLOO, ONTARIO N2J 4K5
  (519) 886-2000

  SUNWALL OF CANADA
  195 WALKER DRIVE
  BRAMPTON, ONTARIO L6T 3Z9
  (416) 791-8788

- **TEKNION FURNITURE SYSTEMS INC.**
  1150 FLINT ROAD
  DOWNSVIEW, ONTARIO M3J 2J5
  (416) 661-3370 **Pg. 224, 225**

- **TELLA SYSTEMS INC.**
  124 BERMONDSEY ROAD
  TORONTO, ONTARIO M5A 1X5
  (416) 752-7750 **Pg. 226**

▶ WESTERN CANADA

ARTMET
15935 114TH AVENUE
EDMONTON, ALBERTA T5M 2Z3
(403) 452-7522

SMED MANUFACTURING INC.
4315 – 54TH AVENUE SE
CALGARY, ALBERTA T2C 2A2
(403) 279-1400

- **ALPHA GLASS AND MIRROR**
1670 MIDLAND AVENUE
SCARBOROUGH, ONTARIO M1P 3C2
(416) 752-6370 **Pg. 260, 261**

BEAUMARK MIRROR PRODUCTS
1490 BIRCHMOUNT ROAD
SCARBOROUGH, ONTARIO M1P 2E3
(416) 752-8772

C.L.O. GLASS LTD.
237 TORYORK DRIVE
WESTON, ONTARIO M9L 1Y2
(416) 749-6161

CAMBRIAN GLASS
176 NOLIN STREET
SUDBURY, ONTARIO P3C 2U3
(705) 674-7571

- **CLASSIC CRYSTAL LTD.**
50 DRUMLIN CIRCLE
CONCORD, ONTARIO L4K 3G1
(416) 738-2073 **Pg. 259**

- **DESIGN AG**
1 SULTAN STREET
TORONTO, ONTARIO M5S 1L6
(416) 963-9422 **Pg. 263**

- **E.J.B. GLASSWORKS LTD.**
1-1244 CARTWRIGHT STREET
VANCOUVER, B.C. V6H 3R9
(604) 684-8332 **Pg. 262**

GELLMAN, MIMI – GLASS DESIGNER
517 WELLINGTON STREET WEST
TORONTO, ONTARIO M5V 1G1
(416) 593-8494

INKAN
14 INDELL LANE
BRAMPTON, ONTARIO L6T 3Y3
(416) 793-4747

ITALIA DESIGN OF CANADA
1357 – 109TH STREET
EDMONTON, ALBERTA T5J 1N3
(403) 420-0270

LALIQUE DESIGNERS INC.
73 ALNESS STREET
DOWNSVIEW, ONTARIO M3J 2H2
(416) 665-0434

QUALITY CRYSTAL
35 EAST BEAVER CREEK
RICHMOND HILL, ONTARIO L4B 1B3
(416) 764-0777

SGO CUSTOM GLASS WORKS
2700 DUFFERIN STREET
TORONTO, ONTARIO M6B 3R1
(416) 440-0140

- **VAST INTERIORS**
96 BOWES ROAD
CONCORD, ONTARIO L4K 1J7
(416) 738-1170 **Pg. 264, 265**

VIVAFORM INC.
1364, AVENUE GREEN
MONTREAL, QUEBEC H3Z 2B1
(514) 931-5520

► QUEBEC

APPELLO SALES & MARKETING INC.
103 LAKESIDE ROAD
KNOWLTON, QUEBEC J0E 1V0
(514) 534-3334

AVAN-GARDE FABRICS LTD.
7955, RUE ALFRED
VILLE D'ANJOU, QUEBEC H1J 1J3
1-(800) 361-8886

**CONNAISSANCE FABRICS &
WALLCOVERINGS LTD.**
1632 SHERBROOKE STREET WEST
MONTREAL, QUEBEC H3H 2L4
(514) 931-2437

J.T. DILLON DECOR
555 CHABANEL
MONTREAL, QUEBEC H2N 2H8
(514) 384-7440

EGAN-LAING INC.
204, PLACE D'YOUVILLE
MONTREAL, QUEBEC H2Y 2B4
(514) 288-6122

MASONITE CANADA LTD.
418 GOLF AVENUE
GATINEAU, QUEBEC J8R 6K2
(819) 633-5331

NOVAX WALLCOVERINGS
740 PLACE TRANS-CANADA
LONGUEUIL, QUEBEC J4G 1P1
(514) 651-7120

SICO INC.
740 PLACE TRANS-CANADA
LONGUEUIL, QUEBEC J4G 1P1
(514) 651-0273

TELIO & CIE.
1407, RUE DE LA MONTAGNE
MONTREAL, QUEBEC H3G 1Z3
(514) 842-9116

VAL ABEL TEXTILES LTD.
55 MT. ROYAL AVENUE WEST
MONTREAL, QUEBEC H2T 2S6
(514) 842-9503

► ONTARIO

BARWOOD SALES (ONTARIO) LTD.
220 MIDWEST ROAD
SCARBOROUGH, ONTARIO M1P 3A9
(416) 751-7811

BAUMANN FABRICS LTD.
302 KING STREET EAST
TORONTO, ONTARIO M5A 1K6
(416) 869-1221

W.H. BILBROUGH & CO. LTD.
326 DAVENPORT ROAD
TORONTO, ONTARIO M5R 1K6
(416) 960-1611

BRUNSCHWIG & FILS
320 DAVENPORT ROAD
TORONTO, ONTARIO M5R 1K6
(416) 968-0699

CANADIAN GENERAL TOWER
457 REYNOLDS STREET
OAKVILLE, ONTARIO L6J 5C8
(416) 844-3213

CROWN WALLPAPER CO.
88 RONSON DRIVE
REXDALE, ONTARIO M9W 1B9
(416) 245-2900

DECOUSTICS
65 DISCO ROAD
ETOBICOKE, ONTARIO M9W 1M2
(416) 675-3983

EGAN LAING LTD.
1067 WESTPORT CRESCENT
MISSISSAUGA, ONTARIO L5T 1E8
(416) 670-1100

FABRA-WALL
3464 KINGSTON ROAD
SCARBOROUGH, ONTARIO M1M 1R5
(416) 269-5757

• **FABRICS INTERNATIONAL**
1090 AEROWOOD DRIVE
MISSISSAUGA, ONTARIO L4W 1Y5
(416) 624-5104 **Pg. 239**

B.F. GOODRICH CANADA INC.
409 WEBER STREET NORTH
KITCHENER, ONTARIO N2H 4B1
(519) 742-3641

GREEFF FABRICS INC.
170 BEDFORD ROAD
TORONTO, ONTARIO M5R 2K9
(416) 960-8222

HABERT ASSOCIATES LTD.
321 DAVENPORT ROAD
TORONTO, ONTARIO M5R 1K5
(416) 960-5323

INTERNATIONAL WALLCOVERINGS
151 EAST DRIVE
BRAMALEA, ONTARIO L6T 1B5
(416) 791-1547

JEFF BROWN FINE FABRICS LTD.
1785 ARGENTIA ROAD
MISSISSAUGA, ONTARIO L5N 3A2
(416) 821-3666

JOHNSON, CRAIG & ASSOCIATES INC.
110 DAVENPORT ROAD
TORONTO, ONTARIO M5R 1H7
(416) 975-1867

KOBE FABRICS LTD.
5380 SOUTH SERVICE RD., P.O. BOX 939
BURLINGTON, ONTARIO L7R 3Y7
(416) 639-2730

LAURII TEXTILES
354 DAVENPORT ROAD
TORONTO, ONTARIO M5R 1K6
(416) 922-5514

McFADDEN HARDWOODS LTD.
2650 RENA ROAD
MISSISSAUGA, ONTARIO L4T 3C8
(416) 677-4272

MILNE & ASSOC. INC.
170 ROSEWELL AVENUE
TORONTO, ONTARIO M4R 2A6
(416) 322-5533

MORBERN INC.
80 BOUNDARY ROAD
CORNWALL, ONTARIO K6H 5V3
(613) 932-8811

ONTARIO WALLCOVERINGS
462 FRONT STREET WEST
TORONTO, ONTARIO M5V 1B6
(416) 593-4519

PRIDE OF PARIS FABRICS LTD.
WEST RIVER STREET, BOX 130
PARIS, ONTARIO N3L 3E9
(519) 443-6351

**PRIMAVERA
INTERIOR ACCESSORIES LTD.**
160 PEARS AVENUE
TORONTO, ONTARIO M5R 1T2
(416) 921-3334

RODA WALLCOVERINGS LTD.
80 TYCOS DRIVE
TORONTO, ONTARIO M6B 1V9
(416) 782-1168

• **RODGERS WALLCOVERINGS LIMITED**
415 HORNER AVENUE
TORONTO, ONTARIO M8W 2A5
(416) 253-1600 **Pg. 241**

SAMO TEXTILES LTD.
67 ST. REGIS CRESCENT NORTH
DOWNSVIEW, ONTARIO M3J 1Y9
(416) 636-7273

SAMO INTERNATIONAL
320 DAVENPORT ROAD
TORONTO, ONTARIO M5R 1K6
(416) 920-3020

SANDERSON & SON
320 DAVENPORT ROAD
DOWNSVIEW, ONTARIO M5R 1K6
(416) 323-1168

• **STRETCHWALL + CANADA LTD.**
2215 MIDLAND AVENUE
SCARBOROUGH, ONTARIO M1P 3E7
(416) 297-8672 **Pg. 242**

SUNWORTHY WALLCOVERINGS
195 WALKER DRIVE
BRAMPTON, ONTARIO L6T 3Z9
(416) 791-8788

TELIO & CO.
113 DUPONT STREET
TORONTO, ONTARIO M5R 1V4
(416) 968-2020

VICRTEX, L.E. CARPENTER CO.
1200 AEROWOOD DRIVE
MISSISSAUGA, ONTARIO L4W 2S7
(416) 624-4614

WALTER L. BROWN LTD.
17 VICKERS ROAD
TORONTO, ONTARIO M9B 1C2
(416) 231-4499

▶ WESTERN CANADA

ITALIA DESIGN OF CANADA
10357–109TH STREET
EDMONTON, ALBERTA T5J 1N3
(403)420-0270

▶ BRITISH COLUMBIA

CROWN WALLPAPER CO.
910 WEST, 6TH STREET
VANCOUVER, B.C.
(604) 736-4541

DAYCOR WEST WALLCOVERINGS
2131 BURRARD STREET
VANCOUVER, B.C.
(604) 731-4174

DESIGN SOURCE INTERNATIONAL LTD.
923 WEST, 8TH STREET
VANCOUVER, B.C.
(604) 733-1714

ODISSEY DESIGN PRODUCTS LTD.
1310 WEST 6TH STREET
VANCOUVER, B.C.
(604) 734-7667

SELECT WALL COVERINGS LTD.
106 EAST, 7TH STREET
VANCOUVER, B.C.
(604) 872-8181

WALTER L. BROWN LTD.
911 HOMER STREET
VANCOUVER, B.C.
(604) 683-2564

TILES

▶ QUEBEC

APPELLO SALES & MARKETING INC.
103 LAKESIDE ROAD
KNOWLTON, QUEBEC J0E 1V0
(514) 534-3334

CERATEC INC.
414, ST-SACREMENT
QUEBEC, QUEBEC G1N 3Y3
(418) 681-0101

ENTREPRISES TUILES MONGIAT
10972 ESPLANADE
MONTREAL, QUEBEC H3L 2Y6
(514) 331-4761

MASONITE CANADA LTD.
418 GOLF AVENUE
GATINEAU, QUEBEC J8R 6K2
(819) 633-5331

NORTRA DISTRIBUTIONS
5375 DES GRANDES PRAIRIES
ST-LEONARD, QUEBEC H1R 1B1
(514) 326-0062

PROMOSTYLE INTERNATIONAL INC.
6969 TRANS-CANADA HWY., SUITE 121
ST-LAURENT, QUEBEC H4T 1V8
(514) 336-3646

• RAMCA TILES LTD.
1085 AVENUE VAN HORNE
MONTREAL, QUEBEC H2V 1J6
(514) 270-9192 **Pg. 252**

WORLD MOSAIC INC.
9545 ST. LAWRENCE BLVD.
MONTREAL, QUEBEC
(514) 388-1118

▶ ONTARIO

ACME SLATE & TILE CO. LTD.
21 GOLDEN GATE COURT
SCARBOROUGH, ONTARIO M1P 3A4
(416) 293-3664

CENTRAL SUPPLY
53 APEX ROAD
TORONTO, ONTARIO M6A 2V6
(416) 785-5165

COUNTRY TILES
321 DAVENPORT ROAD
TORONTO, ONTARIO M5R 1K5
(416) 922-9214

FERLEO IMPORT-EXPORT CO. LTD.
315 HUMBERLINE DRIVE
REXDALE, ONTARIO M9W 5T6
(416) 675-0075

• FORMGLAS INC.
250 RAYETTE INC.
CONCORD, ONTARIO L4K 2G6
(416) 669-5111 **Pg. 270**

• MARBLE TREND LTD.
710 ROWNTREE DAIRY ROAD
WOODBRIDGE, ONTARIO L4L 5T7
(416) 738-0400 **Pg. 251**

NEW ENGLAND SLATE LTD.
P.O. BOX 503
ST. CATHARINES, ONTARIO L2R 6V9
(416) 892-5793

OLYMPIA FLOOR AND WALL TILE CO.
1000 LAWRENCE AVENUE WEST
TORONTO, ONTARIO
(416) 789-4122

ONTARIO CORK CO. LTD.
26 ASHWARREN ROAD
TORONTO, ONTARIO M3J 1Z5
(416) 630-9702

PHOENIX FLOOR & WALL PRODUCTS
111 WESTMORE DRIVE
REXDALE, ONTARIO M9V 3Y6
(416) 745-4200

• QUARELLA INC.
135 EAST BEAVER CREEK
RICHMOND HILL, ONTARIO L4B 1E2
(416) 764-0141 **Pg. 251**

• RAMCA TILES LTD.
354 DAVENPORT ROAD
TORONTO, ONTARIO M5R 1K6
(416) 781-5521 **Pg. 252**

ROCKFORD MARBLE CENTRE LTD.
160 PEARS AVENUE
TORONTO, ONTARIO M5R 1T2
(416) 922-6122

STEPTOE & WIFE ANTIQUES LTD.
322 GEARY AVENUE
TORONTO, ONTARIO M6H 2C7
(416) 530-4200

• T.M.T. MARBLE SUPPLY LTD.
900 KEELE STREET
TORONTO, ONTARIO M6N 3E7
(416) 653-6111 **Pg. 253**

THAMES VALLEY BRICK & TILE
14 DORCHESTER AVENUE
TORONTO, ONTARIO M8Z 4W3
(416) 252-5811

▶ ATLANTIC CANADA

**ATLANTIC
VENETIAN BLINDS AND DRAPERIES LTD.**
22 WADDELL AVENUE
DARTMOUTH, NOVA SCOTIA B3B 1K3
(902) 463-2263

▶ QUEBEC

AVANT-GARDE FABRICS LTD.
7955, RUE ALFRED
VILLE D'ANJOU, QUEBEC H1J 1J3
1-(800) 361-8886

**CONNAISSANCE
FABRICS & WALLCOVERINGS LTD.**
1632 SHERBROOKE STREET WEST
MONTREAL, QUEBEC H3H 1C9
(514) 931-2437

DRACO LTD.
605, BOULEVARD IBERVILLE
REPENITIGNY, QUEBEC J6A 2C2
(514) 581-6600

SALETEX FABRICS LTD.
4716 THIMENS BOULEVARD
ST. LAURENT, QUEBEC H4R 2B2
(514) 334-7533

TELIO & CIE
1407, RUE DE LA MONTAGNE
MONTREAL, QUEBEC H3G 1Z3
(514) 842-9116

VAL-ABEL TEXTILES LTD.
55 MT. ROYAL AVENUE WEST
MONTREAL, QUEBEC H2T 2S6
(514) 842-9503

▶ ONTARIO

ACCESSORIES CANADA
P.O. BOX 1273
GUELPH, ONTARIO N1H 6N6
(519) 836-3283

AVEBLA LTD.
442 BRIMLEY ROAD, UNIT 9
SCARBOROUGH, ONTARIO M1J 1A1
(416) 264-4345

BAUMANN FABRICS LTD.
302 KING STREET EAST
TORONTO, ONTARIO M5A 1K6
(416) 869-1221

W.H. BILBROUGH & CO. LTD.
326 DAVENPORT ROAD
TORONTO, ONTARIO M5R 1K6
(416) 960-1611

BRUNSCHWIG & FILS LTD.
320 DAVENPORT ROAD
TORONTO, ONTARIO M5R 1K6

CANADIAN WINDOW COVERINGS
55 JUTLAND ROAD
TORONTO, ONTARIO M8Z 2G6
(416) 252-3751

CURBSUN SYSTEMS INC.
555 HANLAN ROAD
WOODBRIDGE, ONTARIO L4L 4R8
(416) 656-0394

D.C.S. DRAPERY LTD.
334 LAUDER AVENUE
TORONTO, ONTARIO M6E 3H8
(416) 651-5757

**EMHART CAN. LTD.
INTERNATIONAL HARDWARE DIVISION**
P.O. BOX 396, 180 COLEMAN STREET
BELLEVILLE, ONTARIO K8N 5A8
(613) 394-6651

• **FABRICS INTERNATIONAL**
1090 AEROWOOD DRIVE
MISSISSAUGA, ONTARIO L4W 1Y5
(416) 624-5104 **Pg. 239**

HABERT ASSOCIATES LTD.
321 DAVENPORT ROAD
TORONTO, ONTARIO M5R 1K5
(416) 960-5323

HUNTER DOUGLAS CANADA LTD.
2155 DREW ROAD
MISSISSAUGA, ONTARIO L5S 1S7
(416) 678-1133

JEFF BROWN FINE FABRICS LTD.
1785 ARGENTIA ROAD
MISSISSAUGA, ONTARIO L5N 3A2
(416) 821-3666

• **JOANNE FABRICS CO. LTD.**
1090 AEROWOOD DRIVE
MISSISSAUGA, ONTARIO L4W 1Y5
(416) 624-2744 **Pg. 239**

JOHNSON, CRAIG AND ASSOCIATES INC.
110 DAVENPORT ROAD
TORONTO, ONTARIO M5R 1H7
(416) 975-1867

KIRSCH CANADA
233 SIGNET DRIVE
WESTON, ONTARIO M9L 1V1
(416) 745-8860

KOBEFAB INTERNATIONAL INC.
BOX 939, 5380 SOUTH SERVICE ROAD
BURLINGTON, ONTARIO L7R 3Y7
(416) 639-2730

LAURII TEXTILES
354 DAVENPORT ROAD
TORONTO, ONTARIO M5R 1K6
(416) 922-5514

LOUVRE DRAPE CANADA LTD.
6310 VIPOND DRIVE
MISSISSAUGA, ONTARIO L5T 1J9
(416) 670-2869

**MODERN WINDOW SHADES LTD.–
AVENUE CUSTOM SEWING**
267 DAVENPORT ROAD
TORONTO, ONTARIO M5R 1J9
(416) 927-0292

PRIDE OF PARIS FABRICS LTD.
WEST RIVER STREET, BOX 130
PARIS, ONTARIO N3L 3E9
(519) 442-6351

**PRIMAVERA
INTERIOR ACCESSORIES LTD.**
160 PEARS AVENUE
TORONTO, ONTARIO M5R 1T2
(416) 921-3334

RODA WALLCOVERINGS
80 TYCOS DRIVE
TORONTO, ONTARIO M6B 1V9
(416) 782-1167

SAMO INTERNATIONAL
320 DAVENPORT ROAD
TORONTO, ONTARIO M5R 1K6
(416) 920-3020

A. SANDERSON & SONS LTD.
320 DAVENPORT ROAD
TORONTO, ONTARIO M5R 1K6
(416) 323-1168

SEWING ROOM, THE
170 BEDFORD ROAD
TORONTO, ONTARIO M5R 2K9
(416) 961-5536

SILENT GLISS
705 PROGRESS AVENUE, UNIT 63
SCARBOROUGH, ONTARIO M1H 2T1
(416) 431-3330

SOLARFECTIVE PRODUCTS LTD.
22 MOWAT AVENUE
TORONTO, ONTARIO M6K 3E5
(416) 588-6682

STURDI-BILT WOOD PRODUCTS LTD.
275 DON PARK ROAD
MARKHAM, ONTARIO L3R 1C2
(416) 475-1050

TANDEM FABRICS INC.
320 DAVENPORT ROAD
TORONTO, ONTARIO M5R 1K6
(416) 964-6744

TELIO & CO.
113 DUPONT STREET
TORONTO, ONTARIO M5R 1V4
(416) 968-2020

WALTER L. BROWN LTD.
17 VICKERS ROAD
TORONTO, ONTARIO M9B 1C2
(416) 231-4499

▶ WESTERN CANADA

ITALIA DESIGN OF CANADA
10357–109TH STREET
EDMONTON, ALBERTA T5J 1N3
(403) 420-0270

COMMUNICATIONS AUDIO/VISUALS

BRACK ELECTRONICS
129 JARVIS STREET
TORONTO, ONTARIO M5G 2H6
(416) 364-5002

EGAN VISUAL INC.
300 HANLAN ROAD
WOODBRIDGE, ONTARIO L4L 3P6
(416) 851-2826

ELECTROHOME LTD.
809 WELLINGTON STREET NORTH
KITCHENER, ONTARIO N2G 4J6
(519) 744-7111

GUTMAN, KARL INC.
605 EDUCATION ROAD
CORNWALL, ONTARIO K6H 5V6
(613) 932-0108

INTALITE INC.
9855 MEILEUR STREET
MONTREAL, QUEBEC H3L 3J6
(514) 382-2793

3M CANADA LTD.
P.O. BOX 5757
LONDON, ONTARIO N6A 4T1
(519) 451-2500

PHASE THREE AUDIO & LIGHTING
358 KING STREET EAST
TORONTO, ONTARIO M5A 1T1
(416) 363-9489

PHILIPS ELECTRONICS LTD.
601 MILNER AVENUE
SCARBOROUGH, ONTARIO M1B 1M8
(416) 691-7372

ROBLOK LIMITED
880 WELLINGTON STREET
OTTAWA, ONTARIO K1R 6K7
(613) 237-7236

• **SOUTHAM AUDIO VISUAL GROUP**
189 DUFFERIN STREET
TORONTO, ONTARIO M6K 1Y9
(416) 533-6511 **Pg. 177-180**

TALBOT KELLY ASSOCIATES LIMITED
2 BERKELEY STREET
TORONTO, ONTARIO M5A 2W3
(416) 360-7915

CORPORATE SERVICES

EXECUTIVE CORPORATE SERVICES INC.
400 SUMMERHILL AVENUE
TORONTO, ONTARIO M4W 2E4
(416) 920-1921

**GERRY BROWN & ASSOCIATES INC.
HOSPITALITY CONSULTANTS**
50 GERVAIS DRIVE
DON MILLS, ONTARIO M3C 1W2
(416) 449-6444

**SALLY FOURMY & ASSOCIATES
CORPORATE FASHION CONSULTANTS**
30 DUNCAN STREET
TORONTO, ONTARIO M5V 2C2
(416) 593-4676

• **ULTIMATE SOURCE RELOCATION SERVICE**
855 HARRINGTON COURT
BURLINGTON, ONTARIO L7N 3P3
(416) 827-6445 **Pg. 147**

INTERIOR CONTRACTORS

ARTEK
150 WEST 1ST AVENUE
VANCOUVER, B.C. V5Y 1A4
(604) 876-2131

B.M.P. INC.
1320 BAS DE L'EGLISE SUD
ST-JACQUES DE MONTCALM, QC J0K 2R0
(514) 839-2419

• **BEGG & DAIGLE**
195 NANTUCKET BOULEVARD
SCARBOROUGH, ONTARIO M1P 2P3
(416) 285-8500 **Pg. 168, 169**

BOZZI CARLONE
101 YORKVILLE AVENUE
TORONTO, ONTARIO M5R 1C1
(416) 925-6824

BRADLEY CAMPBELL
125 TRADERS BOULEVARD EAST
MISSISSAUGA, ONTARIO L4Z 1W7
(416) 890-5400

• **CAS INTERIORS INC.**
549 OAKDALE ROAD, UNIT 38
DOWNSVIEW, ONTARIO M3N 1W7
(416) 743-6291 **Pg. 167**

• **CAMERON – McINDOO INTERIORS LTD.**
20 UPJOHN ROAD
DON MILLS, ONTARIO M3B 2V9
(416) 447-3301 **Pg. 170**

**CENTRE LEASEHOLD
IMPROVEMENTS LIMITED**
STE 3306 ROYAL TRUST TOWER, P.O. BOX 184
TORONTO, ONTARIO M5K 1H6
(416) 363-6131

DESICON PLUS INC.
146 WEST BEAVER CREEK ROAD
RICHMOND HILL, ONTARIO L4B 1C2
(416) 731-7151

• **CORPORATE NATIONAL LTD.**
21 KERN ROAD
DON MILLS, ONTARIO M3B 1S9
(416) 449-1991 **Pg. 171**

• **DECORA CONTRACTING INC.**
160 TRADERS BOULEVARD
MISSISSAUGA, ONTARIO L4Z 3K7
(416) 568-4211 **Pg. 172**

JAS. F. GILLANDERS CO. LTD.
33 ATOMIC AVENUE
ETOBICOKE, ONTARIO M8Z 5K8
(416) 259-5446

HOLMAN DESIGN LTD.
160 LESMILL ROAD
DON MILLS, ONTARIO M3B 2T7
(416) 441-1877

**INTERIOR CONSTRUCTION
SPECIALISTS INC.**
151 NASHDENE ROAD
SCARBOROUGH, ONTARIO M1V 2T3
(416) 292-4041

INTERIOR DIMENSIONS
980 YONGE STREET
TORONTO, ONTARIO M4W 2J5
(416) 922-7165

K.P. MANUFACTURERS LTD.
7403 30TH STREET SE
CALGARY, ALBERTA T2C 1N6
(403) 279-7727

LOGULLO INDUSTRIES LTD.
3836 27TH STREET NE
CALGARY, ALBERTA T1Y 5K7
(403) 291-1024

PANCOR INDUSTRIES LTD.
7105 PACIFIC CIRCLE
MISSISSAUGA, ONTARIO L5T 2A8
(416) 670-2910

• **PATELLA CONSTRUCTION INC.**
161 STERLING AVENUE
LASALLE, QUEBEC H8R 3P3
(514) 364-1964 **Pg. 173**

PHILLIPS & ASSOCIATES
1263 EAST 2ND AVENUE
VANCOUVER, B.C. V6A 3T9
(604) 253-4480

**PROCARIO CONSTRUCTION &
MANAGEMENT INC.**
1020 MATHESON BOULEVARD
MISSISSAUGA, ONTARIO L4W 4G9
(416) 625-6666

**PROFESSIONAL CONSTRUCTION
CO-ORDINATORS LTD.**
575 EGLINTON AVENUE WEST
TORONTO, ONTARIO M5N 1B5
(416) 486-9772

QUALITY GENERAL CONTRACTING CO.
140 BENTLEY STREET
MARKHAM, ONTARIO L3R 3L2
(416) 475-1315

RAE BROTHERS INC.
512 KING STREET EAST
TORONTO, ONTARIO M5A 1M2
(416) 364-8656

• **RICHWAY CONSTRUCTION LTD.**
1035 TOY AVENUE
PICKERING, ONTARIO L1W 3N9
(416) 683-5150 **Pg. 174**

SCALI-DURANTE FURNITURE MFGS. LTD.
5371 REGENT STREET
BURNABY, B.C. V5C 4H4
(604) 291-7551

SUSS WOODCRAFT
1165, AVENUE HICKSON
VERDUN, QUEBEC H4G 2L3
(514) 768-1165

• **URBACON LTD.**
5 LOWER SHERBOURNE STREET
TORONTO, ONTARIO M5A 2P3
(416) 865-9429 **Pg. 175**

WALWOOD CONSTRUCTION LTD.
65 WEST BEAVER CREEK ROAD
RICHMOND HILL, ONTARIO L4B 1K4
(416) 889-8607

WOODRITES CUSTOM BUILDERS AND RENOVATORS LTD.
940 QUEEN STREET WEST
TORONTO, ONTARIO M6J 1G8
(416) 532-9621

LIGHTING · ENGINEERING CONSULTANTS

H.H. ANGUS & ASSOCIATES LTD.
1127 LESLIE STREET
DON MILLS, ONTARIO M3C 2J6
(416) 443-8200

CROSSEY ENGINEERING
4141 YONGE STREET
TORONTO, ONTARIO M2P 2A8
(416) 221-3111

JACK A. FROST LTD.
3245 WHARTON WAY
MISSISSAUGA, ONTARIO L4X 2R9
(416) 624-5344

GIFFELS ASSOCIATES LTD.
30 INTERNATIONAL BOULEVARD
REXDALE, ONTARIO M9W 5P3
(416) 675-5950

INTERIOR ENGINEERING
790 BURNHAMTHORPE ROAD WEST
MISSISSAUGA, ONTARIO L5C 4G3
(416) 848-2233

LIGHTING PERCEPTIONS INC.
7305 WOODBINE AVENUE
MARKHAM, ONTARIO L3R 3V7
(416) 495-9023

• **PHILIPS ELECTRONICS LTD.**
601 MILNER AVENUE
SCARBOROUGH, ONTARIO M1B 1M8
(416) 292-5161 **Pg. 237**

• **SOUTHAM AUDIO VISUAL SERVICE**
189 DUFFERIN STREET
TORONTO, ONTARIO M6K 1Y9
(416) 534-6622 **Pg. 177-180**

INTERIOR LANDSCAPING

BEACH McLEOD NORTHERN
116A VICEROY ROAD
CONCORD, ONTARIO L4K 2M1
(416) 669-5777

BOTANICAL INTERIORS
260 KING STREET EAST
TORONTO, ONTARIO M5A 1K3
(416) 866-2176

BRUCE JENSEN NURSERIES INC.
RR NO. 2
NEWCASTLE, ONTARIO L0A 1H0
(416) 283-3065

HYDRO-GRO INTERIOR LANDSCAPE
3226 LENWORTH DRIVE
MISSISSAUGA, ONTARIO L4X 2G1
(416) 238-9168

INTERIOR LANDSCAPE GROUP INC., THE
70 WHITMORE ROAD
WOODBRIDGE, ONTARIO L4L 7Z4
(416) 851-9057

MOORHEAD FLEMING CORBAN
33 BRITAIN STREET
TORONTO, ONTARIO M5A 1R7
(416) 366-9238

• **SILK DESIGN**
12 ONTARIO STREET
ORILLIA, ONTARIO L3V 6H1
(416) 472-0726 **Pg. 273**

SILK-SCAPING LTD.
110 RIVIERA DRIVE
MARKHAM, ONTARIO L3R 5M1
(416) 477-8733

TOUCAN TROPICAL PLANTS & DESIGN INC.
83 GALAXY BOULEVARD
ETOBICOKE, ONTARIO M9W 5X6
(416) 674-6881

PAINT

BENJAMIN MOORE & CO. LTD.
139 MULOCK AVENUE
TORONTO, ONTARIO M6N 1G9
(416) 766-1173

• **CLASSIC ARCHITECTURAL COATINGS**
2700 DUFFERIN STREET
TORONTO, ONTARIO M6B 3R1
(416) 789-7887 **Pg. 256, 257**

• **INTERNATIONAL COLOUR COATINGS**
339 CANARTIC DRIVE
DOWNSVIEW, ONTARIO M3J 2P9
(416) 665-3569 **Pg. 258**

• **MULTIFLEK PAINT SYSTEMS INC.**
111 GRANTON DRIVE
RICHMOND HILL, ONTARIO L4B 1L5
(416) 886-9733 **Pg. 255**

PAINT COLORS UNLIMITED
502 ADELAIDE STREET WEST
TORONTO, ONTARIO M5V 1T2
(416) 366-2941

PARA PAINTS CANADA INC.
25 RACINE ROAD
REXDALE, ONTARIO M9W 2Z4
(416) 743-7860

SIGNAGE

CLAUDE NEON
555 ELLESMERE ROAD
SCARBOROUGH, ONTARIO M1R 4E8
(416) 759-5685

COOPERCO
2220 MIDLAND AVENUE
SCARBOROUGH, ONTARIO M1P 3E6
(416) 293-6700

THE MARKLE BROTHERS LTD.
226 STEELCASE ROAD WEST
MARKHAM, ONTARIO L3R 1B3
(416) 475-6900

• **NEW STYLE SIGNS**
596 KING STREET WEST
TORONTO, ONTARIO M5V 1M1
(416) 596-6533 **Pg. 159**

PRINTART
41 BRITAIN STREET
TORONTO, ONTARIO M5A 1R7
(416) 869-1986

• **TECHNISIGNS**
5510 AMBLER DRIVE
MISSISSAUGA, ONTARIO L4W 2V1
(416) 238-9322 **Pg. 162**

SPECIAL EFFECTS

ANSELMO ART STUDIO & ASSOCIATES INC.
280 AVENUE ROAD
TORONTO, ONTARIO M4V 2G7
(416) 966-3856

• **DE FOREST STUDIOS CORP**
42 VICTORIA PARK AVENUE
TORONTO, ONTARIO M4E 3R9
(416) 696-8971 **Pg. 164, 165**

HANNIVAN, DAVID & CO.
1 PHOEBE STREET
TORONTO, ONTARIO M5T 1A6
(416) 597-0298

JANNA DECORATORS
580 FRONT STREET WEST
TORONTO, ONTARIO M5V 1C1
(416) 467-0624

KURTZ MANN DESIGN
390 DUPONT STREET
TORONTO, ONTARIO M5R 1V9
(416) 927-0353

LA BOITE DU PINCEAU D'ARLEQUIN
760, RUE ST-FELIX
MONTREAL, QUEBEC H3C 2B8
(514) 878-9166

WIEGAND, ERIC DESIGN/DIRECTION
143 MADISON AVENUE
TORONTO, ONTARIO M5R 2S6
(416) 928-0790

WYERS, BRIAN DESIGN
2661 KINGSTON ROAD
SCARBOROUGH, ONTARIO M1M 1M3
(416) 287-2345

VENEERS · LAMINATES

CERATEC – NEVAMAR
1550 JULES PORTRAS
MONTREAL, QUEBEC H4N 1X7
(514) 334-4713

CONTOUR DISTRIBUTORS
3615 WESTON ROAD
TORONTO, ONTARIO M9L 1V8
(416) 747-7877

FORBO · ARBORITE INC.
385 LAFLEUR
MONTREAL, QUEBEC H8R 3H7
(514) 366-2710

FORMICA CANADA INC.
2735 MATHESON BOULEVARD EAST
MISSISSAUGA, ONTARIO L4W 4M9
(416) 238-3526

• **GENERAL WOODS & VENEERS LTD.**
P.O. BOX 1059, STATION A
MONTREAL, QUEBEC H3C 2X6
(416) 674-4957 **Pg. 266**

OCTOPUS PRODUCTS LTD.
200 GEARY AVENUE
TORONTO, ONTARIO M6H 2B9
(416) 531-5051

• **WILSONART**
1500 SUPERIOR PARKWAY
WESTLAND, MICHIGAN 48185
(313) 721-3600 **Pg. 267**

ART · ANTIQUES

▶ ATLANTIC CANADA

THE GALLERY
282 DUCKWORTH STREET
ST. JOHN'S, NEWFOUNDLAND A1C 1H3
(709) 753-1511

MORRIS ART GALLERY LTD.
221 UNION STREET
SAINT JOHN, NEW BRUNSWICK E2L 1B2
(506) 657-6860

▶ QUEBEC

ALLENCO-TRICON ARTS DECORATIFS
4650, BOULEVARD ST-LAURENT
MONTREAL, QUEBEC H2T 1R3
(514) 849-3892

CANADIAN GUILD OF CRAFTS (QUE.)
2025 PEEL STREET
MONTREAL, QUEBEC H3A 1T6
(514) 849-6091

GALERIE ALMAN INC.
4557, BOULEVARD ST-LAURENT
MONTREAL, QUEBEC H2T 1R2
(514) 849-2908

GALERIE ELCA LONDON
1616 SHERBROOKE STREET WEST
MONTREAL, QUEBEC H3H 1C9
(514) 931-3646

GALERIE VERRE D'ART
1518, RUE SHERBROOKE OUEST
MONTREAL, QUEBEC H3G 1L3
(514) 932-3896

GALERIE WADDINGTON & GORCE INC.
1504, RUE SHERBROOKE OUEST
MONTREAL, QUEBEC H3G 1L3
(514) 933-3653

▶ ONTARIO

ANCERL-CUTLER, ZANA
238 DAVENPORT ROAD
TORONTO, ONTARIO M5R 1J6
(416) 787-2631

ART COLLECTION CANADA OF TORONTO LTD.
315 QUEEN STREET WEST
TORONTO, ONTARIO M5V 2X2
(416) 977-4456

ASHTON'S
267 QUEEN STREET EAST
TORONTO, ONTARIO M5A 1S6
(416) 366-6846

• **AVENUE ANTIQUES**
2 ELGIN AVENUE
TORONTO, ONTARIO M5R 1G6
(416) 960-5913 **Pg. 182**

BAAS STUDIO GALLERY
322 KING STREET WEST
TORONTO, ONTARIO M5V 1J2
(416) 979-2705

BENITZ, JEAN
120 CARLTON STREET
TORONTO, ONTARIO M5A 4K2
(416) 926-1632

BRASS ROOTS
220 BAYVIEW DRIVE
BARRIE, ONTARIO L4N 4Y8
(416) 698-1353

CHRISTIE'S AUCTIONEERS
94 CUMBERLAND STREET
TORONTO, ONTARIO M5R 1A3
(416) 960-2063

BARBARA COLE FRAMERY AND GALLERY LTD.
223 AVENUE ROAD
TORONTO, ONTARIO M5R 2J3
(416) 924-7780

CONTEMPORARY FINE ART SERVICES
411 RICHMOND STREET EAST
TORONTO, ONTARIO M5A 3S5
(416) 366-9770

CORPORATE ART SERVICES OF CANADA
114 RICHMOND STREET EAST
TORONTO, ONTARIO M5C 1P1
(416) 947-0691

• **DESIGN COLLECTIONS INC.**
366 KING STREET EAST
TORONTO, ONTARIO M5A 1K9
(416) 360-7015 **Pg. 183**

DU VERRE GLASS LTD.
307 QUEEN STREET WEST
TORONTO, ONTARIO M5V 2A4
(416) 593-0182

GALLERY DRESDNERE
12 HAZELTON AVENUE
TORONTO, ONTARIO M5R 2E2
(416) 923-4662

GALLERY MOOS LTD.
136 YORKVILLE AVENUE
TORONTO, ONTARIO M5R 1C2
(416) 922-0627

GALLERY 133
74 BATHURST STREET
TORONTO, ONTARIO M5V 2P5
(416) 361-6099

ISAACS GALLERY, THE
179 JOHN STREET
TORONTO, ONTARIO M5T 1X4
(416) 595-0770

• **SHELLEY LAMBE FINE ART**
2 MATILDA STREET
TORONTO, ONTARIO M4M 1L9
(416) 778-0700 **Pg. 184**

MICHAEL REEVES ANTIQUES
171 QUEEN STREET EAST
TORONTO, ONTARIO M5C 1S2
(416) 368-0257

MIRRA GODDARD
22 HAZELTON AVENUE
TORONTO, ONTARIO M5R 2E2
(416) 964-8197

NAVARRO GALLERY
33 HAZELTON AVENUE
TORONTO, ONTARIO M5V 1M5
(416) 921-0031

PAISLEY SHOP LIMITED
889 YONGE STREET
TORONTO, ONTARIO M4W 2H2
(416) 923-5830

PASU GALLERIES
401 RICHMOND STREET WEST
TORONTO, ONTARIO M5V 1X3
(416) 599-9869

PRIME
229 QUEEN STREET WEST
TORONTO, ONTARIO M5V 1Z4
(416) 593-5750

● **PROGRESSIVE EDITIONS LTD.**
418 QUEEN STREET EAST
TORONTO, ONTARIO M5A 1T4
(416) 860-0983 **Pg.185-188**

MARCIA RAFELMAN FINE ARTS LTD.
466 ST. CLAIR AVENUE EAST
TORONTO, ONTARIO M4T 1P5
(416) 482-0944

SANDRA AINSLEY ARTFORMS
55 AVENUE ROAD / HAZELTON LANES
TORONTO, ONTARIO M5R 3L2
(416) 968-8685

**STEINER CORPORATE
ART CONSULTANTS INC.**
2729 BAYVIEW AVENUE
WILLOWDALE, ONTARIO M2L 1C3
(416) 865-9377

STEPHEN R. BAILEY CONSULTANTS
40 HAZELTON AVENUE
TORONTO, ONTARIO M5R 2E2
(416) 924-4240

UPTOWN ART INC.
260 KING STREET EAST
TORONTO, ONTARIO M5A 1K3
(416) 360-6881

● **VALENART & ASSOCIATES INC.**
238 DAVENPORT ROAD
TORONTO, ONTARIO M5R 1J6
(416) 860-1733 **Pg. 189**

WADDINGTON & SHIELL GALLERIES
33 HAZELTON AVENUE
TORONTO, ONTARIO M5R 2E3
(416) 925-2461

▶ B R I T I S H   C O L U M B I A

ARTWORKS LTD.
400 SMITHE STREET
VANCOUVER, B.C. V6B 5E4
(604) 688-3301

CANADIAN ART PRINTS
736 RICHARD STREET
VANCOUVER, B.C. V6B 3A4
(604) 681-3485

MAH, BARRY PHOTOGRAPHY
72 WEST CORDOVA STREET
VANCOUVER, B.C. V6B 1C9
(504) 682-3881

PEKARSKY NOBLE & ASSOCIATES LTD.
1926 MATTHEWS AVENUE
VANCOUVER, B.C. V6J 2T7
(604) 681-5614

RENDERERS

▶ Q U E B E C

GRAPHI-PERS INC.
1122 BOULEVARD LAIRD
MONTREAL, QUEBEC H3R 1Z2
(514) 345-0102

**SCHNEIDER, FRANK
ARCHITECTURAL RENDERER**
2024 PEEL STREET
MONTREAL, QUEBEC H3A 1W5
(514) 843-6462

▶ O N T A R I O

ARCHITECTURAL RENDERINGS
2025 SHEPPARD AVENUE EAST
WILLOWDALE, ONTARIO M2J 1V7
(416) 496-0635

FENWICK BONNELL DESIGN ASSOCIATES
363 ADELAIDE STREET WEST
TORONTO, ONTARIO M5H 1Y2
(416) 593-5041

G.A. DESIGN
31 SILVERTON AVENUE
DOWNSVIEW, ONTARIO M3H 3E7
(416) 638-4933

GRICE GORDON ARCHITECT ILLUSTRATOR
878 QUEEN STREET WEST
TORONTO, ONTARIO M6J 1G3
(416) 536-9191

HEART RENDER INC.
1027 YONGE STREET
TORONTO, ONTARIO M4W 2K9
(416) 964-1545

HEWSON, JAMES
21 HILLSBORO AVENUE
TORONTO, ONTARIO M5R 1S6
(416) 921-8059

● **KEOGH RENDERING**
10 GRENOBLE DRIVE
DON MILLS, ONTARIO M3C 1C7
(416) 423-2412 **Pg. 191**

McCANN, MICHAEL ASSOCIATES LTD.
2 GIBSON AVENUE
TORONTO, ONTARIO
(416) 964-7532

● **MORELLO DESIGN & CO.**
2 GIBSON AVENUE
TORONTO, ONTARIO M5R 1T5
(416) 963-4315 **Pg. 192**

TED NASMITH
37 RANDOLPH ROAD
TORONTO, ONTARIO M4G 2R8
(416) 423-2124

● **THE RENDER GROUP**
277 MACPHERSON AVENUE
TORONTO, ONTARIO M4V 1A4
(416) 960-0028 **Pg. 193**

RENDERING ASSOCIATES
55 INDIAN TRAIL
TORONTO, ONTARIO M6R 1Z8
(416) 767-8438

SULLIVAN STUDIOS
880 QUEEN STREET WEST
TORONTO, ONTARIO M6J 1G3
(416) 588-5153

VERSTEEG DESIGNS LTD.
600 MARKHAM STREET
TORONTO, ONTARIO
(416) 537-9641

YUJI YOSHIZAWA – ILLUSTRATION
14 GLENDOWER CIRCUIT
SCARBOROUGH, ONTARIO M1T 2Z2
(416) 754-4674

▶ A L B E R T A

CREATIVE GROUP DESIGN LTD.
300 B 17TH AVENUE SW
CALGARY, ALBERTA
(403) 263-8100

ODIN CREATIVE DIMENSIONS LTD.
6216 TOUCHWOOD DRIVE NW
CALGARY, ALBERTA
(403) 274-4886

PHOTOGRAPHERS

▶ Q U E B E C

ALLARD, PHOTOGRAPHERS INC.
1394 MONT ROYAL EST
MONTREAL, QUEBEC
(514) 526-1691

**DRUMMOND, MICHAEL
DESIGN & PHOTOGRAPHY LTD.**
1235A, AVENUE GREENE
MONTREAL, QUEBEC H3Z 2A4
(514) 933-5205

McNEIL, BRUCE PHOTOGRAPHIE
267 LAGAUCHETIERE OUEST
MONTREAL, QUEBEC H2Z 1C7
(514) 861-3969

**MONGEAU, PIERRE LOUIS
PHOTOGRAPHE INC.**
11 KILLARNEY GARDEN
POINTE-CLAIRE, QUEBEC H9S 4X7
(514) 871-3962

PRODUCTIONS MILNOX, LES
1573, RUE DUCHARME
MONTREAL, QUEBEC H2V 1G4
(514) 279-1352

STUDIO ALAIN ENR.
7562, ST-DENIS
MONTREAL, QUEBEC
(514) 279-9225

VACHON, JEAN
95, RUE PRINCE
MONTREAL, QUEBEC H3C 2M7
(514) 395-2227

• **VAN DUSEN, RAY**
2062 BELGRAVE
MONTREAL, QUEBEC H4A 2L7
(514) 486-5054 **Pg. 199**

▶ ONTARIO

ALKIN, GILL PHOTOGRAPHY
41 SHANLY STREET
TORONTO, ONTARIO M6H 1S2
(416) 534-2259

AMESTOY, JUAN PHOTOGRAPHY
67 MOWAT AVENUE
TORONTO, ONTARIO M6K 3E3
(416) 534-7729

APERTURE
40 LOMBARD STREET
TORONTO, ONTARIO M5C 1M1
(416) 368-0783

BARR PHOTOGRAPHY
1275 EGLINTON AVENUE EAST
MISSISSAUGA, ONTARIO L4W 2Z2
(416) 460-7996

BELL, RICHARD AND ASSOCIATES
5 SOHO STREET
TORONTO, ONTARIO M5T 1Z6
(416) 444-7425

BRODIE, RALPH PHOTOGRAPHICS
1499 QUEEN STREET WEST
TORONTO, ONTARIO M6R 1A3
(416) 536-9463

• **DESIGN ARCHIVE**
276 CARLAW AVENUE
TORONTO, ONTARIO M4M 3L1
(416) 466-0211 **Pg. 194, 195**

DUFF, JOSEPH PHOTOGRAPHY LTD.
56 THE ESPLANADE
TORONTO, CANADA M5E 1A7
(416) 363-7081

EAGER, JIM
327 WINONA DRIVE
TORONTO, ONTARIO M6C 3T2
(416) 652-3832

ELMY, RON PHOTOGRAPHY INC.
56 THE ESPLANADE
TORONTO, CANADA M5E 1A7
(416) 363-7081

DAY, FRASER PHOTOGRAPHY
34 BARBARA CRESCENT
TORONTO, ONTARIO M4C 3B2
(416) 463-9052

EVANS, STEVEN PHOTOGRAPHY INC.
27 DAVIES AVENUE
TORONTO, ONTARIO M4M 2A9
(416) 463-4493

• **HOZ, GADI PHOTOGRAPHICS INC.**
105 DOLOMITE DRIVE
DOWNSVIEW, ONTARIO M3J 2N1
(416) 665-2233 **Pg. 196**

INTERIOR IMAGES
100 WOODMOUNT AVENUE
TORONTO, ONTARIO M4G 3Y4
(416) 467-5104

• **KILBURN, ELAINE PHOTOGRAPHY**
353 EASTERN AVENUE
TORONTO, ONTARIO M4M 1B7
(416) 466-9270 **Pg. 197**

**LEITH, IAN & ASSOCIATES
PHOTOGRAPHY**
17 CARLAW AVENUE
TORONTO, ONTARIO M4M 2R6
(416) 462-2966

LENSCAPE INC.
222 EASTERN AVENUE
TORONTO, ONTARIO M5A 1J1
(416) 368-9567

McELLIGOTT, JIM
150 CATHCART STREET
OTTAWA, ONTARIO K1N 5B6
(613) 594-5955

MELLOWS, IAIN PHOTOGRAPHY INC.
56 THE ESPLANADE
TORONTO, CANADA M5E 1A7
(416) 363-7081

NARVALI PHOTOGRAPHY LTD.
5 SOHO STREET
TORONTO, ONTARIO M5T 1Z6
(416) 593-0813

PANDA ASSOCIATES PHOTOGRAPHERS
524 WELLINGTON STREET WEST
TORONTO, ONTARIO
(416) 593-9266

PAROW, LORRAINE C.
85 DRAYTON AVENUE
TORONTO, ONTARIO M4C 3L8
(416) 461-3847

PHOTOCOM
P.O. BOX 173, ST. N
TORONTO, ONTARIO M8V 2T2
(416) 251-9309

RAHMER, LUCY PHOTOGRAPHY
20 AVOCA AVENUE
TORONTO, ONTARIO M4T 2B8
(416) 925-2029

SAMSON PRODUCTIONS
100 WHITEHORN CRESCENT
TORONTO, ONTARIO M2J 3B2
(416) 493-1131

SPALDING-SMITH, FIONA
70 HOGARTH AVENUE
TORONTO, ONTARIO
(416) 463-5073

ELLEN B. TAUB PHOTOGRAPHY
44 CHARLES STREET WEST
TORONTO, ONTARIO M4Y 1R7
(416) 968-7175

WHITTAKER, DAVID PHOTOGRAPHER INC.
276 CARLAW AVENUE
TORONTO, ONTARIO M4M 3L1
(416) 466-0558

YARWOOD, TED
1179A KING STREET WEST
TORONTO, ONTARIO M6K 3C5
(416) 531-4615

▶ WESTERN CANADA

BILODEAU/PRESTON LTD.
100 – 1615 10TH AVENUE SW
CALGARY, ALBERTA T3C 0J5
(403) 245-1804

KOPELOW, GERRY PHOTOGRAPHICS
18 EINARSON
WINNIPEG, MANITOBA
(204) 775-5113

• **LIGHTWORKS PHOTOGRAPHY**
715 – 4A STREET NE
CALGARY, ALBERTA T2E 3W1
(403) 276-4321 **Pg. 198**

▶ BRITISH COLUMBIA

FULKER, JOHN
1755 – 29TH STREET
W. VANCOUVER, B.C.
(604) 922-6857

MAH, BARRY PHOTOGRAPHY
72 WEST CORDOVA STREET
VANCOUVER, B.C. V6B 1C9
(504) 682-3881

OTTE, GARY PHOTOGRAPHERS LTD.
21, 1551 JOHNSTON STREET
VANCOUVER, B.C.
(604) 681-8421

SCOTT, SIMON ASSOCIATES LTD.
1627 W 2ND
VANCOUVER, B.C.
(604) 733-9797

SHERLOCK, JOHN
225 SMITHE STREET
VANCOUVER, B.C.
(604) 683-2614

▶ QUEBEC

**L'ACADEMIE INTERNATIONALE
DE LA MODE ET DU DESIGN**
C.P. 55 MART D-36 DAWSON
PLACE BONAVENTURE
MONTREAL, QUEBEC H5A 1A3
(514) 875-9777

CEGEP VIEUX MONTREAL
C.P. 1444, SUCURSALE N
MONTREAL, QUEBEC H2X 3M8
(514) 284-7137

**DAWSON COLLEGE
DELORMIER CAMPUS**
2120 SHERBROOKE STREAT EAST
MONTREAL, QUEBEC H2K 1C1
(514) 931-8731

▶ ONTARIO

**ALGONQUIN COLLEGE OF APPLIED
ARTS AND TECHNOLOGY**
COLONEL BY CAMPUS, 281 ECHO DRIVE
OTTAWA, ONTARIO K1S 1N3
(613) 237-5343

**CONFEDERATION COLLEGE OF APPLIED
ARTS AND TECHNOLOGY**
P.O. BOX 398
THUNDER BAY, ONTARIO P7C 4K1
(807) 475-6110

• **DURHAM COLLEGE OF APPLIED ARTS
AND TECHNOLOGY**
SIMCOE ST. N. CAMPUS, P.O. BOX 385
OSHAWA, ONTARIO L1H 7L7
(416) 576-0210 **Pg. 275**

**FANSHAWE COLLEGE OF APPLIED ARTS
AND TECHNOLOGY**
520 FIRST STREET
LONDON, ONTARIO N5Y 3C6
(519) 452-4225

**GEORGIAN COLLEGE OF APPLIED
ARTS AND TECHNOLOGY**
1 GEORGIAN DRIVE
BARRIE, ONTARIO L4M 3X9
(705) 728-1951

**HUMBER COLLEGE OF APPLIED ARTS
AND TECHNOLOGY**
P.O. BOX 1900
REXDALE, ONTARIO M9W 5L7
(416) 675-3111

**INTERNATIONAL ACADEMY OF
MERCHANDISING & DESIGN LTD.**
31 WELLESLEY STREET EAST
TORONTO, ONTARIO M4Y 1G7
(416) 922-3666

**NIAGARA COLLEGE OF APPLIED ARTS
AND TECHNOLOGY**
WELLAND CAMPUS, P.O. BOX 1005
WOODLAWN ROAD
WELLAND, ONTARIO L3B 5S2
(416) 735-2211

• **ONTARIO COLLEGE OF ART**
100 McCAUL STREET
TORONTO, ONTARIO M5T 1W1
(416) 977-5311 **Pg. 276, 277**

RYERSON POLITECHNICAL INSTITUTE
350 VICTORIA STREET
TORONTO, ONTARIO M5B 2K3
(416) 979-5188

**SENECA COLLEGE OF APPLIED ARTS
AND TECHNOLOGY**
YORKDALE CAMPUS, 2999 DUFFERIN ST.
TORONTO, ONTARIO M6B 3T4
(416) 491-5050

**SHERIDAN SCHOOL OF
CRAFT AND DESIGN**
1460 SOUTH SHERIDAN WAY
MISSISSAUGA, ONTARIO L5H 1Z7
(416) 274-3685

**ST. CLAIR COLLEGE OF APPLIED ARTS
AND TECHNOLOGY**
2000 TALBOT ROAD WEST
WINDSOR, ONTARIO N3A 6S4
(416) 979-5188

▶ MANITOBA

UNIVERSITY OF MANITOBA
DEPARTMENT OF INTERIOR DESIGN
FACULTY OF ARCHITECTURE
WINNIPEG, MANITOBA R3T 2N2
(204) 474-9386

▶ SASKATCHEWAN

COLLEGE OF HOME ECONOMICS
SASKATOON, SASKATCHEWAN S7N 0W0
(306) 966-5823

▶ ALBERTA

LAKELAND COLLEGE
VERMILION CAMPUS
VERMILION, ALBERTA T0B 4M0
(403) 853-2971

MOUNT ROYAL COLLEGE
4825 RICHARD ROAD SW
CALGARY, ALBERTA T3E 6K6
(403) 240-6100

▶ BRITISH COLUMBIA

KWANTLEN COLLEGE
5840 CEDARBRIDGE WAY
RICHMOND, B.C. V6X 2A7
(604) 273-5461